Praise for
Guts & Borrowed Money

"In my library of business writings about the road maps to success, *Guts & Borrowed Money* is probably the most direct, precise, and logical I have had the pleasure of studying.**"**

—Edward Lowe
Founder, The American Academy of Entrepreneurship

"A must-read for any entrepreneur or aspiring entrepreneur! This practical guidebook provides the "nuts and bolts" of starting, operating, and growing your business. *Guts & Borrowed Money* gives experienced advice and suggestions to the entrepreneur in the trenches on the problems common to all small businesses. Use this advice to gain a competitive edge.**"**

—Nancy Upton, Ph.D.
Director, Baugh Center for Entrepreneurship
Baylor University

"This is the book I wish I had had, not only when I was starting out, but during my entrepreneurial career. It truthfully lays out the path that most entrepreneurs follow, and then proceeds to answer most of the everyday problems that frustrate so many small-business owners. It is the best reference book of its kind I've seen.**"**

—Glen Dorflinger
Managing Partner, Partners for International Development
1988 Entrepreneur of the Year, Entrepreneur of the Year Institute

"Tom Gillis draws on his successful experiences as founder, owner-manager, lawyer, CPA, and business consultant to give advice on the day-to-day problems of running a business. An added advantage to the woman business owner is that *Guts & Borrowed Money* gives an excellent description of the attitudes and practices of men who run their own businesses and how the game of business is played from the male perspective. Its straightforward style makes it a mental spark plug; you can't help but come up with fresh ideas for improving business performance.**"**

—Helen I. Hodges
Past Director
National Association of Women Business Owners

GUTS & BORROWED money

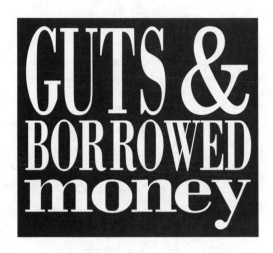

GUTS & BORROWED money

STRAIGHT TALK FOR STARTING & GROWING YOUR SMALL BUSINESS

Tom S. Gillis

Bard Press

GUTS & BORROWED MONEY
Straight Talk for Starting & Growing Your Small Business

Printed in the United States of America

Permission to reproduce or transmit in any form or by any means, electronic or mechanical, including photocopying or recording, or by any information storage retrieval system, must be obtained by writing to:

> Bard Press, Inc.
> 1515 South Capital of Texas Hwy., Suite 205
> Austin, Texas 78746
> Phone (512) 329-8373 Fax (512) 329-6051

To order the book, contact your local bookstore or call 1-800-945-3132.

ISBN 1-885167-20-2 trade paperback
ISBN 1-885167-19-9 cloth

Library of Congress Cataloging-in-Publication Data
Gillis, Tom S., 1921–
    Guts & borrowed money : straight talk for starting & growing your small business / Tom S. Gillis.
        p.   cm.
    Includes bibliographical references and index.
    ISBN 1-885167-20-2 (trade pb). -- ISBN 1-885167-19-9 (hc)
    1. New business enterprises--Finance.   I. Title.
    HG4027.8.G55   1997   97-771
    658.15'92--dc21   CIP

The author may be contacted at the following address:

> Tom S. Gillis
> 175 Sage Road, Houston, Texas 77056
> Phone (713) 622-2818   Fax (713) 622-0887
> E-mail: TGILLIS@BAYOU.UH.EDU or TGILLIS @ SILVERFOX.ORG

A BARD PRESS BOOK
Developmental Editing: Lianne Mercer
Copyediting: Jeff Morris
Text Design/Cover Design: Suzanne Pustejovsky
Composition and Page Layout: Round Rock Graphics, Inc.
Proofreading: Deborah Costenbader, Doreen Piano
Indexing: Linda Webster
Project Manager: Sherry Sprague

CONTENTS

■

PART ONE

THE STAGES OF THE GAME:
How Your Business Grows

1 The Idea Stage   3

Guts . . . Money—Raising Capital . . . Finding a Need and Filling It . . . Preparation and Conditioning for Action . . . Entrepreneurs vs Volunteers . . . The Entrepreneur's Personal Agenda—Independence . . . Learning on Someone Else's Money . . . Sharing the Idea with Others . . . From Idea to Business Plan . . . Time of Decision . . . The Essence of Entrepreneurship . . . Common Milestones along the Way

2 The Survival Stage   21

In a Fight for Your Life . . . Business Incubators and Government Activities . . . Paid Full-Time Employees . . . Additional Personnel and Skills . . . Unending Quest for Money . . . Record Keeping and Government Reporting . . . Turning Your Dream into Your Company . . . Freeing Your Company to Grow . . . When All Else Fails . . . Skipping the Survival Stage . . . Congratulations! You've Created a Company . . . Common Milestones along the Way

PART TWO

SUCCESSFUL STRATEGIES FOR PLAYING THE GAME:
Starting, Surviving, and Growing Your Small Business

DEDICATION

This book is dedicated to my gracious and loving wife, Frances.

She raised two fine children and built the nest while I tried to build a business. We have worked to find balance in active and productive lives with many friends. Time has been kind to us.

She has patiently supported everything I have tried, but writing this book consumed more time than expected. The process included many hours in front of a computer, mixed with consulting, mentoring, and business, over a four-year period. She remarked that if she were called on to identify my body, she would request that it be turned over because she could recognize my back more readily than my face.

I would marry her again, only faster.

who should read this book?

You should read it . . .

- if you have always wanted to realize the American dream of being in business for yourself.

- if you want to learn what it takes to start and run a successful business.

- if you have or expect to have as few as zero or as many as 200 employees.

- if you are an unemployed manager and want to go into business for yourself.

- if you want to understand the stages of growth your company will experience or is going through, and how things can change without your realizing it.

- if you have survived long enough to realize you need guidance and knowledge to achieve more of your dreams.

- if you're puzzled by the changes in your business that happened just because it grew.

- if you don't understand why growth has stalled when you still do things the way you used to.

- if you have invested in your business every cent you own and all you can borrow, and you still need more.

- if you are searching for a mental spark plug to give you new ideas and knowledge for solving your most pressing problems.

- if you think business is a game and money is the way to keep score.

why I wrote this book

I wrote this book because it's one I wish I'd had when I was in business. Like most entrepreneurs with start-up businesses, I felt lonely and searched for help to accomplish my dreams. Now that I'm a consultant and mentor, it's the book I want my clients to have.

This book is also to assure you that you're not alone. Similar problems have occurred and been solved in many small businesses. It is comforting and enlightening to talk straightforwardly to other entrepreneurs and small-business owners. I encourage you to join a CEO roundtable and get a CEO mentor. You'll find both are educational, profitable experiences.

I'm a firm believer that for every reasonable business problem there's a reasonable business solution—if you can correctly identify and define the problem. After that, if you can't find the solution, you can find someone who can. There's always more than one solution for every problem. Which one you choose is a matter of your own judgment, experience, value system, ego, and managerial style.

Like most unrepentant entrepreneurs, I think business is the most fascinating and complex game I know. It's played non-stop around the world 24 hours every day. Some event, new discovery, or idea that influences your business is happening somewhere on that playing field all the time. You can never know all there is to know about your market and your business.

The theories and suggestions in this book came from many sources: from years of practicing as a CPA and later as a lawyer; from the hard knocks of 24 years of managing my own manufacturing business as it grew larger every year; from reading all the management books I could get my hands on; from participating for many years with fellow entrepreneurs in a CEO roundtable;

from the Silver Fox Advisors (a local consulting group of which I'm a member); and from a lifetime of for-fee and for-free consulting and discussions with friends and business associates. Except for four years with the U.S. Army in World War II and one year with an international marketing firm, all my work experience has been with small businesses.

This advice is general because the book is intended to be of benefit to all types of businesses (construction, service, retail, manufacturing, distributing, etc.). I've included both a theoretical and a practical approach to good small-business management for the 80 percent of business problems common to all businesses, regardless of their product or service. This book is not specifically oriented toward the 20 percent of your business problems that are unique to your specialized business as a service provider, retail operation, wholesaler, contracting firm, or other.

Contradictions occur among these general principles, just as they do in the wisdom of clichés: "Look before you leap," but "He who hesitates is lost." Which principle you finally apply to your problem depends on your facts and your managerial judgment.

No rules, including those in this book, are absolute or apply 100 percent of the time. These generalizations are true most of the time, or else I've given you the guiding principle on which to base your decision after considering your facts. I've tried to tell it like it is.

My conclusions aren't substantiated by documentation, because in the heat of battle I didn't tabulate each detail for later statistical analysis. I stayed alert, tried to stay on my feet, and kept score mentally as my wounds healed and while I considered what went wrong and how to make it right.

I don't claim originality for much of the material presented here. I'm a product of all I've met in my business and professional career. I first learned about the stages of growth during a University of Colorado seminar presented by Dr. Alan C. Filley and Dr. Laurence L. Steinmetz. I attended because I was confused and didn't understand some of the changing attitudes of my trusted older managers. I learned that my company was well into the growth stage and that we were changing to different, more effective management methods. This book mixes those theories with 50 years of personal business experiences.

I would gladly give other specific credit where it's due, but I truthfully can't remember where some of the material came from. I don't remember where I first heard "Business is a game and money is the way to keep score." But I've used that expression a million times, and it's a significant feature in this book's organization. No slight or offense to anyone is intended.

Also, I intend no offense to the many women entrepreneurs and managers who now brighten the business scene. Although I have tried to use gender references as random alternatives, where the terminology is masculine or feminine please understand all such terms to include the equivalent of both genders.

The format for part two of this book follows that used by Bill Townsend in his marvelous book *Up the Organization,* first published in 1970. His book was a best-seller, but it was pointed strictly toward big businesses. I've tried to adapt the same style and format to this book for small businesses. It lets me give more information on more subjects, with both a title and a subject index, and helps you find the information more easily.

The condensed comments and advice written here on many subjects cannot explain all the details you'd like to know on some difficult problems. Many times I've referred you to other books or sources treating various subjects in greater depth. I have no financial interest in any of these books or materials. The authors are unaware that I've recommended their books or software, which I purchased from retail stores, until they see this in print.

There's no such thing as par for the course in growing a successful business, nor can anyone else prepare a road map for you. You must draw your own, using your own knowledge, judgment, energy, personality, and managerial style. You and your business are truly unique.

To say that money is the way to keep score is not to say that materialism and money are the most important things in business. A game with no competition and no way to keep score is no fun. Like Adam Smith, I think you'll make the most money by serving the most people—customers and employees. They are your bosses. Money is made by dealing straightforwardly and honestly with your associates, your employees, and your customers. Money is not made by chicanery, sharp practice, misrepresentation, or manipulation.

I admit freely and up front to being prejudiced. After working for a lifetime with small businesses, it's impossible to be completely unbiased. I know a few things that work and many things that don't. It would be stupid of me at age 75 not to have conclusions and firm convictions based on these experiences and observations.

I'm prejudiced in favor of the capitalistic system and a free-market economy, hard work, common sense, common courtesy and decency, honesty, integrity, family, the Golden Rule, God and Country.

If you're the exceptional entrepreneur who survives the dire statistics of failure, and if your company takes off like a skyrocket instead of growing at the pace of an oak tree, I salute you. You've beaten the odds, and you don't need my warnings and advice. You and your performance are far above the averages. I bid you Godspeed and wish you well.

Lastly, I wrote this book because I want to tell you to keep your eyes and mind open, to think smarter, and to work hard. If entrepreneurship were easy, there would be a lot more rich folks. Persevere. Don't find excuses—find solutions.

I wish you every success.

Tom S. Gillis
Houston, Texas
January 1997

PART
one

THE STAGES OF THE GAME

Your Business Grows

*J*ust as a person grows through infancy, childhood, adolescence, and adulthood, the successful business normally progresses through four identifiable stages of growth: idea, survival, growth, and big business. This progression is not inevitable; nor is it necessarily smooth or without trial and error, reversals, triumphs, tragedies, or slow, unnoticed, neglected slides.

Progress from stage to stage has no direct relation to time, sales volume, number of employees, legal structure, changes in control, centralization of management, decision processes, or invested capital. The lines between stages are not absolute; often they are not even distinct.

You'll be better able to anticipate and plan if you know two things: a normal, growing business goes through these stages, and the entrepreneur's managerial skills must grow faster than the company. It's impossible to determine precisely the time when your business passes from one stage to another, but you'll know in retrospect.

Although these stages are a framework for progress and growth, few companies go the whole route to big business. Some operations stop growing after they reach a profitable stage that the owner considers adequate. The owner is comfortable with modest but steady earnings and wishes to stay in tight control and in touch with everything. Few companies leave the growth stage as long as they're owned and operated by the founder.

The big-business stage, if it occurs, usually happens after at least one change in ownership and management, and when there are many more than 200 employees.

I hope you'll read these first four chapters straight through. They're the foundation for the rest of the book, and they contain knowledge you'll need to grow and understand your company.

THE IDEA
stage

MOST PEOPLE THINK AN IDEA for a product or service is all they need to go into business and become financially independent. You *do* need a unique idea or approach to a market, but you also need two more things.

Years ago, when I was asked, "What does it take to go into business for yourself?" I answered, "Guts and borrowed money." Time and experience have reaffirmed my conviction that these are the two absolute essentials, the bedrock requirements you must have to go into business for yourself. If you have guts and seed money, you'll find an idea that turns you on.

Every company starts with an idea in the mind of one person. The idea doesn't have to be

3

original, new, or unique. It must be something you can do for customers for money. It must be something you believe in.

The idea stage is your dream time. Everyone dreams of riches and wishes for better things. The difference between a wish and a burning desire is the difference between failure and success.

GUTS

G uts is the most important quality for the beginning entrepreneur. Without guts, neither money nor an idea will entice you to enter and play the exciting game of business. You need guts to start a business and to keep going after failure and rejection. You need the commitment to *make* things happen, not just *watch* things happen. There's no substitute for fire in the belly—a burning desire to succeed, to achieve, and to be your own boss. It isn't so much the size of the dog in the fight as the size of the fight in the dog.

The desire "to make a lot of money" is too vague to light the fire. Your idea must be specific: "to make money furnishing customers an easier way to trim lawns" or "to make money furnishing customers a faster, more convenient printing service." To become successful, you must have a specific idea about how to do something better or different from what's now available to your future customers.

You must be willing to do anything and everything required by the business. Tom Fatjo, founder of BFI, started with one truck and one contract to pick up garbage in one subdivision. So the truck could carry more on each load, Tom, who was driving, asked an employee to jump up and down on the garbage in the back to pack it down. When the employee refused, Tom switched places and did it himself.

MONEY—RAISING CAPITAL

Y our plan must include accumulating or raising capital for initial expenses or assets. Backing the idea with money separates the doers from the dreamers and talkers.

Getting enough money is the biggest obstacle most entrepreneurs face. There's never enough. The amount of money you spend just getting ready to do business may seem large, but it's usually small compared with your future needs if you grow. Conserve your cash in every possible way. I've never seen an entrepreneur who didn't think he or she was handicapped by lack of capital. Get used to it.

Over 85 percent of initial financing for start-up companies comes from the entrepreneur's own bank account, assets, family, or friends. While you're in the idea and survival stages, you won't be able to borrow from a bank.

The amount you need for start-up varies with the type of operation you've chosen. If you're performing a service, you can start from your bedroom or garage with a minimum of tools and equipment. Heavy manufacturing is capital intensive because of the large machinery required. A retail store usually requires a large amount of money because the minimum amount of merchandise needed to begin is large, and the business expands in large increments.

Initially you'll see cash outflow for recurring expenses with little or no sales income. Obviously, the more quickly you produce an income stream from sales of services or products, the smaller your start-up cash requirement will be.

FINDING A NEED AND FILLING IT

I deas come easily. The idea of going to the moon has fascinated man since the beginning of time. It became reality only after a tremendous amount of planning, financing, and working. Similarly, your idea will become a real business only after you plan, find money, and work hard to make it happen.

Finding a market or an unfilled need is better than finding a product and then searching for the market. Your idea should be to do something to satisfy a need you've already found. If you don't have a specific product or service in mind, consider buying an existing product, company, or franchise that already fills a need.

Sometimes the idea stage is short. If you have guts and money, you may recognize your idea sooner; however, don't make a snap decision. The more time and money you spend, the more you discover. You'll either become more committed or decide to search further.

My idea stage lasted nine years, from the time I got out of the army until I finally got into business for myself. Since American production capacity had helped us win World War II, I was favorably inclined toward manufacturing, but I didn't have any idea of a specific product. I wasn't an engineer, but I had a high mechanical aptitude. I went to work for a small petroleum equipment manufacturing company as their seventh employee, driving the pickup truck in the morning and keeping the books in the afternoon for $1.25 an hour. The owner had invested $350,000. I didn't have, nor could I get, that much money.

During the nine years, as I worked and investigated, my idea changed four times. Often, simultaneously, I had full-time and part-time jobs or went to school. I used the "learn on someone else's money" approach I recommend later in this chapter. Three of the four times, after working for others for one to three years, I decided that what they were doing wasn't the right idea for me. I finally returned to my first idea, manufacturing, because time had allowed me to accumulate capital and taught me how to get around the limits that stopped me the first time.

Thomas Edison said, "Genius is one percent inspiration and 99 percent perspiration." Entrepreneurial ideas may take a little more than one percent, but not much; execution is always 99 times harder than dreaming and imagining. The military adage is "A poor plan well executed is better than a good plan poorly executed." It's not the idea, it's the execution of the idea that's most important to success.

If you don't have a specific idea, at least narrow your search to what interests you. Write down what general type of business you want to be in— retail or wholesale, service, construction, manufacturing, food, computers, and so on. Decide what geographical area you prefer, near your

> **SUCCESS SECRET #1**
>
> *Originating an idea doesn't make an entrepreneur. Backing an idea with guts and money and building a business does.*

home but with access to the largest number of customers. Is the growth potential of this business large or small? Do you feel comfortable in this business?

If you're still drawing a mental blank, read local business-for-sale ads or flip through the yellow pages of your phone book and see which businesses excite you. Analyze why they interest you. Why don't others? The more specifically you can describe what you're looking for and will accept, the more likely you are to find it soon.

PREPARATION AND CONDITIONING FOR ACTION

T he dreamer who becomes an active entrepreneur is usually conditioned by temperament and early training to be original in thought and to be action oriented. The conditioned mind selects and grows the idea. Conditioning the mind and having the desire is the real making of an entrepreneur. You have most of this conditioning, or you wouldn't be reading this book. Many Americans are somewhat conditioned and programmed by their parents to want to be in business for themselves, but not all are willing to act.

When circumstances force an employment decision, it may not occur to you to go into business if you haven't had this early preparation. With family conditioning and youthful experience in earning and handling money, guts and circumstances may give you enough confidence to look for an idea and strike out into a new business; but no one can predict exactly when and how this may happen.

Not everyone is suited to be an entrepreneur (see ENTREPRE-NEURS—ARE THEY BORN OR MADE? in part two). However, anyone with the necessary confidence, energy, and desire can begin. The failure rate is high, because wherever there's an opportunity to succeed, there's also an opportunity to fail.

What sort of person is likely to succeed as an entrepreneur? There's been a lot of study on this subject. If you're interested, you'll find many books discussing or testing your aptitude for being an entrepreneur. None of these tests is more than 85 percent accurate and none can measure guts or the "fire in the belly."

As an entrepreneur, you're an optimist and a practical dreamer. The profound break from thinking and dreaming to acting doesn't happen instantaneously or without preparation. Sooner or later you must couple your idea with action.

ENTREPRENEURS AS VOLUNTEERS

The only important dreams are those you act on. This job can't be assigned by your parents, teachers, bosses, or government. America has always had many volunteers because most of our citizens either came to our shores as volunteers or descended from volunteers.

Some family companies suffer because second and third generations don't volunteer. Unfortunately, family pressures, perceived heirship obligations, or the path of greatest reward and least resistance sometimes places descendants in control of the family business without the burning desire or knowledge to run it.

THE ENTREPRENEUR'S PERSONAL AGENDA—INDEPENDENCE

Entrepreneurs volunteer to strike out on their own and take complete control of their lives. Confident of their ability to produce a financially independent future, beginning entrepreneurs always work for themselves for less than they could earn working for someone else. They want to be their own boss, to acquire fame and fortune, and to experience the joy of achieving. Analyze your motives: What do you expect from having your own business?

Most entrepreneurs realize that business is a complex game and money is the way you keep score. Many like the challenges of the survival stage more than the growth stage. At times, profit is almost a by-product rather than a principal objective.

The skill that creates a company and jobs where none existed before is creativity of the highest order. You'll be a good citizen, a good capitalist, and a good businessperson if you successfully run your enterprise and give rewarding, steady employment to yourself and one or more other families. It isn't necessary that one of your goals be to become a member of the Fortune 500.

LEARNING ON SOMEONE ELSE'S MONEY

A fter you've chosen an idea or the specific field that your idea is in, learn all you can on someone else's money while you gather required experience, knowledge, and skill. If you aren't already doing so, go to work for someone who owns a similar business, sells to the same market, or uses similar means of production. Better still, do that and then do it again. Quit the first job when your rate of learning slows (usually after one or two years), and go to work for a similar company in a different capacity. No business, including yours, does everything perfectly. Learn from multiple companies, and learn more than one good way to do things.

Many excellent technicians and craftsmen think that because they're the best welder or printer they would be the perfect owner of a welding or printing company. Although entrepreneurs must know and understand the work being done, successful owners with more than a few employees must manage the work of others to satisfy customers, not do the work themselves. Technical skills aren't the same as people-organizing and managing skills.

If you go to work for a company with the idea of going into business for yourself, you'll be one of the best employees that company could have because of your broad interest, open mind, dedication, and willingness to assume responsibility. Figure out what mistakes the owner makes and how you'll do things better. Help the owner all you can; you're helping yourself at the same time.

Give a good day's work for a good day's pay, and then some. When you leave, break clean. Take only the knowledge in your head and the experience of having worked in your chosen field. Remain friends if you can; the same thing may happen to you when you're a business owner.

SHARING THE IDEA WITH OTHERS

O riginally, the idea exists solely in your mind. As you discuss and perfect the idea, you'll probably share your dreams with others, particularly family members. You may be looking for future associates or employees. To be acceptable, these people should be able to make significant contributions of skill or money and be of compatible attitudes, ethics, and work habits.

Once your operation gets going well and involves a group of people, the idea will take on a life of its own. Others will have their own view of your idea and will offer their opinions, sometimes disagreeing with you. Clear up disagreements and misunderstandings as soon as you recognize them.

You can take multiple routes to your own business. Most of this discussion applies directly to the classical route of finding your idea and starting your operation. Alternatives, discussed in part two, include buying all or part of an existing business or buying a franchise operation, which is the same as buying a detailed, proven business plan.

FROM IDEA TO BUSINESS PLAN

T he *idea* grows and develops into the nucleus of the *plan,* the next action step to make your idea become reality. I strongly recommend that you write a business plan. This requires detailed mental planning; it should attempt to solve all foreseeable problems. Checklists or other people who have business experience may point out problems you don't yet recognize.

Actually, a business plan is seldom written this early. Few start-up companies have a business plan, and only about one in ten growth companies do. I must admit I didn't do it. When I was starting my business, such planning was called corporate planning, and only very big companies did it. It used to delight me when any business associate showed me samples of corporate plans used by one of the "big boys."

Modern management practices recognize the basic importance of this planning procedure for companies of all sizes. If business planning is new to you, search for help from others, from books, or from computer software. Although I didn't have a written business plan, I did have a written set of lifetime objectives, which I wrote after reading Napoleon Hill's *Think and Grow Rich*. Several paragraphs of that plan concerned business. I revised them every two or three years.

One trigger for finally going through the mental agony of thoroughly thinking, planning, and writing down your future actions is lenders or investors who won't loan you money until they approve your business plan. A business plan can't possibly anticipate everything that will come up; however, your plan must answer these hard questions:

- Have you found the best market for your product or service?

- What is the profile of your ideal customer?

- How can you reach and sell to this customer?

- What sales price will produce greatest volume and profit?

- What is a realistic sales volume for your first year?

- How much money do you need?
- Do you have the required skills or have access to them?
- How long will it be until you can make a steady profit?

For the first year, plan on getting by on 50 percent of your expected sales. This can be a sobering experience.

As planning progresses, and as papers, materials, and supplies begin to accumulate, your garage or a room in your house or in another location will likely become the focus of your activity. You might build models, prepare samples, print preliminary sales brochures, telemarket, or make engineering drawings. You'll choose a name and a logo, get permits and licenses if required, and arrange a business address and phone number.

> **SUCCESS SECRET #2**
>
> *Identify a product or service you believe in and a niche market you can serve best.*

You'll probably do all this planning in your spare time, on nights and weekends, while you continue to work full time at your old job. Until the plan and your commitment to action are complete, it's not wise to quit your old job.

TIME OF DECISION

The crucial decision point in the economic life of most individuals occurs between the ages of 25 and 35. By working for various others until that time, bright, energetic individuals have learned to manage more money and resources than they've ever owned. Due to seniority and increasing skills, they have probably reached a comfortable financial level.

At this point, individuals can either continue to climb some corporate or business ladder or select a career in the uncharted world of the self-employed. Ultimately, some trigger event occurs, or people find enough courage to set a deadline to quit the old job and start a new, full-time operation of their own.

When you commit your energy and your entire future to making your idea a reality, you're no longer a dreamer. You've become an entrepreneur. You've left the idea stage and launched your business into its survival stage.

Preparation, experience, and planning make it a little easier than jumping off a cliff. Some people get pushed off the cliff by being laid off. Since they already have experience, market knowledge, and some money, they may make a rapid start.

The final trigger for many entrepreneurs comes when they realize that no matter how much their present or future employer is paying them, they are earning more than that amount, including a profit for the company. Entrepreneurs want everything they can earn. The only way you get to keep everything you earn is to work for yourself. That is, you get to keep whatever is left over after all the employees and bills are paid, whether great or small.

If you choose the entrepreneurial life, your standard of living will take a step backward. A period of financial sacrifice and belt tightening is necessary while all your available funds go into the business. If you and your family can't or won't pay this price, you shouldn't go into business for yourself.

THE ESSENCE OF ENTREPRENEURSHIP

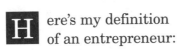ere's my definition of an entrepreneur:

> *An entrepreneur has the guts to risk everything—money, time, and future—to develop as owner an embryonic undertaking into a successful enterprise. When entrepreneurs succeed, the rewards are valuable services for customers, employment for others, and fulfillment and wealth for themselves and their associates.*

The creative thing that only an entrepreneur can do is to give an idea life and substance of its own by committing guts and money to its growth. Until then, no one can buy the idea or its products. No one can sell anything to it or buy from it. There can be no employees or customers. Until then, managers have nothing to manage.

Although this is the essence of entrepreneurship in the classical sense, there are also entrepreneurs who have the guts and the money to assume the controlling position in a small company or operation, thereby taking over someone else's not yet fully developed or proven idea. They, too, risk their money and future on their ability to make a company grow larger and stronger.

> **SUCCESS SECRET #3**
>
> *The people who win are the people who think they can. Believe so strongly in yourself and your idea that you risk your fortune and your future on that belief.*

When several customers pay real money at a competitive price for your product or service, your business is launched. A halting, unsteady stream of sales and cash has been started. Now you want to keep it coming, make it bigger, and prove that your dream can become reality. You've launched a business and become an entrepreneur. Your company's struggle for survival has begun.

COMMON MILESTONES

along the way

These events typify the idea stage for many companies, although they may not all happen or may not occur in this sequence. These milestones are intended to give you a more specific idea of what to expect during this stage.

- Examine yourself as to motivation, psychology, and personality type. Do you have entrepreneurial qualities?
- Search the yellow pages for business ideas.
- Recognize an opportunity, a need, or a saleable product or service. Find a need or market niche you can fill.
- Work for a company in an operation similar to the one you're considering.
- Based on experience gained while learning on someone else's money, change your concept or idea, or make your commitment to risk all, to plunge ahead into the unknown.
- Plan to bring this idea to market and form a company.
- Consider buying a franchise if you have no specific product or service in mind.
- Accumulate or solicit capital. Plan a way to finance your operation.
- Bring in others to share and develop the idea, the plan, or the dream.
- If you don't own 100 percent, decide on initial equity percentages for other contributors.
- Plan or produce the product or service. Make samples or pilot models, or determine in a practical way that the idea will work and be acceptable to customers.
- Decide on a pricing and billing structure.

- Accumulate supplies, equipment, or raw materials.
- Design sales literature or brochures.
- Organize your activities. Write a business plan, including a marketing plan.
- Make a cash forecast for the first 18 months of operations.
- Revise the product or service as additional ideas are presented.
- Sell personal assets to raise money.
- Sell to a large enough number and variety of customers to be convinced of the market validity of the product or service.
- Quit your old job. Work full time on the new venture.

FROM IDEA STAGE INTO SURVIVAL STAGE

What does it take to get your business from the idea stage into the survival stage? Energy, work experience, and the following:

Guts

THIS IS A COMBINATION OF SELF-CONFIDENCE AND THE DESIRE and willingness to take control of your life. Guts includes not only the initial spark that lights the fire in the belly, but the commitment to continue, bounce back, and recover from inevitable setbacks and failures. The ultimate question is this: Are you willing to risk everything—your fortune and your future—on *your* belief in your ability to carry out your dream?

If you think you'll lose, you've lost,
For the out in this world you'll find
Success begins with a fellow's will—
It's all in your state of mind.

Life's battles don't always go
To the stronger or faster man;
But sooner or later the man who wins
Is the man who thinks he can.

—Walter D. Wintle

Seed Money

HOW MUCH DOES IT TAKE? Enough to survive your mistakes and cover personal and business expenses until your total gross profit or gross margin (total sales minus cost of sales) covers all expenses.

Trying to borrow start-up financing from a bank will get you a prompt, polite, but firm refusal. The best and usual source of start-up financing is from your piggy bank or from the bank assets you've been accumulating for years.

To conserve your scarcest commodity—cash (discussed in greater detail in part two)—let me give you a few hints now:

- Always keep a cash reserve for payroll, payroll taxes, or absolute emergencies.
- Don't buy land, or a building, or real estate.
- Be sparing with fixtures or machinery.
- Don't buy what you can rent.
- Contract out to others for production or whatever you can.

- Don't buy more than a bare 60-day supply of anything.
- Never hire people for future needs in a service business, or any business.
- Until you've checked out the unknowns and are positive you have a winner, make no unnecessary financial commitments.

Your Unique Business or Idea

THIS IS WHAT YOU'RE GOING INTO BUSINESS TO DO. If you're not an inventor (most of us aren't), find a product or service to sell. Your idea doesn't have to be patented or involve rocket-science technology. Do something better than others; get it there faster, cleaner, better, easier, or cheaper. It can be as simple as providing better service, better location, greater selection, or easier, more convenient, faster delivery.

A small company can always react, serve, and deliver faster with more customized products than a big company. Identify and focus on your sustainable, competitive advantage.

Customers

THE PURPOSE OF YOUR BUSINESS IS TO CREATE CUSTOMERS. Never mind your product, technology, or good intentions, without customers who pay money for a product or service you have no business. The technical excellence of your product, the enthusiasm and skill of your management, your soaring dreams of greatness will come to naught if you have no customers.

People

YOUR MOST IMPORTANT RESOURCE IS PEOPLE: first, selecting, then motivating, then guiding and training them. Many entrepreneurs, especially those with strong technical backgrounds, fail to realize how much success depends on people skills and the ability to keep many people pulling harmoniously together toward the same goals. More businesses fail from lack of people skills or managerial skills than from lack of technical skills.

Don't scrimp on people. You're much better off with first-class people doing first-rate jobs than you are with second-class people doing second-rate jobs.

Self-Starting Ability

MAKE THIS YOUR MOTTO: *If it's to be, it's up to me.*

In times of confusion and doubt, entrepreneurs push ahead into the unknown, confident they can handle the situation. Bureaucrats and managers retreat into the security of the known, proven environment.

Imagination and Innovation

YOU MUST CONTINUALLY VISUALIZE and see in your mind's eye things that do not now exist. This entails finding new solutions to old problems, or solutions for problems others may not see at all.

You'll make mistakes. Not every new idea is a good one; some changes make things worse. Constantly search, compare, question, and consider alternate and multiple ways of doing everything. Always look for innovative ways to make manpower time more productive, to reduce total cost, and to reduce the time span between order and final delivery.

THE SURVIVAL stage

 OUR INITIAL, LIMITED SALES to real customers for competitive prices have demonstrated but not proven the commercial validity of your idea. Your objective now becomes survival, then growth.

Early in the game, your greatest pressure is dealing with long hours and low personal income, both of which happen when you start from scratch. Overcoming problems in the survival stage is a matter of dedication and intense personal effort.

21

Sales are irregular and unpredictable. You have many bad months and some good ones; sometimes big orders, sometimes none. During the lulls, you try to figure out why. You listen eagerly to customer comments and suggestions. You note the need for revisions or changes in your product or service to make it more appealing and more saleable. You work harder to increase sales. Hopes, dreams, and reality now ride an emotional and financial roller coaster together.

Increased business activity and potential for future growth require that you quit your other job to devote all your time to your new operation. Part-time employees and workers can serve as an effective balance between needed work and limited funds for hiring, but part-time management absolutely won't work. At this stage, management is a full-time job—at least 60 hours a week.

The survival stage is the only growth stage in which you cannot linger forever. It's like bleeding to death. Unless you have an unlimited supply of money or blood to lose, there's a limit to how long you can survive without running out. Your immediate objective is to get enough customers and get so good at running your business that your gross revenue covers all expenses. At this point, you'll hit cash break-even and shut off the outflow of cash.

Each month of profit makes you stronger. Every month in the red makes you weaker. Continuation of either course for a prolonged period has a tremendous cumulative effect.

IN A FIGHT FOR YOUR LIFE

Y ou, your dream, and your business are almost one at this stage. Should something happen to you now, your company will probably be liquidated rather than continue. Your idea is not yet so crystallized, organized, and proven as to be capable of continuing life on its own.

Continued operation exposes defects in your original plan or product. You modify your plan over and over, each time with high hopes that the new product or service will result in more sales, better acceptance in the marketplace, or less cost to produce. Remedying defects in existing inventory costs money and time. There are no guarantees.

Survival means you must provide enough cash each month to cover payroll, taxes, and operating expenses until you have

> **SUCCESS SECRET #4**
>
> *Only you can guarantee your success: "If it's to be, it's up to me."*

sufficient cash income from sales. Every payday and every month-end bring high blood pressure and a crisis until sales get high enough to cover expenses—which could take several years.

You're fighting a battle against time. Produce sales at a profitable price and in sufficient volume before cash runs out, or die. Peter Drucker, the most widely accepted authority on business management today, says you must have enough money to survive your mistakes.

Be alert. Listen to how you talk about the market. At this early stage, many times you'll catch yourself talking about what the market *should* buy and not what it *is* buying. As founder, you're often more dedicated to products than to profits or customers. If you hold too long to your dream of how things should be rather than how they really are, you will have a problem.

BUSINESS INCUBATORS AND GOVERNMENT ACTIVITIES

I f you're located in or near a large city, you may find a business incubator you can fit into. A business incubator is a collection of administrative facilities that provides small entrepreneurial businesses with affordable rental space and low-cost facilities shared with other survival-stage businesses. These facilities include secretarial services, receptionist, answering service, copying and fax machines, and possibly warehousing, shipping, and receiving.

The sponsoring agency is frequently a government agency or educational institution, although some are run by entrepreneurs on a for-profit basis. In addition to furnishing most required facilities at low cost, they also provide business counseling, a helpful, sometimes life-saving service.

Such a facility allows you to get further with less money and fewer employees than owned facilities. After you've passed a certain size or time limit, you must move out to make room for another beginning firm. (See INCUBATORS FOR START-UP BUSINESSES in part two.)

Most large cities, states, and several departments of the federal government have active programs to identify, encourage, counsel, and help prospective entrepreneurs in every way except by furnishing money. Most of these programs are sound and are usually free or at nominal cost to the recipient. Many programs are pointed directly at the start-up or survival-stage business. Usually a different set of programs, administered by other departments of the same agencies, are pointed toward growth-stage companies.

PAID FULL-TIME EMPLOYEES

Y our first paid full-time employee may be a hired worker, partner, or associate. It takes real courage and confidence to guarantee a regular paycheck to someone else when you know that you may not get one. Your spouse, usually unpaid, may help in uncounted ways.

Hiring the first employee is sometimes necessary to get started. Hiring the second employee is a momentous decision— you're doubling your fixed payroll!

Your second paid full-time employee, as well as each additional one, makes you grateful for the increased sales volume that she brings (and that pays her), and more anxious every payday about your increased fixed-dollar overhead.

Your employees are motivated because they're working side by side with the boss. You see who and what procedures are productive. You know everything that goes on. You can't avoid knowing whether operations are profitable, because all money coming in or going out passes through your hands.

ADDITIONAL PERSONNEL AND SKILLS

At this stage, in addition to production workers, you need associates and employees whose skills cover your weaknesses or whose funds you may need. Basic functions or skills required are sales, production, and minor bookkeeping and administrative duties. Depending upon your technology, a strong production manager may also make a contribution.

When you employ or associate with people whose strengths cover your weaknesses, your enterprise will have competence in most required areas. Two partners strong in the same skill are destined to disagree about handling problems within the area of their common expertise. As a lawyer, I've dissolved more partnerships than I've formed, often because both partners are strong in the same skill.

The best operations I've seen are run by a strong sales-oriented person coupled with a strong administrator or manager. These skills complement each other nicely and cover almost all the bases with only two people. Throughout the survival stage, this is what my company had. I was the administrator with reasonable people skills.

In the survival-stage company, there's no room for part-time management or management by committee. A domineering entrepreneur who knows everything that's going on, makes all the decisions, and controls the smallest details has a beneficial impact on operations. This condition usually lasts through survival. Later, in the growth stage, this operating style stops the company's growth; the limitations of the one person become the limitations of the company.

No formal organization chart or employee structure exists or is needed. Your company is one big family inspired by and motivated by you. Without any organization chart or guidance from you, employees will instinctively divide themselves into official family, trusted employees, and transient workers. Sales, product specialization, and minimal administrative capability may be loosely organized and recognizable. There may be a chief technician, if needed. When you're small and don't have a lot of Indians, you can't afford many chiefs.

> ## SUCCESS SECRET #5
>
> *Dedication to service and quality will make you rich faster than dedication to profit.*

Basically, people do what they think needs doing without specific job assignments or titles. Aggressive people take over many jobs. Nonaggressive ones don't, but they work hard doing what they think is necessary.

UNENDING QUEST FOR MONEY

On several occasions your bank account will run out and you'll look frantically for more money. Establish credit everywhere you can. Within reason, defer paying bills coming due. Sell something you own. Advances on personal credit cards have financed crises for many small businesses. When all else fails, go to friends, family, and employees. A temporary loan for "just 30 days, just to tide us over" probably cannot be repaid and remains invested in the business. Banks are not yet receptive.

It's essential that paychecks (for everyone except yourself) go out on the scheduled payday every time, regardless of anything else. Employees' families depend on those checks to pay their bills, frequently live on pocket

> **SUCCESS SECRET #6**
>
> *As an entrepreneur, you get whatever is left over after all employees and bills are paid— even if it's a deficit.*

cash, and cannot skip a payday without missing meals. If you don't get paid, you have the owner's privilege of making up the deficiency from other sources so the company can continue to pay its bills.

The discipline of short money forces you to refine your judgment of the marketplace in order to get more money from more customers. This cruel treatment eliminates those who don't learn the lessons the capitalist world teaches.

RECORD KEEPING AND GOVERNMENT REPORTING

S tart your first financial records with a simple bookkeeping system that keeps track of your bank account, your payroll and payroll taxes, who owes you what, and how much you owe whom. A simple system that's current is better than an elaborate system that's four weeks behind. Manual records, provided they are current, will do fine if that's all you can manage.

I shudder when no current financial statements with reliable, detailed information are available to run and control businesses intelligently. Computers are so inexpensive and accounting software is so simple and helpful that it's easier to record cash receipts and checks currently than to neglect them. Correct financial statements are then available whenever you want them.

Your cash flow will be faster if you invoice customers as rapidly as you can. To start the customer's paperwork processing, send the invoice along with the merchandise. Get advances from customers on future work, if that's acceptable practice in your industry. Your accounts-payable person must learn which payments may be deferred without the vendor complaining too much or refusing to ship essential materials.

Government reports and payment of payroll taxes and sales taxes are very important. Many survival-stage entrepreneurs are surprised at the speed and indifference with which taxing authorities will confiscate your bank account or shut your doors for continued late payments of these taxes, regardless of your good intentions. (See INTERNAL REVENUE SERVICE (IRS) IS A PREFERRED CREDITOR in part two.)

TURNING YOUR DREAM INTO YOUR COMPANY

Y our company has nothing that can really be described as management. Your company has just one boss: you. No private knowledge or private lives exist within the survival-stage company. Everyone knows whose children are sick and each other's dietary preferences. Everyone works long hours, frequently without extra pay.

Ingenious, inexpensive solutions to problems are common. An early portable computer company torture-tested its new products by putting them in the trunk of the boss's car, which the boss drove a lot of miles over bumpy roads. If the model still worked properly after two weeks, it was declared okay.

You continuously, agonizingly reappraise (either consciously or unconsciously) all aspects of your plans and operations. Why aren't more customers buying? Why aren't you getting rich and growing faster? What more must you learn about your market, your customers, your competitors, your craft, and your costs? How can you do it faster, better, and at less cost?

Finding answers requires dedication and long hours. Two young partners, before starting their business, declared that they wouldn't conform to the usual mold of overworked business owners. Instead, they would observe 8-to-5 office hours and spend weekends relaxing with their families. They weren't going to become slaves to their business. Their money ran out and they folded in less than a year.

Your company now exists in the hearts and minds of your employees and yourself. It's found a need in the operations of some repeat customers. The company has become separate from your personality and your original idea because associates and customers are also involved. Since the time and habits of others are affected, changing your company is no longer as simple as waking up with a new idea.

FREEING YOUR COMPANY TO GROW

Your company started as a one-person company, but if it remains so (with you making all managerial decisions and supervising every detail), its growth will be limited. The restrictions of a 24-hour day and your physical stamina limit growth by causing late decisions, late deliveries, neglected operations, and inefficiencies.

> **SUCCESS SECRET #7**
>
> *The purpose of your business is to create and serve customers.*

Survival-stage growing pains are often overlooked as mere operating inefficiencies. If the national economy or business activity in your industry turns down, these growing pains can become terminal.

To get bigger, delegate duties and responsibilities and begin to work through managers. In the growth stage, you'll be managing managers rather than employees, so get accustomed to delegating.

Your relationship to your company is similar to a mother's relationship to her child. You're always aware that a tender, growing thing needs your constant attention, thought, and best efforts. Not all your time will be spent in direct help or contact, but that awareness nags continually no matter what you are doing.

In the survival stage, you're committed to a product that will satisfy a need, but you may have trouble describing or identifying your market. In order to grow, you must move from being product oriented to being market oriented.

WHEN ALL ELSE FAILS

My fondest hope and dream is that this book will help you become a better, more creative entrepreneur and help you avoid becoming one of those awful statistics of new businesses that fail.

If at some point after you've gotten started you're unable to obtain the necessary customers and sales volume to cover your expenses and you end up insolvent and out of business, don't think it's because someone is mad at you or that you're not a decent American citizen. The capitalist system is telling you that the job you've been doing is either unnecessary or inefficient. Customers, who vote with their dollars in a free-market economy, are saying that you judged them incorrectly. They can get what they want elsewhere more easily or for less money. You should try something else.

SKIPPING THE SURVIVAL STAGE

I f you have enough money, plus desire and knowledge in your chosen business field, you can almost skip the survival stage by buying a well-selected franchise from a national firm. Investigate to be certain that you're getting a repeatedly proven plan, for a business you can operate profitably, from a reliable and friendly franchiser. This may require more start-up money, but you'll get know-how, instruction, supervision, and a detailed, proven business plan. Usually, you'll begin and end with almost the same size business.

If you choose to acquire someone else's going business, you'll either skip some of these start-up problems or discover greater ones. You'll undoubtedly have to solve many problems the previous owner was wrestling with.

CONGRATULATIONS! YOU'VE CREATED A COMPANY

B ecause of what you've built into your company by the time you're into the growth stage, you've created something greater than yourself, something that may survive your mortality and your original objectives. You've achieved takeoff and are now headed for steady growth.

You've found something you can profitably and repeatedly produce and sell into a known and proven market. You have an income stream large enough to cover all costs (including your own modest salary) with enough left over to start paying off debts and buying more assets and to justify some bank borrowing.

The best working environment you can create is one that rewards and encourages teamwork and better, faster service to customers. You've succeeded when the harder your employees work making money for themselves, the more they make for the company and for you.

COMMON MILESTONES

along the way

These events typify the survival stage for many companies, although they may not all happen or may not occur in this sequence. These milestones are intended to give you a more specific idea of what to expect during this stage.

- Make more than a few isolated sales of your product or services.
- Hire your first full-time paid employee.
- Search for more money as you run short. Get turned down by a bank; go to friends, family, and employees.
- Set up a simple record-keeping system for your own information and government reports.
- Decide to incorporate or to operate as a partnership or proprietorship.
- Get an account number and instructions from state and federal taxing authorities.
- Double your work force. Hire a second full-time employee.
- Delay introduction of new models until old inventory is sold or until you can afford to make changes.
- Learn shortcuts to increase production and lower costs.
- Fight despair when sales are low or nonexistent.
- Take a course in salesmanship or marketing.
- Hire a part-time or full-time bookkeeper.
- Find new sources to supply important components or services.
- Acquire equipment or fixtures to increase productivity or improve quality.

- Hire production workers, but not managerial people. New employees are untrained but enthusiastic. Expect them to learn after they arrive.
- Continually revise product or service to make it more appealing and more saleable.
- Spend more time promoting sales.
- Run out of money again.
- See for the first time income from sales exceeding expenses (but not regularly or continuously).

FROM SURVIVAL STAGE INTO GROWTH STAGE

Methods and skills that successfully managed three people won't work with thirteen or one hundred thirty. If your management methods don't evolve and develop, your company won't grow and can easily go downhill.

Some of these skills are the maturation or continuation in a larger context of the requirements to get started discussed in the last chapter. To get actively into the game of business and succeed as a major player, you should have the following:

Managers, Associates, or Partners

ALTHOUGH ENTREPRENEURSHIP IS USUALLY A SOLO ACT, inspired managers or partners who contribute skills to cover your areas of weakness, and maybe contribute money too, are a desirable asset. Choose the smartest, strongest managers or partners you can find and afford. *Hire people smarter than you are, thereby proving you're smarter than they are.*

During the survival and growth stages, your objective with partners is to give maximum performance incentives with minimum loss of equity or control. Until you're absolutely certain of long-term compatibility of temperament, attitude, work habits, ethics, competence, and areas of authority with the partner involved, give cash bonuses or percentages of operating profits as incentives rather than percentages of equity. If you make a mistake, it's easier to terminate the relationship with fewer strings attached.

Ability to Organize and Delegate

YOU HAVE ONLY 24 HOURS IN YOUR DAY. Your stature as manager increases when you learn that you needn't do everything yourself. Organize, prioritize, and delegate. If you don't change or grow in managerial competence, you will quickly reach your level of incompetence or the invisible wall of management.

To survive and grow, you must become the coach of a team of many players, then the coach of a team of managers. A growth-stage company needs multiple decision makers, with different areas of expertise and authority, bound together by teamwork and incentives. Delegation allows functional specialization—production, sales, accounting, and technology—if required.

The president's job is to carry the torch and lead the way, to set goals and allocate resources and people according to priorities. Leadership and charisma become more important as the organization gathers more people.

Commitment to Excellence

BUILD YOUR REPUTATION FOR QUALITY. Start with the first customer you serve. Erratic or undependable quality, service, and policies build neither a good reputation nor a strong, loyal customer base.

Word-of-mouth advertising is the best kind you can get. Quality comes first, quantity later. If you don't have quality, quantity will never come.

Dedicate yourself to improving service and lowering the cost to the customer. Get your organization to join you. Set the example, create the team, give the incentives, and share the rewards.

Vision

YOUR VISION ISN'T A MISSION OR A GOAL. Your vision is guidance to live by, without end or time limit, while you accomplish missions and surpass intermediate goals. People with widely varying motives can march to the same drummer if they understand and share the same vision. Employees' mental pictures control their actions.

Visionary companies stand out by setting ambitious goals, communicating them to employees, and living their ideology, which becomes a purpose beyond making money. Tom Watson, founder of IBM, used to tell people that they weren't just doing business, they were building a company.

Self-Discipline

YOU WON'T SUCCEED IF YOU CAN'T keep your time, attention, and money focused on the vision you're building. You must have the self-discipline to make short-term sacrifices in favor of long-term gains and to defer self-gratification and pleasure until after the work is done.

With self-discipline, you'll continue to work on solutions. Without it, you're part of the problem.

Ability to Adapt to Continuous Change

BE PREPARED FOR CONTINUOUS CHANGE, both inside and outside your company. Prepare for it. Make it happen. Don't be scared by it.

No matter how hard you try, you can't stop changes. The way you did business last year, last quarter, may not work as well this year, this quarter. Neither bad nor good times last forever. Grow during the good times. Don't shrink too much during the bad. Remain open-minded and alert.

You must grow faster than your business. The only thing that endures is change.

Market Focus and Expertise

THE GRAVEYARD OF DEAD COMPANIES is full of those with complacent managers who neglected personal contact between top management and customers, and who continued to read their old market rather than the changed one that exists today or will exist tomorrow.

The strongest position your company can have is a solid, preferential relationship with your customers as well as a thorough knowledge and understanding of what your customers are doing with your product and why. Only then can you say you know your market.

Negotiating Skill

YOU'LL GET NOT WHAT YOU DESERVE, but what you negotiate.

Almost nothing of importance that you will decide or acquire during your business career is absolutely fixed in all its terms on a take-it-or-leave-it basis. The required skill is continuous weighing of what you think the values are and what you think the other person may think the values are. Your views will differ from his or hers. By knowing these differences, you will know when to press to make a deal and when to walk away and look elsewhere.

THE GROWTH stage

NOW THAT YOU'VE FOUND A WINNING FORMULA and proven it repeatedly with profitable sales, your whole world brightens. There's usually no specific event that you can celebrate with a company party, but the continuous, month-to-month burden of impending financial disaster begins to seem a little lighter.

Consistent profits allow you to dream and make many more plans than a few dollars can accomplish. Since survival seems assured, sustaining and increasing growth becomes a specific objective. With no encouragement, your dreams can quickly outrun reality.

Your physical involvement is greatest in the survival stage. The impending crisis atmosphere and intense personal interaction with fellow employees and customers can be exciting. Because of the challenge and your deep involvement, you might prefer to extend the control and management methods of the survival stage into this new, profitable level.

ATTITUDES TOWARD GROWTH

Your growth-stage company may cease to grow at any time, through either conscious effort or unconscious neglect on your part.

Some entrepreneurs think, correctly, that small can be beautiful. You may deliberately choose to remain small if your financial and social needs have been satisfied.

By the time you're in your mid-50s, you may have become comfortable with your lifestyle. You're a successful capitalist and entrepreneur, pleased with your dependable income, the steady build-up of your net worth over time, staying out of debt, and avoiding complications. Your outlook has slowly shifted from increasing your total fortune to preserving what you have. You may not be willing to fight harder for more, nor to risk losing what you've gained.

Some companies cease to grow because they fail to react to the evolving marketplace. Older, lazier management may not even recognize that the market and its competitors are changing. The company just quits growing.

An established, mature company could quit growing and stay in slow or static existence mode for years if the market did not evolve. However, in most of today's fast-changing markets, management must change just to stay alive.

TRANSITIONAL PROBLEMS

Big may not be better, but it is definitely different. If you choose to grow, as most companies do, you and your employees will begin to notice problems. The increasing volume of orders, shipments, paperwork, and production spotlights bottlenecks and unforeseen control problems you didn't notice at lower levels of operation.

When the job of management goes beyond what one person can do efficiently—when you feel overloaded—you'll never get around to dealing with some critical priorities. A tip-off is when you begin to be surprised by results and distressed by problems brought to you that you didn't even know existed. Customers complain about things you were completely unaware of. These are signs that you can no longer manage 100 percent of the business by the seat of your pants or during your 24-hour day.

Some owners recognize problems and react to correct them sooner than others. Experience and background determine priorities for detecting and solving these growing pains.

If you have a technical or mechanical background, you'll be more sensitive to the need for production equipment and will more readily spend time and money in this area. If you have strong sales or marketing experience, that's where you'll spend more readily while you neglect other functions. Thus the company will progress more rapidly in some areas than in others.

> **SUCCESS SECRET # 8**
>
> *Build a working environment that encourages everyone and shares rewards for teamwork and better, faster customer service.*

Usually, neither you nor anyone else recognizes or acts on the necessary changes in managerial style and methods. After several crises have passed and been analyzed, you realize that a trained, alert employee might have averted them. Someone, not necessarily you, realizes that a new procedure or policy would make things simpler, faster, or safer.

Begin to shift your time and attention from your personal productivity to planning and managing. Your planning time is now more important than the physical work you used to do.

Any consideration of expansion demands hard decisions regarding space, financing, equipment, managerial time and talent, additional permits, and government requirements.

Your two continuing and overriding concerns in the growth stage and during your entire business career will be to increase sales volume and find the money to finance it. The rest is easy.

MAKING MANAGERS OUT OF ENTREPRENEURS

In the early days of your business, entrepreneurial instincts predominate. Later, managerial talents assume greater importance.

All entrepreneurs have some ability as managers, even though that may not be their greatest talent. A person is really neither 100 percent entrepreneur nor 100 percent manager; every entrepreneur and manager must be some of both. The proportion needs to change as the company grows.

A quick definition of the difference is that entrepreneurs lay new track into the wilderness, while managers keep things moving smoothly along track already laid. The entrepreneur has a high level of guts and probably a lower level of managerial skill. The manager has a low supply of guts and a larger supply of managerial skills.

Before you're out of the survival stage, the need for you to set priorities, assign responsibilities, and follow schedules gets more important. As your management responsibilities increase, as more people and assets become part of the company, it's important that you thoroughly develop and use this talent.

Fortunately, management can be learned from others and from books, seminars, and instructional videotapes. Your business education is an essential part of growing faster than your company.

Also, mentors, your CEO roundtable, advisory board members, and consultants can readily review your company's current situation to help you quickly solve problems and learn better man-

> **SUCCESS SECRET #9**
>
> *Multiply yourself by managing managers rather than employees. You must grow faster than the company.*

agement skills. You're not the only entrepreneur to have had these problems. You can work your way through them faster with experienced guidance.

PASSING YOUR LEVEL OF INCOMPETENCE

U p to this point, you've been the company's biggest asset. You were sales manager, production manager, and first-line supervisor for everything.

But now, if you want your company to grow far beyond survival, you must get off the sales floor or out of the shop. Concentrate on marketing to develop the added sales necessary to reach higher levels. Learn to accomplish more by working through others, by becoming more of a manager and less of a technician. If you don't, you can slowly and imperceptibly become your company's biggest liability. If you decide to continue as a happy technician rather than a frustrated manager, hire someone as general manager to handle the rest of the company.

This level of incompetence is permanent only if you're unaware of the problem or choose not to change. You *can* learn to perform at a higher level. Select and hire qualified people. Delegate both authority and responsibility to them.

Step back from day-to-day performance. When you do, you'll be out of constant contact with many of your operation's activities. Your company's success now depends on your ability to work effectively through middle managers who are in close touch with daily performance.

Learn to control the company on a second-hand basis from what managers tell you, from financial and operating reports, and from personal observation. Of course, you'll maintain a friendly dialogue about progress in each manager's area, but to function smoothly, you and your managers need an accurate, timely reporting system.

Communication problems and misunderstandings will arise between you and your managers. Previously, you'd personally solve the problem, but now, if you make decisions for the managers, you undercut them and discourage them from making decisions on their own.

The growth-stage company needs team-centered leadership. This leadership requires shared knowledge and commitment from each team member toward the common goal.

EMPLOYEE PROBLEMS

Internal politics begins among employees. "So-and-so has a better computer, better parking spot, or better office than I do." Egos, status, and office perks cause clashes and envy. Internal communication becomes a problem. Not every department or employee gets the news or information at the same time, or even the same information. Certain power-hungry managers begin building empires.

Some early employees are no longer comfortable in such a structured atmosphere. They may or may not have been chosen for promotion to the managerial level. They feel insecure about their importance and their place in the firm, so they leave, usually to work for another small company where they feel at home.

Common complaints or comments from departing employees include these: "I no longer know what's going on." "Meetings are a waste of time." "We spend too much time putting out fires." "If you want it done right, do it yourself." "Not enough hours in the day."

Although your dream is becoming the vision, those employees' personal dreams are shattered. During the early days of shared, close work, they also dreamed of wealth and glory. Now you have a Cadillac, but theirs hasn't arrived. You didn't promise them a Cadillac, but they assumed they'd get one too. Their attitude is "We used to be equal in this, but now we're different."

> **SUCCESS SECRET #10**
>
> *Don't scrimp on people. You're better off with first-class people doing first-rate jobs.*

After you've developed written policies and procedures, if you break or bend a rule for the benefit of a long-time, trusted employee, she will be happy and ten others will be angry because of favoritism.

MANAGING THE MANAGERS

Now the company needs an organization and an organization chart to show employees the lines of authority and responsibility. As more departments and subdepartments begin to appear, so do more procedures and manuals. Some big-company policies and procedures are put into use. You've begun to manage the managers, not the employees.

Most turnovers in middle managers occur in the late survival stage or early growth stage. Most turnovers in top managers occur in the last half of the growth stage or in the transition to the big-business stage.

Because changes come so rapidly, you should make it clear that policies and procedures are to be reviewed annually—either calendar year-end, fiscal year-end, or some other prearranged time. This is particularly true of bonus plans, commission plans, automatic pay-raise plans, and other things that employees are likely to assume are set in concrete for perpetuity.

Future growth and developments can make a plan that seems sensible today become totally unreasonable after volume has doubled. Or this year's difficult goal may become easy pickings by next year. It is essential that you adapt your policies to the realities of unforeseen future conditions without offending employees or customers.

A scheduled periodic review to determine whether policies and procedures still serve company objectives helps avoid painful backtracking and employee resentment that you're changing the rules while the game is in progress. Your guarantee to everyone is fair treatment at all times, not that a given formula or plan will never be changed.

HIRING MANAGERS

With additional employees or partners come managerial problems that your survival-stage company didn't have. Selecting, hiring, and training senior managers becomes a critical need. The business now needs skills that early or current employees may not possess. They deserve promotions, if training or seminars can make them proficient, but if you require proven experience, you must search outside the company.

> **SUCCESS SECRET #11**
>
> *Choose the smartest, best-qualified, strongest managers the business can afford. Build an organization run by a team.*

With limited opportunities for internal training, hiring a qualified outsider is faster. Prepare the newcomer for hostility from old-timers who wanted the job or who resent any managerial employee who didn't suffer through start-up pains with the family of early employees. The business needs people with the best knowledge and skills, whether they started with you or not.

If you select people because they know less than you do or don't threaten your authority and control, future operations will suffer. You don't need to fear anyone you hire. Your security is your ownership. Your company will be stronger when you select and motivate the smartest people you can find.

BANK FINANCING BECOMES AVAILABLE

Y our record of steady earnings makes bank financing easier to arrange. Each time you negotiate, you have definite plans to pay off the loan, but as long as your company continues to grow, you probably won't ever pay it off. You'll need more inventory, more accounts receivable, more employees, and more space. All these require more capital—probably more than earnings provide. Your increased financial strength will convince both you and the bank that you need and can handle more money, not less.

From the time I qualified for my first bank loan until I sold the company, I was never totally out of debt to some bank, because we kept growing. In 24 years, we never failed to show an increase in sales volume, although sometimes it was small.

My manufacturing business was capital intensive because of the need for heavy machinery and inventory. At one time, the total indebtedness for business real estate, equipment, and working capital loans for my operations totalled over $4,000,000. I personally endorsed everything except the real estate loans. I changed banks three times, getting better terms and a larger line of credit each time. All the debt got paid.

If your situation is still too shaky for the normal bank loan you need, you may be able to qualify for a Small Business Administration (SBA) guaranteed loan or other types of financing. Factoring companies may immediately advance you a high percentage of any valid invoices you have. Advances against inventory are more limited, depending upon the ready saleability of the merchandise. Interest rates and service charges from factors are always higher because of the increased risk and the increased services required to protect the collateral.

Some finance companies will loan on automobiles, equipment, and furnishings. You may not like to pay the higher interest and charges, but if that's your only option, negotiate the best terms, sign your name, pay, and go on.

Extremely rapid growth, no matter how profitable, can cause severe financial problems. Financing ever-larger inventory and accounts receivable can strain your financial and managerial resources to the limit. If this lovely problem arises, quickly call in professional consultants—marketing, financial, managerial, or technical—to help manage your growth.

In such a situation, you may not have time to learn everything yourself, and you need the help *now*. Don't flub this once-in-a-lifetime opportunity. Many companies go broke by over-expanding, usually because of bad managerial decisions on pricing, capacity, and direction of expansion, but sometimes because of a runaway product or service. You can always slow the growth and help your finances by raising prices.

DECISION MAKING

A nother influence on your company's growth is your ability to make decisions regarding your own time and effort. You know of 50 things that need to be done. The obvious solution is to do first things first. As Peter Drucker comments, "There is nothing so useless as doing efficiently that which should not be done at all."

Your most important job is prioritizing your list of things to do, both for yourself personally and for your company. But when ten alligators are snapping at you, it's difficult to concentrate on your most important objective of draining the swamp.

A growth-stage entrepreneur whom I encouraged to establish priorities and put his long-term plans in writing said, "My long-term plan lasts until the phone rings with a new crisis."

Not every decision you make will be correct. You'll continue to make mistakes—even bigger ones now, because you're playing with bigger chips. Use your management team to plan major projects. Once it has been thoroughly considered and decided on, give the new program your best efforts and a fair trial. If it proves wrong, don't let ego stop you from cutting your losses. Three words that can save money, some businesses, and many marriages are "I was wrong."

To solve problems, the management team begins to communicate more in writing. Both internal and external communications grow more difficult because more people are involved. The business becomes more impersonal. Not all employees know each other.

Some companies put out employee manuals early, some late. Some get detailed accounting or cost accounting early, some late. Some get budgets early, some not at all. Some buy new machinery or fixtures early on, some not until later. The ability or willingness to make a poor-boy start with used equipment and clever make-do substitutes has gotten many companies into the growth stage with less capital and therefore higher equity for the owners.

At one point my company needed pipe racks for storage in the warehouse. One of the men who bid the job said, "If you don't have too much starch in that white collar, I'll save you money by building these racks out of rusty used pipe, and they'll work just as well."

It's easy to confuse activity with results. Clerical and bureaucratic people are experts at busywork—shuffling papers, making phone calls, working on computers, and checking correct procedures with no regard to results produced or the lack thereof.

SALESMANSHIP EVOLVES INTO MARKETING

S alesmanship is the skill necessary for an individual to motivate other individuals to favorably consider or buy a product or service. Marketing is the process of creating the product and the environment that facilitates the greatest sales volume. Marketing includes salesmanship.

Salesmanship expands into marketing as you add products and services. The sales focus goes from how to sell one product or line to how you can better sell and service needs of customers in your chosen market.

> **SUCCESS SECRET #12**
>
> *To grow, move from product orientation to market orientation. Identify the customers you can best serve and focus 100 percent on pleasing them.*

In order to market more effectively, your company participates in trade organizations and trade shows. Market penetration comes with expansion into new territories or with additional services and products. You begin to keep track of competitors and mentally compare their strengths and weaknesses with your own.

Marketing needs a comprehensive sales program as well as catalogs, price lists, descriptive literature, policies, and discount sheets for distributors. Production scheduling becomes much more difficult.

EMERGING VISION

During the survival stage and early into the growth stage, you've been trying to sell the service or product that has been your idea. To grow, you must begin to think about other products, other locations, and other customers. Your horizon expands to the market you're trying to serve.

The idea for the product and the plan for the company contribute over time to the vision. The vision includes not just the product or service, or the market you wish to grow in, but the kind of company you're trying to create, its position and reputation in the marketplace, as well as internal things like corporate culture and your attitude toward employees. Whatever you focus your attention on, every manager and employee will soon focus on also.

The vision is intangible but very significant. It has taken root and grown in your mind. Your employees sense it and shape their behavior and emphasis accordingly. It should be formalized in writing.

This vision develops personally and motivates you as the controlling owner. It can't be transferred intact to the next owner. If you die or sell the company, new management (even if it's family) will sooner or later create and follow a different vision. Growth will usually be in a different direction and may either slow down or accelerate, depending upon how the new vision motivates employees and relates to the realities of future customers.

GETTING RID OF PARTNERS

I f you have continued to grow, at some point you probably shared equity ownership with individuals you thought would be helpful to your project. If you're lucky, you were right and everyone is still happy with his contribution and equity position.

If all your equity partners are active in the business, you share daily all information and business knowledge and are easily able to resolve problems. If you have inactive equity partners whose only contribution has been financial, the active managers often feel that these absentee owners are now riding in the wagon rather than helping push it.

Once you feel you're on solid financial ground and no longer need these outside partners, it's easy to forget the value of their financial contribution during the survival stage, the riskiest time your company may ever go through. What to do in this situation depends upon the circumstances, the closeness of your relationships, the personalities, performance, and continuing contribution of the people involved. If things are going smoothly, don't screw up a good deal for everybody by trying to get them out.

GROWTH BY ACQUISITION

I f you decide to continue to grow, growth by acquisition rather than internal expansion is now a real possibility. You might acquire another company to get product lines, market share, better technology, increased capacity, or more highly skilled technical or managerial people. In addition to supplying money, you must also supply management to run the new acquisition. Realize that you're buying problems as well as assets.

Investigate the proposed acquisition carefully. Get technical or financial help in areas where you don't feel confident. Use an experienced consultant. Unless you can write a business plan and a detailed three-year forecast of how you expect to operate both companies profitably, don't do it. It's easy to underestimate the additional managerial time and skill the combined operations will require.

BUSINESS LIFE AS A GROWTH COMPANY

Y ou can spend your entire business life as a growth company. Most of the privately owned businesses that line the streets of America (not listed on any stock exchange) are in the growth stage. They will continue to be so until they're either purchased or absorbed by another company, until they fail in the hands of later generations (usually the third), until the market changes, or until the owner-manager becomes lazy.

If you've spent years working on a growing company, the gradual buildup of sweat equity can be huge. Usually, your only means of cashing in on that value is to sell the entire company. (See GETTING OUT—HOW TO HARVEST THE FRUITS OF YOUR LABOR in part two.)

Between the survival stage and the big-company stage, the company will go through several reorganizations and possibly change its name as you restructure to obtain new financing, admit new partners, or add or acquire new plants or products. The basic operation and the market or customer base continues and grows. You intend all changes to build future growth. If the company joins or is purchased by a larger growth-stage or big-business company, it may be swallowed and absorbed and thereby lose its identity.

Because of the changes continually required in managerial methods, the same management seldom stays in control of the company during all operating stages.

COMMON MILESTONES

along the way

These events typify the growth stage for many companies, although they may not all happen or may not occur in this sequence. These milestones are intended to give you a more specific idea of what to expect during this stage.

- Frequently set new sales records at prices that cover all costs, including the owner's wages. Have steady profits to pay loans or expand.

- Experience months of profitable operation more often and closer together.

- Obtain your first bank loan (personally endorsed), usually a short-term loan for working capital. Use some proceeds for long-term or equipment purchases.

- Use outside accountants or larger accounting firms and have a full audit statement.

- Pay off loans and enjoy (for the satisfied owner who doesn't want to delegate or grow larger).

- Raise capital by sale of stock to employees, relatives, or new investors.

- Establish sales incentives or commissions.

- Start a written employee policy or manual.

- Discover petty thievery by an employee.

- Install computers to speed up your billing and collection cycle, inventory control, and purchasing.

- Waste time and money on a new product or service that flops because you misread or misunderstood the market.

- Take in a financial partner or investor for growth capital.

- Put together a sales catalog or brochure. Develop a written sales or distribution policy and discounts.

- Refurbish, repaint, and rearrange showrooms or offices. Insist on better and neater housekeeping.

- Standardize your production or procedures. Use quality-control manuals.

- Reach the founder's level of incompetence or the invisible wall of management. Growth slows or stops until competence is raised and responsibility and authority are delegated.

- Lay off employees as sales plunge.

- Get a mentor to improve your management and profit.

- Schedule regular management meetings.

- Hire outside managerial people and professionals due to lack of in-house skill or experience and training facilities.

- Start to manage the managers, not the employees.

- Define pay scales for groups of similarly qualified employees, except for a few old-time employees with excessive pay.

- Cut prices. Competitors react. Cut more. Profits fall.

- Install a computer network and a larger, separate information system (IS).

- Make budgets and financial plans.

- Experience substantial loss because a careless employee has an automobile accident, injures a customer, or spoils material or merchandise.

- Obtain your first long-term bank loan, probably to purchase equipment, payable in installments over a period of years.

- Change your sales distribution policies and methods over the objections of long-time salespersons.

- Face the family of a seriously injured employee.

- Increase managerial skills and knowledge by sending yourself and other managers to seminars and training classes.

- Lose early, trusted employees who have not been made managers or arrived at their level of satisfaction, feel "left out," and go to work for smaller companies.

- Defend your company from charges of employee discrimination or violation of hiring/firing laws.

- Find a lawyer or law firm for more frequent consultation.

- Appoint or hire a full-time, qualified human resources (HR) person.

- Install a 401(k) or other tax-sheltered employee benefit plan.

- Improve technology; conduct in-house research or hire outside consultants.

- Receive an assessment, including fines and penalties, following an IRS examination.

- Broaden your product line with more models, choices, and services.

- Consider a real estate purchase; buy or build? Should you and your senior managers own it and rent it to the company?

- Fight off an organization attempt by a labor union.

- Adopt a formal incentive plan for senior and middle management.

- Discover an employee taking kickbacks from vendors or skimming money from the company.

- Find that the company has outgrown the competence of early, loyal employees. Send them to school or seminars for training.

- Revise incentive plans for senior and middle management.

- Hire or appoint a safety manager.

- Consider growth by acquiring another company, location, or related product line.

- Engage outside professionals other than lawyers and CPAs, for mentoring, marketing, financial planning, insurance, environmental protection (management), human resources, or other functions.

- Join a CEO roundtable. Begin to participate in trade organizations and trade shows. Join your trade association.

- Indulge. Buy previously denied luxuries and deluxe equipment. Buy bigger, better cars and more expensive clothes; take better vacations, maybe abroad.

- Publish your first color brochures or catalogs. Use a professional advertising agency.

- Put your first outside director on the board of directors.

- Keep written minutes of directors' meetings.

- Change your banking connection to get a bigger loan or better terms.

- Hire or appoint an environmental manager.

- Reorganize the company and amend your company name to take in a new partner, to acquire a new product or market, or to acquire a major new asset.

- With new affluence, lose focus on minute business details. Quit working nights and some weekends.

- Schedule departmental or supervisors' meetings.

- Make sophisticated financial forecasts by department or product line. Make long-range plans and financial forecasts.

- Advertise in periodicals, newspapers, or a mass distribution medium.

- Search for more real estate, other locations, or other cities.

- ■ Obtain a bank loan from a new bank that isn't personally endorsed.

- ■ Sell out (or the founder quits, dies, or turns it over to the kids). A larger growth company or big company or family member takes over and slowly changes the corporate culture and employee attitudes.

THE BIG-BUSINESS stage

A S I'VE STATED, this book is for entrepreneurs with zero to 200 employees. The reason I've included this chapter is just to recognize that big business is the last in the stages of growth and to point out a few major differences that occur if you get there.

A big company isn't just a matter of size. The real difference is managerial attitudes, motivations, and bureaucratic procedures, which trickle down through all levels to all employees. The structured controls, lethargy, and bureaucracy of big companies emphasize procedures over results, procedures developed and revised over many years.

Most big companies are overstaffed and over-managed, or at least were until recently. Organizational reappraisals, reengineering, and downsizing are raising concern for customers, cost consciousness, and employee incentives in big companies that are progressively managed. They're moving back toward their entrepreneurial roots.

MANAGERIAL ATTITUDE

M any intelligent, accomplished people manage and run existing operations; few choose to start from scratch. Most senior executives and corporate managers have plenty of ideas plus all the skills required to run a company, a division, or department, but earlier in their lives they lacked the burning desire to make the break, to risk all their money and future on their own capabilities.

So—what differentiates successful entrepreneurs from these other capable people? Guts and borrowed money.

In the survival and growth stages, you, the entrepreneur, radiate self-reliance and a "Let's make it happen" attitude. You and your management team share the feeling of being in control of your own destinies. The controlling interest is owned by active managerial employees. Management's attitude is "We own the place. We're working for ourselves. We get to keep most of the money, and we're not afraid to take a calculated risk with our own money. Our managerial philosophy is BYA (Bet Your Ass)."

In contrast, the attitude of big-business management, and therefore also of the employees, is "We're working for *them,* the remote, unknown stockholders. If we make some money, they'll give us a little bit of it. We should take little or no risk with their money. Our managerial philosophy is CYA (Cover Your Ass)."

The managerial attitude in big businesses, where active officers own only a small percentage of the total stock, becomes that of managing assets and people for the benefit of someone else and making a good return on someone else's investment, with limited risk-taking. The wider the stockholding among employees, the better, and the more incentive value it has. But in big business, the incentives of stock ownership are a severely watered down version of those in small, entrepreneurial companies.

This difference in motivation is directly related to, and a result of, the degree of ownership or control exercised by the active managerial group. Inactive ownership and management won't work at all in survival- and growth-stage companies, but it has to suffice for big companies.

The survival rule for managers in big companies is to keep a CYA file of documents on everything they do. Promotions go frequently to the manager who's made no major mistakes in his or her corporate career, rather than to the bold, innovative person who's made some mistakes by trying new things.

Most of the time in directors' meetings is spent allocating resources—financial, technological, marketing positions and strength, personnel, and productive capacity—for the greatest return to all shareholders. Directors in big businesses spend most of their time worrying with and working on the corporate balance sheet, managing assets and liabilities. Owners, managers, and directors of growth companies spend most of their time managing the operating statement—working on sales income and expenses.

> **SUCCESS SECRET #15**
>
> *Top management must stay in intimate touch with the changing needs and desires of customers.*

INTRAPRENEURING—MAKING ENTREPRENEURS OUT OF MANAGERS

L arge companies are becoming increasingly interested in encouraging and reintroducing the entrepreneurial spirit into their companies. This is called *intrapreneuring.*

As the company grows larger, the direction and operations become fully defined and widely understood. The framework and organization within which everything operates becomes increasingly structured. Limits of authority and responsibilities are carefully defined and redefined. Lack of these controls in a large organization can create chaos.

Under these conditions, however, individuals with strong entrepreneurial tendencies feel confined and thwarted. They do not willingly accept such restrictions, especially for a prolonged period, and usually find other employment. But the need for entrepreneurial attitudes and action never disappears from business.

Intrapreneuring is often accomplished by separating or setting up a smaller division that gives selected managers and employees large incentives and increased freedom of decision making, more freedom than it's possible to grant throughout the whole company. This setup reaches a kind of middle ground within the large company framework. It provides strong incentives and wider authority to people whose income is directly affected by their own decisions and actions.

> **SUCCESS SECRET #16**
>
> *Managerial attitudes and policies must be as entrepreneurial as possible.*

An example of intrapreneuring at its best is *The Great Game of Business,* by Jack Stack with Bo Burlingham (New York: Currency Doubleday, 1994).

The other choice is to change the corporate culture of the whole company, which some progressive large companies are doing today. This apparently requires changing over 60 percent of top management.

CHANGE IN ATTITUDE

T o get to the big-business stage, an organization must undergo many evolutionary changes—but these may not bother you. Seldom does the same management own and stay with the company all the way from the idea stage to the big-business stage.

When my growth company sold to a company listed on the New York Stock Exchange, there were 17 shareholders, including me. By the time I completed my three-year contract as chairman, 15 were no longer employed there. No one was fired; there was no unpleasantness, criticism, or confrontation. They just didn't feel comfortable in the bureaucratic atmosphere. They drifted away to jobs with other small companies, started businesses of their own, or retired. Of course, they also had money in their pockets from the sale of their stock, which made them feel more independent.

The final word on the stages of growth of entrepreneurial companies has not yet been written. It's likely that further study by academic and informed researchers will show that the growth stage should be subdivided. Not all parts of companies grow at the same rate, nor will they be at the same level or stage of progress.

> The world's best companies tend to be entrepreneurial rather than managerial; they have faith in a future vision, and stick to it; they resolve the tension between authority and participation in such a way that employees feel as if it is their company, and yet feel a part of something larger than themselves; they feel secure that they are the best, yet insecure because they are not perfect.
>
> —Ken Auletta in *The Art of Corporate Success*
> *(New York: Putnam, 1984)*

COMMON MILESTONES

along the way

These events typify the big-business stage for many companies, although they may not all happen or may not occur in this sequence. These milestones are intended to give you a more specific idea of what to expect during this stage.

- Neither bank financing nor any other financing is personally endorsed by any individual. The credit rating of the company is stronger than that of any of the individual shareholders.
- Most of the directors do not work for the company.
- Company-wide pension or deferred profit-sharing plans have been installed.
- A complete job description exists for every job.
- A full-color stockholders' report is published.
- The board of directors has an audit committee and a compensation committee and meets monthly or quarterly.
- A revised, written policy for almost everything is developed.
- Whole departments work on nothing but planning, procedures, reporting, or taxation—functions that do not really produce products or services for sale to customers.
- Most employees never talk to a customer about business or know any other employee who does.
- The company has in-house legal counsel in addition to outside lawyers.
- Periodically, special task forces or committees decide which product lines or services are no longer profitable and should be disposed of.

- Management worries about the loss of niche markets to smaller competitors who specialize and give better and faster service.

- The company remains self-insured for many risks because of its size and diversity.

PART

two

Starting, Surviving, and

SUCCESSFUL STRATEGIES FOR PLAYING THE GAME

Growing Your Small Business

I hope you'll consider Guts and Borrowed Money to be your personal consultant offering guidance plus advice on a multitude of individual subjects significant in the growth process of your business.

This part contains information you'd like to get from experienced friends, knowledgeable employees, outside advisors, or gray-headed businessmen who succeeded when they were in your shoes. This information comes in the form of 265 alphabetized items covering everything from Accounting Is Not an Exact Science to Management—

Style and Ego to You Are Sole Guardian of the Bottom Line to Women-Owned Business (WOBs). Skim these items to learn what and where they are. Read now the ones pertaining to your present problems. Then put this book within easy reach for future reference.

TROUBLE-SHOOTING GUIDE

To help you find related discussions more easily, topic titles are listed below under major subject matter headings. Almost every subject is discussed from several different points of view and indexed and cross-referenced to related materials. Many titles are listed under more than one subject.

FINANCIAL PROBLEMS—SEVERE

GUTS—STARTING AND RUNNING YOUR BUSINESS

ENTREPRENEURS

OWNERSHIP, EQUITY, PARTNERS, AND SHAREHOLDERS

WISDOM FOR BUSINESS OWNERS

Business Plan   116

69

70

OUTSIDE HELP— CONSULTANTS, LAWYERS, OTHERS

71

72

WINNING THE GAME OF BUSINESS

EMPLOYEES

CUSTOMERS AND CUSTOMER RELATIONS

MARKETING AND SALES

73

MANAGEMENT AND MANAGERS

74

INCENTIVES AND MOTIVATION

77

Accountants—Selecting Yours

AS LONG AS ALL THE MONEY involved in your business is your own, the only accounting you're required to do is to file state and federal payroll tax reports and possibly sales and use tax reports, and to comply with income tax rules. If you choose, payroll services can relieve you of these requirements.

If you, a trusted associate, or a spouse has the ability and time to crunch these numbers, you don't need any other accountant. But if you want to know what's going on in your business—and to grow, you must know—then you must have timely and accurate financial information and statements.

78

If no one in the company can provide the necessary financial information, use a part-time accountant or bookkeeper until you need or can hire an in-house accountant. Many small accounting firms keep books on a part-time basis. Many accountants employed full time by other companies keep books on the side.

When you must have a full-time, in-house person, find one who'll do more than just gather and rearrange your numbers. Ideally, you want someone who has greater business knowledge and experience than you do. You need someone to guide you, principally in financial areas, but also in other business and tax-related matters.

Eventually, you'll need outside accounting help, business advice, and information about other governmental requirements that begin to apply as you get larger. You also want the outside accountant's loyalty, opinions, business knowledge, and help in setting up internal control procedures to deter employee fraud. You'll need greater knowledge of ever-changing tax laws, both state and federal.

The graveyard of small businesses and broken dreams is filled with companies that didn't have either current or enough financial information to run the company.

Expect to build a close relationship of confidence and trust with your chosen accountant over the long term. After getting recommendations from friends and associates, make appointments for exploratory interviews with each candidate. Speak to the owner or partner of the accounting firm and request that the accountant who will actually work at your company be present.

Discuss your goals and problems frankly, both financial and otherwise. Ask about the accountant's professional education and experience, particularly regarding your type of operation, as well as possible conflicts of interest with close competitors. Do not hesitate to discuss fees, services that you both agree could be of benefit to your company, and the total costs and benefits of using this particular accountant's services.

Such discussion interviews are free and are a necessary part of selecting and building the confidential relationship you need to get the full benefit of the accountant's knowledge. After several interviews, choose the individual or firm with whom you feel most comfortable and in whom you have the most confidence.

Your choice will certainly not be one of the Big 6 national accounting firms. It will probably be a small to medium-sized local firm where you'll get more personal attention for a smaller fee. Ask for an engagement letter that outlines the services, fees, and payment terms.

When outside investors or lenders such as banks or the SBA have money in your business, some will insist that you have an audit, or that some outsider do enough work to assure them that your statements are correct. One local bank now has a loan limit of $30,000 unless outside-audited statements are available. Beyond that amount, owner's numbers are no longer acceptable.

Good luck selecting your accounting and financial personnel, either inside or outside the company. They, or the reports they produce, will provide significant information for every business decision you make.

Accounting and Record Keeping

A CHRONIC PROBLEM WITH MANY small businesses is lack of enough current financial information to manage the business. This is because many entrepreneurs find accounting boring. It's like homeowners' attitudes toward plumbing—they want it to work, but they don't care to understand the details of how it works.

In general, entrepreneurs consider accountants bad news and accounting a necessary evil. They use outside accountants only because the bank or governmental reporting requires it. At the very least, the IRS and other state and federal agencies demand that you keep adequate records to file their reports.

However, if you believe that business is a game and money is the way to keep score, you need reliably recorded information in terms of both dollars and units (production, people, performance, shipping, and other data) to keep score and to make intelligent managerial decisions.

Your business decisions can be no better than the information and numbers on which they're based.

Insist that whatever decision-making information you need be accurate and timely. Using old accounting information as a basis for current decisions is like driving while looking only in the rearview mirror. When your operating information is over ten days old, it's just recorded history—too old to help you make a decision involving current problems. Up-to-date records, properly analyzed, will tell you whether your instincts about the market and the productivity of your company and employees are correct.

Within your accounting system, information is gathered into organized sections (accounts receivable, accounts payable, shipping, utilities, etc.) so you can get detailed reports on each section's

A

80

performance. Combining segments into departments gives summarized reports of these larger divisions' performance, activities, and profitability. Finally, combining all departments results in one operating statement covering a specified time period plus one balance sheet of assets, liabilities, and owner's equity as of the end of the operating period.

Think of all this accounting information as a pyramid with a large number of detailed transactions at the bottom and one set of summary financial reports at the top, with many layers of intermediate reports in the middle. From the summary at the top, you can trace down through layers to a lower divisional summary or to the bottom to find exactly what happened. Every transaction, small or large, is included in the totals of each higher report. It will show up in some way on both the operating statement and balance sheet.

If your books are current, they provide you with 20/20 vision covering today and the recent history of your business. This is your basis for knowing where you are, making current operating decisions, and predicting the future. Otherwise you're operating in the dark.

If you ever intend to expand your operation, you must have financial knowledge and control of your operations. A good financial reporting system gives you quick feedback that lets you make corrections and adjustments before it's too late. Begin early to establish an effective internal control system that discourages and detects fraud.

Your financial statements are like a sports scoreboard. They give you gratification if you're ahead and increase your anxiety and motivation if you're behind.

If you understand them, they can tell you what you're doing wrong. (See FINANCIAL RATIOS—WHAT THE NUMBERS MEAN.)

Accounting Is Not an Exact Science

THE ACCOUNTING PROFESSION HAS AGREED upon, and American business has accepted, a set of "Generally Accepted Accounting Principles," known as the GAAP rules. The objective is to report and present business data uniformly and correctly on financial statements.

GAAP rules are the best approximations known and approved to tell you your cost of doing business and the results of your operations during stated time periods. But when your accountant tells you that it cost precisely X dollars to produce and deliver your product or service, be mildly skeptical. Ask how overhead or indirect costs were applied. If you don't understand, ask for more explanation.

Your accountant may know more about accounting than you do, but you certainly know more about your business than she does. All incurred costs must be added or applied somewhere. Unless you understand what was included in overhead and several asset and expense categories, and how indirect costs were applied, you and your accountant aren't talking the same language. Based on the facts, there are many judgment calls about presenting data.

The federal government, through Internal Revenue Service regulations, exercises the strongest influence on principles of accounting. The IRS enforces its rules with this simple policy: Keep your records and reports almost any way you wish, but when you file your tax returns and compute the amount of taxes you owe, you must conform to IRS accounting rules. Since it's difficult (and not recommended) to keep two sets of books, almost everyone follows IRS rules.

A

81

It's better to be approximately correct and to know immediately than to be precisely wrong and not know it until it's too late to change anything.

All accountants I know are sticklers for consistency. If you use a different reporting or recording theory this year than last, comparative reports lose meaning and validity. Discuss with your accountant the basic rules you should use, especially those in the next section, ACCOUNTING POLICIES.

Accounting isn't a tax avoidance system. It's a managerial tool for gathering and distributing information to business people as a basis for making decisions and taking actions to generate a profit.

It's an educational system that depends on accurate input and quick processing to get out meaningful reports, which are the basis of your future actions.

Information costs money to gather, process, and record. Sometimes accountants can be penny wise and dollar foolish in chasing pennies to three decimal points. If this information is for a report no one uses, quit gathering it. Don't turn every special report into a routine report. Make old reports justify themselves as a continuing need.

A

82

Accounting Policies

ACCOUNTING MAY NOT BE an exact science, but it's still the best way to find out how you're doing financially.

Within the boundaries of Generally Accepted Accounting Principles (GAAP; see ACCOUNTING IS NOT AN EXACT SCIENCE), and even within the requirements of IRS regulations, you have room to make judgments and decisions about how to report your results. Early in the survival stage, discuss accounting policies with your accountant to be certain that you are talking about the same things. Agree on the theory that will correctly report your results. Your banker or investor will ask about the policies you use for certain financial reporting purposes.

Once you've reached sound decisions on these policies, make changes slowly, and only for good reasons.

The following are some of the things you should understand and discuss.

Bad Debt Reserve
If you do any business on credit, you will have some customers who don't pay. The bad debt reserve is your educated guess as to the amount of these losses. Should you use a fixed percentage of all sales, or of the total accounts receivable? Should you reserve against only specific accounts, or against all accounts over a certain age? Your policy should decide additions and deductions from the reserve as well as the total amount of the reserve.

Capitalization of Assets
What is the minimum dollar amount of the purchase you will capitalize and de-

preciate rather than charge to current expense? $250? $500? $2,000? The larger the company, the larger the minimum.

Depreciation Policy

After you've capitalized any purchased asset, how will you depreciate it? Straight line? Sum of years digits? Double declining balance? Accelerated depreciation methods? Service life is currently limited to 3, 5, 7, 10, 15, or 20 years (except for real estate) by the Tax Reform Act of 1986. Here IRS regulations have their greatest impact, through the Modified Accelerated Cost Recovery System (MACRS). In some cases you get a new choice with each new asset purchased. Adopt a conservative policy you can live with for a long time.

Inventory Valuation Policy

The method you use to evaluate your inventory for balance sheet and IRS purposes is a significant choice. It has a tremendous basic influence on your financial reporting and your taxes. (See INVENTORY.)

Intangible Assets

What are you going to do with the legal and accounting charges of organizing and reorganizing your company? Research and development costs? Patents and copyrights? Customer lists? Excessive advertising costs with long-term benefits? Be conservative. Your banker and other creditors will quickly subtract from your net worth the value of all intangible assets identifiable on the balance sheet.

Creativity is great— but not in accounting.

Application of Burden or Overhead to Direct Costs

Depending upon practices within your industry, there are many ways of doing this: per dollar of sales, per hour worked, per direct labor dollar, per machine hour or operating hour within a cost center, per unit of product, per employee, per square foot, per dollar of material cost, per ton, and so on.

Your decisions concerning these and other accounting policies can have a tremendous effect on your profit accounting, your understanding or misunderstanding of your cost of sales, and the managerial decisions you make based on your cost of goods sold. The better you understand these things, the better your decisions will be and the less likely that you'll need to change things later.

83

Acquisition—Growing By

ACQUIRING A GOING COMPANY becomes attractive in any of three situations: (1) when you haven't found "the idea" that really turns you on to starting a business, but you find it in an existing business; (2) when you have more money than you have time to start a business from scratch; or (3) when you want to grow but lack a compatible product, service, location, or particular advantage now available from an owner who wants out.

Any business can be duplicated if you have the time, the money, and the will. Your question for acquisition is this: What do I gain by acquiring this business that I can't do better myself?

The worst thing you can do is acquire a company either because you think it's a bargain or without a specific plan for action afterward.

While I was in business, I made five acquisitions of whole or parts of other businesses. In each case the objective was to expand our marketing opportunities with compatible product lines. Two of these proved to be mistakes that were finally resolved by reselling after a few years at break-even or a slight loss. One was liquidated after an expensive effort to change customers' buying habits. One was resold at a large gain after six years because it was no longer compatible with our changed marketing direction. The last one, after complete redesign and re-tooling, was the basis of the greatest

growth the company ever had. When the company was sold, we were number one in the market with this product.

I tried to acquire three other companies; fortunately these negotiations failed. I also tried twice to sell my company. Both times these negotiations failed, and in retrospect, were premature. None of this would have been in my business plan, even if I'd been smart enough to have one.

Acquisition is a complex subject. These pages provide only a superficial discussion of basic considerations. Read a lot of books about acquisition. Talk to experienced people. Hire a consultant. This isn't a good field for amateurs—too many things can go wrong.

Negotiate and discuss all you want, but before you sign any papers, hire a good lawyer, one who specializes in handling sales and purchases of companies. Not all lawyers have this expertise. Many have never seen one of these transactions and don't know what's important.

Get all the representations and warranties that you can from the owners. This forces full disclosure and keeps you from buying too many unknown problems. Always try to buy assets, not stock. Leave all the liabilities, known and unknown, for the seller to worry with, if you possibly can.

When you spend your money, you don't legally require a due diligence investigation, but you're being foolish with your money if you don't protect yourself with more than the due diligence investigation of a prudent business person.

Advantages and Disadvantages

The acquired company already has an established track record, some kind of customer base, and a tested list of suppliers and service people. You'll inherit trained employees who will help you learn the business. Start-up costs and headaches and other unknown risks have been handled by a previous owner. Your entry is easier because you don't have to select plant location, employees, suppliers, and customers, or go through false starts.

On the downside, you may be inheriting ill will and incompetent employees. You're buying the reputation of the acquired company, its unknown competitive position, employee inadequacies and problems, possibly antiquated or inadequate facilities, obsolescent inventory, threatened lawsuits, or other unknown problems that may now be encouraging the owner to sell.

The unknown is always fearful. You can't learn all you'd like to know before the acquisition. But try to determine exactly why the present owners want out. Don't accept the first answer at face value.

Operating Plan

The most important things are your detailed evaluation of exactly what you expect to accomplish by acquiring this business and your detailed operating and financial plans for what you're going to do with it after you own it. List the tangibles and intangibles you expect to gain. List things you don't want or will have to change. Remember that there will be a new load on you and your management team: running a larger, unknown operation with unknown people.

How will the joint operations of both old and new companies pay off the debt you're taking on to make the acquisition? What additional management must you furnish? What new funds will you need? What changes will be needed in work force and managers? What will customers' reactions be? What will your sales volume be in one year? Three years? Five?

Always look at the company with an eye to potential growth opportunities the current owner doesn't see or is unable to exploit. Don't buy something you can't make grow.

Valuation, Terms, and Payment

Valuation, terms, and payment are too complex to be treated here. Generally, if the company being sold has earnings, the sale price is a multiple of earnings. If there are no earnings, then assets are sold to an entrepreneur who believes he has the managerial skill to get the assets to produce earnings.

Never buy or sell with future payments based on net profits. It's impossible to define costs and earnings unambiguously; it's too easy for others to dispute or manipulate the result. Structure the deal so that both buyer and seller have strong incentives to maintain profits, increase volume, transfer customer and employee loyalty, and work harmoniously together during the transition. You want to owe the seller money until you're satisfied that you got what you paid for.

If you can muster the down payment, urge the owner to finance the balance of the purchase price on a payout. You want to keep the owner involved and working on her behalf as well as yours.

Your negotiating skills and reading of the seller's strengths are very important. Nothing is fixed. I know of no business that's been sold for the original asking price and terms. You need to have the right to deduct deficiencies or losses from future payments if the present owner's representations and warranties weren't 100 percent correct.

A service business is more difficult to take over than a product business because personal relationships are more difficult to transfer. If it's successful, you'll probably pay more than if you started it from scratch, but you'll become profitable faster and with less trouble.

Just like marriages, no two acquisitions are quite alike, because no two businesses are alike. An acquisition or merger is similar to a marriage between two corporate cultures, two groups of people, two different viewpoints, two different backgrounds, two different bosses, and two different visions. There are certain to be problems and adjustments.

After the Acquisition

After you've acquired a company, the following suggestions may be helpful:

- Don't immediately change a lot of policies or the name. Make changes slowly.

- Find the parts of the business crucial to the operation and learn them as quickly as you can.

- Ask for employee feedback, but don't lose control.

- Pick the seller's brains as thoroughly as possible, but slowly replace her vision with yours.

- Listen to customers; they're the real bosses who determine your future success.

- Husband your cash reserves until you know where to spend them most wisely.

If you're considering an acquisition, it's well worth your time to learn more about the procedure. A good book to read is *How to Buy a Business: Entrepreneurship through Acquisition,* by Richard A. Joseph, Anna M. Nekoranec, and Carl H. Steffens (Chicago: Enterprise–Dearborn, 1993). But you should still get a knowledgeable lawyer and some experienced help when you buy a going business.

Advertising

YOUR GOAL IS TO GET YOUR MESSAGE to selected, ideal customers in the most specific, attention-getting, impressive, and least expensive way. Balance what's needed to accomplish an aggressive plan with what your company can afford.

In the survival stage, you usually advertise through business cards, brochures, and carefully chosen sales pieces, plus phone calls, shoe leather, and gasoline. Individually delivered giveaway items (knives, coffee mugs, drinking glasses, pocket tissue, cosmetics, etc.) make introductory and lasting impressions. Direct mail and telemarketing work with some products but are expensive. Appearances at trade shows help spread the word.

Later, in the growth stage, advertise first in trade publications and then in more general magazines. Finally, if you get big enough, use institutional advertising. This builds the company's image and favorable reputation without being too specific about products or prices, but it's too expensive for small companies.

Selling a product to a buyer unfamiliar with your company or your product is the same as asking the prospect to go down an unpaved road to an unknown destination. Advertising, or any method of familiarizing prospects with your company or products, means you're beginning to pave that road. With time and a favorable reputation plus advertising, prospects feel as though they're going to a familiar place on a wide, paved highway.

Advertising, like road paving, is expensive. But, unlike paving, you can't really see the results. If this isn't your area of expertise, you can go through all the motions, spend your money, and still have practically no results.

Even though you'll have little advertising at first, whether you have brochures, handouts, or sales pieces, have them professionally done. Amateurish advertising makes your business look amateurish. Professionally printed materials help create the impression that you're a large, stable company.

In my manufacturing company, customers were scattered over almost 20 states and hardly ever visited our plant. Everything we passed out to customers was professionally done by a young, up-and-coming, inexpensive advertising team. We once had a sales representative from a distant state come in to visit our only plant. He stood in the two-room office and then in the middle of the 3,200-square-foot shop and said, "Is this all there is?" The quality of our advertising, people, products, and operation had convinced him that we were a much bigger company.

When you select an advertising agency, look for a good growth record and active participation by the agency's owners. They should have a creative knack

A

87

for your situation. Check their client list and comments from representative accounts. To judge their performance, tell them you want to take a look at some of their past campaigns. Do they now or have they ever represented your competitor? Would representing you create a conflict of interest? Previous representation may be more beneficial than harmful; working for your competitor may have taught them the best and least expensive way to reach your market.

When you do repetitive or expensive advertising, take a hard-nosed viewpoint with the salesperson or advertising consultant. "How is this advertising going to increase my sales? How can I measure the increase that results from your advertising?" These are tough questions to answer. Let them know you won't spend advertising dollars unless you get satisfactory answers.

What's your message? What's the best medium to carry that message? What's the best way to get the message in front of selected, prospective buyers? How can you be certain your dollars are producing adequate results?

Advertising works only when everything else is securely in place. Once motivated by advertising, your customer must be able to find and buy your products.

My small company had some large competitors with large advertising budgets. A pushy advertising agency recommended an elaborate and expensive campaign that they said would make us a major player in this market. The total cost was beyond anything reasonable for

our size. When they continued to insist that the results would pay for the ads, I finally told them, "If you wish to spend your money doing this, go ahead and I'll repay you from the increased sales, but I'm not going to spend my money on it."

A good public relations (PR) firm can frequently get you more results for less cost than an advertising agency. Find a small PR firm that has handled public relations for successful products. Interview them; look at their proven results. Then get them to plant some stories for you and your products. The cost may be small compared with buying advertising.

Advertising is paving for the road your salespeople must travel.

I knew a small retail firm that went into business in a ski resort with the usual specialized clothing and merchandise line. They were neither well established nor well known. The husband-and-wife team started off by spending $20,000 to produce and mail full-color mail-order catalogues. They used an unproven mailing list and got practically no sales. The following season, their doors didn't open.

We can learn two lessons from this: First, they should've gotten professional help with their disproportionately large advertising budget. The husband didn't know how to get value in advertising, nor did he go to someone who did. He didn't even ask his wife, because he thought he knew enough. Second, he bet everything he had on this program without small-scale testing of the mailing list or the process to prove their effectiveness.

The most famous ad concerning advertising is one used by McGraw-Hill, which pictures a tough, bald-headed industrial buyer sitting in a wooden swivel chair, wearing glasses, staring the reader straight in the eye, saying, "I don't know who you are. I don't know your company.

I don't know your company's product. I don't know what your company stands for. I don't know your company's customers. I don't know your company's record. I don't know your company's reputation. Now what was it you wanted to sell me?"

Choose your professional help carefully and test them on small projects. Insist on getting identifiable results for the dollars you spend.

A good book for further information is *AMA Complete Guide to Small Business Advertising,* by Joe Vitale (Lincolnwood, Ill.: NTC Business Books, 1995).

Advisory Directors

TAKING ADVICE DOESN'T COME EASILY for most entrepreneurs. However, you'll frequently need additional information and especially experience and judgment. Here's one way to get it.

Your official board of directors in the early years of your corporation usually consists of you, your spouse, and maybe an associate, an investor, or your lawyer. The early board's primary function is to meet legal requirements, which include annual elections, and to affix signatures and the corporate seal to official papers. These directors have a legal responsibility to your company and to others for the way the company is run.

Formal meetings are seldom held except to satisfy bank or liability require-

ments. Formal minutes are seldom written until an auditor or banker asks for them; then there's frantic scrambling to write minutes for nonexistent past meetings and get required signatures.

Establish a functioning formal board when you have more shareholders or greater outside financial participation (loans, leases, or investor money). You need more formality when operations require multiple levels of management or when you decide you want continuity and direction to perpetuate your dream.

Growth-minded, progressive CEOs realize at some point that they can't always get needed knowledge or experience from inside people. They search outside the company for ideas, suggestions, and contacts. If you're searching, consider joining a CEO roundtable, hiring a mentor or consultant, seeking informal advice from good friends, or using one or more outside directors. You will feel comfortable and challenged with one or more of these activities as a source of business wisdom and knowledgeable advice. (See CEO ROUNDTABLES OR PRESIDENTS' CLUBS; MENTORS AND MENTORING; CONSULTANTS; MASTERMIND ADVISORY GROUP.)

When you formally include one or more outsiders on the board or in an advisory group, choose someone with a proven record of accomplishment, perhaps retired from her business or your industry. Rather than full-time participation, the value added by outside directors comes from their wider business experience, greater professional knowledge, and their ability to contribute an experienced, unprejudiced view of managerial problems.

> **The first essential of getting good advice is knowing when you need it. The next is knowing where to get it.**

They also serve as a sounding board to help you make major decisions. You normally don't need such expertise for day-to-day activities. Add one board member first and another later. Three may be all you ever need.

The board should provide a perspective that you cannot get from your management team. Expect board members to disagree with you or with other board members from time to time. Your company needs the creative input of individuals willing to express their opinions without fear of bruising egos or hurting feelings.

A significant issue with outside directors is the boundary between advisors, who only give advice, and management, which has executive authority, acts, and is legally responsible for such actions. In most states, the difference between being an advisor and being in control is having the right to vote, which may also make the board member legally responsible for actions taken or not taken. Check with your lawyer as to your local laws. For these reasons, outside executives are hesitant to be full directors with authority to vote because they don't want to accept the accompanying liabilities.

Create opportunities for board members to visit your business so directors, senior managers, and family members can personally know each other. Keep outside directors informed of company plans and progress. Attending a brief meeting to render advice or decisions without proper advance knowledge and full familiarity with the subject matter is futile.

The board can help maintain continuity in a closely held business and should meet at least quarterly. Meeting dates should be set six months or more in advance. Board members should receive an agenda and a meeting package to review several days before the meeting. Meetings should have a time limit and focus more on the future than on rehashing the past.

Provide reasonable compensation for time spent in meetings, preparing for meetings, and becoming knowledgeable about company operations and personnel. The advice should be worth paying for. Probably the only person you can expect to do this for free is an old family friend.

Analyzing Results

IF YOU WANT TO IMPROVE your operations and make your business grow, take time to critically analyze the reports, data, people, facts, and impressions available to you.

If you have the imagination and innovation described in part one for success as an entrepreneur, you won't be able to stop making these analyses and comparisons during most of your waking hours:

- Which are your most profitable products?

- Who are your most profitable customers?

- From what source do you get most of your customers?

- Which employees are productive?

- Which services are profitable?

- What change will most increase your income?

- What will cut production costs most?

- Which product models draw the most complaints?

- Which models require the most callbacks or warranty costs?

- Which areas or machines are most productive?

- Which activity produced the most new inquiries?

- Why did my competitor do that last week?

91

While you're driving or walking or sitting in a waiting room, while you're in bed or enjoying moments of solitude, while you're on the throne or holding on the phone, ask yourself questions such as these. The entrepreneur who asks himself and others the right questions, and who recognizes the right answers, no matter where they come from, will have the best company. Continual questioning and analysis is a basic requirement.

Good data should come from your reporting system. If you don't have good accounting for both dollars and units (hours, tons, boxes, pounds, customers, employees, and so forth), you can't make an intelligent analysis.

Sometimes the only way to get accurate, timely data is from subordinates who keep their own records when your management information system (IS) doesn't give them what they need to do their jobs. Encourage the flow of information any way you can.

Don't shoot the messenger when he gives you bad news. Or let people tell you what they think you want to hear. When you encourage the mediocre and the nonproductive at the expense of the creative and productive, you encourage problems.

A

92

> *You'll improve your future by intelligent and continual analysis of your past.*

You will probably receive plenty of good suggestions and ideas. Consider them all. Don't be too proud or too egotistical to look at something from your employees or your competitors. Then *you* pick the best suggestion or idea.

Angels

THIS TERM COMES FROM BROADWAY, where financial backers of new or unknown Broadway shows have traditionally been referred to as angels. If you're looking for seed money or start-up money, you, too, will consider anyone who gives it to you an angel. In venture-capital circles, the term refers to an entrepreneur's first investors, who put money in before there's a proven product or demonstrated customer appeal.

Angels are most often friends, relatives, or business acquaintances who believe in an entrepreneur's abilities or in the value of her ideas. They're willing to invest significant sums before the business is established. Retired successful entrepreneurs often help new entrepreneurs get started.

Angels are typically unsophisticated investors. They are investing their own money. Their investments are usually poorly documented rather than well thought out or structured. What the angels receive in return may be poorly defined.

If you value friendship with and commitments to your angels, take pains to discuss the structure of your relationship and the exact amount of stock or equity you're promising in return for the investment. You may need to return to these angels for another miracle in the future, so it's important that you and they have specific understandings and realistic expectations of the first investment. If it isn't feasible to involve lawyers, at least write and sign a letter detailing your understanding. (See HANDSHAKE DEALS.)

Arbitration and Alternate Dispute Resolution

AS FULL-SCALE LITIGATION gets more time-consuming and more expensive, many businesses search for acceptable alternate means of resolving disputes.

Fortunately, alternate means of dispute settlement are available. The oldest organization actively promoting this, the American Arbitration Association, is over 70 years old. Other associations that provide somewhat similar services to disputants are the Judicial Arbitration and Mediation Services, Inc. (JAMS) and Judicate, Inc., an organization whose stock is publicly held.

Opposing parties may always agree to enter either mediation or binding or nonbinding arbitration. The disputing parties should meet to decide which of several procedures they choose to follow. They should reach a written understanding concerning the procedure and how binding the results will be on each party.

Mediation

Mediation is a voluntary way to resolve a dispute. Courts in many states order parties in pending litigation to mediate. The chosen mediator, an individual experienced in dispute resolution, will try to get voluntary agreement between the parties by emphasizing the points on which the parties agree, in hopes that this will lead to agreement on the entire controversy. The mediator will seek common ground for additional agreements on other disputed points.

The experienced mediator may be a former judge or lawyer, or someone with knowledge of the industry in question. This individual will hear each side's position and the issues in dispute, then assist each to make a realistic evaluation and find creative ways to resolve the dispute voluntarily.

Lawyers aren't absolutely necessary but are often useful in helping each side evaluate its position. Each side should agree in advance whether or not to use lawyers. The mediator, after initial presentations, usually meets privately with each of the parties, reviews the issues with the lawyers and their clients, and discusses the strengths and weaknesses of the case.

Mediation often reduces the emotional intensity of the dispute, clarifies issues, eliminates unnecessary discovery procedures, and sets the groundwork for cooperative settlement and discussion.

A

93

Arbitration

A lawyer friend who is still practicing tells me that unless the amount in dispute is over $100,000, hiring lawyers to file a lawsuit isn't economically justified. To start alternate dispute resolution procedures, you or your lawyer should talk to either the opposing party or her lawyer.

In arbitration, both parties must agree on a procedure and an organization. Arbitration may be either binding or nonbinding; the procedure is basically the same in either case. Lawyers are usually involved. Each side presents evidence and its position before a presiding officer, who renders a specific decision on the award at the end of the proceeding.

Usually, binding arbitration is mandatory only if it is agreed on between the parties in their original contract. If the award is binding, then settlement is final and cannot be appealed. If nonbinding, the award serves only as a factor in further settlement negotiations.

Nonbinding arbitration is typically used where the parties want a realistic evaluation by a person qualified because of training, experience, and knowledge. The arbitrator may assist the parties in developing settlement options.

Binding arbitration is the submission of a dispute to one or more impartial persons with the understanding that the decision will be final and nonappealable. It's used where the parties, by stipulation or contractual agreement, seek a final and conclusive determination by an impartial, experienced judge.

In this case, evidence is presented as in a nonjury trial. Then the arbitrator may consider affidavits or other hearsay evidence. Counsel usually makes closing arguments and may present briefs in support of their positions. The arbitrator then renders an order or decision, usually within 30 to 60 days.

Commercial arbitrators are compensated on a per diem basis. Whether one or more, they are selected by agreement of the parties. They usually provide arbitration at a fair cost.

If it's an American Arbitration Association (AAA) case, they are bound by the code of ethics for arbitrators in commercial disputes adopted by the AAA and the American Bar Association (ABA) in 1977. That code requires an arbitrator to disclose any facts that might indicate bias or an appearance of bias.

Rules of evidence usually aren't quite as strictly enforced, and minutes or records usually aren't kept, so there's little need for a court reporter. You're submitting your case to credible, knowledgeable people, seeking a fast, inexpensive way to get an impartial ruling or decision.

Mediation usually lasts one day or less and can cost less than $2,000. Arbitration costs more, depending upon the length of the hearing, and often takes three to six months to resolve the dispute. However, this is faster than the court systems in most states and usually more economical.

The American Arbitration Association's home office is at 140 West 51st Street, New York, NY 10020-1203. The address of the National Headquarters of Judicial Arbitration Mediation Services, Inc. (JAMS) is 500 North State College Blvd., Orange, CA 92668. JAMS uses principally former judges and people with judicial experience to handle the proceedings it supervises. (See LITIGATION.)

Audits and Opinions by CPAs

AN AUDIT IS A METHODICAL REVIEW of your financial transactions by a qualified, disinterested third party. It's conducted by an independent accounting firm with a high degree of technical knowledge and independence that allows the firm's opinion to be accepted by other parties. Three levels of examination by outside accountants are recognized, leading to three levels of opinion and responsibility by accountants for the company's financial statements.

Remember that the financial statements are yours. Only the opinions are the auditors'. Because of their usually greater knowledge of GAAP, auditors are inclined to insist that your statements be presented in a certain way, based on the facts as they know them. If you know additional facts that justify your position, you must present them.

The highest level is a full audit, which requires the examination of financial statements in accordance with generally accepted auditing standards. A full audit costs more money because the CPA does a lot more work.

The auditor or his deputy is required to personally observe and test the inventory. The auditor writes letters containing self-addressed, stamped envelopes to a selected sample of your accounts receivable and accounts payable, requesting that they state in writing the amount of money due to or from your company as shown on their books. If their amount differs from yours, the differences must be reconciled. Sampling and verification of many internal accounting procedures must be checked. These tests and procedures are also intended to detect dishonesty or embezzlement by employees.

This is a complete audit, at the end of which your independent auditor attaches to your financial statements a letter expressing his professional opinion on them. The wording of the opinion and the work required to formulate the opinion are specified by the American Institute of Certified Public Accountants.

The opinion may be either qualified (the auditor doesn't agree with something shown in your statements) or unqualified.

A
95

An unqualified opinion is the highest type, expressing the auditor's opinion, without qualification, that the statements are substantially correct and in accordance with GAAP rules.

Be not the first by whom the new is tried, nor yet the last to cast the old aside.

A qualified opinion says that the statements are correct except for some minor described procedure or event shown incorrectly in the statements. If the exception is major, the auditor is required to express no opinion. If it's severe, canons of ethics require the CPA to express no opinion, withdraw from the engagement, and have nothing to do with the statements.

An intermediate-level audit is called a review. No outsiders are contacted, and only limited internal work is reviewed by the auditors. The CPA's attached opinion mentions her limited work and states that she isn't aware of any material deviations from GAAP rules.

A compilation is not an audit. It consists only of helping the company describe and arrange its information on the pages in the customary financial format. No opinion is expressed on compliance with GAAP rules or the fairness of the presentation.

If all the money invested in your business is your own, you don't need a full audit because you should already know what's happening to your money. If you have outside people with a major financial interest in your company (bankers, major creditors, or other stockholders), they will want a full audit, or at least a review, for their own information and protection.

You'll need a full audit with an unqualified opinion for at least the last two full years before you sell your company, have an Initial Public Offering (IPO), or get involved in major financing.

Banks and Bankers

BANKING IS A COMPETITIVE BUSINESS like any other. And banks are as different as retail clothing stores. Some banks want only big-company business, others want primarily small-company business, and others want a mixture. Some are hungry for business. Others aren't. Just because one bank tells you no doesn't mean that every bank in town will tell you no.

If you qualify for a loan, you'll get a different reaction and loan proposal from each bank. If you can, find out what the bank is likely to do if you have bad times. Some banks will work with you. Others are more likely to shut you down.

Once you have a bank connection, keep friendly relations with a second bank in case your lead bank changes ownership, management, or policies, or does something you can't live with.

Choosing a Bank

Find two banks that specialize in small and medium-sized businesses, and cultivate good relations with both. Your business friends will tell you where they bank, or you can just walk into a medium-sized bank and ask to speak to a business loan officer.

Before asking either bank for a business loan, do personal banking (an automobile or home-improvement loan) while you build a good credit history and personal relationships. These loans will probably be from a personal loan officer,

but let the business loan officer know that you're in business and that you may be a future customer.

Keep each banker informed of your business plans and progress as you finance your business with funds from your own resources. Before a banker loans you the bank's money, she will want to know how much time and money of your own you've already invested in your business.

Before you ask either banker for a business loan, write a well-thought-out business plan stating what you intend to do with the borrowed money as well as how and when you intend to repay it. Get help with this if you need to. The banker will judge your future performance and ability to repay by your performance record on these personal loans, plus reports from other credit-reporting agencies.

If you have had credit problems or trouble in the past, be sure you are able to give a reasonable explanation. The realization that you squarely faced your problem and behaved well in bad times can be a plus factor.

In addition to your business plan, the banker wants written descriptions of your entire operation plus biographies of key managers. Impress the banker. Present your business and your application well. Know how much money you need, what you can accomplish with it, and how you expect to pay it back. (See BORROWING BANK MONEY FOR THE FIRST TIME.)

When times are good and your business is doing well, changing banks is easy but usually unnecessary. The new banker will know that you're changing. He must pay off the former bank. It's customary that the new bank writes the payoff check to the old bank to secure the release of collateral, so the new bank can place its new lien on the same assets.

When your business is doing poorly and your company is distressed, a new or unfamiliar bank won't want to loan you money. However, one you've known and had a relationship with might.

Be a good account for your banker. Let him make a fair return on your transactions. If you're not a good account for him, he will be less inclined to stretch something for you in either good times or bad.

Bankers

Bankers have tough jobs. What they hear from every new entrepreneur boils down to this: "With *my* idea and *your* money, I'm going to make a million dollars."

Bankers don't think the way you think. They're not entrepreneurs and are suspicious of those who are. They're particularly suspicious of promoters and inventors.

Bankers are continually risking someone else's money and their own jobs. They'd like to help you and make a profit for the bank with the interest you're going to pay, if they're absolutely certain you can repay the principal, but they will take little or no risk. They're restrained by rules plus layers of bosses and examiners looking over their shoulders. Often they already know that the loan committee won't let them do what you've requested, but they want to let you down easily and maintain your friendship.

One of their loan limits is a specified percentage of your company's net worth. If they loan too much, they might have more money invested in your business than you do—something bankers are reluctant to do.

I once met a banker during a tennis match and afterward answered all his questions concerning my business. When he asked whether I was satisfied with my present banking connection, I replied that the bank wouldn't loan me any amount in excess of my net worth. He commented that if my operations were as described, I had just barely gotten started on borrowing money. My secret thoughts were, "I've found myself a banker!" I changed banks, ultimately owed his bank over $4,000,000, and served on his board of directors. That was in the late '70s, when banking policies were totally different from what they are today.

Bankers are professionals who don't like to think that you're shopping around. After you decide which bank to use, you must make a moral as well as legally binding commitment to that bank as your lead bank. Then, as long as they honor their commitment and meet your business needs, do all your business banking there, because your collateral can't be split. Those who loan you money deserve your business and your loyalty for a long time.

When bankers turn you down for a loan, ask nicely why you don't qualify. They will give you good reasons, or at least give you the bank's reasons, and you can use this information to improve your plan before you go talk to the next banker. If three bankers tell you the same thing, you'd better change your business to meet their qualifications.

Ask for more money, maybe twice as much as you think you'll need. It's easier to get the necessary funding the first time than when you go back the second time after missing your forecast.

My company was growing nicely after 10 years with the only bank we had ever used, and I had found an acquisition that would add to our strength and position. I made thorough analyses and projections, negotiated the deal, and submitted a complete, written proposal to the bank for the amount of money I needed. After several meetings, they offered about two-thirds of my request. In retrospect, they seemed to still be thinking of my company as the small, weak one they had known so long.

I took the same proposal and the documents described in BORROWING BANK MONEY FOR THE FIRST TIME to another banker I knew. After meetings and an inspection trip, the new bank agreed to finance the full amount.

My contacts at the first bank were shocked when I informed them that I was going to change banks, said they did not realize how badly I wanted the money, and asked if I would stay if they met the other bank's offer. I replied that it was not good if I had to pound on the desk to get what I wanted after 10 years. Also, after they had refused, the other bank and I had made a commitment, and I was bound by that commitment. We parted friends.

Be conservative. Try to equal or exceed your promises and predictions of the future. Build credibility in your management, operating, and forecasting skills. Don't lie to your banker. Tell it like it is, even when the news is bad. Your banker has heard bad news before. Neither of you should panic.

Generally, give your banker too much information rather than too little. She will file away your written information, budgets, and forecasts. At expiration time, she will haul it out and say, "Last quarter (year) you told me you were going to do so-and-so by now. What happened?"

Your banker really wants you to succeed. Your success will be a feather in her cap. The bank can then make more money by loaning you more money.

Take your banker to lunch on a personal basis at least once every six months. Do it when you're not in trouble and don't immediately expect to ask for anything. Keep the conversation friendly and personal, but don't hesitate to discuss informal information off the record.

Bigger Isn't Necessarily Better

B

100

START SMALL. Try everything new on a small scale. Work out of your house as long as you can. Don't buy new equipment. No impressive office or reception room. The most impressive things you want are smiles on your customers' faces.

Sacrifice time, of which you have plenty, to save money, always in short supply. A poor-boy start in a make-do office with used equipment isn't as spectacular, but your chances of survival are much improved. Do enough customers come into your office to justify a grand impression? I have yet to see a company survive that starts with all-new equipment and an early real estate purchase.

Learn to make every dollar do the work of a dollar and a quarter. Believe me, you'll have plenty of need later for every dollar you save now. Card tables, apple crates, and folding chairs have started many good companies. You can always upgrade when prosperity allows.

You don't have to grow larger. When some owners realize they're holding back their own growth, they would rather stay with what they have than change their style. So be it. If you own the company, that's one of your privileges. Watching the company go backward, however, is less fun and sometimes less controllable.

Being small is a bigger advantage than most small businesses realize. Your company can react more quickly to customers' requests. You can customize your services or products in a way no large company can.

I remember an old western movie in which James Cagney, a short, feisty actor, was looking up to a much bigger cowboy and punching on his chest as he said, "I learned long ago that the strong take it away from the weak, and the smart take it away from the strong." By being smart and small, you can take business away from the big guys.

The larger you get, the more you're a target for government regulations, environmentalists, pressure groups, labor unions, and other groups with rules and regulations designed to make your life miserable. Keeping your number of permanent employees below a certain level allows you to escape some regulations. (See GOVERNMENT REGULATIONS YOU SHOULD BE FAMILIAR WITH.)

Keep it fun. If it isn't fun, why work so hard? Maybe you shouldn't be doing it. Find what you're good at, where you're comfortable, and what you enjoy; in other words, find your niche. You don't really have to get any bigger or get out of that mode unless that's part of your goal.

As long as you're small, you can keep control. You can carefully select and retain 20 to 50 skilled, trustworthy, dependable, stable employees. You'll know each of them and their families by name. You can have a splendid life and pleasant relationships with employees, vendors, and customers.

Steady accumulation of profits over a long time will support a comfortable lifestyle. After you reach this stage, you won't have to work very hard, and your heirs will have a lot of money.

Just because a little bit of something is good doesn't mean that a lot more is better. Use moderation in everything you do.

B

101

Bonus and Incentive Plans

NO WELL-MANAGED GROWTH-STAGE company should be without bonus and incentive plans. Financial incentives and rewards are the best method of creating your business utopia—an operation in which the harder people work to make money for themselves, the more money you make, too.

During the survival stage, earnings are so erratic that an incentive formula based on earnings isn't practical. Arbitrary bonuses are the only effective kind. (*Arbitrary* means that the amount each employee gets is based on opinion or an unmeasurable result, frequently called favoritism.) Whenever something really good happens, pass out cash or something highly desirable to an employee, the manager, or to all employees (I used to use $50 bills). Doing so reinforces the concept that if the company does well, employees will do well, too.

For the growth-stage company with enough stability, a fixed formula based on measurable performance is better than an arbitrary bonus plan. Arbitrary bonuses have some motivational effect, but not as much as those calculated by a simple formula. Sometimes arbitrary bonuses or splitting a known bonus pool arbitrarily among the participants becomes a popularity contest rather than a performance reward.

In smaller companies, the best bonus plans put all members of each peer group in the same boat and keep them working toward the same goal. Don't give any one person or group an incentive that could make work more difficult for others. Everyone should draw from the same pool of funds accumulated as a bonus, measured by a known formula, and paid out to designated individuals in an understandable way.

The only exception is salespeople's bonuses. Their job is to produce sales at prices determined by management. Everyone else's job is to produce and deliver high-quality products and/or services on time with lower cost. (See COMMISSION COMPENSATION FOR SALESPEOPLE.)

There are many different incentive systems. In larger companies that use a different basis for measuring the output of different groups or departments, a system can be devised in which, although one group gets more or less than another group, all employees still consider it fair.

Start with owners, partners, and managers. Anyone who exercises independent judgment, whose decisions and actions significantly affect the bottom line, should have a financial incentive and reward for doing it better. This is how you encourage everyone to watch the bottom line and to thoroughly consider all options before asking to increase expenses.

When you're fully organized, you'll have three tiers of incentive bonus pools: one for senior managers, one for middle managers, and one for hourly paid or production workers. Percentage-of-base-pay bonuses generally include everyone but the sales department. You don't want a system that pits managers against workers or vice versa. You want a system that encourages people to understand one another's problems and to work things out together for their mutual benefit.

Annual calculation and payment eliminates problems that arise when you deduct monthly or quarterly losses from bonuses already paid or from a previously profitable period. Managers understand these annual incentives, but hourly employees don't always plan that far in advance.

Everyone's underlying belief must be "When the company makes money, everybody makes money."

Use an easily understood formula. Some version of the KISS principle (Keep It Simple, Stupid) is best. Bonuses are perceived to be fair when they're calculated as a percentage of base pay or regular compensation. It's acceptable and recommended that middle managers receive a higher percentage of base pay than employees, and senior managers an even higher percentage of their base pay.

After years of experience as owner and consultant, I'm even more convinced that incentives, properly placed, designed, and administered, are one of the best guarantees of successful operations.

Whatever plan you start with doesn't have to be a permanent commitment. Announce it as the next year's bonus plan, subject to change in the following year after you've had some experience with it. Don't ever change the rules in the middle of the game; just start the next game with more equitable rules.

Books—Business and Managerial Books Worth Reading

UNTIL THE EARLY 1980S, almost all business books were written principally for big business and the Fortune 500. Now, bookshelves have not only books for these groups but also a growing number written specifically for small business.

The following books have proven their merit over a long period. I've given the original publication date and publisher, but many of them have been republished, sometimes as paperbacks. A used-book store near you may help you find copies of those out of print. Your local library is certain to have copies. If you want to improve your knowledge and understanding of your business, I recommend them to you.

Cohen, Herb. *You Can Negotiate Anything.* New York: Citadel Press, 1980.

Drucker, Peter F. *The Effective Executive.* New York: Harper and Row, 1966.

Peter Drucker, a professor of social sciences at Claremont Graduate School in California, is the most widely acclaimed and respected thinker in the field of management.

Drucker, Peter F. *Innovation and Entrepreneurship.* New York: Harper and Row, 1985.

Drucker, Peter F. *Managing for Results.* New York: Harper and Row, 1964.

Drucker, Peter F. *The Practice of Management.* New York: Harper Business, a division of Harper Collins, 1993.

McGregor, Douglas. *The Human Side of Enterprise.* New York: McGraw-Hill, 1960. This first presented Theory X and Theory Y as philosophies of how employees should be treated.

B

103

Peters, Tom, and Nancy Austin. *A Passion for Excellence.* New York: Random House, 1985.

Townsend, Robert. *Further Up the Organization.* New York: Alfred A. Knopf, 1970. This revised edition of *Up the Organization* was written for big businesses but is direct, sincere, and stunning with its advice and logic. It's still in print. I've borrowed Townsend's format for this book, which is pointed toward survival and growth-stage companies.

If you don't like to read or don't have the time, Soundview Executive Book Summaries, 5 Main St., Bristol, VT 05443-1398, publishes an eight-page condensation of the most important ideas from each of 30 selected new business books each year.

If you'd rather listen to tapes while driving, Audio-Tech Business Book Summaries, 566 W. Adams, Ste. 701, Chicago, IL 60661-3627 (1-800-776-1910) can send you taped summaries of 36 new business books each year.

B

Books—Inspirational Books Worth Reading

THE ENTREPRENEUR'S EMOTIONAL roller-coaster ride has times of despair and doubt. During such times, or for emotional reassurance that you're not alone, inspirational books serve a worthwhile purpose.

It's necessary to remain optimistic, think positively, and at times ignore negative remarks and advice from others. However, you must also be honest with yourself and face reality. (See MISTAKES—ADMITTING THEM.)

Excellent new inspirational books appear all the time because spiritual sustenance is a significant part of most people's lives. The books recommended here have proven their excellence and stood the test of time. Most of them are still in print, but your local library is certain to have copies.

Bettger, Frank. *How I Raised Myself from Failure to Success in Selling.* New York: Prentice-Hall, 1949.

Bristol, Claude M. *The Magic of Believing.* New York: Cornerstone Library, 1979.

Carnegie, Dale. *How to Win Friends and Influence People.* New York: Simon and Schuster, 1994. First printed in 1936, this is still the most famous book on dealing with other people.

Hill, Napoleon. *Think and Grow Rich.* New York: Fawcett Crest, 1960. Republished many times, this book has probably inspired more entrepreneurs than any other. Napoleon Hill coauthored several other inspirational books before he died.

Hill, Napoleon, and W. Clement Stone. *Success through a Positive Mental Attitude.* New York: Prentice-Hall, 1960.

Maltz, Maxwell. *Psycho-Cybernetics.* North Hollywood, Calif.: Wilshire Books, 1960.

Peale, Norman Vincent. *The Power of Positive Thinking.* New York: Prentice-Hall, 1952. A powerful message by a powerful writer.

Schuller, Robert. *Tough Times Never Last but Tough People Do.* Nashville, Tenn.: Thomas Nelson, 1983.

Schwartz, David J. *The Magic of Thinking Big.* New York: Prentice-Hall, 1959.

Borrowed Money—Three Types of Loans

DURING THE SURVIVAL STAGE, financing will most likely be from your savings and from family and friends. You probably won't be able to borrow money from banks except by pledging to them a valuable security you already own.

In the early growth stage, all your loans are going to be short term, secured by your signature, with everything the business owns pledged as collateral. After you have a proven profit record, and after the bank has developed confidence in your managerial skills and ability to repay, you'll be able to borrow a greater total amount by keeping your borrowing and your collateral in the three types of loans described below.

Think of it this way: A man with a closet full of clothes has sports clothes, business suits, and a tuxedo. To have a closet full of borrowed money, you need a working-capital loan secured by working-capital assets; one or more equipment loans secured by specific equipment with a life of over three years; and long-term loans secured by real estate, major equipment, or whatever you can arrange that may be due over a period of 10 years or more. Each type of loan may be made by different institutions, with different policies, security, and payment terms. The main differences are length of time to repay and type of collateral pledged for security.

Working Capital Loans

Your first loan will be a working-capital loan for a maximum stated term of one year. This loan should be used for and secured by accounts receivable and inventory. The amount to be loaned may be determined as a fixed percentage of the total amount of these assets. This works well if your business has a seasonal peak or if you're continuously growing at a fast rate.

Natural lenders for working capital loans are banks. This is their cup of tea. These loans are always short term because your working capital turnover should be short term. If your company continues to grow, you may never get working-capital loans off your balance sheet. With each short-term note or loan, the bank reviews your credit situation. If all is well, the new note pays off the old, frequently with different terms and amounts.

In larger, more established companies, these are called *revolving loans,* or *revolvers.* For such loans you will have a lengthy loan agreement with your bank with positive and negative covenants, carefully detailed and negotiated. When you refer to your line of credit, it usually means the maximum amount of working-capital loan your bank will allow you to draw at one time.

The way to minimize a problem is to anticipate it and prevent it.

This type of loan automatically adjusts to the size of your operation and to business cycles, going up and down with volume. The interest rate is prime plus probably 1 to 2½ percent, depending upon your financial strength and general economic conditions. A commitment or standby fee of ½ percent may be charged on the part you don't borrow, in return for the bank's commitment to keep those funds available for you.

Depending upon your customers' credit ratings, you can borrow 75 to 90 percent against your current accounts receivable. You may also be able to borrow 0 to 60 percent of the value of your inventory, depending upon how readily salable your merchandise is in the general market.

If your profits or general credit rating isn't especially good, a factoring company may give you a working-capital loan. Factoring is the pawn-shop end of the lending business. The interest rate will be about 3 percent more than the bank loan and will require more reporting and control. If you must have the money, sign your name to the factoring contract and pay, but carefully read the termination clause.

Equipment Loans or Personal Property Loans

These loans are used for and secured by chattel mortgages or personal property mortgages. Personal property is any property that can be moved. The mortgage must be registered either in the county courthouse or at the state capital in order to complete the lender's right to foreclose and take possession of the property. If your state has adopted the Uniform Commercial Code, this is called a UCC registration.

These loans and registrations are used

for automobiles, production equipment, office equipment, computers, shelves, racks, forklifts, and other items, capital assets with a useful life of usually three to five years. This is called *asset-based lending* because repayment is secured by asset value rather than operating earnings.

Usually, on new equipment you must be able to make the down payment of 10 to 20 percent of the purchase price. Repayment terms will be in equal monthly installments, which include both principal and interest, over a period equal to about two-thirds of the actual useful life of the equipment.

Most banks make such loans on new, common, or easily resold equipment. Banks usually aren't interested in specialized or highly technical equipment. Used fixtures and equipment are more difficult to finance.

Many equipment manufacturers have standard leases available, often with the opportunity to buy equipment for a favorable price at the end of the lease. (See EQUIPMENT—RENT/LEASE OR BUY.)

Long-Term Loans or Real Estate Loans

Long-term loans are often secured by mortgages on land and buildings that you own or occupy. Mortgage companies and long-term lenders make these loans, which are typically amortized over 15 years or more. The front-end costs of appraisal, survey, title policy, and legal and other fees make arranging them a slow, expensive process.

The only other long-term loans you will get will be from investors, friends, or stockholders, because you have no other collateral to pledge for security. Frequently, such debt must be subordinated to any or all of the above-described financing—meaning that this debt won't be repaid until another debt is paid first. In effect, such loans are second mortgages, because all the lenders above insist on and will have valid first mortgages. Legally, such debt has a right to payment only after all other debt to which it is subordinated is paid off.

Banks and other first-mortgage lenders consider subordinated debt to be equity, and it usually serves that function. The lender expects return of the money only after the company is financially secure. Subordinated debt of this type is often convertible into stock.

One of the prospective purchasers of my company remarked, "Tom, you sure do know how to borrow money." I was deeply in debt because my business was capital intensive. Some of the large machines cost over $250,000 each.

I'm not encouraging you to go into debt as heavily as you can. If you're too heavily in debt in good times, bad times can sweep you away when you're unable to make all the payments you so easily promised when the future looked good. Being overextended with debt, frequently because of attempted rapid expansion, is one of the easiest ways I know of to go broke.

Borrowing Bank Money for the First Time

YOU DON'T HAVE TO TRY MANY TIMES to learn that borrowing money isn't easy. Bankers are a skeptical, questioning lot because other business people have made presentations and promises that they found weren't true. If you choose a bank where you have a checking account or car loan, a banker there will be familiar with you and maybe your company.

Your initial visit to a new banker for a business loan should be friendly and inquisitive. If banking times are hard, the banker may call on you at your business. If banking times are good, you will probably call on the bank. If you don't know a specific banker, tell the receptionist you wish to discuss a small business loan with a bank officer.

The objective is a pleasant exchange of information—from you about your business and from the banker about the bank. Consider this visit a first date, the beginning of a courtship. The banker will ask plenty of questions. Don't be hesitant about doing the same thing.

You usually know by the time you leave whether there's any point in having additional conversations. If things have gone favorably, the banker will start a file on your company and ask that you furnish more information on your next visit. He will probably want to visit you at your business.

Hold preliminary conversations with your banker to feel him out about loan prospects. Save yourself and the banker trouble and embarrassment by discussing the situation in detail before you make a formal request. The banker will indicate the bank's policies, what's reasonable in your situation, and what he thinks the loan committee will approve.

If these conversations aren't encouraging, then decide whether to modify your plans or to find a more agreeable bank. If you're new to the second bank, they will need even more information than the first, familiar one.

For your first loan from any bank that doesn't already have a written history file on your business, you will have to furnish a stack of papers that thoroughly describe your operations. Don't walk into a strange bank for the first time with all this material under your arm, but be aware that the need is there, and be prepared for it.

Much of the information you'll ultimately need when you apply for a loan is in your business plan. (You do have a business plan, don't you?) The prospective lender is also interested in how much money you want and what you're going to do with it.

To reasonably expect anyone to loan you money, you must make a complete disclosure of your present business situation and your personal situation. Even if the banker knows you and your company well, bank supervisory people and government bank examiners are looking over the banker's shoulder. Even if the banker wants and intends to loan you the money, there still must be a written file adequate to satisfy these additional people that the loan is sound.

To persuade bankers or any other lender to loan you money, you must clearly show them, probably in writing, the following things:

- The amount of money you want and on what borrowing terms. Display enough business and financial knowledge to know what your reasonable needs and possibilities are. Don't try to borrow short-term money for long-term needs. (See BORROWED MONEY—THREE TYPES OF LOANS.)

- What you're going to use the money for and how it will benefit the business. Do you need all the money at once or as certain progressive steps are completed? Your answer demonstrates your knowledge of your business, its operations, and how the financing will improve its operations.

- How and when you will pay the money back. This involves planning, forecasting, and budgeting. (See FORECASTING AND FINANCIAL MODEL BUILDING.)

- Certainty of the fund's safety and security for the duration of the loan. This means providing an alternate

source to recover the bank's money if expected profits don't appear. You must pledge assets or collateral, including your personal guarantee.

Most of these general matters should be worked out in your preliminary conversations. When you reach a verbal agreement, the banker will have the necessary papers prepared for signature on your next visit.

If you have significant problems to discuss, make an appointment so the banker can be prepared and have others present if needed. Discuss the problem, answer any questions, then leave written material you've prepared for the banker to go over at leisure. Before you leave, ask when to make contact again or when to return to discuss the matter further. You want to give the banker, and whoever else needs to read your material, plenty of time to do so.

Generally, give your banker too much information rather than too little. Your banker will file away the written information, budgets, and forecasts, then haul them out at the expiration of the forecast period and say, "Last year (quarter) you told me you were going to do so-and-so by now. What happened?"

By the time you get your loan, you can expect most of these things to be in the bank's files:

- A cover letter of not more than two pages explaining and summarizing your overall proposal and program

- Three years of financial statements (five years is better), preferably from outside auditors

- Interim financial statements for the year to date and most recent month you have closed—without audit, but compared to budget

- Federal income tax returns for the last three to five years

- Biographies of owners and managers

- A list of your board of directors, if any

- Sales literature, including market surveys, if any—something about your competitive market position and marketing plans

- A list of what you plan to spend the money for, and when, and an explanation of business benefits

- A financial forecast for the next three years, showing the results of using this new money

- Current aging of accounts receivable and accounts payable

- A list of assets and depreciation that balances with the balance sheet given, noting which assets are pledged as collateral for loans

- A list of your 10 largest customers, or any customer who buys over 10 percent of your total sales volume

- Status of your real estate or location; a copy of all significant equipment or location leases; an explanation of location or terms under which you occupy your real estate

- A description or copy of significant long-term contracts

- A list of general insurance coverage (your insurance agent can help here)

- The total compensation paid to company officers, including yourself, for the last year or several years

B

110

Boss Sets the Example and Attitude

YOU'RE THE BOSS. Whatever attitude you have toward your employees, your company, and your customers will be reflected by all your employees.

You set the tone for integrity and attitudes toward work. When you treat employees with respect and dignity, intermediate managers will do the same thing. Whatever actions and attitudes you dis-

play will be observed and followed by all.

If you are dedicated to superior quality and customer service, this attitude permeates the whole organization. Your enthusiasm and style will be a powerful factor in building a great company.

If you're disorganized, your business will be disorganized. If you cheat on your expense account, charge personal expenses to the business, play favorites, or act unethically, you can't blame alert, intelligent employees when they copy your behavior.

What you do will speak so loudly your employees won't hear what you say. For better or for worse, your actions have a multiplier effect. The attitude of everyone below is this: "If the boss doesn't care about this, why should I?"

During World War II in Europe, one of my assignments was to bring updated technology and instruction, under combat conditions, to all heavy antiaircraft artillery batteries in Third Army. My team started working with radar, range finding, and gun crews as soon as we arrived at a new battery, often before meeting the commander. We soon became adept at forming opinions of their commanders from the attitudes, morale, and responses of the men we dealt with.

Good habits don't trickle up. The trickle-down theory works perfectly within a business. A production worker or clerk who has pride and excellence influences one or two people nearby, but if that

behavior isn't reinforced by management, the company won't change.

Resist any temptation to cheat your employees, your customers, or yourself. If you give in to it, you'll be hypocritical when you tell others not to. You will have opened the door for other associates to do the same thing.

If you don't take care of your customers and employees, someone else will.

Keep everything up front. If you set the example, you're in a strong position to clamp down hard on any employee or associate who takes advantage of the situation, the company, another employee, or a customer.

When I was an employee, I came early and left late to impress my boss. As boss, I came early and left late to impress my employees.

B
111

Break-Even Point

ALWAYS BE CONSCIOUS OF THE VOLUME of weekly or monthly sales it takes to break even. The break-even point is the sales volume at which gross margin or gross profit covers all fixed expenses. By keeping track of daily sales or shipments,

you'll know whether you're having a good month or a bad month, and you'll get a rough idea of your profitability.

In the survival stage, you don't regularly reach your break-even point. It changes so frequently, and operations are so irregular, that knowing precisely at what sales volume your gross margin covers your expenses is difficult. You made the most intelligent estimates you could in your original business plan, but actual performance is always different. Once you regularly achieve break-even, recompute your break-even point whenever growth or changes require it.

Note that break-even means that your operating statement will show no loss and no gain. Your cash flow may still be negative because of note payments, equipment purchases, or increases in accounts receivable or inventory. If you ask your accountant to compute your break-even point, she will compute it in a complicated manner by analyzing all your expenses and classifying them as either fixed or variable, or maybe as semi-fixed or semivariable.

Think of fixed costs as those that remain the same over a reasonable period, perhaps several months, until you make a significant change in productive capacity. Fixed costs are such things as rent, insurance, administrative and sales salaries, office supplies, repairs and maintenance to office facilities and equipment, and routine monthly expenses— expenses little affected by sales volume.

Variable costs relate directly to the amount of productive work being done— materials, hourly labor, shop supervision, field overhead, and supplies consumed or needed for production. These costs vary directly with your operation's activity level or the amount of services or products produced and sold.

If you're in the manufacturing or distribution business, you will probably classify fuel, utilities, and transportation costs (or a large portion thereof) as variable expenses applying to the shop, but service and some retail businesses classify these as fixed. In some service businesses, almost all expenses are fixed. When in doubt, call the expense fixed.

The quick and dirty way to compute break-even is to find your average gross-margin percentage (average gross profit divided by average net sales). Divide that amount into the average total of your sales and administrative expenses. The result is your average break-even sales volume. Verify by multiplying gross-margin percentage times calculated break-even sales. The result should be your total fixed expenses, such as sales and administrative expenses.

Many things can keep this calculation from being a fixed, precise number. Changing product mix or operating efficiency alters the gross margin. Any change in sales and administrative costs (for example, hiring more people) affects the result. But within a reasonable time span and at a similar operating level, this procedure works.

This break-even figure is based on operating income and expenses only, and has nothing to do with cash flow, collections on receivables, capital expenditures, owner's withdrawals, or buildup or drawdown of inventory. Other miscellaneous income and expense are usually ignored, although interest charges on current notes should be considered a fixed expense.

Budgets

A BUDGET ISN'T A TOOL for increasing productivity or making money. A budget helps you allocate the time and resources necessary to accomplish your objectives. This means that you have objectives and a time line for reaching them.

In the survival stage, you're so busy surviving that you don't really know what your resources or your objectives are. But the larger and more stable you become, the more necessary a budget becomes.

In the survival stage, your business plan and business forecast become your budget. They help you estimate whether you have the resources and whether your goals are within reach. Forecasts or budgets have definite value because they require you to think through logically and undertake a sequence of activities to carry out a specific, identified program. Budgets also provide a means of determining the cost of alternate paths of action and give you a yardstick against which to measure progress and results, or lack thereof.

If you aren't committed to the budget and treat it loosely, it can quickly fall into disrepute with subordinates and have no real significance for cost control.

As a manager, you should be responsible for budget preparation for your own operating unit. Don't expect the accounting department or someone within your department to put together a bunch of numbers for you to submit further up the line. Money is spent at the operating level.

The company budget is the assembled, reviewed, and reconciled total of the budgets of all subordinate units. Middle managers don't have a perspective beyond their own department or division. They need guidance from the top about objectives for the coming year. They must know whether the financial estimate or forecast includes growth, new plans, new products, or other changes in market conditions.

The first, most basic requirement for the entire budget is the sales forecast. Until you get an intelligent sales forecast made by the best brains in your company, the budgeting function is without significance, because although budgets may control the outflow of money, only the sales forecast estimates control the inflow.

The budget isn't an authorization for the manager to spend monies regardless of what happens to the sales forecast. You need quarterly and semiannual checkpoints. If sales aren't meeting the forecast, make budgetary changes. Many companies make mid-course corrections at six months. To be ready during the first month of the new year, begin budget preparation during the last quarter of the preceding year.

Preparing the budget or the sales forecast is a teamwork proposition. You're

B

113

asking people to commit to operating within or at certain levels, and to produce results that are as good as or better than the budget. Many people are reluctant to make budgets. They think they must feed back to top management the numbers it wants to hear. They feel they're being forced to help design the club they'll be beaten over the head with for the next twelve months. For this reason, sometimes there's a tendency to sandbag a little, to make conservative estimates. People want to be able to beat the numbers rather than to do poorly. This isn't all bad. Managers must still carefully consider their course and what they consider to be realistic results of their own actions.

Managers should be accountable only for budgeted expenses they have control over, which they agree are chargeable to them. Overhead assigned from other departments or sources over which they have no control shouldn't result in any penalty.

Departmental budgets show the department's contribution toward the overall profit. These significant numbers don't have to be the bottom line or total profit responsibility for the entire company. Include bonus or incentive compensation amounts within the overall expense budget.

With or without a budget, you're going to have surprises. Budgeting either helps you eliminate many surprises or prepares you to handle them. Let your accountant examine and critique your budget so you won't be surprised by questions your banker may ask. (See FORECASTING AND FINANCIAL MODEL BUILDING; FORECASTING SALES.)

Bulletin Boards

BY LAW, YOU'RE REQUIRED to notify your employees about many things. Your official communication channel is one or more bulletin boards, plus your employee handbook.

If information appears either on the bulletin board or in your employee policy manual or handbook, then employees can't claim official ignorance of specific policies or matters. Be prepared to prove that they were told to read the bulletin board or that they received a copy of the employee handbook.

Your employee policy manual or handbook should state that all employees are responsible for knowing information posted on the bulletin board. It should also state that nothing may be placed on the bulletin board without the prior approval of your personnel or human resources manager.

Put bulletin boards in high-traffic areas or highly visible locations, such as the coffee bar, time clock, snack room, locker room, or any place employees frequently visit or linger.

All bulletin boards should have a glass cover and be locked. The manager who keeps the key should check all the boards every morning to be sure no official notices have been removed and that no prankster or disgruntled employee uses the official communication channel to play pranks or spread fun or venom. The same manager should remove notices or communications after the specified exposure time, and keep a file copy of all notices placed on the board, noting date posted and date removed.

Some state and federal laws require that certain notices be permanently posted on your bulletin board, such as the Equal Employment Opportunity Commission (EEOC) notice, the Workers' Compensation Insurance Coverage notice, the Occupational Safety and Health Act (OSHA) notice, and other required state notices. Put permanent notices in one section of the bulletin board or on a separate but equally prominent bulletin board. Leave room for temporary notices elsewhere.

Use your bulletin board to boost morale and give employee recognition by announcing employee accomplishments; company progress; news or articles about your industry, customers, or competitors; explanations of problems or new policies; and letters the company has received from customers.

Keep your bulletin board alive and attractive. Purchase colored posters that call attention to personal safety, customer service, product quality, or an aspect of personal improvement. Employees should want to read what's on your bulletin board because it's interesting and informative.

B

115

Business Cycles

WITHOUT THE DOWNS, the ups wouldn't be so good.

During boom times, when living is easy and sales seem to increase almost without effort, it's easy to become sloppy about cost controls, pass out fat wage increases, and create numerous other luxurious-but-not-essential continuing expenses. Wise management doesn't add that extra layer of fat, even in good times, and keeps itself lean, mean, and productive.

As the total market grows in good times, enjoy it, grow faster than the market if you can, but stay prepared for bad times. Take all the growth you can finance by trying to increase or at least maintain market share of existing products or services. Caution: During boom times, don't overexpand capacity or payroll or create financial burdens that can't be carried by reduced activity during a downturn.

Follow market trends and events.

Downturns are almost always unexpected, sudden, and fast, but the following upturn, with its rebuilding of confidence and volume, is always slow. Always try to cut costs in both good times and bad.

You're not a seasoned business manager until you've survived both an economic boom and an economic bust.

116

When a major economic downturn occurs that isn't seasonal (over 10 percent) or that affects your whole industry, quickly cut back on expenses and payroll. Try not to lose money. Make less money on reduced volume until better economic times allow slow market recovery. A recession magnifies bad or sloppy management; a well-managed, mature company can make money at any level by adjusting expenses to the current level of income.

The first time you experience a major decline, you may resist taking action you know is necessary: slicing overhead. Cutting expenses is hard but usually impersonal. Cut out all the expenses you can—particularly overhead, overtime, and fringe benefits—before you consider cutting personnel. It hurts to lay off employees—it's cutting muscle, not just fat.

People are expensive, but not just because of paychecks. They receive benefits, use supplies and telephones, and spend money. They need space, equipment, taxes, and insurance. People are at the center of both your productivity and your overhead.

Start by weeding out expendable employees—the least productive, and those performing nonessential tasks. (See LAYOFFS OR REDUCTIONS IN FORCE (RIF).) Trying to maintain the overhead you needed when volume was higher can quickly cost you much of the surplus it took you so long to accumulate.

When your business increases rapidly, use temporaries. When the decline comes, temps are easier to let go. The psychological damage is less severe for you and for them.

During bad times, consider new products, services, or areas, as well as affordable expansion opportunities. Buy into or develop opportunities at lower prices. Lay your foundation for growth into the next boom. Pursuing increased market share with extensive sales programs in a falling market is a recipe for disaster.

If your company is having a bad season while competitors or other firms similar to yours are doing well, you have internal managerial or product design problems that you can't blame on the business cycle.

Business Plan—Outline

THIS BOOK DOESN'T HAVE DETAILED instructions on how to write a business plan, but your local book store or library has plenty of books that do. A good one is *The Ernst & Young Business Plan Guide,* by Eric Siegel, Brian Ford, and Jay Bornstein (New York: John Wiley & Sons, Inc., 1993). In addition, some software programs contain helpful outlines.

No business can be all things to all people. Your plan must clearly identify the specific niche you intend to fill.

In particular, update financial sections of the plan as time goes by. Keep actual performance numbers up to date, as well as the forecast. Revise other sections as appropriate. Below are descriptions of the sections usually found in a business plan.

1. Executive Summary

The most important part of the plan is the executive summary. If you're submitting the plan to prospective investors, the executive summary is your first and possibly only chance to capture their attention. Venture capitalists are deluged with plans, and their analysis time is limited. If five minutes of initial review fail to give a good impression, they'll either return or discard your plan.

The summary must be a thumbnail sketch of the business, emphasizing key points of the plan. One and one-half pages is an excellent length. Three pages is maximum.

Include a description of the basic product or service and a discussion of the market. State how the product is different from its competition and why it will succeed. Introduce the management team, refer to financial projections, and provide a schedule regarding financial results. Finally, state the amount of funding you're seeking and how you intend to put those funds to use. Write this last, after you've completed the other sections.

2. Table of Contents

Include a list of headings along with page numbers.

3. Company Description

Discuss the nature of the business, including major products or services, and the final use of the product. Point out present and future social, economic, or technical trends that will influence market growth, your product, or your customers. Include a paragraph on what you consider the greatest strengths and greatest weaknesses of the operation you're describing.

4. Market Analysis and Strategy

Realistically assess the marketplace. A venture capitalist or banker knows that every business is market driven. The bottom line is making money; that means selling the product or service. Describe in detail the customers you seek. Describe your industry, its outlook, and the specific target markets you want to cover. Enumerate your national, regional, and local competitors. Never underestimate your competition. Describe the current total size of the market that you can expect to serve.

Also, describe your marketing activities and summarize the marketing plan you are using or anticipating using. Include product pricing and how it is to be determined. Show how you think your marketing strategy will persuade people to buy your product; don't say that the product will sell itself. State whether you will sell directly to the final consumer or through sales representatives, distributors, or retail outlets.

5. Technology, Research, and Development

This section is necessary if you have a distinctive, new, or different technology, process, or product. Otherwise, include this explanation in your market analysis and strategy section.

6. Production Operations

If manufacturing is involved, indicate your plans or your present operating or production situation as well as how you furnish goods or services. What are your sources of supplies and raw materials? Assess your supplier relationship, production quality, and production costs. What's your production or operating capacity? How can your facilities be expanded and at what cost? Do you need skilled labor? Are unions or zoning a

problem? Discuss whether you plan to make or buy your product.

7. Management and Ownership

Persuade people to invest in people. Include résumés of officers and important managers on your team. Describe their professional backgrounds or experience within your industry. To be complete, your team must have a marketing expert, a financial manager, and someone competent in production and in the development of additional technology or operations.

Investor confidence comes from seeing that you have recruited associates with good track records in your industry. Describe the equity investment of each manager. List the members of the board of directors and their credentials.

8. Organization and Personnel

Describe how your management people will work together. Provide an organization chart and show the division of duties and responsibilities.

9. Funds Required and Their Uses

If you're using the plan to raise money, show how much financing the company will need and when. Include a realistic estimate of the future. Explain any debt financing or creditor financing required, as well as the desired terms of anticipated financing.

Describe why it's appropriate to introduce the product or service at this time. The professional investor has many alternate investment opportunities. You must demonstrate that your chances for success are better than other investment opportunities awaiting the venture capitalist's consideration.

If possible, provide a way for the investor to get out in three to seven years with lots more money than she put in. Explain how this will happen. Exit plans frequently mean taking the company public, selling the company to a larger entity, or buying back the investor's interest. The latter is usually a gradual plan, because there's never enough money internally to do it in one lump sum.

Don't underestimate your capital requirements. Financing is most easily obtained when the market considers you an attractive candidate. Differentiate funds required and their future use from past financial data, although they are closely related.

10. Financial Data and Forecasts

In condensed columnar form, include a minimum of the last three operating years or whatever actual history you have; five years is better. Show the current year to date, projections for quarterly profit and loss, cash flow projections for the next two years, and annual projections up to five.

It's best to err on the conservative side. It's much easier to explain why things turned out better than you planned than to explain what went wrong. For your own security and peace of mind, you should prepare and know, if asked (no need to include it in full in the presentation), an optimistic estimate (150 to 200

percent of the sales volume) and a pessimistic estimate (50 percent of the realistic sales volume). Compute a break-even point.

The forecast depends on your best estimates of sales as well as expenses. In your forecast, include balance sheets showing assets and liabilities to go with operations and most of the financial ratios. Cash flow projections are significant. (See FORECASTING AND FINANCIAL MODEL BUILDING; FINANCIAL RATIOS—WHAT THE NUMBERS MEAN.)

Whatever is sufficient to get us to this point is insufficient to get us further.

B

119

List and explain your assumptions; these will demonstrate how sophisticated and knowledgeable you are about running your business. If you put statements in common-denominator form, you can tell whether or not your predictions conform to your own history and to good business practices. (See HOW ARE YOU DOING COMPARED WITH INDSUTRY STANDARDS?) If your forecasts don't reflect industry standards, give some reasons or explanations.

11. Administrative Considerations

If your operations have special network, database, or customer-tracking problems, explain how you are going to handle them. Mention any significant administrative or personnel problems and their solutions; eliminate this section if you have none.

12. Appendices or Exhibits
Include your sales literature, pictures of your products, market studies, articles from trade journals covering your market, and any other information that would be of concern to a person interested in your company.

Business Plan—Why You Need One

A BUSINESS PLAN IS A WAY of running your business instead of letting it run you. The plan helps identify problems quickly and monitor company performance on a regular basis. A written plan is essential if you're trying to persuade a banker, investor, or venture capitalist to put money into your business.

Many a business starts, lives, and dies without ever having a formal business plan. However, the sooner you get one, the better off you are. Your plan can't foresee every contingency or accurately forecast the future, but the discipline required to think through and reduce to writing all aspects of your proposed or present operation will clarify and improve your understanding of your own business. It's hard-copy proof that you have your thinking and your act together. Write one as soon as you can.

A written plan makes it easier for you to communicate your basic plans, dreams, and methods to associates and managers. When it's in writing, others can understand it, share it, and help you make the plan real.

You can start on the back of an envelope. Discuss everything with your associates. They will think of things that you don't. While writing and talking, you're building the team and training your managers to plan the company's future. This gives managerial teamwork a tremendous boost and leads to everyone's shared commitment to make it happen.

Put down what you think a stranger would like to know about your business. Put down what you think an investor or banker would like to know. Put down what you think an astute customer who depends upon your company as a source of supply would like to know. Refine the document every time you think of a better way to express or clarify something.

Internally, a business plan ensures unity of purpose, goals, and understanding among all managers. It improves performance by obtaining agreement and commitment, provides a basis for measuring performance, and establishes a framework for making key decisions by middle managers during the ongoing process.

Externally, use your business plan to explain to bankers, venture capitalists, investors, and other interested parties exactly what you're trying to do. It helps gain support from shareholders, investors, and banking institutions. You'll probably make revisions or additions to the basic components of the documents to shape them for the purpose at hand.

To write the best business plan you're capable of, you need several things: your financial statements, a list of identified business risks, and an ability to look honestly at the strengths and weaknesses of your current operation and ask "What if?"

Key questions to ask yourself are these: Why should potential customers give money to me rather than to my competitor? What kinds of customers do I expect to give me money? Identify this target market as precisely as possible. How many of them are there? Where are they? How can I reach them as economically as possible? What's the potential for loss? How sensitive to recession is my business? What happens if a new product outdates mine? What if a major supplier or customer goes out of business?

If you don't know where you're going, any old road map will do; you'll never get lost, and you won't know it when you get there.

In the final analysis, your budget, your business and strategic plans, and your financial forecasts are all different expressions of the same basic principle of business management: Understanding the past and present, and thinking and planning for the future, is the best way to make good things happen.

B

121

Business Problem Identification

FOR ANY NORMAL BUSINESS PROBLEM, there's at least one normal business solution. Don't think you're the only one who has ever faced and dealt with this problem.

The problem that walks in your door is already in the crisis stage. As boss, your real job is to find and solve problems before they become crises. An old navy proverb is "A good admiral roams the ship." While roaming, he's searching for problems.

Find the root of the problem and strike at it. Don't just whack at the branches. Many people can show you problems among the branches, but finding the decay in the root is your goal. Your solution will usually include fast and temporary treatment of the symptoms (like treating the cough and runny nose—not curing the cold) while you work on the root problem over a longer period. You know the alligator and swamp story. (If you don't, see LONG-RANGE PLANNING.)

It is harder to ask the right questions than to find answers for the wrong questions.

To identify a problem, talk to customers, managers, employees, or vendors, preferably on their turf. Have an open-door policy. Be alert to what's going on in your business. If you get enough account-

ing reports and numerical data, you'll see the trends. You'll find problems before they become crises. Often the problem is related to one or more people, typically managers. Firing them isn't the answer; motivating and training them usually is.

If you have trouble identifying the root problem or defining a specific problem, discuss it with the managers and trusted employees most closely involved. They will have differing views of the problem and different solutions. All usually think someone else is at fault.

If you're not satisfied with their analyses, definitions of the problem, or suggested solutions, present what you think is the complete problem to each member of your mastermind group or advisory directors—one at a time, not collectively.

Each time you present the situation and redefine the problem to people whose opinion you respect, the root problem will become more clear. When you can describe it simply and straightforwardly, the solution will usually also become clear. If you have a mentor or are a member of a CEO roundtable, discuss it with these people. (See CEO ROUNDTABLES OR PRESIDENTS' CLUBS; ADVISORY DIRECTORS.)

Buy-Sell Agreements with Other Shareholders

ENTREPRENEURS ARE VERY CAREFUL about who owns the stock of their company. Other than shares you must sell or option to outsiders to raise capital, you should share stock ownership only with people who are active, full-time employees of the business.

The advantages of having employees

share the incentives of stock ownership are discussed in EMPLOYEES AS STOCK-HOLDERS. But whenever you sell stock to any other employee who will become a minority shareholder, you should have the employee and spouse execute a written buy-sell agreement. Have a business lawyer draw up such an agreement, and print on the face of the shares that are issued that the sale or transfer is subject to such an agreement.

The agreement we developed and used over the years had the following principal terms:

1. The original sale price to the employee was for five times the after-tax earnings per share, calculated on a three-year moving-average basis. The mandatory sale price at termination was seven times the earnings per share, on the same basis. The computation was made by the company's outside accounting firm using federal income tax returns as filed.

    The intention of the pricing method used here was to keep everyone's attention focused on earnings, a view we all shared. The buyback at seven times earnings gave the associate a break and a greater incentive. Other values that could be used are book value per share, appraised value, or an updated agreed value for the following year (which is usually out of date when needed). An arithmetical formula that can be easily calculated is best.

2. Termination of employment for any reason—including death, discharge, or disability—activated the agreement that the employee or heirs must sell and the company must buy the stock.

3. Payment from the company to the shareholders could be a lump sum paid within 90 days, or at the discretion of the company, 25 percent within 90 days, and the balance in three annual installments with interest. This provision was designed to provide the departing employee with immediate cash without unduly burdening the company. If the cash amount was manageable at the time, the company paid in full. If the amount was large, the company reserved the right to make payment over a three-year period.

4. If the employee engaged in a competitive activity, the total price to be paid dropped to a multiple of five rather than seven. We didn't want to be in the position of financing a former employee who quit and wanted to use our money to compete with us. This seemed fair because the employee paid only five times earnings originally. We never had occasion to use this provision.

We didn't develop this written agreement until after we were well into the growth stage, although similar prices were used for the few transactions that occurred before then. Under the formula, the value per share went slowly and steadily upward. I paid $1 per share for my stock, and so did one of the other two employees I started with. Later he quit as vice president and production manager to go into a business of his own. We bought his stock back for $6, and we're still good friends. All but three shareholders paid less than $20 per share. When we sold our company to the corporation listed on the New York Stock Exchange, we had 17 shareholders. The purchaser paid $190 per share. Everybody smiled.

If you don't invest very much, then defeat doesn't hurt too much and victory is not very exciting.

Cash Management

IN ALL STAGES OF GROWTH, business is like a table-stakes poker game: when you're out of cash, you're out of the game. You're finished. It's over.

To stay in the game, you *must* manage your cash and make cash projections. In survival-stage companies, profit is an accounting concept. Cash is king.

As long as you have enough cash to pay all your bills, you stay in business. It doesn't matter whether you get cash from your nest egg, from bank or other loans, or from customers for services rendered.

When you're insolvent and don't have enough cash to cover your bills or your note payments, you're out of business or you soon will be. It doesn't matter whether this lack of cash happened because you started with too little, bought too much inventory, equipment, or real estate, took too large a paycheck for yourself, or had too costly a product or service.

The accounting definition of cash flow is the sum of after-tax earnings (profit after taxes) plus depreciation, plus any other noncash charges to operations, such as amortization of intangible assets. Managers need this number to plan growth and debt repayment. Bankers need it to feel secure in their credit position. Many businesses are evaluated and sold as a multiple of cash flow.

Anyone can manage a company as long as there's money in the bank. Making the proper decisions when there's little or no cash tests your management skills. I cannot overemphasize that you must conserve cash in absolutely every way you legally can.

To improve your cash flow, issue invoices daily. People can't even start to pay until they receive your invoice showing exactly how much they owe you and why. Get your paperwork into the payer's processing and paying cycle as quickly as possible.

Other than increasing sales, you can improve cash flow by any procedure that accelerates receipt of income or delays actual date of payment. To bring in money faster, take advance payment on large contracts, take deposits at the time of the order, set up a closer due date or shorter payment terms, or give cash discounts. To keep your money longer, put equipment purchases on installment notes. Just don't make late payment habitual.

Run your business on OPM (Other People's Money) as much as you can. This requires collecting quickly and paying slowly to the greatest extent possible without offending your customers or creditors.

The best thing you can do is collect in cash from your customer before you have to pay for the merchandise or services you furnish him. Payroll cannot be deferred, but many other payments can.

125

When my business was small (three employees), I left invoicing up to the man who managed the office and the warehouse. One month almost no checks came in, but volume and expenses went on as usual. When I investigated, I learned that this employee (also busy and overworked) had decided to save himself some time by invoicing the entire month's shipments at once at the end of the previous month. That solved his problem, but it created big cash problems for me.

You need cash to grow. You need it to buy something, to take advantage of a golden opportunity, or to cover a rainy-day catastrophe. You'll need cash as long as you're in business; don't spend it except on essentials. You'll never have enough money to waste it. Your business should be a lean, mean, money-making machine. (See CASH TRACKING AND FORECASTING.)

Sometimes spending one penny is too much. Sometimes spending several thousand dollars is too little. The cliché you've heard is true: The first million is the hardest. That breaks down also to the first $100,000, to the first $10,000, and to the first $1,000.

Keep your line of credit open, with some of it unused, as your source of emergency funds. This is your sinking fund when your cash in the bank runs low.

Your two financial focus points are cash and profit: cash, because it's the mother's milk your business needs to grow; profit, because it's your long-term source of future cash.

Cash Tracking and Forecasting

ONE MORE REMINDER about the importance of cash: When you're out of cash, you're out of business. Even if you don't forecast or control anything else, record and forecast cash as an early-warning system that trouble is coming.

Other sections discuss understanding and handling your cash. This section discusses only cash tracking of yesterday or the last period as the key to forecasting the coming period in more detail than the cash section of the PRESIDENT'S DAILY/WEEKLY REPORT. For this report, use the same kind of multiple-column accounting form mentioned there.

This is the relationship you're trying to control and get on paper in understandable numerical form:

Cash available at beginning of time period,

Plus cash received during the time period,

Minus cash spent or checks released during the time period,

Equals cash available at the end of this period, which is the beginning of the next period.

The period used may be from one day to one week. Longer than one week is dangerous; trouble can arise too quickly. Start daily. Lengthen the period as you gain confidence and knowledge. Start by recording what actually happened yesterday; then budget or project what you expect to happen tomorrow.

If your outgo exceeds your income, then your upkeep will be your downfall.

Forecasting or budgeting future collections comes from analyzing your past collection history to determine the usual payment time in days, as well as the payment cycle, indicating the times of the month or week when the most and the least cash are received. You will know whether other borrowed funds become available, fixed assets are sold, or additional investment is expected.

Cash spent or checks released during the period should be broken down into payroll and payroll taxes, payments on accounts payable, new assets purchased, and other payments such as taxes, note payments, and interest. Use the same breakdown for forecasting.

If you don't have a simple way to determine these figures, work with your accountant to get adding-machine tapes from stacks of checks released or to be released. Such accurate estimates are acceptable for interim reports. But reconcile and correct every amount on the report to general ledger numbers as often as possible, at least at month's end.

The cash balance at the end of the period tells you whether you're above or below your comfort amount and whether the trend is up or down. When you're familiar enough to forecast several periods ahead, you'll be able to get real control of the race between the calendar and your cash.

The moral of the story: Don't ever allow your company to run out of cash. Easy to say, difficult to do.

A sample form you can use on your green accounting pad or print from a spreadsheet is shown as figure 1 on page 128. Modify it to suit your operations and your needs.

127

	Date or First Period		Date or Second Period		Date or Third Period	
	Actual	Budget	Actual	Budget	Actual	Budget
BEGINNING BALANCE						
Expected Cash Receipts						
Cash Sales						
Accounts Receivable Collections						
Other Cash Received						
Total Cash Received						
Expected Cash Paid Out						
Payroll and Payroll Taxes						
Accounts Payable						
Materials and Inventory						
Production Expenses						
Sales and Administration						
Plant and Equipment						
Other, Taxes, Interest						
Total Cash Paid Out						
ENDING BALANCE						

Figure 1. Cash Report and Forecast

C

128

Catastrophe—When You're Faced With

EVERY ENTREPRENEUR LIVES WITH the haunting fear that some unforeseen catastrophe will wipe out his business. Something out there beyond your knowledge or control can unexpectedly threaten everything you own.

When a catastrophe threatens, ask yourself these questions: What's the worst-case scenario? Could I lose my business? Will I have to sell something to raise money? Will the bank increase my loan to cover what I need? Will I survive? Will my business survive? How can my family come out of this okay? Can I recover? Can I delay the catastrophe and use the time to find a solution?

After you consider the worst things that could happen, figure out what you can do to prevent them. Maybe you can cut the bill in half with offsetting claims or get long-term payout terms. Even the IRS will negotiate if they think you're sincerely trying to pay them. Maybe the lawsuit will be tied up in the courts for three years. Can you live with these results? Who's the most knowledgeable, experienced person you can find to help you? Try your mentor, CEO roundtable, or advisory director.

After a few days or weeks of contemplating the event and possible courses of action, take the action most likely to save your business and yourself, or at least the most important parts. Work to soften the disaster's effects, to recover, and to work

into a better situation. Believe the old adage, "Turn your stumbling blocks into stepping stones."

I acquired a company knowing that it was in difficult financial condition but thinking I could straighten out the problems and make a profit. If it hadn't been in bad shape, I couldn't have afforded to buy it. Several months after the purchase, the largest single customer requested permission to return a large volume of products from South America because of cancellation of a project. The value of the material was more than two months' total sales volume. The material had been shipped and paid for two years before. Trade practice was such that if I did not accept the return, no one would buy from me because I was not standing behind my products.

I thought I would go bankrupt. After much soul-searching and review of all possible alternatives, I went to the customer's home office and proposed that if they would pay the freight, we would accept the return. Credit was to be issued as a merchandise credit (payable only in other merchandise) against future purchases, to be issued as a cash credit each month equal to 20 percent of the current month's purchases. They accepted.

Two years later, I personally delivered the last credit memo to a company officer, and that firm remained one of my best customers as long as I was in business.

C

129

Of course, I refurbished and resold the inventory to others as soon as possible, thereby getting an immediate cash infusion. Years later, at a trade show, company officials told me they had no choice other than to accept my offer because otherwise they would have recovered no value at all from this equipment.

We cannot direct the wind, but we can adjust our sails.

When you can see the reasonable end of the situation, say to yourself, "It could've been worse, and it would've been worse if I hadn't done so-and-so." Be comforted by the thought that you're not the only person who has ever faced that problem. I do not believe that everything works out for the best all by itself. Everything works out for the best because you work at it to make it the best. Find a solution that works for you; the result is almost never as bad as you first imagined it might be.

An understanding spouse, as well as active assistance from your partners, advisors, and everyone in your company, will help you overcome your problems. Alcohol won't.

CEO Roundtables or Presidents' Clubs

ACTIVE PARTICIPATION WITH OTHER entrepreneurs, owners, and chief executive officers (CEOs) in a CEO roundtable is one of the least expensive, most rewarding ways to improve your managerial skills and business understanding and an excellent way to relieve your entrepreneurial loneliness.

The specific purpose of a CEO roundtable is to mutually assist members to manage their businesses by counseling, coaching, supporting, motivating, and holding each other accountable. The objective is the improvement of managerial practices and profitability for every member, and the dedication of all to each other's business success.

In this group you seek answers to questions that can't be raised within your company or with other associates because of their confidential nature. You might hesitate to discuss these problems with your accountant, lawyer, banker, or insurance person because these people may not be objective or knowledgeable, or they might be influenced by their own position in or dependence on your company.

A CEO roundtable provides a private forum for confidential discussion of your most serious problems with a group of peers who know you, want you to succeed, and share similar problems. This forum encourages honesty, respect, and the willingness to share intimate feelings and strong opinions. Members should feel safe discussing their most sensitive problems. Group continuity over a long period develops trust. Members usually receive both immediate and long-range benefits; later they credit these roundtables with many specific contributions to their growth and success.

A CEO roundtable isn't a networking group. Normally, little business is transacted between member companies, although members talk frequently with each other by phone. Membership is usually limited to CEOs of noncompeting small companies in which the CEO owns effective financial and operating control.

Membership should be limited to 10 to 15 active members, so that 8 to 12 will attend meetings. Each member must be compatible with and unanimously accepted by all other members. You may wish to select principally CEOs of service companies or CEOs of companies that are capital intensive, but diverse viewpoints contribute knowledge and experience to the entire group. Being part of such a group is like having knowledgeable consultants at your beck and call.

I was fortunate to have been a member of such a CEO roundtable over 30 years ago. The assistance, ideas, and moral support I received helped me tremendously. Other members experienced similar results. Friendships were formed that have lasted to this day.

We didn't have a mentor for the group, but I think an experienced elder participant can definitely make a positive contribution. A retired former CEO and owner should be able to earn a free meal, if there is one, by bringing experience and maturity to an eager young group.

A panel of qualified CEOs can knowledgeably discuss any and all business problems of growing businesses, such as incentive plans, compensation, organization, diversification, finance, advertising, sales, personnel, tax planning, and forecasting. They can support one another's plans for actions.

Members benefit from the additional eyes, ears, education, experience, opinions, and contacts of other CEOs. In effect, group members become consultants and advisors for other entrepreneurs in the group. (See ADVISORY DIRECTORS; MENTORS AND MENTORING.)

There are several kinds of roundtables. Local and national consulting groups assist in forming CEO groups within a city or a particular geographical area, or within an industry or type of business. Some groups charge a fee to furnish a consultant to facilitate monthly meetings. Many business-oriented government and nonprofit agencies, such as chambers of commerce, help set up CEO roundtables within their activity areas. Some industries put together geographically separated and therefore noncompeting CEOs with almost identical operations. One such group is the Petroleum Equipment Institute.

If you can't find a ready-made CEO roundtable to join, you can fairly easily form one of your own using the ideas given here or with help from existing groups or interested local agencies.

To start a roundtable yourself, call three to five CEOs of noncompeting businesses with whom you think you'll be compatible. You should be geographically accessible to each other. Propose a date for an initial meeting. Send photocopies of this write-up or other appropriate literature. Let common need and business judgment guide you.

Each member in rotation usually fills the office of facilitator or president for six months or a year. The facilitator sends notices; schedules programs; arranges meeting places, food, or payments, if any; and keeps the administrative wheels in smooth motion. I recommend holding monthly meetings; if food is involved, share food costs or pay individually.

To cover the many program possibilities, the most helpful and interesting practice is for each member to take turns being responsible for the program. The presenter uses the opportunity to present the most difficult managerial problem that she has been wrestling with for the last several months for suggestions, discussion, and solutions. The presenter leads the discussion and paces the meeting to cover all aspects of the problem or the agenda within the allotted time. Hold nothing back when presenting your problems; participate frankly and positively in discussing the business problems of other members.

The following are examples of serious problems you cannot easily discuss with others outside such a group:

- Should I fire my vice president?

- Should I undertake a major expansion?

- Should I refinance, take new partners, or kick out the old ones?

- How can I handle family members in my business?

- What bonuses or incentives will motivate my employees?

- How can I overcome my competition?

- How can I improve marketing or production?

- Why aren't we growing faster?

Furnish exhibits or financial statements to explain the problem or possible solutions, but collect them for destruction at the end of the meeting.

Format is important. Presenting real problems and inviting assistance and coaching requires profound levels of thought and sharing and can create a deep bond of understanding between members. The atmosphere must be informal, friendly, and as close to one-on-one discussion as possible. Ask questions or make suggestions for possible solutions at any time. This encourages the greatest interchange of ideas and understanding of the problem and alternate solutions. Everyone benefits to some degree because the same fundamental problems are found in almost every organization.

Alternative programs may be any subject requested in advance by a member with a specific problem. Choose a business topic and ask each member to come prepared to discuss her experience handling it. Or invite an outside speaker to talk on a subject of current interest.

Each group develops its own dynamics and character and establishes a workable format. During the early part of the meeting, former presenters should inform members of their progress and results since last meeting. Much of the meeting's value comes from members' holding each other accountable for results.

> *Peak performers concentrate on solving problems rather than placing blame for them.*
>
> **—Charles Garfield**

The presenter or another member may want to bring an associate from his company to benefit from the discussion. To be certain there are no conflicts or violations of confidentiality, visitors usually aren't allowed except by unanimous consent.

New members may be proposed by a member-sponsor, who furnishes a résumé of the prospect to the group for approval.

Several other members should have a get-acquainted lunch with the prospect to confirm compatibility. The prospective member may then visit one or two meetings. The unanimous approval of all current members must be obtained before accepting the prospect as a member.

Three to six meetings after acceptance, the new member should make a presentation covering in detail her company history, a company mission, important personnel, operating statistics, and goals and financial statements. Some roundtables have this meeting at the new member's plant or office to get a guided tour and a better understanding of the nature of the new member's business.

In the roundtable of which I was a member years ago, we admitted a new member who was introducing the use of plastic sheeting to agricultural and construction markets for protection against the weather. His financial statements were eye-popping, showing him bringing almost 15 percent to the bottom line after taxes. One of our members remarked, "Bill, take those financial statements and get out of here before we try to give you some advice." On other occasions, we discussed ways members who were losing money could make their turnaround.

I strongly recommend that you join or form your own CEO roundtable. The Greater Houston Partnership (the equivalent of the Chamber of Commerce; 1200 Smith St., #700, Houston, TX 77002-4309) has a successful CEO roundtable for local companies.

C

133

Change Your Mind—It Will Cost You Money

YOUR DECISIONS ARE BASED ON KNOWN information, perceived facts, and your opinions on the question at hand. Once you make a decision, you begin to act and spend money on it. So do others within your organization. Soon a whole chain of events has occurred, accomplishing or approaching the goal you decided on.

Changing your mind has major consequences. Changing directions or reversing processes already begun will certainly cost you money. Some of the things that were bought or some of the work already done is now wasted. This can cost you credibility with associates and employees. They dislike a boss who frequently changes his mind and requires them to do work that ends up wasted.

If you're in the contracting or construction business, you can use this to your advantage. Many a contract has been bid and taken from original drawings at a break-even price, with the bidder knowing very well that higher-than-normal margins can be charged on all changes the customer wants. Major contracts are almost never completed without multiple changes. The entire profit in such jobs may be in the change orders.

I'm not saying don't ever change your mind. Like everyone, you'll make mistakes. Correcting a major mistake may be the smartest and least expensive thing you can do now. (See MISTAKES—ADMITTING THEM.)

Consider your decisions carefully. Then realize that if you have to change your mind it's going to cost you money, but perhaps less than if you continue on a path that isn't productive.

C

134

Changes—How to Make Them

CHANGE YOUR KNOWLEDGE and your management style as your company size and operations change, or you'll hit an invisible wall. Human nature doesn't change. You cannot change stupidity, but you can change ignorance.

If something doesn't work, change it. Stupidity is doing the same thing this year that you did last year and expecting a different result. If nothing has changed, you'll get the same result regardless of wishful thinking. If you have an employee whose work is unsatisfactory, ask this: "What will you do next year to make your work different from and better than last year?"

Resistance to change is proportional to the size of the change. The larger the business, the harder it is to change. This is one reason large companies don't react as fast as small ones. Changing one person is easy, as is changing the procedure one person follows, but changing procedures used by a large group of people is difficult, slow, and confusing.

Make small changes rather than drastic ones. By the inch is a cinch; by the yard is hard. Those changes can be digested and handled, even if unexpected problems arise; corrective action can be taken before problems become serious.

Employees understand changes that appear to be part of a larger plan with a logical goal. Frequent changes that appear to be the result of irrational whims or pique, or that have no visible cause-and-effect relationship, create anxiety, frustration, and loss of confidence in management. Resistance to change decreases when you include employees in recognizing and understanding the problem and planning the change. Teamwork makes a difference.

Keep in mind that the first effect of almost any change is a loss of productivity because of confusion and the newness of the activity. Resistance to change, a natural human attitude, is only part of the reason.

> **Unless your business is doing something new and different this year, it won't be here five years from now.**

Resistance to change gets greater as the company gets older and more accustomed to doing things the same way. When the first question is "How did we do it last year?" your company has the big business mentality, and you should consider retirement.

I used to wonder why things in my company seemed to go more smoothly when I was gone than when I was present. Then I discovered it was because I was the one who changed things. When I was gone, no one made changes, and everything went smoothly.

Constant change is a way of life for a small business.

C

135

Changing Your Customers' Buying Habits

WE'RE CREATURES OF HABIT, resistant to change, accustomed to doing things the same old way, following the path of least resistance. Changing prospective customers' habits of buying from your competitor to buying from you is the only change you should try or can afford if you're a small company with limited marketing resources.

> **Try to make it easier for your customer to buy from you.**

Unless your product or service has an unquestionable technological advantage—unless it offers an obvious, favorable, sudden improvement—don't try to change your customers' other habits. Trying to reeducate an entire market about a new distribution method, a new and different product, a new place or type of store for buying, or any major change in old habits is too much for a limited marketing budget. Most major changes in customers' buying habits come slowly and at great expense, no matter how logical or rational the change may appear to you.

Know your market well enough to generalize about the group habits and group thinking of customers you already have. You need this logical basis to find your ideal customers and to understand how and why they buy your products. Focus your marketing program on how to get more of these customers to buy more of your products.

Commission Compensation for Salespeople

ENCOURAGING THE EMPLOYEES WHO CAN find customers and make sales benefits the entire company. Red Motley was right in saying that nothing happens until somebody sells something. Good salespeople work harder and smarter when they have a financial incentive they consider rewarding and fair.

Salespeople often work alone. More than managers, they must be rewarded for their measurable individual performance results, but they must also share and feel rewarded for joint efforts with other sales or service personnel.

Bonus or incentive plans for managers and other employees are usually based on teamwork, with everyone sharing proportionately in the earnings produced by all. When you consider sales incentives for your operation, decide whether selling is a teamwork effort, an individual effort, or a mixture of the two.

No two sales incentive programs are exactly alike, because no two companies are alike. After consulting with salespeople, you and your management team must decide what size incentives effectively reward those sales or service people who most often produce the results the company wants to achieve.

For an effective sales program with commission incentives, you must address the following subjects.

Kinds of Sales to Encourage

Generally, salespeople are unconcerned with the operations or profitability of the production process, although all other management and production people spend most of their time working on these problems. The incentive for sales departments should be to sell whatever carries the greatest gross margin, if your information system (IS) can quickly and accurately produce a commission check computed on that basis. Few small companies can do this, but it's an objective worth working on. You are really trying to produce the maximum amount of gross margin, not the maximum amount of sales.

Historically developed percentages of gross profit by product line may be accepted as accurate and used for computation purposes. If you can't differentiate your products or operations or products by profitability, or if all things are equally profitable (are you sure?), then just encourage sales of everything you profitably produce or deliver.

Giving the Most Incentive for the Most Profitable Sales

If an identifiable salesperson acting alone is responsible for a sale, then any commission should go to that person. If, however, multiple salespeople contact and work on the same sale or same customer, the incentive should encourage teamwork. This means splitting the commission or paying it into a pool to be split among those who contributed. Generally, although service people serve the customer, their portion of the commission is usually less than that of salespeople. The split or division must reward most those who contribute the most, i.e., the split doesn't have to be equal.

For the best interests of the company, avoid setting up a system that encourages employees to work against other employees rather than with them.

Base Pay or Draw against Commissions

Sales compensation based 100 percent on commissions is applicable only to limited operations. Some combination of base pay or draw against commission, with an added incentive (to put frosting on the cake), is usually best.

Base pay should be adequate to cover hamburgers, shoes, a family home, and a "comfort level" to keep the family from worrying. Frills and luxuries should become affordable from the incentive part of the compensation. The harder and smarter salespeople work, the more frills and luxuries they should be able to afford.

Base pay should also include fringe benefits. Take all deductions from base pay; add merit or length-of-service raises. Deal fairly with salespeople's expenses— automobile, travel, entertainment, and other expense accounts.

Dealing with House Accounts and Problems

The most controversial question in any sales incentive program is the reservation of house accounts on which lesser or no commission is paid. Excluding from the

C

137

plan accounts on which no sales commissions are paid is a demotivator to every salesperson, because no customer can be continuously and permanently retained without sales effort.

A basic rule of business economics is that a salesperson or sales department can't change or lower product price or terms of sale unless by so doing she reduces her commission more than she lowers the company's profits. The incentive must be to sell products at the price that makes the company the most money, either the highest price or the price established by management. It doesn't take a salesperson to give products away.

The trigger event that means commissions are due or payable may be either issuing the invoice, signing the contract, completing the job, or collecting money for the job. The plan must include provisions for later deductions against future commissions for returned merchandise, credit memos, and changed or cancelled contracts.

Many salespeople take the view that a commission plan is a lifetime contract between themselves and the company, that their territory and their commission will never be reduced or changed. However, continuous changes in the marketplace require continuous changes in management's plan.

Review the formula or plan after six months, and annually thereafter, to adjust to changing market conditions, additional personnel, new products, new

advertising, competition, and the company's ever-developing operations.

Administering a Commission Incentive Plan

Make the final plan simple and easily understood. Put it in writing and discuss it. A simple plan with a few inequities is a better motivator than a complicated plan people don't understand or believe in. The company's commitment is to incentives and to fairness, not to specific terms or decisions made in the first or subsequent plans.

Furnish written commission statements to each salesperson with each check, showing how the commission is computed. Someone in accounting or sales must be prepared to answer questions and correct mistakes.

The basic principle is that if the company makes more money, the individuals most responsible should also make more money. No two salespeople will earn exactly the same total compensation. The best should earn more than the worst. Making and adjusting these assignments is the sales manager's job. With every change, someone will get more and someone else will get less. Management must have a good reason and use good judgment to make these changes.

What your company really wants from salespeople is the highest possible gross margin, in total and per job. This should be the same as the highest sales volume, but it seldom is.

C

138

Committees

BIG COMPANIES HAVE TOO MANY committees. Growth companies usually have several that are temporary.

In the survival stage, the entire company is one happy committee. Keep everyone informed and coordinated, aware of and working on current problems and trends. Because of small size and intimate working conditions, this will happen naturally.

Ad hoc or temporary committees should have a definite objective and go out of business as soon as that objective is accomplished. Standing or permanent committees usually have a regular meeting whether or not anything needs doing. When you're large enough, your board of directors will have two standing committees—audit and compensation.

A past president of General Motors has declared that the best kind of committee is a committee of one. Many times, a committee is a managerial excuse for putting off decisions. If not overdone, committees can serve valuable purposes gathering facts and getting a consensus. The purpose is to accomplish something, make decisions or set policies, not just to meet.

A committee is a group formed to report on progress in lieu thereof.

In your growth company, begin team building, but remember the difference between a management team and a committee, which is mainly commitment and action. Committees discuss and disseminate information. Management teams decide and act, either individually or collectively.

Committees and management teams should include people based on their expertise or authority or on the committee's goals, not on the basis of titles or seniority.

C

139

Communication

IN THE SURVIVAL STAGE, communication is verbal and frequent. So little is written and so few people are involved that infrequent misunderstandings are easily corrected. As your company gets larger, the problems of misunderstanding or just not getting the word become more serious. By the time you have 10 employees or work from more than one location, many important matters must be written. Use e-mail if your network allows.

If you have trouble writing clearly and concisely, find someone in the company or a secretary who can. Write your memo or letter, then let the other person read it for comprehension and clarity before you send it.

> *How well you communicate is measured by how well your message is understood.*

To test its effectiveness, ask a recipient to explain what your written communication means to her. You can test your own understanding of a communication from someone else by saying, "What I understand you to mean is. . . ."

If necessary, hire a writing consultant to bring you up to speed. Written communication should go from the general to the specific, from the simple to the complex, and from the known to the unknown.

Remember, communication is a two-way street. You want to talk and write to your associates, and you want them to talk and write to you. Sometimes, as members of your official family, they will want to be able to get things off their chests, either orally or in writing. When they do, listen carefully but don't shoot. (See LISTENING; DON'T SHOOT THE MESSENGER.)

Competing with Customers

AN ECONOMIC FACT OF LIFE in almost all industries is that you cannot sell to your customers and then also sell to their customers. If you do that, you're a competitor, and they'll no longer be your customers.

When you write your business plan, decide what level of what market you're in. Don't go up or down the distribution chain for more customers until you get very big and know your industry well.

Put yourself in your customer's shoes. Would you buy from a supplier who competes by also selling to your customers?

For example, your retail clothing store serves its customers by buying manufactured clothing lines and selling them retail. If one of your manufacturers opens a factory outlet in your neighborhood, selling the same merchandise to your potential customers, you'd be foolish to continue representing that product line.

Competitors—Knowledge Of

A GOOD GENERAL WOULDN'T CONSIDER going into battle without knowing all he could about the opposing forces and their commander. You, too, must do your homework on your competitors.

Shop in your competitors' stores or buy their products. Test performance and quality. Take products apart; analyze their design. Estimate their origin, cost, and cost savings. Analyze their catalogue and pricing policy.

Look at your competitors' public operations, displays, or showrooms. Talk to their salespeople; you'll be surprised at the information you'll pick up. When you attend trade shows and conferences, collect competitors' sales brochures, descriptive materials, price lists, and catalogues. You'll find their latest products and innovations, price changes, and the direction of their development and marketing. They will, of course, be analyzing your products and operations in the same way.

Count the number and types of cars in your competitors' parking lots—both employees' and customers'. This is one way to estimate a competitor's size and activity level.

Talk to your customers; let them tell you what they like about your competitors' policies and products. If you lose a sale or a client to a competitor, ask why.

Specifically, ask lost customers about your sales approach, your product, your service, your quality. Find out what your customers like and do not like about your personnel or operations and those of your competitors.

Other questions are these: What do successful competitors do that you don't? What do they omit that you think is important? Do they have an appeal to customers that you do not have?

If one of your competitors' former employees applies for a job at your place, you may find out even more. How does your competitor handle the same problems you have?

C

141

> ## *People buy things from people they like and respect.*

Get to know your competitors personally and form your own opinions. Learn how to play your strengths against their weaknesses. Then you'll know better how to persuade customers to buy from you rather than them.

Competitors—Policy Toward

AS MUCH AS POSSIBLE, MAINTAIN friendly relations with your competitors. You'll probably find yourself in some business association with them and see them at conventions and trade shows. You share common problems in your industry, politics, economics, and local business attitudes. You should be able to discuss these things in a friendly atmosphere.

Your best policy with them, openly expressed and agreed upon, is not to lie to each other. Either tell them the truth or tell them it's none of their business. You have your trade secrets that you won't share, and they have their trade secrets that you aren't supposed to know about. However, you'll no doubt have some favorite customers who will tell you everything your competitor is doing and let you look at his literature or products.

Greet your competitor warmly when you meet in the customer's waiting room. Expect your competitor to do his honest best to sell the customer, and do the same yourself. After hours, buy him a drink and talk shop in a neutral way.

Antitrust laws are strong and can result in your being fined triple damages. The most common antitrust charge is conspiracy to fix prices or decrease competition. If you are in a trade association meeting where the talk turns even close to such things, quickly and politely leave the room. Do not at any time or in any way discuss pricing or terms or engage in any conversations or plans that might tend to decrease competition.

Complaints from Customers

CUSTOMER FEEDBACK OR COMPLAINTS are the best information you can get about why you don't have more customers. For everyone who complains, three to ten others think the same thing about your products or services but don't take the time to let you know. Their opinions will influence their future buying habits and shift them away from you. They'll just quietly disappear.

Anything can happen once, but as soon as you see a pattern of complaints or comments emerging, move quickly to correct the situation. This valuable customer information must sooner or later find its way to you if you're always seeking ways to get more customers. Review complaint reports personally, or make sure that information on complaints isn't kept from you.

Depending on the nature of your business and the seriousness of a customer's complaints or a product failure, you shouldn't be the first person to greet an angry customer. If the boss is there, the customer expects a decision on the spot from the one with ultimate authority to make it—and at this point, you don't yet know all the facts.

The first person to face the complainant should be a fact finder who can

---

Customer complaints are the schoolbooks from which we learn.

---

listen without getting angry and who completely drains the customer of all information about the complaint. Someone should then search company records to determine what was ordered, the size or model, when it was shipped, and all internal facts.

This necessary information should get to you as soon as possible after the complaint report. Then, as quickly as you can, go out to greet the customer and resolve the matter. The customer will feel flattered to have the attention of the owner or a senior manager taking care of her problem.

The greater the time lapse between receipt of the complaint and its resolution, the greater the damage to your company's reputation.

143

Complaints from Employees

AN OPEN-DOOR POLICY THAT INVITES all employees to speak to the boss is essential for the free flow of ideas from bottom to top. Through that door will come petty and serious complaints, excellent and silly suggestions. Whatever you do, don't shut off the flow of truthful information from any level by either shooting the messenger or discouraging sincere suggestions. (See LISTENING.)

Make it easier for employees to talk to you by going to them. Walk through the store or shop several times a day or each week. A good admiral roams the ship.

Be aware, however, that some employees will use the same open door to jump the chain of command and undermine the authority and effectiveness of your middle managers. When an employee complains to you about a matter his supervisor should have taken care of, your first question must be "What did your supervisor say when you told her about this problem?" And if the employee hasn't yet given the supervisor a chance to correct it, ask the employee to do so. Invite him back to see you if that doesn't solve his problem.

If the employee says he talked to the supervisor but didn't receive a satisfactory answer, refuse to take any action until you have a chance to talk to the supervisor and review the facts. In all but the most unusual cases, you must back the supervisor. If you don't, you've damaged the confidence that all managers must have that you'll back up the authority you've given them. If it gets to this, you and the supervisor involved should inform the employee of your decision in a joint meeting where the manager feels supported rather than accused.

Most employee complaints are related to the way someone else within the company is treated. The complaining employee doesn't think he has been treated equitably—doesn't receive the same pay, doesn't enjoy the same privileges or benefits, or doesn't have the same working conditions. Perhaps rules have been bent to allow someone else a privilege, but not for the employee. The employee might be right. At any rate, he thinks he is.

Hear the employee out. Ask enough questions to be certain you're hearing the whole story and getting to the root of the problem. Did the employee's actions contribute to the problem? Present the problem from the company's viewpoint, or discuss the reasoning behind the rule or decision. Then ask the employee this: "If you were running this company, what would you do? What do you think would be fair?"

The final result should leave the employee feeling as though his concerns have been seriously considered and fairly handled. And if a manager is involved, that manager should feel that the owner has confidence in her ability to handle such things.

Computers—Those Most Marvelous Management Tools

AS WITH THE OPPOSITE SEX, you can't live without computers, and sometimes you can't live with them. You have to show tender loving care to keep them happy and working. They're a wonderful management tool. I'd hate to consider doing business without them.

A computer won't solve a poorly defined problem. It won't save money by eliminating workers. It won't clean up mistakes or solve your scheduling problems. It won't always be right.

The computer is only a tool, but it's one of the most important tools you've got. You don't have to push the keys yourself or even be an expert. But you should understand its capabilities, limitations, and frustrations, or your competitor, who is an expert (or has one), will put you out of business.

A company I'm familiar with used to take three days from receipt of an inquiry to the production of a firm quotation. The enlightened owner, over a five-year period, made all his data and procedures accessible on a computer network, trained his employees, and slashed the response time. The company can now give a firm quotation and firm delivery date within 30 minutes of receipt of the inquiry. His customers have noticed.

Your own temperament and desire to know will determine how intimately you get involved with your information system (IS). Learn to work with your system, not against it. A computer makes a marvelous slave; don't let it become the master.

Information is power. Knowing what's happening in your company in time to take action is crucial. Knowing which products you make money on and which ones you don't is essential. You need rapid, accurate data to make timely managerial decisions. Nowadays, that information almost always comes from a computer.

If you don't understand computers and haven't used them before, it may be advantageous to start your IS with easy things like payroll and accounting. The computer will do things you already know how to do, but faster and more easily. Since you know the process and the result you expect, you can readily tell if the computer is programmed to do it right.

If you're already computer savvy, be hard-nosed about making computers cost effective. If a proposed system won't do something better than you do now by hand, or if it won't give you more information faster, don't buy it. Give your smart computer jobs that are impossible to solve or information that is impossible to collect rapidly by hand, such as production costs; tracking customers, inventory, and orders; or getting useful, complex information that is unavailable in a timely manner from your present system.

Do not be afraid of computers. Be afraid of the lack of them.

Electronic files can be displayed in multiple places and summarized faster and more easily. In effect, you end up with one big electronic database that can be accessed by authorized persons more quickly and readily than it ever was by hand. A caution: the more data you put into your IS, the more important security and backups become.

If you have a growing company, your IS will never be finished. You'll always be tinkering with it and asking it additional questions.

Something you expect to do only once or fewer than 10 times doesn't justify setting up a computer spreadsheet. But repetitive tasks justify the setup time. The computer does precisely what it's told, which sometimes makes it frustrating.

Ensure the integrity of the input data, or the output will be unusable. Putting a poorly thought out, confusing procedure or handwritten system into the computer won't make it better and will probably make it worse.

To err is human, but to really screw things up takes a computer.

Con Men

A CON MAN IS THE MOST TALENTED PERSON in his chosen sales field—more talented even than a promoter. But he's totally lost his moral compass and his conscience.

He can sell something he may have mentally manufactured out of the clear blue sky but which he can make appear real to his victim. On a scale where the top salesman ranks a 10, the con man is a 13. (See LEVELS OF SALESMANSHIP.)

The con man thrives in areas where you expect to meet new people and must form opinions quickly without the opportunity to check with friends or your usual sources. He usually targets one person or couple, not a group. As your business grows and you make decisions involving more and more money, you become his ideal target. You have some degree of affluence, and you're a decision maker, acting on your own impressions and opinions without too much reliance on others. He tries to obtain your trust, and then, because you trust him, you lower your business guard. By the time you discover your mistake, it's too late.

Be suspicious. If what the con man offers is too good to be true, it probably is. Try to verify what he tells you. Check out names, dates, companies, and anything questionable. Personally call the phone numbers he gives you. In one case I know of, the man's big-company phone number was an answering service.

Pay for a professional credit check and criminal history investigation before you enter a major financial deal with a stranger who has no visible resources or reputation except a smile, a charming manner, a high-priced car, and a lavish lifestyle.

The absence of a verifiable record should be more disturbing than finding a bad record. It probably means he's hiding something. He could be using an alias, fleeing from previous failures, or hiding a prison term. But he's a likeable character; if you don't like him, he can't succeed in his chosen profession.

I've had dealings with four con men. One of them was the smartest guy I may have ever known. After a tip-off, we found his prison record. He damaged the lives and pocketbooks of several people, including me, before he disappeared again. My wife, with a woman's knack for reading character, became suspicious before I did.

Confidentiality Agreements

TWO TYPES OF CONFIDENTIALITY agreements cover two different situations, both involving transfer of information.

Inside the company, certain employees, especially those involved with high technology, research, or the discovery or use of significant secret business knowledge, need to recognize that secrecy and not disclose it to unauthorized parties.

Outside your company, intelligent business conversations concerning selling, licensing, merger, or acquisition are often impossible without disclosing trade secrets or patent applications. Before engaging in such discussions or negotiations, the disclosing party should seek to protect herself against use of the secret information if the transaction isn't consummated. (See TRADE SECRETS; PARENTS; NON-COMPETE AGREEMENTS.)

Before one businessperson discloses important confidential information to another, she frequently wants the person or firm receiving this information not to use it unless and until certain financial terms are met, and, further, to agree to keep the information confidential. This can present real problems for each side.

When you hire any employee who may use or be involved in the research or development of material considered trade secret, require the employee to sign a confidentiality agreement as a prerequisite of employment. Discuss with your attorney how to get a binding agreement with employees already on your payroll.

The biggest problem is defining what information is to be kept confidential. It's a matter of defining exactly what is new and different that's being disclosed and is therefore to be kept confidential, as distinguished from what the other party or many other parties already know.

If you have a patent, patent laws protect your disclosure for 20 years from the filing date. If you have only a patent application, which may or may not result in a patent, the problem of defining and agreeing on the information disclosed is difficult. If sale of a company or product line is being considered, confidentiality agreements are commonly used.

When signing a confidentiality agreement with someone outside your company, make sure the agreement

147

- specifies an expiration date, typically one year;

- excludes information that is in the public domain, already known by the general public;

- excludes present industry practices, processes, and knowledge; and

- excludes any agreement as to liquidated damages in the event of disclosure or violation.

Ask your attorney to give you a form concerning the confidentiality of trade secrets for use with employees.

Confrontation

CONFRONTATION CAN BE USEFUL or detrimental. When you have employees who have problems or don't perform as expected, face the truth squarely and confront them in a constructive way. Next to firing such employees, which is usually the last step, this is often the most difficult part of your job.

If you can't confront a poorly performing employee when good business considerations require it, you won't have a smooth-running organization. Your authority comes from being the owner. You don't need to adopt blustery, confrontational tactics to get your points across.

Ninety-nine percent of people shrink from confrontation, argument, visible conflict, or strong differences of opinion with other people. The remaining one percent have an advantage because they're not afraid to make their ideas and feelings known to others. However, if they become overbearing, they can dominate a meeting or an interview and disrupt the orderly flow of decision making.

People who have learned to get what they want with raised voices and intimidating conduct are sometimes referred to as madaholics. Sometimes they don't realize that others are offended or afraid to speak out after an outburst, which the madaholic quickly forgets.

A diplomat is one who can disagree without being disagreeable.

Confrontation tactics aren't a substitute for merit or logic, but some people use them to get their way when these other methods fail. This demolishes teamwork.

When you must confront someone, do it constructively.

Consultants

YOU'RE NOT EXPECTED TO KNOW everything, even though your ego tells you that you should. Don't be embarrassed to admit what you don't know. We all hire consultants in areas we're unsure of.

Don't pay others to do what you can do for yourself, unless you don't have the time or the skill to do it. There are two situations in which you should hire outside professionals:

1. When they have knowledge that you need and don't have either within yourself, your group, or in house. You're better off with 20 percent of the time of a knowledgeable, experienced brain than you are with 100 percent of the time of a mediocre brain.

2. When you're trying to complete a project by a deadline that in-house personnel don't have time to meet. One or more outsiders with the required skill and a single mission can push the project through on time while in-house people continue with their normal jobs.

Selecting a Consultant

Look for a consultant knowledgeable about small businesses in general and your type of business in particular. You want someone with practical experience as well as specialized knowledge.

When you're compiling a list of candidates, first solicit recommendations from business friends. A CEO roundtable is a good place to get others to tell you their experiences. Word-of-mouth success stories are the best kind, whether you're buying or selling.

Hiring personal friends brings added relationship problems, but if you hire a friend, handle the relationship professionally. Decide whether you want free advice from a friend or professional advice you expect to pay for. And be sure to discuss hourly rates or estimated total cost before you start problem solving.

Look for quality, not bargain rates. An experienced advisor can save you money in the long run. The hourly rate isn't as important as the benefit received.

A proven consulting procedure is for the consultant to hold in-depth interviews with senior and middle managers associated with the problem, asking what they think the problem and solution are. After getting a consensus from this group, the consultant writes a report and presents it with the bill.

If you and your employees have good communication, or if your ego isn't offended by asking opinions and help from subordinates, you can do the same thing for yourself. This communication teamwork should go on freely all the time as a normal part of business.

Ask for a résumé or professional literature from a prospective candidate, and the names of three business owners to contact. If the candidate says the business is so private he can't give you references, don't hire him.

When you check references, ask these questions:

- Did the consultant stay within budget?

- Was the consultant finished when he said he would be?

- Did loose ends need tying up, resulting in extra cost?

- How good were the consultant's actions and relationships with staff and owners?

C

149

■ Did you get a satisfactory, lasting result?

Be sure you agree on which people or departments will be responsible for carrying out the plan. Ascertain whether the person you're talking to is actually going to do the work.

A word of caution: quacks and phonies can call themselves consultants, too; they're usually the ones who push themselves on you too hard. Beware of people with large egos. Large egos influence presentations and relationships, and they may overshadow the consultant's talent. A consultant who keeps telling you how great he is usually isn't. If you have a large ego too, it's worse.

Consulting Fees

Don't be afraid to discuss fees. First visits are almost always free. If you don't like the consultant's fee, discuss it again with her or with another consultant. Your confidence in the quality of the work to be performed is more important than the hourly rate.

At least one-third to one-half of the consultant's time (and therefore her fee) is spent educating her on what the problem is and the solutions you've already tried and found ineffective. The consultant must diagnose the problem before she can prescribe possible solutions.

You'll save yourself time and money if you prepare a written presentation defining the problem as precisely as possible, with supporting data to speed the consultant's education.

Before you sign a contract, get a written proposal outlining the scope of the work, the rates, the agreed-upon problem, the nature of a favorable outcome, and whether or not a final report will be included. Build in progress review points. Make progress payments as agreed for intermediate accomplishments.

Working with a Consultant

Plan to spend some of your time and some staff time to acquaint the consultant with the problem. Expect him to ask a lot of questions. When you discuss the consultant's perceptions of your problem and ways it might be solved, get a timetable for progress reports and completion. Check with him often to see whether any unexpected problems have turned up. When appropriate, send a memo after each meeting reviewing the topics discussed and specifying which of them you will handle and what you expect the consultant to do.

A consultant can't work magic without your participation.

Insist that the consultant's solution be tied to some person or group in the organization for execution—probably the person he works with most closely, the person closest to the problem. The new plan must be introduced, understood, and pushed long enough to replace the old system. Resistance to change is human nature. Without backing from the top, change won't happen. The best plans or programs in a well-written report that ends up at the bottom of the boss's private file drawer accomplish nothing.

Part of the consultant's task is to work himself out of a job. Once he is sure of progress and ultimate completion, release him or offer another assignment.

I know an excellent consultant who never makes a recommendation—he only asks questions. But he asks such penetrating questions that by the time management has answered them, the real problems have been identified and several possible solutions are apparent and ready to be evaluated. Once you find the key question and answer it, the rest becomes obvious.

Consulting is like giving a hungry man a fish—you solve one problem with one fish. Mentoring is like teaching the hungry man how to fish—it takes more time but yields more benefits.

Controlling Interest and Minority Interests

151

EXPLAINING TO AN ENTREPRENEUR the advantages of owning the controlling interest in his company is like telling Noah about the flood. One of the main reasons most entrepreneurs go into business for themselves is to be masters of their own destiny.

Control means different things to different people. You should keep control of your enterprise, but you may have to compromise to grow. For growth, especially rapid growth, you will need more money. People who put up money want part of the ownership. Your dilemma is either to find many small investors, none of whom can effectively exercise control, or to slow down growth and live within available capital.

I'm sure you're thinking that giving up control means losing enthusiasm and dedication—it would become a different ballgame. But what investors really want is assurance that their money will be safe and will make a large profit. They don't want to run your company on a day-to-day basis, but the assurance they require gives them the right to take control if they see their money going down the drain. They'll give you huge incentives to make money for yourself and for them, but their fallback position to protect their money is to take control.

Before you solicit funds from people who aren't your employees, see your lawyer. Every state has "blue sky" laws (to prevent promoters from selling worthless pieces of blue sky to earthly people for their life savings), and you must be certain that you comply. The penalties are usually more severe than just giving the money back.

Take control of
your life,
or someone else
will do it
for you.

C

152

Your best outside investors are often other successful entrepreneurs. They probably understand your problems, capabilities, and plans better than passive investors who have never managed their own company.

From your viewpoint, maybe it's not quite as important to own 51 percent as to be sure that no other single person or group owns 51 percent. If you know and trust the individuals with whom you're in business, a number of them collectively may own more stock than you do. You can live with this, particularly if you have the right to buy them out when you or the company is capable of doing so. If more than 50 percent of these people agree that what you're doing is wrong, they're probably right.

A minority interest in outside hands is really more of an irritant than a practical,

powerful force. It's also of little use to its owner, because it will probably never pay dividends and it's unsalable except to the corporation or another shareholder. These practical realities make it difficult to find minority investors who aren't your family or good friends.

State laws put legal restrictions on the controlling interest. For example, it may take a vote of at least 80 percent of the stock to dissolve the corporation, or 66⅔ percent to change the voting rights of existing shares, but only 51 percent to elect directors and to make normal operating decisions.

Other provisions of your charter and state laws concern cumulative voting for directors and shareholders' preemptive rights. Cumulative voting means that if five directors are being elected, each share gets five votes, all of which may be either cast for one director or spread among several. This device allows minority shareholders to elect at least one representative to the board.

Preemptive rights are the rights of a corporation's shareholders to maintain their percentage ownership of all outstanding stock. If new shares are issued, present shareholders have the preemptive right, on the same terms as the new stock, to purchase or acquire enough new shares to maintain their original percentage of total outstanding shares.

Check your charter, bylaws, and state statutes to see what governs your corporation. (See CORPORATIONS—HOW CONTROL IS EXERCISED.)

Corporation, Partnership, or Proprietorship—Forms for Doing Business

GOOD OPERATIONS WILL PROSPER and poor performance will go broke, regardless of the legal form of your business. No magic or additional profit occurs whether your business operates as a proprietorship, partnership, or any type of corporation. You can make just as much money, or lose just as much, within any structure, except for a few administrative costs. Your customers, the real source of your wealth, probably won't know or care what form you use; your creditors and the IRS care a great deal. The operating relationships with your associates, legal partners, and shareholders are quite different in each structure, especially as regards control.

When you start with no formalities, in your back room or garage, you're an individual proprietorship. If you grow or have important associates, consider taking in one or more partners to form a partnership. Although this should be a written partnership agreement, it frequently isn't.

Further growth, or the inclusion of more partial owners, almost requires some kind of corporation, which is an independent legal entity separate from its owners and employees. All old, large companies are corporations. You may start this way if you wish, but additional legalities, red tape, and expense are involved in creating and maintaining this intangible, legal entity.

Sole Proprietorship

When you start in business, you're a sole proprietor. You own the company and everything in it. Choose your name and location, get a phone number, and you're in business. Register at the county seat under the assumed-name act or whatever law your state requires. Depending on the nature of your business, you may also need a state or county license or permit.

You don't need any legal papers. If you run your operation honestly and above board and pay your debts, no one will interfere with you. You must still comply with all laws concerning employees, the environment, insurance, and so on. Sole proprietorship attracts the least attention from all governmental authorities. Honest ignorance on your part is a reasonable defense for your first offense in most minor matters.

You and your company are the same. Any money you make, you get to keep (after taxes, of course). If you decide to shut down the operation, all you do is pay off your debts, liquidate your assets, lock the door, and go do whatever you wish.

You are the sole recipient of all profits or the payer of all losses. The disadvantages of sole proprietorship are your unlimited liability for all debts. Depending upon your state laws, all your personal assets are also liable for both your business and nonbusiness debts.

C

153

You will have difficulty raising outside money for a proprietorship because business funds and personal funds are so intermingled. If you die while owning this business, your sole proprietorship terminates and your estate takes over.

Partnership

If you want company in your business, or if you need additional high-quality managerial talent, sales, or technical skills in order to succeed, consider a partnership—if you can find the right person or persons. This is a bigger warning than it sounds like, because the right person is hard to find. A partnership requires a little additional paperwork, and you file a different tax return.

Partnership involves a definite commitment to each other concerning shared responsibilities, shared control, and shared profits or losses.

Don't go into a partnership with only an oral understanding and a handshake. For your future peace of mind and for a good relationship, ask a lawyer to draw up your partnership agreement. She will discuss your questions about control, sharing of profits and liabilities, partners' duties and responsibilities, and what will happen on termination.

There are operational problems as to who is in charge and who has the final say in various matters. Obtaining capital from outside investors is difficult. Disposing of your partnership interest to an outside party is also difficult, if not impossible. It's best to consider these things when you go in, rather than at a later date when bitterness and misunder-

standing could cause more problems.

Business decisions or actions taken by any of your partners can legally bind you because each partner is the agent of all other partners. A contract signed by any partner is binding on all.

All general partners (there must be at least one) have unlimited liability for all business debts or activities of all other general partners. Limited partners put up only money, and their liability is limited to what they've invested. They can't be active in the business in any way or they become general partners. If one general partner can't pay a partnership debt, the creditor can ultimately get the entire indebtedness from one of the other general partners who can pay.

Be especially careful of going into business with close friends or relatives where friendship, blood relations, or personal loyalties can interfere with business judgment. In a partnership, it's advisable to know your partners as well as you know your spouse. Breaking up can be just as messy. In my legal and consulting practice, I've dissolved more partnerships than I've formed.

A partnership is easily formed, and with compatible associates it is a reasonably stable business form. It's also more free of government control and special taxation than a full corporation. The partnership itself pays no taxes but files an information tax return allocating all earnings or losses to the partners in proportion to their percentage interest, whether or not the funds are withdrawn in cash. The death of one partner generally terminates the entire partnership.

C

154

C Corporation

A corporation is defined as an inanimate, intangible entity created by the state and existing only in contemplation of the law. State laws and the corporate charter allow and control the association of persons for some common legal purpose. Each state has its own requirements for the creation of these artificial entities, although there are many similarities. A corporation is recognized as a legal entity that has an existence of its own, independent and apart from its shareholders.

After making decisions about name and operating matters, you will obtain a charter from your state capital. The charter is your right to do business as a corporation within your state, subject to the requirements and limitations of state laws. If you do business in other states, your corporation must comply with their laws as well.

The same person will usually act in multiple capacities in small companies, such as employee, shareholder, officer, and director. The duties, rights, and responsibilities of each person when he acts in each of these several corporate capacities have been carefully defined by law and by judicial decision. The corporation exists independently of shareholders and managers, who may come and go.

The corporation name usually must include "Inc." or "Corporation," which puts creditors on notice that they can look only to the company for payment of business debts. This limited-liability feature and the opportunity to include different people in different stages of the management leads almost every long-existing company ultimately to the corporate form of doing business. If you have more than three equity owners, a corporation is almost your only practical choice.

The death of one of the shareholders, employees, officers, or directors doesn't terminate the corporation. It continues to exist until either the state cancels your charter, or you fail to pay your annual franchise tax, or you're out of business for some other reason. You also avoid personal liability in the event that business debts exceed the business's ability to pay. Under normal circumstances, your liability is limited to what you have invested in the corporation.

Banks and other lenders prefer to deal with a corporation because this separate entity doesn't get mixed up with personal finances and personal liabilities. Disadvantages are additional administrative costs, problems administering the corporation, and some additional tax problems.

C corporations have tax problems that individuals don't have. The corporation files its own tax return. It pays income taxes at corporate rates, after deducting the salaries and expenses of its employees. Since the dividends it pays aren't deductible to the corporation but are taxable income to the recipient, few small corporations pay dividends.

Advantages of a corporation are limited liability, ease of securing capital, and permanent existence. Disadvantages are a tremendous amount of paperwork and government forms. In addition, your losses aren't deductible unless you're an S corporation. Corporations come under immediate government regulations of all

C

155

sorts. Taxes on your earnings can be considered double taxation. (See CORPORATIONS—HOW CONTROL IS EXERCISED.)

S Corporation

Originally called a Subchapter S corporation, an S corporation is taxed like a partnership rather than as a C corporation. The S corporation isn't individually taxed by the IRS, even though it's a distinct, separate entity from the shareholders. All incomes and losses are passed directly to its shareholders for tax purposes. This amount must be included in their individual returns, whether or not the cash is distributed. Generally, shareholders and management make annual distributions of enough cash to each shareholder to pay his taxes on reported income.

This corporation is popular when individual income tax rates are lower than corporate tax rates. It lowers taxes while the corporation is operating, as well as when it is sold.

The present requirements for qualifying as an S corporation under IRS rules are strict. There may be only one class of stock. No shareholder may be a corporation, and there may not be more than 35 shareholders. Because of the complexities of S corporations and the peculiarities of taxation, consult your lawyer and your accountant concerning these features.

If you elect to be taxed as an S corporation, the company must pass a formal resolution at a directors' meeting and send the IRS a copy. The time and procedural limits on changing this election require professional help.

Limited Liability Corporation

Over two-thirds of the states have now enacted some kind of legislation concerning limited liability corporations (LLCs), and the IRS has accepted the concept. An LLC is treated as a corporation under state law. It resembles and is taxed as a partnership by the IRS but offers the benefit of limited liability to all partners, just like corporations, as long as certain tests are met. It eliminates double taxation on dividends. Because an LLC resembles a partnership, in most states its benefits aren't available if a single person owns the entire corporation.

Because of this newness and confusion, many open questions have not yet been decided. For example, if you form a limited liability corporation in a state that allows it and do business in a state that has not yet adopted such laws, will you be treated as a partnership in the other state? The LLC could be more advantageous to you than an S corporation provided you can satisfy yourself or your tax advisor that you aren't exposed to additional taxes or liabilities. Since this is a rapidly developing section of the law, confer with your tax advisor.

An LLC is similar in concept to an S corporation but is more flexible as to ownership and who can be included. For example, owners of an LLC may make their own agreements for sharing deductions, profits, and losses as long as the agreements comply with partnership tax rules. In S corporation distributions, profits and losses must be divided according to ownership interests.

The LLC's advantage over a partnership is the limited personal liability. The LLC form of operation is increasingly used by family businesses, professional service firms, and a wide variety of small businesses. S corporations cannot accept corporations, trusts, or foreign individuals as shareholders, but LLC corporations can. Most states put no limit on the number or types of owners. LLCs are simple to maintain and operate.

The SBA periodically updates a booklet that you might find of interest, *Selecting the Legal Structure for Your Firm,* by Antonio M. Olmi (Washington, D.C.: Small Business Administration). Another good book is *Starting and Operating a Business in [Your State]* (there's a book for each state), by Michael D. Jenkins and The Entrepreneurial Services Group of Ernst & Young (Grants Pass, Ore.: Oasis Press, 1995).

Corporations—How Control Is Exercised

157

THIS BRIEF DISCUSSION WON'T MAKE YOU an expert on corporate law, but it may give you a framework for future learning as you conduct your business life.

State corporate laws differ in some provisions, but all impose some form of franchise tax, payable annually in advance, for the right to operate in the state as a corporation.

Charter

The charter is a document approved by the proper authority of the issuing state. Included within its written provisions are the exact name, duration, and purpose of the corporation. It also gives the address of the corporation's registered office, names of the first board of directors, and the number and type of stock shares the corporation is authorized to issue.

Depending on state requirements, the charter may have clauses concerning amendments, cumulative voting for directors, preemptive rights for shareholders, and other required or optional basic rights of shareholders. As authorized by the charter, shares of stock are issued to stockholders—the real owners of the company.

A copy of your charter is on file in the state capital and is a public record. All other corporate records are private and are kept in the corporate offices.

The stockholders (or shareholders) are required by law to have at least one annual meeting at the time and place specified in the bylaws. Although your charter has only a few pages, your corporation is also governed by a body of state laws usually called the corporate code, which has detailed procedures concerning most things corporations do.

Bylaws

The charter and bylaws are the two most important corporate legal documents. At their first meeting, the stockholders (or, in some states, the directors) adopt bylaws that establish operating rules and other details necessary to conduct corporate affairs. The bylaws contain rules for regular annual stockholders' meetings, special meetings, notices, quorums, election of directors, and so forth. The bylaws also contain rules for the board of directors, such as number of directors, their terms, their compensation, annual meeting, and how to fill vacancies.

The bylaws usually establish an executive committee, a subcommittee of the board with authority to act in certain matters, provided it reports its actions to the next directors' meeting for approval.

Directors

Because stockholders normally meet only once per year, they control the corporation by electing directors to run the company during the time between meetings. Proxies are allowed at stockholders' meetings to ensure that shares are represented, but proxies are not allowed at directors' meetings. Directors must be present and vote in person, or they're absent and do not vote. Every director gets one vote regardless of how many shares of stock she may own or control.

Meetings of directors are held as outlined in the bylaws, with one required annual meeting plus regular and special meetings as defined. Notices of these meetings are specified, as are minutes of all meetings. There may be standing committees within the board— audit committee, compensation committee, and special projects committees.

Since directors' votes actually control corporate actions and policies, directors may have personal liabilities to other stockholders or outside parties. Directors' duties are to maintain a fiduciary relationship with the corporation and to exercise judgment as reasonable and prudent persons to protect the interests of all shareholders equally.

Directors must be careful about possible conflicts of interest concerning corporate matters. This is usually resolved by making complete disclosures of any such interest, and by abstaining from voting on matters in which they may have a personal interest. Directors may not make future commitments to vote in any predetermined way. Fees are normally paid to outside directors, but not to insiders, because the company is already paying for their full-time employment.

Officers

Since the directors cannot be present to run the day-to-day affairs of the corporation, they elect corporate officers and set their compensation for performing these tasks. The bylaws contain a list of the officers to be elected, their duties, and the requirements concerning their appointment and removal. These officers, and the employees they hire, carry on the daily business of the corporation in accordance with policies and instructions established by the directors.

Although these formalities and meetings are necessary to control and run a large company, the same individuals may hold several or all of these positions in small companies. Particularly in small companies, the same person may be a stockholder, a director, an officer, and an employee of the corporation. The capacity in which that person acts at any given time may be significant. Because of intimate daily involvement of all personnel in the operations of small companies, formal meetings aren't always needed to transfer information or reports.

Bylaws and state corporate codes almost always allow any corporate action to be taken by unanimous written consent executed either before or after the event. Since formal corporate actions in small companies are usually unanimous, this allows minutes to be written and other required documents to be prepared and executed as if the meetings had actually been held.

As your company gets larger, and as more people are involved, you will need to document more formally and actually hold some of these meetings.

Creative People—Their Care and Feeding

C

159

CREATIVE PEOPLE ARE FREQUENTLY loners, sometimes inventors, computer programmers, artists, composers, technicians, designers, and engineers. They're able to handle abstract concepts. They imagine things that do not now exist, things that seem unreal to others.

Many creative people don't respond to monetary rewards the way most goal-oriented people do. Often they're not team players but are distinct individualists who march to their own drummer. It's best to ask them what they want. It could be a stand-up desk, pictures on the wall, a flexible work schedule, or background music. If these things are more important than money, try to provide them.

Creativity is a wonderful attribute. The mind that discovers new relation-

ships and new approaches to old problems truly has a gift given to only a few. Creative minds have the ability to comprehend, consider, and resolve abstract problems that most of us may not even be able to identify or understand, much less solve.

You cannot allow such complete freedom for one or more creative employees that it disrupts all other company rules and procedures. If you have that situation, try letting them work at home or physically isolate the office or lab in a remote location. The creativity is needed, but not all other employees understand favored treatment.

Creative people sometimes provide the technological basis for start-up companies and are a significant part of the company's foundation. But it isn't unusual that these talented people lack managerial or personal relations skills. For routine managerial problems, they're worse than bureaucrats. As owners, creative people should include in their managerial team people with sales and administrative skills as well as the ability to organize and get along with people.

You're a creative person if you've formed a business that provides new jobs and new customer satisfaction. This demonstrates a high degree of creativity. You should be proud.

Credit—Four C's Used by Bankers

160

IF YOU WANT TO BORROW MONEY from bankers, you should know how they think. They will evaluate your loan application based on the four C's of credit and banking: character, capacity, capital, and collateral. These criteria are in all the banking handbooks and are freely discussed among bankers. Not all borrowers are aware of them.

Character. Do you have the integrity, the personality, and the historical behavior pattern to pay your bills when they're due? This is often a judgment call on the banker's part, backed up by the best information available from other suppliers or credit sources.

Capacity, or cash flow. Do you or does your firm have the cash flow and the financial and productive capacity as well as managerial and financial strength and ability to pay all debts, including the new one, out of current operations? Or will this debt overload the company beyond its capacity to repay?

Capital. Do you or does your company have adequate capital and resources to conduct its business and pay this debt if it cannot be paid out of current earnings?

Collateral. What collateral are you offering to go with this debt? Can it be foreclosed on and sold or liquidated quickly for the amount of the debt?

If the answer to any of these questions is no, you probably won't get your loan.

Credit—Granting and Managing

MANY A SOLVENT COMPANY has become insolvent because its customers were unable to pay. You may run your business well, but you can go broke if several customers go down the tube while owing you lots of money. You want them to be profitable, so watch their operations and their ability to pay you.

You don't really want to invest money in your customers' businesses, but if they don't pay you promptly, that's exactly what you've done. If you sell something you don't collect for, you've given it away.

Place your credit terms within the commonly accepted range in your industry. Make them competitive with other suppliers in your trade group. If you're in a service industry, you may be able to collect at the time the services are performed or you may have work billed for later payment. If you're a retailer, a high percentage of your sales are normally in cash, with little or none billed on a pay-later basis. Pay-later customers generate accounts receivable. Many retailers are delighted to have credit account customers because they feel these customers are tied to them by the charge accounts they build up.

Adjust your credit department and policies to your industry and your customers. When you grant credit to salaried customers, encourage prompt payment habits but know that payments will sometimes be delayed. If they don't pay you out of the current paycheck, you will have to wait until the next one.

If you're in manufacturing or wholesaling, and selling to other companies for resale, use the way you handle credit and credit terms as part of your marketing strategy. It's a good way to stimulate business and gain a competitive edge. Consider both cash discounts for prompt payments and late-payment penalties or interest charges to help sales and stay solvent.

Send an invoice, packing slip, or delivery ticket with the merchandise, with terms of payment clearly indicated. If each sale involves a substantial amount, don't expect the customer to hand over the cash on the spot, but ask him to sign a contract or agreement. If there's no written contract, the customer should process your invoice and send you a check for the total purchases for the month in due course of business, preferably within the terms you've stated.

Granting and managing credit is a senior management function—at least the policies controlling credit. The person administering them must know when an exception or questionable matter requires the approval of senior management.

State your credit policy plainly. Include the credit application form as well as the extent of data checking to be done

C

161

through independent sources. On a separate page, have your credit manager evaluate the application, indicate approval or disapproval, and set up a credit limit. The terms may be low at first but later raised as favorable experience is accumulated.

He who never climbs never falls.

Sales employees should clearly understand your credit policy and terms. Internal procedures should include a quick, inoffensive way to verify credit and current status of any account before accepting an order or delivery of merchandise. Use a phone or your computer. At every point of sale, system software should be able to flash necessary information for credit approval. Train salespeople to routinely and politely refer unapproved requests to the credit manager for a final decision.

Here are some questions to consider and answer in your credit policies and procedures:

- What are customary invoice and credit terms in your industry?

- What do you need to know before you're willing to grant credit to a new customer?

- Are you going to use a specific Dun & Bradstreet or other credit-report rating?

- What factors indicate that you should limit or not grant credit?

- Who is authorized to grant or approve credit?

- How do you establish the credit limit per customer: analysis of financial condition, historical activity, or universal policy?

- What are your standard procedures for pursuing collection of past-due accounts?

- If you're not going to grant credit, will you still accept business on a COD basis?

- Once you're doing business with a customer, what's your trigger to recheck the credit rating?

- Do you have a procedure to warn you of the sudden ballooning of an account?

Include in your credit procedures a way to monitor customers' accounts regularly to be sure that they stay within approved limits. You also need a policy to collect delinquent accounts, a system that first raises warnings and then cuts off when accounts get overdue. (See PAST-DUE ACCOUNTS—COLLECTING.)

C

162

Credit Rating—Your Company's

YOUR CREDIT RATING, or your company's, is something you'll have to live with as long as you're in business. It would be nice to pay all your bills on a discount-to-prompt basis, but if you do that, you're either growing too slowly or you have a rich partner, which most entrepreneurs never seem to find.

Good credit consists of paying whenever you agree to pay, which may not necessarily be promptly. If you know you can't pay for 60 or 90 days, tell your vendors. If they don't like it, they may not sell to you, but they'll still talk to you and maybe sell to you next time when your situation is better.

During one of its darkest hours, our manufacturing company received an export order that would require two months of our total productive capacity, after a one-month wait for receipt of raw materials. We could not produce such an order nor finance the materials and labor during the time required to finish the job.

After getting from the purchaser an irrevocable letter of credit payable in U.S. dollars against a sight draft with signed ocean bill of lading, I went to our three principal material suppliers and to our bank. At each place, I showed them our order and financing documents and asked them to carry us with sufficient credit and time to complete the order and collect, at which time they would be paid in a lump sum. Each agreed.

As soon as material came in, we went into round-the-clock production. I kept the creditors informed of our progress, and everything stayed on schedule. The check was the largest we had ever received, and we promptly paid everyone. Although we paid none of these people for over 90 days, we had done exactly as promised and finished with a better credit rating than when we started.

Whatever date you've told your creditor you'll pay, do your damnedest to pay. If it's impossible, call your creditor. Explain what happened, and give a date when you realistically think you can send your check.

How do you know when you can expect to have the money to pay your creditor? Keep track of your cash flow, your accounts receivable, and all your other accounts payable (for whom you must also promise a date), and then you'll know enough about your business and its cash flow to make a reasonable cash forecast. (See CASH TRACKING AND FORECASTING; CASH MANAGEMENT.)

Don't lie to your creditors or give promises you know you can't keep. Do not hide. Don't evade. Don't refuse to talk or return phone calls. If possible, don't furnish financial statements. Do not refer them to your banker. Your creditors earn their money the same way you do; they need your money to meet payroll and pay creditors the same way you do.

C

163

Credit is like a rubber band. You can always stretch it some, and when it goes back to normal it's as good as ever. Then you can probably stretch it again when you need to and then maybe a little more. If you have to, stretch it even a little more. Finally, if you continue to stretch too far, it will break. When it breaks, it will never go back to normal. And you won't have any credit or credibility.

Most of your creditors don't know each other, and each one has a rubber band from you. Some will let it stretch further than others before it breaks.

Your credit strength will increase as you build a track record. During your survival stage, you'll have calluses on your knees from begging bankers for money, begging customers to buy, and begging vendors to give you credit. Once you have established all these things, you can get up and walk and maybe run a little. After a while, it gets to be fun.

Customers

"THE REAL PURPOSE OF ANY BUSINESS is to create customers," says Peter Drucker. It can't be said with greater simplicity or eloquence. No matter what your business, success starts with the customer.

When you're starting a business, one of the cardinal rules is to identify the profile and location of your logical or ideal customer. If you don't, you can waste a lot of time and money chasing (and finding!) the wrong customers.

Answer these questions: Why should customers buy from you rather than from the firm down the street? What value do you provide that they don't get elsewhere? What unique things can you do to draw satisfied customers to your business? Your degree of business success will vary greatly depending on how correctly you resolve those questions.

Satisfied customers aren't enough. To get referrals, you must have enthusiastic customers. After five years, over half of your new business should come from referrals by current customers.

Business goes where it's invited and stays where it's appreciated. Create customer consciousness in your organization.

All employees are involved in customer relations, whether they realize it or not. Management's job is to make them aware of it and to get them to act accordingly. If the boss establishes the right attitude toward customers, everyone else will follow. If employees think sales, they'll be sensitive to whatever they might be able to do to enhance sales, from answering the phone graciously to putting something extra into products or services.

You want to find where your new customers are coming from so you can get more just like them. If the nature of your business doesn't automatically provide you with this information, have your employees pleasantly ask every new customer, "How did you find us?" or "Why did you come to our company for this?"

The answers may confirm that your sales efforts are properly directed, or they may open totally new avenues or directions for future sales efforts.

Getting a new customer takes a long time and much effort. That customer can be lost in 15 seconds if an employee treats him discourteously or with a lackadaisical attitude.

Customers—Large

A LARGE CUSTOMER IS CONSIDERED to be one from whom you receive over 10 percent of your revenues. You may have to start with only one or two large customers and be glad to get them as a crutch to get started. Get off that crutch just as soon as you can by developing many other customers.

If you have only a few large customers rather than many smaller ones, you're vulnerable to sudden, substantial drops in business volume and total revenue, because managements change, people die or get fired, and companies get sold, merged, or liquidated.

Bankers and investors will always ask you for a list of customers who provide more than 10 percent of your revenue. They're probing for what they consider vulnerable spots in your operation.

Customers—Repeat

UNLESS THE NATURE OF YOUR BUSINESS requires you to have only one transaction per customer (such as home construction or maybe real estate sales), and unless these customers hardly ever talk to one another, you must build customer friendships that encourage repeat business and long-term relationships. If you can make your money on repeat sales to repeat customers, and not have to find a new customer every time, you'll build a steady sales volume plus a reservoir of good will.

C

165

This reservoir of good will in the minds and opinions of an ever-growing group of customers is the source of future profits, the real basis for value in your company. Almost everything else you have is replaceable or expendable. People may die or the plant burn down, but the company can survive if the good will remains. It's perishable and requires continuous nurturing.

Making the first sale to a new customer is one of the most difficult and expensive things a business does. Because of this high cost, many businesses do not make money from the first sale to a new customer. Unless repeat sales to a satisfied customer follow, your salespeople have wasted a lot of effort.

You know how you like to be treated when you're the customer. Your customers probably like the same things.

CYA File

COVER YOUR ASS: this is the mythical name for any documentary file you keep to prove, if necessary, that you weren't at fault for some big mistake.

Every manager in a big-business company needs CYA files, because promotions go to those who make the fewest mistakes, not always to those who make the most progress.

Avoiding failure isn't the same as achieving success.

This bureaucratic attitude doesn't succeed in an entrepreneurial enterprise. You don't need CYA files for internal purposes, although some of your employees might think they need them because of internal politics. In survival and growth-stage companies, employees don't have the same fear of mistakes. Favorable results from innovation count for more than the avoidance of mistakes.

The owner will find CYA files prudent and necessary for some employee relations, disputed discharges, customer complaints, insurance, or defense against possible lawsuits or Equal Employment Opportunity Commission (EEOC) violation charges.

Danger Signs—Trouble Ahead

A HEALTHY BUSINESS has an aura of efficiency and urgency. Questions get answered. Papers move quickly from place to place and end up where they're supposed to. People do their jobs without confusion or delay. Cash flow and profits increase. Bills are paid on time. Customers and employees remain loyal.

The business headed for trouble appears disorganized to both employees and customers. Frequently, management provides no clear direction, which leaves employees to make up operating rules as they go along. The following are some of the signs that your company is in some degree of trouble:

- Decreasing or no profits

- Decreasing gross margin

- Failure to grow

- Rapid growth without a corresponding growth in profits

- High customer turnover

- Deteriorating customer service without an orderly system to provide it

- Missed deliveries

- Customers holding the phone too long waiting for information

- High employee turnover, especially the good ones

- Slow collection of customers' accounts

- Failure to meet budgets

- Failure to make timely deposits of IRS tax money

- Getting further behind in paying bills

- Overstaffing, with employees standing around talking

- Owner or owner's family withdrawing too much cash

The surest sign of business trouble is that your payables get older and older. You find yourself sifting through invoices deciding which to pay and which to delay. Calls start coming in from creditors seeking payments. Sometimes you answer with evasion, excuses, or promises. Then you don't keep the promises. When bills are running a month overdue, it's time to take notice. When they exceed 60 days, you have a serious situation that requires immediate attention.

Although trouble shows up as financial woes, the real problem is probably the result of other operating or management deficiencies:

- Insufficient sales for the expense level maintained

- Putting out poor or defective products

- Not reacting to a competitor's actions

- Not knowing the market

D

167

- Not giving customers the quality and service they expect

- Poor inventory management or buying practices

- Managerial neglect or incompetence

- Unavailable or inaccurate financial reports that should have warned you of the problems

Recognize that your business has made some mistakes or you wouldn't be in this condition. Identify those mistakes. Admit them to yourself. Unless you do, you'll continue to make them. When you're in a financial crisis, you've already run out of the mistakes you can make. Take full responsibility for the problems and the recovery. Your time is limited.

Now that the financial problems have gotten your attention, you must solve them at the same time you try to solve the basic problems. Using the alligator metaphor, you must fight off the three biting you now while you try to drain the swamp to get rid of all the rest. Identifying the underlying problems—the equivalent of draining the swamp—is critical and not easily done.

Heed early warning signs and make changes. Expect to suffer some pain to achieve any benefit. Deal openly with employees to enlist their support. Pay special attention to key employees. Concentrate on getting the business back on a sound footing.

The first question is this: How much trouble are you in?

Obviously you don't have enough cash to pay your bills. How much cash will it take to pay your bills now? Where can you get it and how long will it take? What problems keep you from having a positive cash flow? What must you do to solve them? How long will it take? Time is always a factor, working either for or against you.

How much cash can you expect from accounts receivable? How many accounts are past due, and by how much? How much can you cut out of inventory? What is your current ratio? What's your gross profit margin? What's your break-even point? What is your gross profit margin compared with the standard in your industry? Are you drawing out too much money? Are there nonproductive people on your payroll? Are your sales going up or down? What are your realistic sales projections for the next three months? If you can't answer these questions and other related ones, you can't make an intelligent plan.

You should have gotten warning signs of trouble some time ago if you had current financial statements and if you analyzed them honestly. If you didn't, examine your most recent financial statements now, or let some knowledgeable person do it. And the statements should be less than 30 days old.

Obtain current profit and loss information from the accounting department. The information they provide must become the basis on which you plot your recovery. (See TURNAROUND OPERATIONS.) Devise your operating plan, and a cash plan to go with it. Then monitor your performance against those plans.

This trouble probably didn't arise overnight. Most likely it won't be solved quickly. Make comparative statements of your last 12 months of operation to determine trends and to show you what was coming and what should have set off warning signals. If you don't have financial statements that answer your questions, get them immediately. Current, accurate financial statements are the first things anyone trying to help will ask for.

How much time do you have? Do you have to act immediately and drastically, or do you have the luxury of acting slowly with more deliberation and certainty? In any event, you will have to cut expenses and cash outflow, even if you can still borrow money and get more investment. If your income is inadequate, then you've got to cut outgoing cash or you'll run out more quickly.

Cutting outgo means cutting employees you like, employees who have been with you a long time, employees with high salaries who don't produce results. Cut to the point where cash outflow and expenses are less than cash income from sales. It's that simple.

What else are you going to cut? That's where your judgment as manager comes in. Cut your own pay. Set the example. If drastic action is called for, take it promptly and decisively. Cutting too deep is better than not cutting deep enough. If you don't cut deep enough, you're dead anyhow. (See KNOWING WHICH EXPENSES TO CUT; FIRING PEOPLE—EFFECT ON THOSE REMAINING; KNOW YOUR COST OF DOING BUSINESS.)

The seeds of bad times are usually sown during good times. The experienced small-business owner is slightly paranoid, always worrying about impending disaster. If you're that attentive, you're less likely to get into trouble.

> *Do what you can, with what you have, where you are!*
>
> —Theodore Roosevelt

One thing that will hover over you from the beginning is the gut feeling that you could go broke. You'll spend your whole life avoiding that. You may have to postpone cherished projects. You'll probably have to perform superhuman feats yourself as well as inspire superhuman efforts from others. Leave no expense account unexamined.

A classic situation that is sure to cause trouble is rapid growth combined with lack of profitability. You may see success in a rapid sales increase, but without profits the growth is funded entirely by debt. In this situation, a market downturn or sudden drop in sales is a recipe for disaster. Survival comes from the ability to reduce expenses and operate at a lower level. Once you pass a certain minimum, you can make profits operating at any level if you do it correctly.

Always act as if your business were one month away from going broke. Don't rest on past successes. Scramble to retain current volume, find new sales, and conserve cash. If you're out of trouble and get back into it, you'll already know how to work with creditors and the bank.

Prepare for the recessions that are an inevitable part of business life, but also be prepared for the growth period that is sure to follow.

A good book for small businesses on this subject is *Save Your Business: How to Avoid Trouble in a New Business or Turn It Around If You Are Already in Trouble,* by Dick Parise (Norfolk, Virginia: Hampton Roads Publishing Co., 1991).

Debt Coverage or Debt Service

D

170

CREDITORS USE THIS RATIO as a measure of the safety of their loan to you. Since you'll repay out of current earnings, the bank seeks to measure your company's earnings in excess of the amount you're obligated to pay on your debt or will become obligated to pay on your new loan. A high ratio (considerably over two-to-one) allows your banker to sleep well at night.

Interest coverage is computed by dividing earnings (before interest and taxes) by annual interest expense. (Since interest is tax deductible, use earnings before interest and taxes.) This measures a firm's ability to meet only the interest payments, and also indicates your capacity to take on additional debt.

For coverage of principal payments, compute net profit after taxes, add depreciation and noncash charges, and divide the result by the current portion of long-term debt. (See FINANCIAL RATIOS.) This measures the number of times your cash

flow can cover current maturities of principal on your long-term debt. Since principal payments aren't deductible, use earnings after taxes as being available. This cash flow is a source of funds for debt retirement. A high ratio means the firm can service existing and possibly future principal repayments.

Anybody can manage a company as long as there's money in the bank. The problems come when you must run it without money in the bank.

The terms *debt coverage* and *debt service* are used loosely by different people. It's important that both parties understand whether they're discussing coverage of principal or interest, or both, and exactly what's included or excluded from the other's calculation.

The time period is always one year—your annual earnings divided by the amount of your debt and interest due to be paid during the same year. If you're a partnership, S corporation, or limited liability corporation (LLC), your operating statement normally shows no taxes at all. In that event, subtract the maximum individual tax rate from earnings before taxes to estimate earnings after taxes. Have your statements prepared showing this amount as taxes, so you won't be tempted to spend it.

If the ratio isn't considerably over two, meaning that your earnings aren't more than twice the amount of principal or interest coming due, you may not get your loan. Your banker will think that a slip in the economic climate could quickly reduce your earnings to only your required payments, leaving nothing for capital investments or increased capital requirements.

D

171

Decision Sheet or Decision Tree

WHEN YOU'RE FACED with a difficult decision, organize your thinking and evaluate all aspects of the problem by making a decision sheet. At the top of the sheet, succinctly state the problem. Then list all possible courses of action or decisions, even if they seem extreme or ridiculous. Usually number one is "Do nothing," which is always an option. The last option might be "Sell out."

If you don't have enough room on one sheet to evaluate all your options, use a separate sheet for each. List advantages and disadvantages; include both tangible reasons and intangible ones that you can't quantitatively evaluate. You can't measure everything, but for each action you may take you must include a factor for the expected reactions of customers, employees, or competitors. Examples of intangibles are "Will it make the sales manager mad?" "Competitors will take it as a sign of weakness." "Sets a bad example for employees."

Make a special effort to separate out the intangibles of pride and managerial egotism. They're expensive luxuries. These intangibles are important parts of every decision, but they're sometimes difficult to recognize and even more difficult to evaluate rationally.

Ask your most concerned manager to evaluate each option, then compare analyses. You may be surprised at how differently someone else defines or evaluates the same problem.

If the resulting action requires more than a single decision or single course of action, make a decision tree—an upside-down tree with the trunk representing your main problem. Each downward fork of the tree is the yes-no decision at that point, which leads to a further yes-no decision at the next branch.

Any fool can criticize,
condemn, and
complain—and
most fools do.

—Dale Carnegie

Identify the resource limits that rule out particular courses of action. However, in your long-term plan, resolve to move back or remove the limits that most hinder your course of action.

How much information do you need to gather about a given problem before you make your decision? It's impossible to gain 100 percent of the information on every question or to foresee 100 percent of the results of every decision and prospective solution.

Divide the information into three categories: "must know," "should know," and "nice to know." "Must know" information is so fundamental you must have it to make an intelligent decision. "Must know" usually amounts to about 50 percent of the information available or required by a particular question.

The middle ground, "should know," contains information that bears secondarily on the problem. Within reasonable parameters, this information is good to know if you can gather it, find it, or talk to someone who knows it. "Should know" is another 35 percent of available, problem-specific information.

The last category, the remaining 15 percent, is "nice to know." However, many things are just unknowable.

Your decision point will occur somewhere between 50 and 85 percent of the available information, probably while you're gathering and examining the "should know" material.

You won't have the time or resources to get 90 percent of the available information on every decision you make, but if you base your decision on less than 50 percent, you're shooting from the hip. If you put off a decision until you have 90 percent of the available information on every problem, you won't survive long as an entrepreneur. (See WHAT IF?)

Default—What to Do When You're in It

DEFAULT IS THE FAILURE of a debtor to fulfill obligations to a lender under an agreement. This event activates substantial new rights for the lender.

Loan agreements are designed to ensure that you're running your business properly as well as remaining solvent and profitable, thereby keeping your company in position to pay off your loan. As long as you're doing these things, your lender is happy.

As safeguards and early warning notices to the bank, the loan agreement usually requires that you maintain the following:

- A certain minimum amount of working capital (current assets minus current liabilities)

- A certain current ratio (current assets divided by current liabilities)

- A minimum amount of net worth (don't lose any money after this point)

- Some restriction on additional borrowing to purchase equipment without permission

- Some restriction on leasing equipment without permission

- Other trip wires that warn the bank that things aren't going quite as well as they should

A properly drawn major loan agreement has so many provisions that it's difficult not to be in default on some provisions sometime during the life of the loan. Usually a company officer is required to certify in writing to the bank each month or each quarter that the company is not in default under any of these provisions (covenants).

Whenever you fall from grace and lapse into default on a loan agreement provision, it's best to notify your lender orally or in person and explain why it happened and how long you think it will take to correct the default. If you expect the violation to last very long, ask for a written waiver of the specific provision, even if only for a specific period. If you have good reasons and are trying to run a tight ship, the lender will usually give you the waiver.

If the default can't be cured reasonably quickly and the banker begins to worry seriously about the loan, the banker may transfer your loan to the "work out" section of the bank, where bad loans are worked out by some means that will get the bank its money. You may have to sell assets, reduce the size of your operation, or do any of several drastic things.

Of course, if you do not and cannot cure the default, the lender's final remedy is to give you written notice that the bank is accelerating the maturity of the loan. The entire indebtedness becomes immediately due and payable in full. This is serious business; you must either find another lender who will loan you enough to pay off the bank, or the bank will exercise one of its many options. These range from taking over your assets and having someone of the bank's choosing operate your company until the bank is paid, to auctioning off the equipment and closing the doors.

Your banker doesn't want your company. He doesn't want to manage your company. All he *really* wants is the bank's money back, plus interest. The banker wants you to succeed and to do well so he can lend you more money in the future and collect more interest from a larger, solvent, operating company. The loan agreement provisions are to protect the bank in the event your dreams become nightmares. The banker will help you, if you convince him that you're not going to lose the bank's money and that you can pay it back.

The cliché among borrowers is that banks will loan money when you don't need it, but won't when you really do need it. Lenders counter that banks are delighted to loan money to someone who they feel will pay it back with interest, but will not loan money when they have any doubt about the ability of the borrower to repay.

When I was a young lawyer, I financed a car purchase with a wise small-town banker. Following my own advice never to sign anything without reading it, I started reading the four printed pages of documentation. He stopped me with this comment: "Tom, there's no point in your reading those papers, for two reasons: (1) if you don't sign them, I can't loan you the money, and (2) all they say is that if you pay back the money plus the interest, as you agree to do, you won't have any trouble. If you don't, you're going to have a lot of trouble." That's the simplest explanation I know.

174

Definitions—Financial Terms

MONEY IS THE WAY to keep the score, so business people talk to each other in financial terms to compare their scores. If you counted only dollars in the bank, the scoring system would be easy. Actually, scoring is very complex, with many interrelated ratios and measurements of one item relative to one or more other items.

The following buzzwords are common in banking and financial circles. If you don't know what they mean, find out so you can speak the language of business with owners and financial people. You can't really run your business without understanding them. Many of these are discussed or defined in section two.

Acid-test ratio

Aging of receivables

Aging of payables

Asset turnovers

Assets per employee

Assets per share

Balance sheet

Book value

Bottom line

Budget

Burden

Burden rate

Capital stock

Cash flow

Compound growth rate

Current assets

Current ratio

Days sales in receivables

Days sales in inventory

Days open payables

Debt coverage or debt service
     requirements

Debt-equity ratio

Direct costs or expenses

Direct labor

Discounted future return

Dividends

Economic order quantity

Earnings

Earnings per share

Earnings on sales (percent)

Equity

Fixed assets

G&A expenses (general and adminis-
     trative expenses)

GAAP (Generally Accepted Accounting
     Principles)

Gross profit or gross margin (percent)

Growth rate

Income stream

Indirect expenses

Indirect labor

Intangible assets

Internal rate of return

Inventory turnovers

Lead time

Liabilities

Liquidity

Long-term liabilities

Margin (percent)

Markup

Market share

Net working capital

Net worth

Operating statement

Overhead

Preferred stock

Present value of money

Price/earnings (P/E) ratio

Prime rate

Retained earnings

Return on equity (percent)

Return on investment (ROI)

Return on total assets (percent)

Sales expenses

Sales per dollar of assets

Sales per employee

Treasury stock

Working capital

Working-capital turnovers

Definitions of these terms can be found in any accounting handbook or textbook. An excellent, complete explanation is con-tained in a small paperback book, *A Review of Essentials of Accounting,* by Robert N. Anthony (Reading, Mass.: Addison-Wesley Publishing Co., 1993). Another good discussion of these terms and their relationships is in the front of the *RMA Annual Statement Studies,* which is described under the heading HOW ARE YOU DOING COMPARED WITH INDUSTRY STANDARDS?

Delegating

D

176

IF YOU CANNOT DELEGATE, you're destined to have a small company and stomach ulcers. One person can do only so much. Twenty-four hours per day is still the limit for all mortals, including the president and the pope.

Every job, large or small, that isn't assigned or delegated to someone else belongs to you by default. Since you can't do them all, choose which jobs to do now and which to put off until later. This is how you establish your priorities.

One of your entrepreneurial privileges is that you get to decide the shape and content of your own job. Choose which responsibilities you wish to keep and which you'll delegate or hire others to do.

Don't delegate jobs that are extremely important; reserve these for yourself. Otherwise, selecting what to delegate depends on the importance of the problem and the skills of both parties. Retain the functions you're best at and enjoy. Let partners or employees do things they're good at.

If you keep too much of the job, you're a poor manager because your subordinates will be waiting and missing an excellent training opportunity while you finish the job. If you delegate too much, you're a poor manager because you're not doing your share and you become unnecessary.

When you delegate, choose someone you think is capable of doing a good job. Be certain that he or she understands the problem and the results you expect. You can't delegate what you can't define and express.

Delegate results, not actions. To build strong middle managers, specify the desired result but don't define too closely the procedure or activity to produce it. Delegate for direct results, for development of the individual, or for evaluation of the individual. Provide times and procedures for reporting back and evaluating interim progress and results.

The key to growing as large as you want to grow is learning to delegate both responsibility and authority to trusted managers who have the knowledge and motivation to perform well.

The span of control is the number of subordinate employees one supervisor can effectively manage and supervise. For a foreman, whose subordinates all do the same thing, the span of control is about 20 people. For a manager, whose subordinates do several different things, it's 5 to 7 senior or major managers, or about 10 minor managers.

Authority comes with responsibility attached. How much judgment are you delegating? Are you delegating the digging of the ditch or the supervision of the ditch diggers? Activity doesn't equal results. What you want is results that flow from activity.

Delegation means giving up some control over the details and day-to-day running of the company, perhaps even part of the ownership, in order to make the company grow. The ability to step aside, forgo total control, and delegate authority separates success from survival and can turn a tiny operation into an empire.

If turning responsibility over to others is a major problem for you, a practical workbook with sound instructions is *Successful Delegation: How to Grow Your People, Build Your Team, Free Up Your Time and Increase Profits and Productivity*, by Frank F. Huppe (Hawthorne, N.J.: Career Press, 1994).

D

177

Disciplinary Problems

SETTING GOOD EXAMPLES and being a good leader aren't enough to ensure that no disciplinary problems will occur. A large part of prevention is to have a clearly established and communicated policy concerning absenteeism, drunkenness, theft, drug abuse, tardiness, and so forth. Include these things in friendly tones in your employee policy manual. Even that doesn't mean everyone will automatically comply.

Disciplinary problems usually involve confrontations in which the employer questions or reprimands the employee for a rule infraction. Most of us shrink from confrontation, but at times it's necessary. If you allow disciplinary infractions to go unpunished, you send this message: "You may violate the rules, because there's no punishment."

Someone in the company, probably you, must have authority and be hard-nosed enough to "kick ass" when required. Whoever does it should do so reluctantly and only when necessary. It must not be done frequently by someone who thinks it's the preferred management method.

For the good of the team and the company, create a climate of positive attitudes and encourage respect for the company. The following suggestions should be of some help.

- Establish reasonable rules or standards. Explain them so that employees also consider them reasonable.

- When feasible, consult employees before adopting any firm rules. Propose them first, at least to selected employees, and ask for their input. This will bring out possible errors or problems before the rule is established as final and unchangeable.

- Put in place an appeal or grievance procedure so an employee who feels that he has been treated unfairly can be heard, by either a higher supervisor or the owner.

- Don't show favoritism. What you expect of one employee, expect of all. If you allow one employee to bend the rules, you'll make ten others angry who don't have the same privilege.

- Many cases involve extenuating circumstances. Every story has two sides. Give an individual the opportunity to discuss her situation to learn whether such circumstances exist.

Your company atmosphere should be such that if employees feel they have a grievance or are dissatisfied with the rules, they can speak to their supervisor or to you to consider interpreting, modifying, or eliminating the problem.

Firing people is governed by detailed laws nowadays. The traditional form of progressive discipline involves an oral warning, then a written warning, then time off without pay, then firing if the offenses continue. Properly documented, this covers the legal niceties, but it doesn't necessarily motivate an employee to do better and to work with the team with good will.

Make the confrontational interview as nonconfrontational as possible. Discuss policies and rules, and be sure the employee understands both. In an extreme case, suggest he take time off with pay and reflect on his conduct rather than harbor bitterness against the company for perceived punishment. Time off with pay is more likely to motivate the employee; time off without pay is punishment.

Tell the employee that upon his return, you expect either his total commitment to acceptable performance in the job or his resignation so that he can look for more satisfactory work elsewhere. Say that the company will accept either decision, but that if the employee elects to stay, then another lapse in conduct will result in immediate termination.

> ### *Shape up or ship out.*
>
> —Old navy saying

This puts the future squarely in the employee's hands. If he wants to "beat the boss to the punch," he may quit. He will think more highly of the company and you as an individual and probably have less incentive for retaliation or sabotage. Unpaid suspension almost never brings an employee back feeling better about his job, his boss, his company, or himself.

D

179

Dishonesty, Theft, and Embezzlement

NOT EVERYONE IS HONEST. This is an unpleasant but unavoidable fact of life.

Design your internal standard procedures to limit temptation. To detect dishonesty, establish other procedures, such as annual audits, enforced vacations, inventory counting, and surprise audits of purchasing and receiving records, accounts receivable and payable, and all cash accounts.

These detection methods are called internal control procedures; they control the opportunities for dishonesty. These procedures should be designed so that dishonesty is possible only if there is collusion between two or more employees.

Discuss internal control, cash control, and early detection with your inside and outside accountants. Forced vacations afford an opportunity to uncover problems. (See VACATIONS.)

When you're in town, you as owner should sign every check other than payroll. This is one of your principal sources of information concerning your business. Each check should be brought to you with the invoice, purchase order, receiving ticket, and voucher attached. When you sign the check, scrutinize the paperwork and ask questions about anything that seems irregular.

When you're out of town, arrange for two signatures on all checks that must go out. Have someone keep the paperwork for you to review when you return, before it goes to the files.

As you get larger, reviewing everything becomes more difficult and time consuming. You might require the corporate treasurer or department heads to sign their checks before they are brought to you. The bank will pay on your signature alone, but the other signature on the check means that a responsible manager is telling you, "This transaction is okay for you to sign."

An important step in preventing losses is to make sure your employees understand you won't tolerate stealing or dishonesty. They must know they will be fired and prosecuted. Your standard insurance policy doesn't normally cover these losses. Either discuss theft and embezzlement policies with your insurance person or carry special coverage, such as bonding employees.

Balance the cost of extra paperwork and duplication of work against what you and your accountant think are your greatest exposures to dishonesty. There are more ways of being dishonest and fraudulently taking money from the company than you can ever imagine. You can't afford to guard against them all.

If you have a high-cash business (the person at the cash register handles your total sales volume), you have a special problem. Without sophisticated cash registers, complex accounting procedures, and large amounts of the boss's personal time, some cash may not get to the bank

or even into the cash register. Even family members or in-laws aren't always trustworthy at the cash register, and they're harder to fire.

My wife's family had a country dry goods store and saloon in the good old days before Mr. Patterson and the National Cash Register Company worked on this problem. Grandfather's general manager died living in a larger house than Grandfather did. Many people couldn't understand why.

If your product or inventory is small, highly desirable, edible, or has a street value, theft from inventory by employees as well as customers is a major problem. In many retail stores, more products are lost out the back door due to employee theft than are carried out the front door by shoplifters.

During the three months we spent upgrading our computer system, we were unable to maintain all our usual internal controls. We then found that the person who ran the computer while printing paychecks was altering data before the final payroll run. After each run, he changed it back. The result was that he added about $60 to his paycheck for overtime hours that he didn't actually work.

We made the discovery in early December. After some consideration, we realized that if we fired him immediately, it would cost us more to train a new person to finish the year's payroll and run the required annual W-2 forms than to keep him on the payroll until he could finish the job in January.

We secretly decided to hire a replacement in January, but we carefully watched our employee steal his $60 per paycheck until he completed the annual government reports. Then we confronted him. In return for our not filing against him, he signed a note for the amount he had stolen and paid us back out of what he earned from his next employer.

Unfortunately, your purchasing agent (or anyone who decides where to spend your money) is often tempted by over-eager vendors. It's easy for the purchasing agent to favor the supplier who gives him presents or pleasures, whether that supplier is deserving or not, but it may be detrimental to your company. I have had to fire three purchasing agents who got their best interests and the company's mixed up.

Check on your purchasing agent every way you can. Limit the gifts she can accept and make this policy known to vendors. An acceptable limit may be any food, drink, or entertainment that can be consumed on the spot or within less than one day. This means no TV sets, guns, vacations, jewelry, or anything else of substantial value. A $40 value or some other fixed dollar limit is also acceptable. (See VENDOR GIFTS TO YOUR EMPLOYEES.)

If you have enough friends among your vendors or within your industry, they may complain to you if they're losing business with your company because your employee is on the take. Auditors may also discover fraud or diversion of funds when they audit purchasing records and procedures.

Discovering that one of your partners or managers is dishonest is one of the worst things that can happen to you. As soon as you're convinced you're dealing with a dishonest person (either inside or outside your company), start looking immediately for the shortest and best way out. Fire the person, quit, or get out of the relationship. Take your losses, but sever the relationship while your losses are small.

Continuing to deal with a dishonest person will only get you into worse trouble. However, you may be legally liable if you act on information you can't prove or if you tell others that an employee was released because of suspected fraud. If your proof isn't ironclad, find another reason for discharging a suspected employee. Carefully save all documentary evidence, including employees' statements. In this instance, you need a CYA file to protect yourself and your company in the event of later damage claims.

Length of service isn't necessarily a vaccination against embezzlement. A previously honest employee in a desperate situation can succumb to temptation. When found out, he will often maintain that the money was intended as a loan—he was going to put it back when the situation allowed. Others might say they thought they were entitled to it; they've worked for so long at such low wages that the company owes it to them.

The Small Business Administration offers a publication called *Preventing Embezzlement,* by Christopher J. Moran (Washington, D.C.: Small Business Administration, 1973). Another good book is *Are Your Employees Stealing You Blind?* by Edwin C. Bliss and Isamu S. Aoki (San Diego: Pfeiffer & Co., 1993).

D

181

Do More Than the Customer Expects

DON'T YOU GET A NICE, warm feeling when you find an unexpected benefit or receive an extra touch of service from a person or company you've bought something from? Afterwards, you might comment to others how nicely you were treated or what a pleasant surprise you had.

Such word of mouth is the best advertising you can get. Establish your policies and convince your employees that they should always do a little more than the customer expects. This will help build your reputation and open your door to an ever-growing source of new, satisfied customers.

Success starts with the customer.

Doing Business with Friends

THE BEST POLICY is to inform one and all that, all things being equal, you prefer doing business with friends, but you won't pay a premium price to do so. A genuine friend wouldn't expect anything more, but you'll find pseudo friends who do.

Making friends with your business associates is better than doing business with your friends.

The problem with friends is that you hesitate to complain when something's wrong for fear it might damage your friendship. If the supplier weren't a friend, you or someone with your company would quickly call and insist on getting the problem fixed. You won't be as hard on a friend as you would be on a different supplier.

As your company gets larger, you'll find that others in your organization also have business friends they want to favor. Keep your policy the same. Vendors and suppliers must earn their business with your company on the basis of merit, not friendship. Merit means price, quality, and service. (See LOOKING OUT FOR #1; VENDORS—POLICY TOWARD.)

Don't Shoot the Messenger

MAKE IT EASY FOR EVERYONE to tell you the truth. The message isn't the messenger's fault—but even if it is, you still should be one of the first to know when there's a problem.

If you react angrily when someone gives you bad news or criticism, that person quickly learns to tell you nothing. Events still happen, but you don't hear about them as soon as you should, or as directly or completely.

Keep your staff small, so they don't fend off this kind of news. Be approachable outside of formal meetings. Go to employees' offices to talk. Take colleagues to lunch or dinner without an agenda—just "What's on your mind?" Let listening dominate. Make your walking around routine and low-key so that your unannounced arrival brings a favorable greeting, not terror. (See GO TO THE OTHER PERSON'S OFFICE.)

Cultivate people who tell you the way it is, not the way you want it to be. These people help you face reality. Take steps to hear opinions and truths from someone other than an underling trying to please you. It's always good to ask someone what she thinks you ought to do. Decide whether information brought to you is important, requiring action, or merely gossip or self-serving. Get all the information you can in person; don't let someone else filter it for you.

When you hear something from one employee that you aren't supposed to know but that you think requires action on your part, find a way to innocently "discover" the information yourself. When you do this, you confirm that it's true, and you don't have to reveal your source.

All it takes is a story going around that a forthright employee was banished to Siberia or fired, and you'll cut off free and easy communication to yourself. Employees won't tell rumors to *you,* but they'll still tell other employees. You'll be the last to know.

One of the problems of success is that the ego expands to become a wall. If you're going to continue to be a success, keep smashing that wall so unpleasant news can penetrate it.

Entrepreneurs need at least one person working for them in a senior capacity who has the honesty and sincerity to tell them when they're wrong.

80-20 Rule

THIS CONVENIENT, GENERALLY ACCEPTED rule recognizes the principle that you can achieve most of your result (80 percent) by concentrating on a small part of the total problem (20 percent). The astute person who first recognized this was Vilfredo Pareto, a turn-of-the-century Italian economist.

For example, probably 20 percent of your salespeople will produce 80 percent of your total sales. And 20 percent of your product line produces 80 percent of your profit. Also, 80 percent of your troubles come from 20 percent of your employees.

And 80 percent of your business volume comes from 20 percent of your customers.

This book recognizes the 80-20 rule. It concentrates on the 80 percent of business problems shared in common by all types of businesses; it doesn't cover the 20 percent of the activities that are specific to your industry or type of business.

Recognizing this principle in many cases allows you to concentrate your scarce resources of time and money where they can be the most effective—on the 20 percent of the activity that produces 80 percent of the results.

184

Employee Education Policy

SMALL COMPANIES NEED TO KEEP their employees' technical and professional skills current with state-of-the-art developments in both general and specialized fields. But small companies don't have the in-house facilities necessary to train new employees or to help current employees increase their skills or stay abreast of developments in their chosen or assigned fields.

Seminars, short courses, trade association meetings, schools, and professional meetings for selected employees are the best way for small companies to accomplish this. Attendance should be on company time and at company expense,

perhaps with a requirement that returning attendees must instruct or share materials with others who didn't attend.

Reward ambitious individuals who want to use their own time for personal development in a business-related field. This includes night school, vocational school, correspondence courses, and weekend courses on everything from basic mathematics, computer usage, repairs, and machine shop to drafting, salesmanship, programming, and other business-related subjects.

After we tried many ways to encourage employees toward self-improvement while also helping the company, we came up with the following policy: An employee who wished to pursue a business-related skill or subject on his own time brought to the human resources office a description of the course or activity, including time required and price. The HR person verified that the skill or knowledge would be of help in our business, as well as helping the person individually, and that this was a legitimate, accredited educational source. The HR manager then obtained the approval of the employee's immediate supervisor.

We then entered into a written agreement with the employee stating that if he completed the specified program and brought us the certificate of completion, the company would reimburse him for two-thirds of the cost of the course. This was written into our employee policy manual.

> *I will prepare myself,*
> *and when the time*
> *comes, I will be ready.*
>
> —Abraham Lincoln

The message to our employees was this: "We want you to improve yourself in the skills that will help our business. If you put in the time and effort, we'll pay twice as much of the cost as you do."

We tried paying in advance several times but found that there are a lot more starters than finishers.

185

Employee Pay Policies

AFTER YOU'VE GOTTEN INTO the growth stage, make some decisions concerning what kind of employees you're trying to hire and retain. You don't have to write down these decisions, but you should seriously consider where you want your company to be on the employee pay scale and how this can best motivate and reward the people you want.

Do you want everyone to be the very best you can find? Can you afford to pay the highest wages? When does a required talent or skill justify hiring from outside rather than promoting from within? Are attitudes more important than productivity? Does the competitiveness of your business require sweatshop pay scales? What percent of total compensation should be guaranteed salary and what percent should be incentive, based on performance? What form of incentive is most effective in your business? Why and how often should you review and adjust the guaranteed base pay?

While your company is small, you aren't setting policy by the way you treat one person. As the number of people increases, each compares her treatment to that of similar employees. At this point, whether you realize it or not, you've set policies by your historical actions. You're breaking policies, and maybe laws, if you treat one employee differently from the others for reasons they don't understand or agree with.

At first I thought everyone I hired into our growing company should be capable of becoming a vice president. It took a while to figure out that not everyone, regardless of capability, wanted to be a vice president. Not everyone thought like I did, wanted the same things I wanted, or was motivated the same way. I also noticed that, even if I paid the highest wages in town, there was no way to be certain I'd cornered the best employees.

Not all performance incentives are measured in money. Peer-group recognition or awards that can be displayed to family and friends can instill pride and build loyalty. The perquisites of a title, a rug on the floor, office location, type of car, membership in a club, or the best and latest equipment also provide incentive and recognition. A good book on this subject is *1001 Ways to Reward Employees,* by Bob Nelson (New York: Workman Publishing Co., 1994).

Somehow my sales manager always drove a better car than I did. When I drove a Ford, my sales manager drove a Buick. When I got an Oldsmobile, he drove a Lincoln Continental. Sam Walton of Wal-Mart drove a pickup truck.

When I was introducing a new product line, the best salesman I could hire wanted a starting salary higher than I was paying myself. My wife thought it was foolish to pay someone else more than the owner was making—so I raised my own pay and hired him.

You're not trying to make money by hiring the cheapest employees you can. You're trying to get maximum production for minimum dollars spent, whether for salary, bonuses, material, equipment, or any other expenses. Working smarter is more productive than working harder. You, your managers, and your employees are trying to make money by providing customers products and services they're willing to pay for. Your job will be simpler, and everybody will make more money, if you have a few well-motivated, trained employees than if you have many underpaid, unhappy, and resentful employees. (See MANAGING PEOPLE—THEORY X AND THEORY Y.)

A few general guidelines concerning pay practices might be helpful. When you establish formal pay grades or pay scales for hourly or salaried people, set up a minimum of four and a maximum of eight grades or steps, with minimum and maximum pay for each grade. Too many grades become an administrative headache and difficult to explain to employees.

There should be some overlap, meaning the top pay in one grade should exceed the minimum pay in the next higher grade. Raises or promotions within a grade should be easier, with different

186

requirements, than promotion to the next higher grade.

Although you don't want to broadcast any employee's specific pay, including yours, don't assume that your payroll is a secret. Such things have a way of becoming known. Don't bend the rules for favorites or old-timers.

Everyone needs financial help now and then, but the person who frequently asks for an advance against the next paycheck can cause a lot of headaches. This person is unable to handle his own finances and expects special treatment, which you can't give to everyone. Put in your policy manual whatever you decide is reasonable and proper (an advance once per

quarter, twice per year, etc). Then try to stick to it.

Concerning deductions from gross pay, take the smallest number of deductions you reasonably can from employee paychecks. Put every dollar you can into take-home pay. That way, employees can decide what to do with their money and can buy what they want to. There are enough required deductions that reduce take-home pay. The more you suggest, authorize, or allow your employees to buy through payroll deductions, the more you're inviting future requests for pay increases. (See RELATIVE PAY FOR CORPORATE OFFICERS.)

Employee Policy Manual or Handbook

THE LARGER YOUR COMPANY GETS and the more people who work for you, the more written policies you will need. But your relationships with your employees are so important that the first policy you should put in writing is your employee policy manual or handbook. Start it either late in the survival stage or early in the growth stage.

In the early stages, when only a few people are employed, everyone knows the policies. Everybody knows everybody else. You can announce something about holiday work hours or the new parking lot, and everybody understands it immediately. You make policy decisions on the

spot as needed. New employees are absorbed into the group and pick up attitudes and policies from older employees as they go.

As the company gets larger and you hire more people, written policies and procedures simplify and shorten the familiarization and break-in period for new employees. When you find yourself spending too much time explaining things to new employees, or when there's confusion, write your policies down.

Begin simply with one or two pages of items you believe are important and concerns that are causing problems. Our first employee policy statement, when we had about 10 employees, was a typewritten page and a half. We added about a page a year and revised everything at the same time.

Written, accessible employee policies and benefits help guarantee that all employees know about them. Written policies also make favoritism less likely to occur. The manual communicates to middle managers and to employees what's expected and ensures that consistent rules are applied.

Make the rules as simple and explicit as you can, but expect employees to interpret them liberally in their own favor. For eye safety, we said the company would pay the cost of safety glasses, custom ground to the worker's prescription, for use on the job. A draftsman came in with a bill for $375 for gold-rimmed glasses. The next revision put a dollar limit on the amount the company would pay.

Computerized software programs and books can help you write your manual. One program is *Policies Now* from Knowledge Point, 1311 Clegg Street, Petaluma, CA 94954. I've included a simple outline of possible subjects as shown in figure 2. (See HUMAN RESOURCES DEPARTMENT.)

Even if you've gotten your draft forms from a good source, today's laws about hiring, firing, and treatment of employees are changing so rapidly that you should get an expert to review each revision for compliance with current local requirements. Although these policies are legal documents that create binding legal obligations, don't allow them to sound stiff. Keep out legalese.

You don't have to accept the "canned" language in the software or book. Without changing the meaning, you or your favorite writer can dramatically change the tone and feeling. Be caring. Be enthusiastic. Treat employees with dignity and respect. Don't talk down or use commanding language. Make clear what you expect. Make no promises or guarantees, but offer opportunities. The tone should be friendly, upbeat, and encouraging, and should create warm feelings within new employees and their families. Include explanations of the tone or attitude you wish to create toward customers and fellow employees.

Give a copy of the manual to applicants who request it and to all newly hired employees in their hiring interview. You want them to read it thoroughly and come to work confident that they're joining a good group of people. The manual should let them know what's expected of them and that they will be treated fairly in the workplace.

Your employee manual is your contract with your employees. It's consummated by performance on both sides, even though you haven't signed an agreement. Be sure your manual doesn't imply that people will have a job as long as they keep their noses clean. Contingent-fee lawyers can infer a contract for a lifetime job in loose language in your formal policy.

Be especially careful with provisions for discharge. Besides listing specific causes, include general language covering poor performance, actions detrimental to the company, and actions that

E

188

189

Figure 2. Employee Policy Manual or Handbook Sample Subjects

damage customer confidence or employee morale. Be sure these statements are complete and legal within your state. If you fire an employee for some reason not listed or covered by the broad language, you may have breached your contract with that employee. (See FIRING PEOPLE—AVOIDING FUTURE TROUBLE.)

Termination at will is outlawed in some states. To preserve whatever rights you may have in this area, your employee policy manual should state that all employment is at the will of the company and may be terminated for any reason. Even with that statement, you are still subject to applicable state and federal laws.

You must be able to prove that employees are familiar with this and all your policies. This is best done by revising and reprinting your policy manual annually and by obtaining a signed receipt from every employee who gets a copy. Getting and keeping this receipt must be part of your hiring procedure.

Later, you'll need different policies for hourly, salaried, and managerial employees, as well as all employees in special groups. And you must follow your own rules. When you bend a rule for the benefit of one employee (usually an old-timer or a favorite), you will offend ten others who think you should have also made an exception for them. (See SEX IN THE WORKPLACE.)

190

Employee Stock Option Plan (ESOP)

AN EMPLOYEE STOCK OPTION PLAN (ESOP) means that groups of employees own company stock under carefully regulated conditions as specified by law. The incentive value of stock ownership by employees cannot be overestimated, but control of stock held in an ESOP is so regulated that its incentive value can be lost because it seems so remote. ESOPs are controlled under government rules and are different from what I've mentioned elsewhere concerning stock options as incentives for managers.

Employee incentives in the form of stock options became possible in the mid-'70s after Congress passed three laws that grant favorable tax treatment to a corporation that provides employee ownership of stock, favorable tax treatment for the ESOP itself, and favorable tax treatment of the interest paid to those who lend money to the employees to purchase company stock. Under these laws, and additional laws and regulations enacted since, employers are allowed to set up plans that qualify.

ESOPs are also a way for the owner to get a portion of the value of her locked-in company equity in cash by giving the employees ownership status with borrowed money. The corporation adopts or creates an ESOP. The ESOP can then borrow funds from a lender bank to buy stock from the corporation or from the owner. The corporation guarantees the loan to the lender and deducts its loan payments to the bank from taxable earnings.

The lender's tax advantage is that only 50 percent of the interest that it receives on the loan to the ESOP is taxable. The advantage to the ESOP is that it purchases stock issued by the company. As it's paid for, this stock is credited to the employees' account. The ESOP pays no taxes. Unlike dividends paid to other holders of stock, dividend payments on stock held by an ESOP are tax deductible.

One advantage to the corporation is that both principal and interest that it pays to the ESOP are tax deductions. Another is that an ESOP is the only deferred-compensation plan that can be used as a means of corporate finance. When marketability of company stock is limited, as it is with privately and closely held companies, the ESOP can provide a needed market for the stock. It can be used to finance acquisition of other companies.

ESOPs also create problems. In a closely held company, determining stock value (it must be done annually) can be difficult. Individual accounts may not be significant enough to justify administrative cost. The ESOP cannot be terminated without possible penalties to the company and the participating employees.

Shares owned by the ESOP must be voted solely in the employees' interests. Initially, they're voted by an administrative committee. Depending on plan provisions, voting rights may or may not pass immediately to employees. Either graduated vesting or vesting after 10 years of service is usual.

The success ratio for ESOPs is 50-50 at best. ESOPs don't always work well in small, privately owned companies. Although I had 17 individual minority shareholders, I never had an ESOP, which is a group ownership approach. A basic and primary decision is whether you ever expect these people to actively control the company. How are they going to pick the CEO, and who is it going to be? Who's going to guarantee the notes at the bank, thereby taking the ultimate credit risk and profit?

Talk to friends who have ESOPs and those who do not; make a thorough inquiry before you decide whether this course of action will benefit you and your company.

The National Center for Employee Ownership (1201 Martin Luther King Jr. Way, 2nd floor, Oakland, CA 94612) has a publication called *Selling to an ESOP*. It also offers, among other publications, *Theory O: Creating an Ownership Style of Management,* a practical discussion with case studies. A balanced account of both sides of the ESOP question is presented in *Employee Ownership: Revolution or Ripoff?,* by Joseph R. Blasi (Cambridge, Mass.: Ballinger, 1988).

191

Employees as Stockholders

THE INCENTIVE VALUE of shared ownership is unquestionable, but shared ownership means shared control. With entrepreneurs, it usually isn't a matter of being selfish about the stock—it's a matter of being in control of their own destiny. (See CONTROLLING INTEREST AND MINORITY INTERESTS.)

Also discussed elsewhere is the suggestion to share income percentages rather than equity percentages until you're certain your associates are competent, compatible, and worthy. (See PERCENTAGE OF EARNINGS COMPARED WITH PERCENTAGE OF EQUITY.)

192

The fastest-growing companies share equity incentives with highly qualified associates sooner rather than later, sometimes from the very start of the company. You get more people working harder with the same motivation you have, but one-person control disappears along the way.

Base your early decision about stock sharing on how much of a solo act you want your company to be. Have your shareholding associates execute a reasonable buy-sell agreement so you can reacquire the stock if a mistake or split occurs. (See BUY-SELL AGREEMENTS WITH OTHER SHAREHOLDERS.)

By the time I had shared ownership with 17 other stockholders, selling them stock individually (usually about two years after they joined the company), I had developed a presentation for the employees and a buy-sell agreement that worked well for me over the years. I wanted to motivate and share ownership with active and contributing associates. I didn't want any inactive shareholders until I considered selling the company. By that time, I had one advisory board member who was also a stockholder.

Preliminary conversations between each qualifying associate and me convinced us both that an offering of shares would be welcome. None of this was secret. Everyone in the company knew who owned stock and who did not.

After the person came to my office, my conversation went like this: "You have earned the right to be a shareholder in this company, if you want to be. I want to be sure that you and your spouse and I all agree on what this means, because good understandings make good friends.

"Please understand that you're not obligated to buy any stock. Whether or not you buy will have absolutely no effect on your employment, your present or future job assignments, or compensation. You've been doing a good job, and I'm sure will continue to, or we wouldn't even be having this conversation.

"Don't feel that you'll be doing me a favor to buy this stock. I don't really want to sell it to you. I feel like I'm selling gold nuggets. I want to keep all of it I can, but you have earned the opportunity to participate in the ownership, if you wish.

"I'm not going to give you the stock, but I will give you the opportunity to buy it. I don't expect you to pay for it now or all at once. If you need help to finance the purchase, I'll cosign the note with you at your bank or mine, with the stock pledged as collateral. If I eventually have to pay off the note, I'll get the stock back, and I'll be delighted to have it. You may apply all or part of your future bonuses to the note or pay it off any way you wish.

"Before you decide, I want you to understand clearly four things: First, I expect to continue to own the controlling interest in this company. Although selling you this stock, as well as what will later be sold to others, decreases my percentage of ownership, I don't expect to sell enough to lose the controlling interest. If you and all other shareholders come to the meeting and vote against me, I'll still win.

"Second, if lack of capital limits our future growth, I still don't intend to sell enough stock to lose control. We'll just grow more slowly.

"Third, you and your spouse must sign a copy of this buy-sell agreement, after you've asked questions and thoroughly understood it, which says that if you leave the company for any reason, you must sell, and the company must buy all your stock, at the price and terms stated in the agreement.

"Fourth, this stock will pay no dividends until we are a much larger company than we are now. Your increase in value will be the increasing value of the company and the increasing value of your stock under the terms of the formula in the agreement. The company is obligated to buy the stock back, upon your death or departure for any reason, based on a formula that depends on earnings. The purpose of this is to keep everyone's attention focused on earnings.

"I don't think these arrangements are unreasonable in a small company. But if you're not comfortable with any of it, then don't buy the stock.

"For the company to buy back the stock is advantageous to you as well as to those who continue to work here. A minority interest in a small, privately held company is generally unsalable and of no use to your family or spouse. The cash provided by the buyout will be advantageous to your survivors.

"If you are interested, you may purchase _____ shares at a price that now computes to $_____ per share, as provided in the buy-sell agreement that we will both sign. Here's a copy of the agreement. Let me explain its provisions.

"Please explain all this to your spouse as you go over this agreement. You may discuss it with your lawyer, accountant, fellow shareholders, or any business friend in whom you have confidence. Please be discreet with any inside information about our business.

"Do you have any questions?

"I'll be glad to meet with you again, or with you and your spouse, to discuss this, answer questions, sign the agreement, or anything else you may wish. Please let me know within the next week what you'd like to do."

193

With each associate to whom I made this offer, the conversation was always much more friendly and open than the blunt comments briefly expressed here.

Because of one unfortunate experience, I always insisted that the spouse know and sign the agreement. A long-time, trusted employee who lived in a frame house asked permission to store his government bonds in the fireproof company vault for safekeeping. During the years when his only child was in college, he cashed these bonds a few at a time to pay the extra expenses. After his death, his widow came to get the bonds, which she knew we were keeping for her husband. Although the boy in college knew that the bonds had been used for his education, I believe the widow to this day thinks I cheated her out of her husband's bond money.

The boss never really knows what an employee may tell a spouse about his or her position or situation on the job, but I want to be able to look any spouse, child, or survivor in the eye and know—if possible, prove—that I've done the right thing and done exactly what I said I would do.

Therefore I insist upon the spouse's signature on all appropriate documents.

As your business grows, you may find that the partner who now owns a large part of the equity because she made a significant contribution in the beginning cannot now contribute at higher levels. You must have the guts to correct such a mistake before it's too late. When you're fully convinced that the progress of the company is being held back by an incompetent or incompatible associate with a large amount of stock, correct it as quickly as possible, regardless of the cost. It's easier to correct the problem now and get the stock back than it is to wait and do it later.

If you have a buy-sell agreement like the one suggested here, it activates at termination of employment for any reason, including discharge. If you have no such agreement, then make an offer the person can't refuse. Offer to pay the placement fee if he or she gets another job. Expect the person to be hostile, irrational, and ungrateful. Check with your lawyer first to be sure that you are not legally exposed.

E

194

Employees Who Quit and Then Compete

IN A CAPITALIST ECONOMY, this happens. If employees break clean and leave your shop with knowledge they can store only in their heads, congratulate them and bid them Godspeed. They, too, are pursuing the American Dream. Maybe they'll even read this book to learn how to get started. You'll see them at future trade shows.

Taking blueprints, customer lists, financial statements, business plans, and the like is neither ethical nor good practice, but it sometimes happens. If it's serious, call your lawyer. Change locks as well as passwords and numbers on security systems and computers.

If you bad-mouth employees who leave to customers or vendors, it reflects poorly on you. Lick your wounds in private. Outsiders are quite capable of forming their own opinions.

If bitterness is evident at the parting, and if harsh words are spoken, they sometimes include grandiose statements or threats about plans for future competition. Such rash statements seldom materialize because of the employee's inexperience and lack of capital.

Should you hire back employees who quit and then want to return? Some companies refuse to rehire. Others think that former employees have seen the error of their ways, and, if their return is voluntary, they're glad to get trained applicants. I have no specific recommendation. Use your own judgment on a case-by-case basis. I have rehired several former employees and haven't had any bad experiences from doing so.

If your business is technologically oriented, get a confidentiality agreement and an agreement not to compete. Even if they aren't legally enforceable in your state, they place a moral burden and give notification to other parties, and that's enough to deter most people. (See NON-COMPETE AGREEMENTS.)

195

Entrepreneurs' and Inventors' Impossible Dreams

THE IMPOSSIBLE DREAM for the inventor begins when the kinks have been mentally worked out, perhaps after a patent has been acquired, or a model has been field tested. Then he may think: "All the hard work has been done. Any idiot can now take my idea and build a multi-million-dollar company around it that will provide me and my family financial support for the rest of my life. And the person who's going to do this easy job deserves only a 5 percent interest in the patent or the company. Any person in his right mind ought to jump at the chance to build the facility, organize and manage the employees and finances, and deliver the product or service to waiting customers." This unrealistic dream will never happen.

If succeeding in business for yourself were easy, more people would do it.

Another aspect of the dream for entrepreneurs is that, after all those years of nose-to-the-grindstone work, they think they can manage the company with one hand tied behind them. They want to take it easy and enjoy their comforts. They think they should get extended time off so they can take things easy while others keep the company running profitably and smoothly.

The good news is that you can find people who can keep things going. You may already have them on board. The bad news is that people so fully capable of running and improving your company will soon have a company of their own— maybe yours. You taught them how and they're not stupid. They may even take your customers and your most profitable employees with them.

If you visualize this as your future, dream on. It will never happen smoothly.

Entrepreneurs and Managers Compared

ALL ENTREPRENEURS HAVE SOME managerial talents, and all managers have some innovational or entrepreneurial skills.

A person who's purely innovative with no managerial or entrepreneurial skills is an inventor. This person just invents, then licenses or sells inventions to others. The inventor has no desire to build a company to produce and sell them.

A manager with no innovative thinking is a bureaucrat. This person's expertise is knowing the regulations and procedures to be followed, with little or no freedom of choice in performing the job.

Entrepreneurs are more innovative than most managers, but the longer they're in business and the larger their company becomes, the better managers they must become. The best managers, those who rise the highest in companies they don't control, have the greatest innovational talents and do the most original thinking.

The rest of this discussion refers to entrepreneurs as people with more innovational skills than managerial tendencies, and to managers as people with greater managerial skills than innovational qualities, even though both of these attributes exist in varying degrees in both types. (See chapter 3, MAKING MANAGERS OUT OF ENTREPRENEURS and chapter 4, INTRAPRENEURING—MAKING ENTREPRENEURS OUT OF MANAGERS.)

Frederick Hayek, the respected Austrian economist who wrote *The Road to Serfdom* (Chicago: University of Chicago Press, 1949), says that the managerial function is different from and always subservient to the entrepreneurial function. The entrepreneur alone makes decisions instrumental in the conduct of business, determining the enterprise's financial structure as well as lines of business in which to employ capital and how much to employ. The entrepreneur decides the expansion and contraction of total business size and internal section size. The execution of the details may then be entrusted to managers.

The difference between an entrepreneur and a manager is the difference between the visionary who starts a company from scratch or puts it on an untried road and the corporate mechanic who can manage any existing company, whatever its type of operation. The entrepreneur lays new track into the wilderness; the manager keeps things running smoothly on track already laid.

Entrepreneurs are more than managers. They're self-starters who risk their all on their ability and judgment. In addition to job and ego, they usually have their life savings at stake. They want to direct their own lives, and they want all the rewards at the end of the game.

Professional managers look for security, not risk. They concentrate on stability and orderly procedure. Their risks are their jobs and reputations. Their personal fortunes aren't at stake, which is what most people prefer. Managers are more conservative and generally aren't motivated to put up their own money to back an idea, even if they strongly believe in it.

The entrepreneur doesn't think like a bureaucrat or a clerk. Avoidance of failure isn't the same as success. Avoidance of failure is a tactic of big corporation managers, who frequently use it to climb the corporate ladder. Success and results are more typically the goals of a survival or growth-stage entrepreneur or owner-manager who's bound to make errors along the way.

> *Managers do things right.*
> *Entrepreneurs and leaders*
> *do the right thing.*

In the survival and growth stages, one person has the authority to start and stop everything. In big companies, it takes a committee, much time, and many recommendations and written reports.

Entrepreneurs create their own jobs with no structure, no known market, no past, and no guaranteed paycheck. They start with nothing; they feel that everything in their business requires their touch and influence. They are concerned with opportunity for gain and improvement, which frequently result in instability and changes in the status quo. They live in the future, crave control, have a vision, and thrive on change.

Professional managers search for jobs with an established company, a company structure, and policies they must live with and cannot change. They don't expect to control their own destinies, nor to have any responsibility for financing the company or its payroll.

Managers live more in the past and its procedures, love order, like the status quo, and see lots of problems in any change; entrepreneurs live in the future, enjoy uncertainty, and see opportunities. Managers follow entrepreneurs and clean up their messes—and without

E

197

entrepreneurs, there would probably be no mess to clean up.

Finding the person with the right mixture of entrepreneurial and managerial skills for each job is a never-ending process. (See ENTREPRENEURS—ARE THEY BORN OR MADE?)

Entrepreneurs—Are They Born or Made?

198

UNTIL THE MIDDLE '80s, no one even asked this question. The only entrepreneurs anyone knew about were not schooled in the process, were therefore born entrepreneurs, and were almost exclusively male. They were all volunteers as well; no one can be assigned to the job of entrepreneur.

These days we know that women are entrepreneurs, too. Probably more women are self-starters and are more self-disciplined than men. They've had little training as risk takers, but they've made tremendous headway in business management. Running a home on a budget and raising kids takes organizational skill, time and money management, self-discipline, independent judgment and action, dedication, and a lot of energy. (See WOMEN-OWNED BUSINESSES (WOBS).)

Until recently, no one tried to teach entrepreneurial characteristics and success in college. Training managers, yes; training entrepreneurs, no. The difference is mindset—entrepreneurs lay new track into the wilderness, while managers keep things running smoothly on track that already exists. It's easier to teach known, proven ways to do things.

In the '90s, all progressive university business schools have departments of entrepreneurship. At the University of Houston, the Center for Entrepreneurship and Innovation selects 30 students per year from business school applicants for a two-year course designed to educate and encourage graduates to go into business for themselves. The first group graduated in 1995. It will be a while before reliable, time-tested results are available.

My experience has been with born entrepreneurs. I include family environment, early upbringing, and heredity in my definition of "born," meaning without formal education or study of entrepreneurship. Studies show that most entrepreneurs are either children of self-starters or of someone who made halting starts toward self-employment in his or her career. Such parents, either knowingly or unknowingly, encouraged or programmed their offspring at an early age to go into business for themselves.

Most present-day entrepreneurs started young, selling magazines, newspapers, or Christmas cards, mowing lawns, sacking groceries, staying busy and productive. They learned the value of money and the cause-effect relationship between work and money. They recognized the importance of selling something customers wanted. They learned to go where customers were and to do something valuable for others in return for dollars. They started early, while their character and personality were still being formed. Historically, this informal home business education has proven effective in encouraging business start-ups.

It may be difficult to start in college to build confidence, ambition, good work habits, and motivation that weren't developed before. It may prove difficult to teach people how to become self-starters and where to find the guts required to risk everything.

There's no shortage of entrepreneurial starters. However, mortality statistics for start-up companies are so high that we obviously have a shortage of successful finishers, or those with the skills to succeed and progress from survival stage to growth stage and beyond. Perhaps with further study we can select which entrepreneurial students are most likely to succeed, but selection criteria can never be 100 percent accurate. The notion that people can go into business for themselves with success guaranteed is false.

Can we find, supply, or nurture the guts or spark needed to get started and survive? For me, that's an unanswered question. Educating managers isn't a problem; we've been doing it for years. However, if by selecting, training, and educating we can substantially decrease the number of entrepreneurial failures, we will have given the economy, business, and many fine people a tremendous boost. The best ways I know of to do this are to use carefully chosen mentors who were successful CEOs or business executives themselves, and to encourage entrepreneurs to share experiences with their peer group through CEO roundtables.

Winning attitudes, more than skills, are the most crucial traits for entrepreneurs.

For me, the jury is still out on the question "Are entrepreneurs born or made?" If you specify successful entrepreneurs, I think the answer may be both. My definition of a *successful* entrepreneur is a person who founded and still manages a company that's at least 10 years old.

Entrepreneurs Set Their Own Wages

NO ONE AND NO THING SETS your wages—and thus your standard of living—except you, by your dedication, skills, judgment, and self-discipline.

You get what's left over after all bills are paid. If nothing is left over, you get nothing. If there's a deficit, you make it up from other resources or borrow it for later repayment. However, if a large amount is left over after you pay the incentives you've provided for others on your team, then you're going to have a large amount of discretionary money. Isn't that a wonderful dream?

Anytime you wish, you may make your own pay large or small, although you should be strongly governed by your company's earnings. If you set your pay too high, you're being unfair to other employees and creditors and setting a bad example for those not on an incentive basis.

Just how hard and how smart are you willing to work?

If you take too little, you're unfair to your spouse and children, and you're not enjoying the fruits of your own labor—you're not having the fun you should be having. (See OWNER'S PRIVILEGES.)

This is where self-discipline comes into play. You *can* take the entire sales volume for the current month. If you tell the accountants to write you a check for that amount, and you sign it, you've got 100 percent of the income. You're also out of business.

You must have the self-discipline to set your own compensation and your perquisites or fringe benefits at a reasonable level. As long as you're in the survival stage and aren't making consistent profits, set your pay at the smallest amount that you and your family can survive on. Provide for necessities, but no luxuries. You want the company to survive, too.

The size of your present paycheck is a balance between living well now, which means a fat monthly paycheck, and building a bigger company, which means living modestly.

In the growth stage, it's best to set your pay at a fixed amount and establish a bonus or incentive system, initially for managers only, later for all employees. You, as well as the employees who share the rewards with you, must live within the system you've established.

There's no such thing as a $50,000- or $150,000-per-year person. You may have earned that in a past job or a particular operation, but in your next job or your own company you may not be able to produce half that. There's no guarantee that your wages won't go down from some plateau that you once were so proud to have reached. You're entitled to whatever you can earn right now, as proven by your own productive work, plus the amount you or your ancestors have previously saved and made available to you from their labor.

Equipment—New or Used?

OF COURSE YOU'D RATHER HAVE the latest and newest equipment, clothing, trucks, and fixtures, if you could afford it. If your survival-stage or early-growth-stage company can afford all-new equipment, you have more discretionary funds available than any start-up company I've seen.

The only reason to consider used equipment is to save your cash, to make each scarce dollar do the work of $1.25. If your discretionary fund is large at first but you draw it down to purchase new equipment, you'll wish later that you had saved part of it for later, more pressing needs.

Although buying secondhand equipment saves precious cash, financing used equipment is much more difficult than financing new. Sellers of major new equipment usually arrange long-term financing; you must make your own arrangements to finance used equipment. Because condition and value are difficult to establish, some banks aren't interested in making used-equipment loans. Since any new equipment you purchase is new collateral, the purchase-money mortgage may be outside your existing loan agreement and can perhaps be arranged with

other companies who specialize in this type of financing.

When customers don't come to your offices or plant, you can save a bit on appearance, but don't let productivity and functionality suffer. Your pride and the pride you want your employees to have shouldn't allow you to buy junk or keep things messy and in disrepair. Used equipment can be cleaned up, repaired, repainted, and refinished, often by your employees. The visual impression you want anyone entering your premises to get is that your business is clean, neat, efficient, bustling, and run by people who know what they're doing. If you want high-quality output and attitude, you must provide a suitable physical environment, tools, and atmosphere.

Clients and bankers are impressed by a lean business that spends money only on necessities that enhance profitability. Smart clients know that any luxuries and expensive surroundings they see are reflected in your prices.

If many other businesses commonly use the type of equipment you need, such as office furnishings, desks, trucks, and filing cabinets, you can generally find

201

decent, usable pieces at going-out-of-business sales, auctions, or secondhand dealers. You'll easily find store fixtures, carpeting, reception and conference room furniture, and ficus trees. You can start your office with something better than apple crates without spending your total equipment budget.

Old fax machines, computers, copiers, or printers probably aren't cost efficient. They're usually technologically obsolete and not worth fixing. Be sure any machine does everything you need it to do; don't buy something you don't really need just because it's a bargain.

General-purpose production equipment and fixtures are available second-hand in conditions ranging from junk to almost new. This includes racks, shelves, trucks, lathes, presses, mixers, cutters, welding machines, hydraulic presses, ovens, and any other kind of general item you need.

If your business is capital intensive, you probably cannot buy enough production equipment brand-new to get started. In fact, I have yet to see a manufacturing business succeed that started with all-new equipment.

Plan your work; work your plan.

Buying new equipment is something older, established companies do. My company was over 10 years old before I bought a brand-new piece of production equipment to do specifically what I wanted—price, $120,000. If you learned your trade while working for someone else, you'll know a good piece of used equipment when you see it. Learn to hold onto your cash dollars.

202

Equipment—Rent/Lease or Buy?

THIS IS ONE OF THE OLDEST business decisions known. Clay tablets from ancient Babylon discuss whether to rent or buy a warehouse and equipment for storing grain. The problem and the arguments really haven't changed much.

The bottom line is this: For equipment you will need on a continuing basis, the total cost of renting or leasing over the complete term almost always exceeds the total cost of owning. However, in the short term, renting or leasing requires less cash outlay on the front end. For that reason, small businesses often rent or lease. The trade-off means paying more total dollars over the total period in order to write smaller checks during the early part of the term.

There's no real difference between renting and leasing. If your usage is temporary, and if others will later use the asset, it's usually called renting. If your usage is longer, particularly if the contract gives you an option to buy, leasing is usually the term used. If none of the lease payments apply in any way to the purchase price, then the lessee is really buying nothing except temporary use of the equipment.

The lease period frequently approximates the depreciable life of the leased equipment. If title later passes under favorable terms, then the lease is merely being used as a long-term financing method. A lease is usually noncancelable, and the lessee always pays maintenance, taxes, and insurance on the equipment. If you plan to use the equipment for longer than five years, owning the equipment is generally more practical than leasing.

For the lessor to make money, the lease contract must provide that you will pay the total cost of the equipment plus interest, as well as the lessor's sales and administrative carrying charges for the term of the lease. Your benefit is that the total sum is payable in small monthly installments rather than one large lump-sum payment.

If you can arrange suitable long-term financing at your bank, you'll probably save money, but you'll need a larger down payment. Many companies specialize in leasing, generally insurance or finance companies (or their subsidiaries) organized for this purpose. Leasing has grown into a billion-dollar industry. Leasing services are frequently offered through trade or financial magazines. If you have a suitable credit rating, 100 percent financing is sometimes possible.

Be sure to specify in your lease agreement who owns title to the leased property, as well as whether the title ever passes from lessor to lessee, at what time, and for what value. The exact terms must be carefully spelled out if you have any hope of assuming ownership. A portion of the lease payments may be applied to your purchase price. The price may be fixed at the end of the lease (fixed residual value), or it may be fair market value at that time, or other terms.

If you can terminate the lease under favorable terms at your option, you may avoid an obsolescence factor by leasing. This particularly applies to computers. A drawback is that the total cost is usually higher; the lessor must be compensated in some way for absorbing the risk of obsolescence.

Study your financial payouts strictly on the basis of in-house economics, not tax savings. The larger you get, the more significant tax planning may become in your business, and the more assistance and knowledge you will have to figure things out. But if any business deal doesn't make good business and economic sense without the tax benefits, you almost certainly shouldn't go into the venture. Tax considerations shouldn't be the determining factor in your leasing and buying decisions.

E

203

Ever-Rising Sales Volume

ONE THING THAT SOLVES more problems than any other is an ever-rising sales volume. This gives you time and money to solve personnel problems, product problems, financial problems, or almost anything else that ails your company.

The catch is that these sales must be at a satisfactory gross margin. Your objective isn't just to produce sales, it's to produce maximum gross margin. You're better off doing without sales that don't produce adequate gross margin. Sales just for the sake of sales volume is an illusory, expensive goal.

204

———

Business is really nothing but logic. Find out what works to satisfy customers and employees, and do more of it.

———

To maintain an ever-rising sales volume, you must be doing most things well, or you won't be earning increased customer loyalty and usage. Even if you're not yet doing your best, if the general economy is good and if every type of business is growing, your business will probably grow. The internal result is the same.

The converse is also true: a declining sales volume is the abomination of small (or large) businesses. Declining volume creates or complicates problems. If your sales decline is long and slow while the general market remains steady or slowly increases, your problem is internal. You may be doing one of the following things wrong:

- You have the wrong sales approach.

- Your product isn't what customers want.

- Your price is wrong for your product.

- Your quality is poor.

- Your location or distribution is slow or poor.

- Your customers think they get better value and service elsewhere.

Your job is to find out what's wrong and to fix it.

If the general market or economic conditions go down, and if you and your competitors have declining sales volume at the same time (in other words, if the tide is receding), then you'll be glad you stayed lean and mean as you grew larger. If you didn't, cut back quickly before your working capital is eaten up by losses. Remember, downturns happen quickly, but recovery is always slow.

Your dream and your plan is never to have a declining sales volume. The reality is that you will, if you're in business long enough. Recognizing this should always be a factor in your plans. The time to prepare for falling sales is when sales are rising. Keep your staff lean. Cut back your overhead. Be the low-cost producer (which means having the largest gross margin). Stay in close touch with your customers; you'll know what market conditions are and what to do about them. However, if you stay in your office, you may or may not know, depending on whether your associates know or feel free to tell you.

If an ever-rising sales volume is the solution to all your problems, isn't it worth a great deal of your managerial time and effort to ensure that it happens?

Excess Capacity

WHILE YOU DREAM of the huge volume of future services and products the world will demand, you must invest today's hard dollars in yet-unneeded capacity. This may be office or plant space, employees, fixtures, computers, inventory, or an advertising campaign.

When you make any of these expenditures, the question is this: "How much capacity for tomorrow can I buy with today's limited dollars?" My suggestion is to provide for your present, proven needs with 15 to 25 percent excess—no more, unless it is proven that the fuse has already been lit on your skyrocket.

If you build or have capacity to produce goods or services you don't have customers for, the cost of carrying that idle capacity or payroll or space or machinery during a market downturn can be unbearable. Rent and purchase payments go on whether you have customers or not.

If you're going to make a mistake, make a little one. One or two big mistakes will put you out of business.

205

I cannot emphasize too strongly that before you make major commitments betting on future customers and demand for your product, you must build pilot plants, test models, or sample programs that will prove the direction and strength of the market with little financial risk for yourself. Before you risk everything you have, find a way to test and prove the product or service as well as market acceptance (including pricing structure). If the test is unsatisfactory, revise based on what you've learned and try again. Time lost in proving your program or product by actual testing is time wisely spent.

It's better to be solvent and growing and unable to serve all your customers than to spend heavily expecting future customers who never come.

Expansion Opportunities

BECAUSE OF LIMITED RESOURCES in terms of both money and manpower, the small business must grow very carefully. Overexpansion is a prime cause of insolvency and business failure.

One of the fastest ways to go broke is to go for an expanded share of a declining market.

Conserve resources. Go by the most direct route—the one that requires the least time and money—to produce an income stream of steady sales. Once something produces profitable sales, add other closely associated increments that can be supported by the existing revenue stream. Add increments of 10 to 20 percent of your existing cost and sales volume, not more. Additions should be like brothers and sisters to existing products

or services, or at least like first cousins—not complete strangers.

Don't try to sell or produce an entire product line or complete range of services at start-up or try to have every asset or fixture you'll later need. Retail businesses are an exception; they must have almost everything they need before they ever open their doors.

In evaluating expansion opportunities, the most important consideration is selling the additional service or product to the same customers you're now serving, rather than selecting something that can be sold from the same location, or produced in the same way, from the same technology. Just because you have idle productive capacity, don't try to go into a whole new market or product that requires you to find new and different customers.

Don't try to break into more than one market at a time. Establish yourself in one market, then expand that effort before going after another. Ideally, your existing business should be able to support the expense and loss stage until the new product or service becomes self-supporting.

If that time never comes, cut your losses. Run field trials and market tests on a small scale before you go all out with a big commitment. The graveyard of defunct companies contains many that became insolvent while trying an expansion move that was too large and unproven.

The best diversification is to a product or service with a countercyclical market—one you expect to go up when your primary market goes down, thus smoothing out your business cycle. When you look at new ventures or new companies, be alert for dishonest promotions or for persons who are only slightly more informed than you are.

> *Good intentions*
> *do not move mountains.*
> *Bulldozers do.*
>
> **—Peter Drucker**

Don't expect quick results from diversifications. They invariably take longer to develop and become profitable than you anticipate.

207

Family Businesses

FAMILY RELATIONSHIPS ARE BASED ON love, forgiveness, and unconditional, continuing relationships. A business is built on accountability and continuing relationships conditioned on performance evaluations. These fundamental differences can create difficult problems for the family and fatal problems for the business.

In most cases, the family depends on income from the company. Any decision that benefits the company will therefore benefit the family. But the reverse isn't necessarily true; a good family decision is often a poor business decision. For example, overpaying a family member, putting a family member in a position beyond her ability, or withdrawing money for the family that the company needs to grow and compete.

As far as possible, keep the family factor out of your business. Make business decisions that are based on meritorious performance and the best interests of the business.

No one ever questions the validity of this advice, but it's difficult to follow and still have peace at family reunions. Even a close family may develop significant conflicts between different adult generations. Family tension also arises when siblings need to dominate or differentiate and establish a sense of self. These conflicts are often played out on the business stage, where they influence important business decisions.

A strong, healthy family can build a strong, healthy business. Historically, the first generation starts the company with fierce motivation and skill, makes money, and builds a prosperous growth-stage company. The founder always sacrifices lifestyle, pleasure, and personal time to build the business.

Members of the next generation reach the top because they were born into the right family. They are close enough to the process of growing the company to see and understand the sacrifices and dedicated effort Mom and Dad made. They learn about the business at the breakfast table, overhear many discussions over the years, and probably work there during summer vacations.

But do they inherit the same motivation and skill? There's no evidence that any of these assets—drive, sense of purpose, guts, the will to win—are passed on in the genes.

The third generation (members of the lucky-sperm club) usually know nothing but affluence. They receive too many toys and gifts from prosperous parents and grandparents. They probably view the company as a fountain from which money flows for their pleasure without effort or sacrifice on their part. They usually feel that the business should make whatever sacrifice it takes to maintain their income and support their personal pleasures and leisure pursuits.

If they've never worked outside the company, they sometimes expect special treatment and think company rules don't apply to them. The problem is worse if some third-generation heirs work in the business and some don't. Negative attitudes and the lack of skills and motivation frequently run the business into the ground, or else it's sold in bad condition.

In summary, both the business and the family will survive and do well only if the family serves the business. Neither will do well if the business is run to serve the family. The cliché is that families go from shirtsleeves (meaning hard work) to prosperity and back to shirtsleeves in three generations.

I've had to advise a surviving second-generation matriarch that she could save either the business or her children and family relationships, but not both. She couldn't bring herself to offend the family. The assets were later sold by the Chapter 11 trustee.

If you have young family members coming along who you expect will participate in managing your business, give them temporary jobs during high school and college summer breaks. Before graduation, they should have jobs in several different departments. Better yet, swap jobs for your kids with other business friends whose kids need experience.

After college, if both you and the younger family members are considering full-time, permanent employment in your business, encourage them to go to work for a few of your competitors for 9 to 18 months each. The learning curve starts to plateau after that time. Use a minimum of string-pulling to place them with well-managed competitors, perhaps in other cities, where they'll learn marketing as well as general business. If you think you have the only well-managed company in your industry for your children to learn from, you're mistaken.

Many family businesses stagnate for lack of an infusion of new methods, technology, and management. Working where Dad or Mom is the boss isn't a normal working environment and doesn't prepare young people for the real world. Working for at least two companies for a total of three years (five or six is better) while they're resilient enough to adapt easily will teach them a lot before they make a mature decision to enter the family business.

When a conflict develops between good business and good family relations, good business should govern. To keep this goose laying golden eggs, you'd better keep it healthy. Your family will last, whether the business does or not. If the family depends on the business, be sure the business lasts, even if it causes temporary hard feelings within the family. Parents try to be fair, but being fair doesn't mean being equal where time, performance, and skill are unequal.

Family members working in the business must be at least as able and hard working as other, unrelated employees. If you're a family member working in a family company, ask yourself, "What would the company pay a nonfamily worker to do my job?"

Staff key positions with nonfamily professionals. No matter how many family members are in management or how effective they are, at least one top job should be filled by a nonrelative who isn't afraid to voice an opinion on business matters concerning the family.

> *There is no on-the-job training for vice president, unless your father owns the company.*

Baylor University's Institute for Family Business says to begin planning family succession as much as 10 years ahead of the time you expect the second generation to take over. Make adequate provisions for parents' retirement income. When operating authority passes, so should stock ownership.

Questions of succession probably shouldn't be unilaterally decided by the founder. The National Family Business Council, at 1000 Vermont Avenue NW, Washington, DC 20005 (202-347-2048), suggests establishing a family council (this used to be called Sons of Bosses, or SOBs). A business council is a good way to resolve family problems.

If Junior doesn't strongly desire to enter the family business, exerting pressure does you and the child a disservice. One of the few times I can remember seeing my father cry was when I told him, after I returned from four years of military service, that I didn't want to go into his independent insurance agency with him. He didn't try to influence my decision, though.

The definitive book on family businesses is *Beyond Survival: A Business Owner's Guide for Success,* by Leon A. Danco (Cleveland, Ohio: University Press, 1975). Danco says that siblings always have a certain amount of competitiveness but shouldn't carry it over into business. He advocates "pruning the bush" to eliminate relatives who feel entitled but who haven't contributed.

Family—Yours

MAKE ROOM IN YOUR BUSY SCHEDULE for your family and its individual members, specifically including children if you have any. You cannot and should not try to make it in business without the understanding and support of your family.

During the survival stage, spouses and family members pitch in to provide much-needed help, typically without pay. You appreciate their help, but when you start appointing vice presidents, it's usually time to phase the family out. Unless genuine performance based on merit and competitive wages is the basis of continued family involvement, other employees whose meritorious performance is essential to the company will resent it. Don't make business decisions influenced by family feelings rather than sound business considerations.

Enjoyment and support of your family outside your business is one thing. Employment, favoritism, and nepotism within your business is something else. (See FAMILY BUSINESSES.)

Did you notice to whom this book is dedicated?

Favorable Success Factors for Start-up Companies

IN THIS LIFE, THERE'S NO GUARANTEE of success, nor is there agreement about what it takes to make a business successful. However, much has been researched and written about the characteristics common to successful entrepreneurs and companies.

In a survey of entrepreneurs who established small start-up companies that had survived at least three years, American Express found that they had these characteristics in common:

- High self-confidence—82 percent

- Initial investment of over $50,000—84 percent

- Good competitive position on service vs. price—80 percent

- Only job, working full time—78 percent

- Previous experience in the industry—80 percent

- Worked 60 to 69 hours per week—80 percent

In August 1993, AT&T asked several experts on entrepreneurship to describe the most important things an entrepreneur must do to successfully grow a company. Their answers, in summary, were as follows:

- Talk to customers. There's no substitute for being in direct contact with your customers and learning about their likes and dislikes.

- Use technology to improve productivity. Personal computers, fax machines, laser printers, 800 numbers, and other technologies enable your business to respond quickly to customer needs at lower cost.

- Use information to your advantage. Collect data, establish your own databases, and use commercial databases.

- Establish business focus. You can't be all things to all people. Decide which

F

211

products or services your business should focus on, and stick to them.

- Monitor cash flow. Small companies have gone out of business, even on the verge of turning a profit, because they ran out of cash.

- Determine where you're making money. Many companies don't know which products or services or accounts are most profitable and which may be losing money.

- Invest in employees. Your employees have the power to make your business successful, provided you give them the training and information they require.

- Find ways to share the wealth. Give employees incentives to work harder and smarter. Figure out approaches that make sense for your business and that you are comfortable with.

- Continually seek ways to lower costs. Continually evaluate the ways you and your employees carry out tasks.

- Be alert to opportunities for expanding your business, including going international.

According to a joint study by American Express and the Federation of Independent Business, the following characteristics are common to most successful entrepreneurs:

- Willingness to work long hours— 60 to 70 hours per week

- Emphasis on rendering service rather than on making a profit

- Self-confidence

- Knowledge of the product

- Understanding how a small business differs from a large one

- Devoting full-time effort to the business

Moreover, the entrepreneur who had worked with the same or a similar product before going into business had a distinct advantage.

Nothing in this book contradicts any of the above.

F

212

Financial Ratios—What the Numbers Mean

FINANCIAL RATIOS ARE THE YARDSTICKS bankers and creditors use to analyze your business. You can use them, too. Once your operations have matured enough to develop a stable pattern, changes in these ratios can warn you of impending trouble and alert you to changes you need to make in your business operations.

Examine these ratios to look for trends during a given period. Compare this quarter to last quarter, this year to last. What ratio is going up? What ratio is going down? Why? What should you do about it?

Learn relationships between the accounts in your financial statements. These comparisons bring a reality check into your business status and trends. If any of your forecasts produce ratios widely different from existing operating ratios, check out the reason to be certain that no error has occurred.

To compute these ratios, you can use financial statements with full dollars and cents, but you're not really searching for pennies. Rounding the numbers to the nearest $100 or $1,000 gives almost the same answer and is easier to work with.

Here are some of the most common, most significant financial ratios to help you understand and run your business. Of course, ratios differ in different industries; I'm giving you an accepted rule of thumb for illustration. Figures 3 and 4 show annual financial statements for a typical retail clothing store (in thousands). To compare your company to others in your industry, see HOW ARE YOU DOING COMPARED WITH INDUSTRY STANDARDS?

Cash and Liquidity Ratios
These ratios tell you how liquid your company is in terms of cash, how fast you're collecting receivables, how fast you're paying your bills, and how fast your inventory turns over.

Current Ratio. This basic liquidity ratio is determined by dividing total current assets, as shown on your current balance sheet, by total current liabilities. Dividing $213 by $87 gives 2.45, or a ratio of 2.45 to 1 (see figure 3). This ratio is a good indicator of your firm's ability to pay its current bills: the higher the ratio, the greater the cushion you have against hard times, and the more current you are in paying existing debts. The accepted rule of thumb is a minimum of 2.0 to 1, meaning current assets should be at least twice as large as current liabilities. If this ratio decreases over time, then you're becoming less liquid and more stretched, and you're paying your bills later.

Quick Ratio or Acid-Test Ratio. This ratio is determined by dividing your cash total plus trade receivables by your total current liabilities. The illustration shows $37 ($16 plus $21) divided by $87 for a ratio of .43 to 1. This leaves out least-liquid current assets (inventory and other current assets), giving you a more conservative or "acid-test" reading on your liquidity. In most industries, the rule of thumb is that this ratio should be 1 to 1. If this month's or this year's reading is lower than it was during a prior period, an unfavorable trend is indicated.

Receivables Turnover and Days of Sales in Receivables. The sales/receivables ratio, or number of days of sales in receivables, reflects how quickly you collect your receivables, which are your source of cash income to pay your bills. When you divide

F

213

Balance Sheet
(in thousands)

Year Ended 12/31/___

Cash and equivalent	$ 16		Notes pay—short term	$ 38
Trade receivables	21		Current portion—long-term debt	7
Inventory	175		Trade payables	17
Other current assets	1		Income taxes payable	2
Total current assets	$213		Other current liabilities	23
			Total current liabilities	$ 87
Fixed assets (net)	81		Long-term debt	73
Intangibles	10		Other noncurrent	21
Other noncurrent	4		Total liabilities	$181
			Net worth	127
Total assets	$308		Total liabilities and net worth	$308

Figure 3. Retail Clothing Store Balance Sheet and Net Worth

Operating Statement
(in thousands)

Year Ended 12/31/___

Cash sales	$809
Credit sales	167
Net sales	$976
Cost of goods sold	660
Gross profit (margin)	$316
All operating expenses	278
Operating profit	$ 38
Interest expense	$ 10
Other (income) and expense	3
Profit before taxes	$ 25
Income taxes	8
Net profit	$ 17

Figure 4. Retail Clothing Store Operating Statement

annual net credit sales (not including cash sales) by average trade receivables, you get the number of times your accounts receivable total turns over during one year. For example, $167 (figure 4, credit sales) divided by $21 (figure 3, trade receivables) equals 7.95. Your total accounts receivable turns over 7.95 times per year. Run a monthly computer printout of aged accounts receivable to get more detailed information.

To compute the number of days of sales in receivables, divide 365 days by the annual turnovers computed above: 365 divided by 7.95 equals 45.9 days. This means you have an average of 45.9 days of credit sales in open receivables at statement time, and that your receivables turnover or your average collection period is 45.9 days. Again, make two comparisons—one with your own past history and one with the industry standards.

You can considerably enhance your own liquidity by improving the turnover in your accounts receivable and shortening the number of days the average receivable is outstanding. Preventing credit losses and keeping fast collection times in accounts receivable is the main function of credit managers. The shorter the average collection time, the more cash you'll have to invest in other things and the healthier your business will be.

Payables Turnover and Days Payables. Your payroll doesn't go through your accounts-payable account, so computing payables turnover from only the completed financial statement is difficult.

The best way to get this ratio is from a monthly computer printout of aged accounts payable.

The race for quality has no finish line.

Anything you do that lengthens the number of days you need to pay your open-account creditors means they will have more money invested in your business. At times, this is your best source of additional money or investment. But remember, to your creditors you're a customer and an account receivable. They want you to pay promptly the same way you want your customers to pay you.

Inventory Turnovers and Days of Inventory on Hand. If you're in a business that requires a product inventory, the turnover of that inventory is a significant figure. In many businesses, inventory is the single largest asset on the balance sheet. The annual cost of goods sold divided by the average inventory during that period (at your cost) will tell you how many times per year your inventory turns over in terms of dollars. In the illustration, $660 (figure 4, cost of goods sold) divided by $175 (figure 3, inventory) yields 3.77 times per year. To convert this to the number of days, divide 365 days by 3.77; the inventory turns over every 96.8 days.

The higher this turnover number (3.77), the more frequently your total inventory turns over, the more liquid your company is, and the more current your inventory is. The lower this turnover number, the more idle dollars your inventory contains and the more old stuff you have on your shelves gathering dust. Idle dollars make you money only when you invest them in other items.

Net Working Capital. Net working capital is the amount of money invested in your business that you use for working capital, not for equipment, buildings, fixtures, automobiles, or fixed assets of any kind. Net working capital is total current assets minus total current liabilities: $213 minus $87 equals $126 (figure 3). Many a financial and managerial problem shows up as a decline in working capital, but this is the result, not the cause. Drawing out too much money or buying too many assets can seriously deplete this precious resource. Watch this number carefully.

Working Capital Turnovers. You can get by with a smaller total investment if you make your working capital work hard by turning it over more frequently. Your net sales (figure 4) divided by your average net working capital computed in the above paragraph ($976 divided by $126 equals 7.75 times per year, or every 47 days) gives you this figure.

Profitability Ratios
These ratios tell you how profitable your operation is by comparing your earnings to other financial statement numbers. If you're not making profits, these will be negative numbers.

Net Profit on Sales. The first profitability ratio everyone looks at is net profit on sales. Divide net profit by net sales to determine the percentage (figure 4). Net profit usually means after-tax profits, but this should be specified. Taxes are a cost of doing business and are not profit in any sense of the word. Using the illustration, $17 divided by $976 equals .0174, or 1.74 percent. This means that for each dollar you sell, the company retains, or has available to pay debts or buy equipment, 1.74 cents.

F

217

Gross Margin Percentage. This is the percentage of the sales price that remains after deducting the cost of goods sold. This percentage is so significant that it's discussed in a separate title. (See MARGIN, GROSS MARGIN, OR MARKUP.)

Return on Equity. The profit-to-net-worth ratio is an indication of management performance. Divide net profit after taxes by net worth at the end of the period. If this percentage is high, management is doing a good job; if it's low, management is most likely inefficient and/or conservative. According to our illustration, $17 (figure 4, net profit) divided by $127 (figure 3, net worth) equals 13.38 percent.

Return on Investment (ROI). This number measures a company's net income in relation to the invested assets required to produce that income. Whether the assets are financed with debt or equity is immaterial in this calculation. The usual measure is net profits after taxes divided by total assets.

To find return on investment in a product line, subsidiary company, or branch operation, divide operating income (after estimated or prorated taxes) by the total operating assets required to produce that income.

> *Good results without good planning come only from good luck, not good management.*
>
> —David Jaquith

Debt-to-Worth Ratio. The overall measure of total debt you can carry from a lending institution is almost always related to your own investment in the company. This ratio, computed by dividing total liabilities by total tangible net worth (net worth reduced by intangibles), expresses the relationship between the amount of capital contributed by the creditors and the amount contributed by the owners. The higher the ratio, the greater the risk being assumed by creditors. The lower the ratio, the greater your long-term financial safety.

Other ratios to track for your own analysis are listed in DEFINITIONS—FINANCIAL TERMS. Significant ratios are sales expenses as percentage of sales, current liabilities to net worth, and bank debt or notes payable to tangible net worth. For debt coverage, see DEBT COVERAGE OR DEBT SERVICE.

Keeping track of these ratios for one month doesn't mean very much. But annualized numbers for the last three months, or for any given quarter, do mean something. On a three-month moving average, pick up the current month and drop the oldest one, so you'll have a current three-month total. Within any three-month period, except in a seasonal business, you can assume one good month, one bad, and one average, so an annualized three-month (quarterly) average is considered significant. To annualize, multiply the three-month operating amounts by four quarters to simulate one full year. Use these numbers as assumed annual numbers. Smooth seasonal or growth variations by averaging twelve months or four quarters of data.

Two good books concerning this material are *What Every Manager Should Know about Financial Analysis,* by Alan S. Donnahoe (New York: Simon and Schuster, 1989) and *Techniques of Financial Analysis,* by Erich A. Helfert (Homewood, Ill.: Dow Jones-Irwin, 1986).

Financial Reporting on Cash or Accrual Basis

YOU MUST BOTH RECEIVE AND understand current financial reports of your operations in order to manage them successfully. Financial reports are compiled for different purposes and in different depths of detail, but all are based on either the cash or the accrual basis of reporting.

At start-up, the cash basis is the simplest accounting system known and has the extreme virtue of keeping you focused on whether or not you have any operating cash. You either have cash on hand (or in the bank) or you don't. That's your final yardstick of financial discipline and progress. If your payout or purchases exceed your receipts or deposits, you're out of cash, and out of business—unless your piggy bank can cover the deficiency.

When you operate on a cash basis, you don't have to write anything down except what the government requires you to report. Your monthly bank statement is a record of whatever you've deposited or written checks for, but it obviously does not record folding-green transactions or goods or services received or delivered but not settled for in cash.

This system, and the reports based on it, recognizes income only when it's received in cash, rather than when services are performed or delivered. Expenses reduce the bank account when paid, rather than when material or services are actually received or used. Asset and inventory purchases, as well as borrowed money or future obligations to pay, are accounted for in memo or ledger form. Depreciation and uncollected debts must also be in memo form.

The cash accounting method is officially accepted by the IRS for businesses with simple accounting problems, such as service businesses and farms. If you have an inventory, you must accrue for Schedule C of your personal tax return at year-end the amount of outstanding accounts receivable, accounts payable, and inventory increase or decrease.

The criterion used by the IRS is this: Does this method of reporting accurately reflect federally taxable income? If you're on a cash basis, making federal government, state payroll, sales tax, and unemployment insurance reports is difficult. A pegboard paycheck system—writing checks with a ball point pen on printed forms held in place on pegs—can produce all required payroll records.

The only way to really tell how you're doing with both cash and profit (these aren't the same thing) is to use the accrual method of financial reporting. Your operating statements on the accrual basis will reflect profits you earned within a chosen time period, whether or not you paid for the goods you purchased and whether or not you collected in cash for products sold or services rendered.

The accrual method achieves the important accounting goal of matching

F

219

every sales dollar with its associated cost dollars, regardless of when either is paid for in cash. You can tell how and where you're accumulating profits, which will later be reflected in cash.

Your balance sheets will also show the amount of cash you have in the bank, amounts due to you from customers, the value of inventory on hand and assets you own, as well as amounts you owe to banks and vendors and for payroll as of a chosen date, even though these obligations haven't been settled in cash.

Using the cash method of accounting for your tax return may save you some income taxes. But if you want to know on a specific date how you're doing and what you need for cash management and other managerial decisions on the basis of your financial reports, make your statements on an accrual basis.

Changing from a cash basis to an accrual basis is not difficult. As your company grows, switch to using the accrual method as soon as possible. No large business can function using only a cash-basis financial reporting system. They don't even try.

Financial Statements

YOU CAN'T MAKE INTELLIGENT business decisions without current and accurate financial statements. *Current* means available to you at least by the tenth business day after the end of the month, except at the end of the year. *Accurate* means not over 10 to 15 audit adjustments at year's end, changing reported profit less than 5 percent overall.

It takes two financial statements—the balance sheet (figure 3) showing assets and liabilities, and the operating statement (figure 4) showing sales, expenses, and profit—to give a complete financial picture of your business. Owners, managers, bankers, and financial people talk to each other and describe companies and operations with financial statements. You must understand and learn to read and speak this language of business. It's a mystery to me how so many owners can think they have a well-managed business when their latest financial statement is over two months old, and the current annual statement doesn't reconcile with last year's, which often can't even be found.

Operating or Earnings Statement

An operating statement (figure 4), or profit-and-loss statement, is a financial picture of the sales and expenses produced by the company's business operations during a specific period. The end of the period and length of time covered must be shown in the heading.

The operating statement has five principal sections, each of which is totaled to show how many dollars were involved in that activity during the period. A summary operating statement may show only large totals, but a detailed statement is always available to show all the smaller categories and each account that makes up the total.

The first section, and the largest number on this statement, is income, sales, or revenues. Your statement may start with net sales or may show details for each department or from each product line or location, minus returns for credit and price allowances. This section ends with net revenues (gross sales to customers minus credits, returns, and price allowances).

The second section shows what it cost to produce the goods or services your customers purchased. This is called cost of goods sold, cost of services rendered, or cost of manufactured products. If you weren't producing products or selling services, you wouldn't need the people, the equipment, or the expenses listed in this section. In a service business, these are sometimes considered fixed costs because you have to have people on the payroll to perform services, but almost every other industry considers these as production costs. Variable costs change approximately in proportion to changes in business volume. Fixed costs are those that are constant for a given period, regardless of business volume.

Subtract the cost of goods sold from net revenue to show gross margin or gross profit. The higher this margin is, of course, the better. The gross margin is small in the grocery business, or any business that has high volume and low profits. It's high in businesses that sell intellectual property, natural resources, or exclusive ideas or technology.

The third section of your statement shows operating expenses unrelated to production of products or services. These usually break down into sales or marketing expenses and general administrative expenses. They may also include research, development, and engineering or design. Whether or not you produced goods or services, these operating costs are related to time. They include rent, office salaries, salaries or commissions for salespeople, utilities, insurance, telephone, entertainment, lawyers' and accountants' fees, office supplies, and all administrative expenses involved in running the office.

Subtract total operating expenses from gross margin to show your operating profit. That's the profit you made based solely on normal company operations. Net revenue, minus cost of goods sold, minus operating expenses leaves operating profit or loss.

The fourth section includes miscellaneous income and expense items that are business related but not required or not routinely the result of the business of serving customers. For example, you may have either interest income or interest expense. If you bought or sold an existing asset, the profit or loss goes down under other expense. If you're amortizing an intangible asset such as organization expense, that goes into other expense.

Sometimes these transactions can be sizable, but they're generally nonrecurring, happen only occasionally, and aren't the direct purpose of company operations.

The total of other income minus other expenses, which may be either additional profit or additional expense, is added or subtracted from operating profit to produce profit before taxes. This total is the net amount earned or lost before you share with your most significant partner, Uncle Sam.

A last section is taxes on profits, both federal and state. Sales taxes collected from customers aren't reported as sales because you're not in the business of producing or selling sales taxes.

Current GAAP rules require that taxes be computed and shown on the operating statement only for C corporations, not for S or LLC corporations, partnerships, or proprietorships. This is misleading. Although a different entity (the owners) must finally pay the taxes, those funds are not available for discretionary expenses. To prevent getting carried away with spending plans when you look at pretax earnings, I suggest that you accrue taxes on your statement on earned income at the highest individual income tax rate. Mentally or actually set that money aside so you will have it when taxes are due and distributions of dividends to individuals take place.

Acronyms are used for net amounts on the operating statement when computing or representing financial ratios or comparing financial results of operations. For example, GP: Gross Profit; OP: Operating Profit; EBT: Earnings Before Taxes; EBIT: Earnings Before Income Taxes; EBDIT: Earnings Before Depreciation, Interest, and Taxes; EBDITA: Earnings Before Depreciation, Interest, Taxes, and Amortization.

The final operating statement summary fits on a single page. Detailed statements of income or expenses that make up the large totals are often shown on separate pages. Amounts shown for any account are usually compared in adjoining columns with budgeted, last month's, or last year's amounts.

You and your managers should continually analyze these statements to see how you can improve performance. After you've been in business a few years, you and your key people should have a mental approximation of your next operating statement before the accounting department gives you an accurate one.

Balance Sheet

A balance sheet (figure 3) is a quick snapshot of the assets, liabilities, and owners' equity in the business at the end of any operating period. One day either before or after this snapshot, some of the numbers would be different.

Balance means that total assets (shown in the left column of figure 3) must always balance and be equal to the total of liabilities plus owner's equity (right column). (Some balance sheets show assets on the top part of the page and liabilities plus equity below.)

An *asset* is anything tangible the business owns. Assets may also include some intangible items that either cost the company money or give the business value. Original organization costs and patents are examples of intangible assets.

Assets are listed on the statement from top to bottom, in order of liquidity, in the major categories of current assets, fixed assets, and other assets.

Current assets includes cash, accounts receivable, inventory, and perhaps other prepaid expenses or deposits. These assets change every day during normal operations. The cash cycle starts with cash, which you use to purchase or create inventory. When you sell inventory or product, it becomes accounts receivable. When you collect receivables, they become cash again.

Fixed assets are items you must have to conduct business but that you do not expect to sell or replace in the normal course of one year's business. Examples are furniture, equipment, buildings, and automobiles. You usually record these items at actual cost and reduce their value by depreciation as they age.

Other assets includes intangible assets and other assets you do not directly use to make products, such as the cash value of your business life insurance.

Total assets is the total of the three items above. This is the largest number on the balance sheet.

All the money you use to buy or hold these assets comes from two sources—borrowed money, which you must someday repay (*liabilities*) and money

permanently invested or retained in the business, which you don't have to repay (*equity* or *net worth*). The total of liabilities and equity (or net worth) must balance and be equal to the total assets.

Trifles make perfection, but perfection is no trifle.

Liabilities are listed in terms of how soon they must be repaid. *Current liabilities* are due within one year. These include short-term notes payable, accounts payable to suppliers, accrued payroll, taxes, and anything else due in less than a year. *Long-term liabilities* are notes or lease obligations due more than one year from the current date.

Equity or net worth always shows amounts originally invested in the company by owners and stockholders, the amount of earnings (or loss) for the current year, and the cumulative total earned since the company started.

Become intimately familiar with your balance sheet and operating statement. These two, or more detailed reports of lesser departments or divisions, will be the financial basis for your most significant managerial decisions. (See FINANCIAL RATIOS—WHAT THE NUMBERS MEAN.)

F

223

Firing People—Avoiding Future Trouble

THE NUMBER OF COMPLAINTS and lawsuits brought by terminated employees charging wrongful discharge or discrimination because of age, sex, or race have increased rapidly over the last decade. Employees who feel they've been unjustly or unfairly terminated must first file their complaint with the Equal Employment Opportunity Commission (EEOC).

You're more likely to be involved in an appearance before the EEOC because of alleged discharge discrimination than to be involved in any other legal proceeding. If the complaint is not resolved there, the employee who feels mistreated can go to the courthouse. If it comes to a trial, juries usually sympathize with workers because employees are the little guys against the big company.

Avoiding such complaints or lawsuits starts with hiring practices. Your prospective employee's signature on his application should authorize you to verify everything on the form and allow you to conduct drug tests and other procedures, as explained in HIRING GOOD PEOPLE. Confirm orally with the applicant (and have the interviewer write a note confirming it on the application) that he has given you the right to do these things, and that he understands that, if employed, his employment will be at the will of the employer.

Carefully check all references. (See QUESTIONS TO ASK WHEN CHECKING REF-ERENCES.) At least verify dates of employment, job titles, and pay scales. Check significant credentials (college degrees, licenses, and professional memberships). All job skills should be tested or demonstrated; keep the test results. Either test supervisory or managerial applicants with recognized and accepted qualification tests, or send them to an outside professional testing organization that will furnish results to you.

During the hiring process, don't make promises you can't or won't keep, or paint a picture of conditions or potential rewards that the employee is unlikely to receive. Be as certain as you can that your employee policy manual can't be considered a contract and doesn't contain undue limits on your rights of management and discharge. Clearly communicate the length of the trial period, as well as other key points of your trial policy, to the prospective employee. Then, during the trial period, monitor the new employee's job performance, attitude, and work habits. (See TRIAL PERIOD FOR NEW EM-PLOYEES.)

You or someone in your company must become familiar with your state and federal laws concerning discharge. Seminars or current publications can keep you up to date in this increasingly complicated area. Discretionary discharge "at will" (at the will of the employer for her own reasons) has become more and more restricted, but you must preserve these rights as much as you can.

Routine performance ratings are losing favor. Managers don't like to explain bad reports, and so tend to conduct perfunctory employee performance rating and review sessions and overrate even troublesome employees to avoid conflict. These reports can be especially damaging when a discharged employee shows a recent performance rating of "excellent" in three of five characteristics.

When you decide that discharge is inevitable, have someone who knows the legal requirements review the documents in the offender's personnel file. You may have warned the employee or discussed unsatisfactory performance with him, but without documenting the conversations or legally notifying the employee. Document such occurrences now, and place the documents in the employee's file. Thoroughly investigate to be certain of your facts. Don't accuse anyone of anything as serious as theft or sexual harassment unless you're sure of the facts and are prepared to prove them in court. Except in emergencies, don't terminate anyone until you have documented evidence supporting a legal discharge.

When you conclude that termination is necessary, handle it in a brief personal interview in a conference room or a private office other than yours. Do this so you can leave when it's over. Always have present at the interview another person, senior or equal in rank to the discharged employee and of the same sex. Your simple, direct, honest explanation should

leave no doubt that the person is being terminated.

Offer the employee the opportunity to resign, but offer no inducements, promises, or changes to get the employee to do so. Give him the opportunity to write it out on the spot. Make it clear that the benefits package is identical whether he resigns or accepts discharge. A resignation saves face for him and may save trouble for you.

Don't allow time for debate. Keep the conversation professional. Remain calm even in the face of emotional outbursts. Don't leave an opportunity for misunderstanding or confusion. Don't air your own frustrations, and don't say "I know how you feel." Don't suggest an alternative such as a transfer or a demotion if it is out of the question. Don't rehash past grievances. Remember, you're not the bad guy in this. Like hiring, firing is an unavoidable part of your job.

Be prepared to answer this request from the employee: "Now tell me again exactly why I'm being let go." The answer you give then must be as close as possible to the one that your lawyer or human resources professional can include in the written reply filed with the EEOC if the employee alleges discrimination or wrongful discharge.

Prepare a final paycheck and present it to the employee as you start discussing the financial settlement. Give a written explanation or check stub of any payments, financial settlements, deductions from the final paycheck, or any open or unfinished financial transactions with

F

225

the company. Provide a prepared statement of any severance benefits or pay, vacation pay, accumulated sick pay, loans or advances, or any other matters necessary to make a clean break. If you provide outplacement services, they should be away from the company's premises.

Whenever you possibly can, tell the employee you will give him a good reference. Ask the employee to reciprocate when talking about you and your company. He will probably interview within your industry and spread stories about you and your company. Protect your image with a good understanding if possible.

The entire session shouldn't last more than 15 or 20 minutes. To avoid arguments, leave immediately after covering all the requirements. If there is no outburst or bitterness, show the employee every courtesy and consideration. Unless security is an issue, don't rush the fired employee to gather belongings and leave the job site. Avoid making an example of the fired employee, and be very careful about how you word announcements.

If there is unpleasantness, a junior supervisor should stay with the discharged employee while he recovers his composure, and accompany him as he cleans out his desk or work station and says farewell to other employees.

Be sure the terminated employee hears about the termination from the boss or a manager and not from a colleague. It's truly humiliating to be terminated by someone the employee doesn't report to, such as a secretary or book-

keeper. Getting the bad news from the boss is more likely to make the employee feel he was treated fairly.

Don't fire an employee when he's on vacation or has just returned. Although the usual termination notice is given at quitting time on Friday afternoon, leaving the employee the weekend to recover emotionally, termination early in the week can get him started hunting a job sooner. He may be depressed and emotionally distraught; the sooner he finds another job, the better off he'll be, and the less likely to file a complaint against you.

You may have to defer firing an individual because you don't have a reason that's bulletproof. You may not have built up the large CYA file necessary under today's labor laws. When the occasion demands it, and when you have several such deferred dismissals, do a company-wide layoff. (See LAYOFFS OR REDUCTIONS IN FORCE (RIF).) The EEOC views a layoff of many employees from different departments during slow business periods entirely differently from a termination of one person for cause.

A good book on this is *Rightful Termination: Defensive Strategies for Hiring and Firing in the Lawsuit-Happy 90's*, by James Walsh (Santa Monica, Calif.: Merritt Publishing, 1994). In questionable cases, check with your human resources professional or your lawyer.

Be consistent and fair. Treat everyone the same way. Helping former employees get other jobs will benefit both them and you.

F

226

Firing People—Effect on Those Remaining

EVERY TIME YOU FIRE one employee, you send a message to those remaining. If they feel that the fired employee was given a fair chance and counseling or warnings about her performance, you will have reinforced the good opinions of the remaining, hard-working employees. If they feel that the dismissal was without warning and without reasonable cause, the message is discouraging.

Since a person's capacity to rationalize is infinite, the fired employee's immediate reaction is going to be that she has been unfairly treated, no matter what you do or say. Maybe she will understand later, maybe not. But if her performance holds back the growth or efficiency of the whole group, you must correct the matter.

Firing people, especially supervisory personnel, is the hardest thing managers have to do. If you can't do it for the greater good of the company, you'll never succeed as a manager. When you finally do it, it usually comes as no surprise to the other party and is a relief for all concerned. She probably wasn't happy and knew she wasn't doing a good job, but couldn't bring herself to quit. Now she has the chance to find self-fulfillment and a better future in a job she likes.

It took me a year to work up the courage to fire my first sales manager. He started with me and helped me when I needed help, but he'd totally lost confidence in our only product. I relieved my own guilty feelings with the reasoning that no matter how much I owed him, if he was now the one holding back the growth of the company, I owed more to the other six families (one of which was my own) living off this small business than I did to him and his family. Afterward, we spent over an hour agreeing on how we would present this to the trade. He told me he would have quit if he'd had more courage, but this was the best title and job he'd ever had.

The example you set by your own conduct and performance is one of the best messages you can send your employees. Most of them will observe, respond, and conduct themselves the same way you do. If several are allowed to underperform or misbehave with no correction or penalty, others will believe they can get away with it too. That's the wrong message.

227

Forecasting and Financial Model Building

THE ABILITY TO THINK AND PLAN ahead is one requirement of an organized entrepreneur and manager.

During the dreaming stage, you plan in terms of dollars about the future of your business. Those dreams have neither the formality nor the substance of a forecast, but they're the beginning of the ideas and procedures that become more formal and dependable as your company gets larger.

For survival-stage companies, forecasting is difficult because there are so many unknown, unproven circumstances. You're sailing uncharted waters. Even though your business plan forecast (if any) is the best you can make it, it will be highly erratic when compared with actual results.

When growth-stage companies begin to show signs of dependable financial trends (less volatile swings in sales and financial numbers), forecasting expected performance becomes easier. The longer you've been in business and the more stable your operation becomes, the longer the forecasting periods should be.

You or one of your key people should always forecast cash requirements and cash availability in writing for at least 30 to 90 days. To do this, you need to know something about your forecasts of sales, accounts receivable, and accounts payable. As you get accustomed to these procedures and know more about your business, you'll get into budgeting and formal planning for expected income and expenditures. (See CASH TRACKING AND FORECASTING; PRESIDENT'S DAILY/WEEKLY REPORT; BUDGETS.)

The forecast includes operating and profit performance forecasts and cash and debt forecasts. It shouldn't be the work of the accountant or the boss alone, handed down to managers and employees as though carved in stone. Input and opinions of senior managers are necessary. You need their cooperation and commitment to make the forecast become a reality. The mental discipline and planning required to visualize the future as accurately as possible is a significant step in management and in team building.

Forecasting can be either simple and general or detailed and complex. It isn't an exact science. At the end of the forecast period, the resemblance between predicted numbers and actual numbers may be purely coincidental.

Forecast for the coming year in either months or quarters. Forecast for year two and maybe year three by quarters; for years four and five by year. Within any quarter, you'll probably have one good, one bad, and one average month.

Forecast in numbers rounded to the nearest $100 or $1,000. Leave off zeros. Forecasting inaccuracies are such that you shouldn't quibble over dollars and pennies that are months or years away.

F

228

Put in your principal forecast what you really think will happen or what you are willing to commit to make happen. Call this your realistic forecast, the basis for your budget. Show this one to your banker, your investors, and employees.

Then make an optimistic forecast that reflects the best results you think could reasonably happen—and a pessimistic forecast, the worst you think may happen. Once you have a forecasting method set up (or a computer model that plays "what if" games), making these alternate forecasts becomes easy, as well as informative, for internal management. Your accountant can be of help, but she is merely a mechanic and observer. To make the realistic forecast come to pass, your senior managers must be emotionally committed to it.

Quantify your forecast whenever possible in terms of both dollars and units. Not just bigger, how much bigger? Not just more customers, how many more? What class of customers or in what territory? How many more units or employees? Will you have the assets and capacity to produce the additional volume? Are you planning unrealistic sales per employee or ratio of sales to total assets? How do your present and your predicted financial statements compare with your past history and with industry standards? (See HOW ARE YOU DOING COMPARED WITH INDUSTRY STANDARDS?)

Your forecast will show how much excess cash you have or how much more cash you need to reach a higher operating level. Depending on the nature of your business, you may need more money when things are very good than when they're very bad.

No forecast is complete without a detailed written statement of the assumptions on which the forecast is based. You may assume that the future will be just like the past. More likely, you'll assume that it will be different in several ways. List your assumptions and attach the list to the resulting forecast. Anyone reviewing the forecast can readily see whether or not she agrees.

Quarterly, if not monthly, the same managerial group that made the original forecast should compare actual performance to predicted performance. Analyzing differences helps you forecast more accurately for the next period.

Revise your forecast at least once a year, or whenever something earth-shaking happens that wasn't predicted by either the optimistic or pessimistic forecast. Minor revisions to make the forecast conform to what's actually happening mean you're just massaging the numbers to make yourself look smarter. Mid-year or six-month corrections to forecasts and budgets are the accepted norm.

Sooner or later, curiosity, skill, or business necessity will propel you into considering complete and formal forecasting. In its highest sense, this includes building a financial model for your company.

Building financial models is more art than science. Since no two companies are exactly alike, no two models are alike. To be applicable to the largest number of potential users, the packaged software for building financial models uses condensed balance sheets and earnings statements. You're forced either to condense and force your financial statements into the standard mold or to modify the mold to fit available financial data. The more details you want, the more customization you need to get results that apply to your specific case. This requires varying degrees of financial and computer skills.

> *Even a good plan must,*
> *of necessity, give way*
> *to a better.*

Spreadsheets and forecasting software now make this process easier. A versatile program I've used for a long time is Bottomline V, by Ilar Systems, Inc., 334 Baywood Drive, Newport Beach, CA 92660. This program can be manipulated and completely customized using Lotus, Excel, Quattro Pro, or any of several computer spreadsheet programs. Bottomline V has modules for budgeting, automatically making a five-year forecast based on your last five years' numbers or allowing you to forecast five years into the future.

One client used this program to build a financial model of her company and projected 20 years into the future, through three of the seven-year business cycles her industry customarily followed. By using this model to play "what if " games, she proved that shortening average accounts-receivable collection time from 55 days to 45 days would save $500,000 in interest charges over 10 years. She immediately hired another person for the collections department.

When you begin to build your model, start simple and add variables as you go. The largest single variable, and the one that drives all the others, is sales. Each new variable multiplies the difficulty considerably. Make a list of the variables you want to include.

The following are helpful suggestions concerning model building.

1. Verify input data. Reverify. Preventing mistakes is easier than trying to find them.

2. Check your answers with the reasonableness test. If the numbers look funny, something is probably wrong.

3. Know that the tough problems at the heart of the process are forecasting cash and short-term debt.

4. Identify each finished forecast for future reference. The name or tag must include a detailed list of the assumptions you used to make the forecast. Be sure to divide the list into *fixed assumptions* (those that don't usually vary from forecast to forecast) and *variable assumptions* (those specifically varied to see what results you get).

5. Your final *realistic forecast* of operations becomes your budget. If you add balance sheets, including capital expenditures, debt borrowing or payments, and cash balances, it becomes a forecast.

6. Keep track of units such as number of employees, number of hours worked, overtime hours, board feet or carloads sold, truck shipments, total payroll, square footage devoted to production, number of vehicles, and so on. Not all data acquired or predicted are financial or in dollar terms.

7. Remember, model building is an art, not a science. After running enough forecasts, you may begin to believe they're true and that the future must happen according to your scenario. Not necessarily.

This is a simplistic presentation of what can be a complex exercise. In larger companies, you get into capital forecasting, departmental forecasting, and sensitivity testing, to see if a small change in input might produce a large change in final results. (See STRATEGIC OR LONG-RANGE PLANNING.)

231

Forecasting Sales

THE SALES FORECAST IS the beginning of your budgeting process and all your planning. You and your managers will unconsciously think about it whenever you make a significant decision. The sales forecast is the least precise and the least subject to your control of the many numbers that crowd into your consciousness. This is because it's based on the future buying decisions of many individual customers.

Sales volume is so important to everything that happens in your company that you must do your best to forecast it accurately, even though you recognize that precision is impossible. No two sets of customers are alike, and most niche markets are unique, so you must find the method that produces the greatest accuracy for your operation. Your customers, whether they're individuals or companies, are also making their future buying plans, which may be based on their growth, the general economy, or the economy of a particular industry.

Your task is easiest if you have a large number of repeat customers. This gives you a starting base, with estimated additions for new customers, new products or services, possible price changes, and effects of the general economy. If your customers are industrial or business, discreetly inquire from appropriate insiders whether they expect to increase or decrease their activity next year. If your customers are individuals, their spending will follow the general economy.

Your salespeople are in closest contact with your customers and have the best reading on which direction they expect to move. Your sales manager (you, unless you've appointed someone else) should be able to take data, opinions, and readings from your salespeople and summarize them into a meaningful forecast.

The total should be the sum of the amounts you've broken down by product line, by geographical location or territory, by type of service rendered, by salesperson, or by whatever segments are significant in your operation.

One basic approach for predicting sales in the industrial market is to identify potential customers and sum up their requirements. If you can pinpoint customers and their usages, you can then estimate the probability of what they will buy. If your customer base is large, these estimates can be quite accurate because overages in one are offset by shortages in another.

Although they should, most small companies don't make a detailed sales forecast. The number they come up with reflects more optimism than reality. Frequently, the WAG (wild-ass guess) method is used, refined after a few years' experience to the SWAG (scientific wild-ass guess) method.

Salespeople start the process by stating a realistic number and committing to fulfilling it. It's a commitment for the entire company as well. Don't pressure them to tell you the number they think you want to hear.

We used to get written sales forecasts for the coming year from our salespeople by product line and by territory. We tabulated and published the total for an annual contest called the "champagne sweepstakes." At the end of the year, the salesperson who made the closest prediction won two bottles of champagne. Of course, commissions and bonuses for exceeding the forecasts were much more valuable, but this kept interest high and injected fun into the process.

What the mind of man can conceive and believe, the mind of man can achieve.

—Napoleon Hill

Discuss the plan, both by segments and in its entirety, with your entire sales organization. You or your sales or marketing manager should lead a series of these meetings. When people approve the final sales forecast, you also want them to agree to specific commitments to one another for the next 12 months to meet the agreed-upon standards.

If you can hit your projections or your budget within 10 percent, you've done well. If you hit within 5 percent, you've achieved the impossible. If you're off by more than 15 percent, review the process, your people, and your managerial skills.

F

232

Franchising

BECAUSE SUCCESSFUL FRANCHISING requires proven business operations at multiple locations with real profits, employees, and customers, the odds are bumped a long way in your favor when you buy a local franchise. Because the franchiser furnishes a detailed, written, oft-revised, well-thought-out business plan complete with policies, procedures, and forms, a franchisee may duplicate that success over 80 percent of the time. An unproven idea with a new owner or manager may succeed less than 20 percent of the time.

This is the best argument I can give you for making a careful, complete business plan. If you start from scratch, you won't have a successful, money-making, operating model to give you details. You can learn most about your chosen business by working for a similar operation (see chapter 1, LEARNING ON SOMEONE ELSE'S MONEY). For a business plan in an unknown business, you must do a lot of thinking, planning, and research just to sound reasonable. The harder you work and the more complete your plan, the better your chances of success.

The benefit of buying a franchise is also the main drawback: you're not going to be in business alone. The advantages are that you get help operating your business, you're part of a larger organization with the advantages of large purchasing discounts, and you may have instant name recognition and proven products to sell. The minuses are that you won't have total independence, you must follow the franchiser's rules, and you're not guaranteed to get rich.

A franchise operation won't run itself. Before you buy, spend several months working for another franchisee. You'll get valuable training while getting paid and a detailed look at the nature and characteristics of the business as well as dealings with the franchiser. You may find that not everything is as represented.

The franchiser gives the franchisee the right to sell a product or service, usually under the franchiser's name, in a specific location or territory. Payments to the franchiser include a front-end fee and usually a percentage of sales or profits, or a requirement that you buy certain materials from the franchiser. The initial investment can range from $10,000 to $500,000. A long, elaborate contract defines your relations with the franchiser, what you can and can't do, and what the franchiser is and isn't obligated to do to help you.

The bloom is off the franchising business. Much litigation has resulted from people who thought a franchise was a guarantee of success without work. It isn't. Look carefully before you leap. Talk to both successful and unsuccessful franchisees. You will learn a lot from the unsuccessful ones.

F

233

A good book is *The Franchise Kit: A Nuts-and-Bolts Guide to Owning and Running a Franchise Business,* by Kirk Shivell and Kent Banning (New York: McGraw-Hill, 1995).

Fun, Fun, Fun

ENTREPRENEURS MAKE LITTLE distinction between work and play, between labor and leisure. They hardly know which is which. They pursue a vision of excellence and independence no matter what they're doing. Others may try to decide whether they're working or playing; entrepreneurs think they're doing both.

Business should be fun, challenging, and rewarding. Enjoy your minivictories and the milestones you've passed, your increased sales volume, the new model brought out, the new territory opened up, the new accounts or customers—however you measure your success.

Yes, there are moments of frustration. Yes, you'll have disappointments and problems. But, on balance, if you don't look forward to going to your job every morning, and if you don't feel that your efforts are justified (not necessarily financially rewarded—that will come later), re-examine your motivation and decision.

> *Teamwork is less "me" and more "we."*

Business is a game. If you're not having fun and don't find your business fascinating and interesting as hell, you're in the wrong game.

Future Shock—Graphical and Audio Communication

AN IMPORTANT AND FUNDAMENTAL CHANGE in the way we live and do business is gathering momentum. The information and communication revolution has been accelerating for the last 10 years. Some people recognize it as the communication revolution, the computer revolution, cyberspace, the information highway, or just the Internet.

All these are facets of the same developments—the impact of unlimited, instant, inexpensive, graphical, and audio communications on business, the economy, and every aspect of our social life, education, and behavior. Changes during the next 15 years are bound to be staggering.

The rapid availability of the following significant capabilities is destroying the presently accepted limitations of time, space, and cost:

- Instantaneous communications, transmitted and received in real time while events are happening and available to multiple interested or involved parties in widely separated places at the same time

- Inexpensive communications, so inexpensive that cost is not a factor once the equipment and standardized procedures have been established

- Graphical, audible, color, bi-directional communication (meaning each party is able to send and receive at the same time)

Business people, end users of these processes, are just beginning to realize the potential impact on their methods. Technological leaders are working frantically to read the future and develop the systems, hardware, and services that each foresees. With changes by law in areas of authorized competition, the giants of communications and services are searching for their place in an unknown future that is vast, rapidly growing, and constantly shifting.

No one can foresee with clarity and certainty where entrepreneurial ingenuity will lead in developing or exploiting these technologies. Many future entrepreneurs will see their niche market in some specialized aspect of these developments. Some will judge correctly and be able to ride the tiger. Others will recognize opportunities or have dreams they cannot move quickly enough to stay on top of.

235

This revolution will touch the patterns and processes of business, society, entertainment, education, and virtually every human activity and experience. It will bring changes in our daily lives as broad as those caused by the automobile, the telephone, the airplane, and television.

These cumulative, earth-shaking changes will open opportunities for some and make other businesses obsolete. Stay in touch with your customers and your market. Improve your services and procedures with newer, faster methods. (See SPEED OF RESPONSE TIME—YOUR BIGGEST FUTURE OPPORTUNITY.)

Getting Out—How to Escape This Mess

236

THE WORST THING is that most of the events described below happen to your company involuntarily—you can't control them. They happen because your business is in trouble and you've waited too long to recognize the real problem or to take corrective actions. Now you've partially lost control of your own destiny.

You don't want to get out under these conditions, but circumstances make it necessary. You have only limited freedom of action remaining. Although you have some rights and are concerned about yourself and your loved ones, you also have legal obligations to others. All these events bring on tax consequences as well as problems with pride and emotions.

To protect your own as well as others' legal rights, you have to deal with lawyers (except when you fade away or perhaps make an informal arrangement with creditors). Your accountant will be helpful in all cases. All these procedures involve some allocation or sharing of available assets, losses, and pain. (See INSOLVENCY AND GOING BROKE.)

Fade Away

This happens to your small business when you just decide to quit. Usually, you make this decision because the operation isn't making money and the loss, if any, is manageable.

You don't want to hurt creditors or your future reputation. You want to pay what you can and work your way out of additional debt. You cease operations, pay employees, padlock the doors, dispose of assets as best you can, and pay off debts with cash or promises.

Dollar amounts of disputed or unpaid items are too small to involve attorneys. Since no one sues or files anything, there's usually no public record and little formal recognition associated with the closing. The statute of limitations on open account items is two years in most states, four years on written notes payable. No one's been badly hurt. Without enough money to pay creditors, there isn't enough to pay lawyers or fight over.

If you have a better idea or opportunity later, you can start over, sadder but wiser.

Informal Arrangement with Creditors

If you're doing business right now, you already have an informal arrangement with creditors. You pay them when you can, within 30 days if possible. There are no written agreements or group actions. When things get tight, you delay payments to 45 days, sometimes 60. Ninety days is about the most time you can go without creditors putting you on credit hold or COD, or requiring payment of back amounts due before delivering more. If you've been doing business with them for some time, you know which ones are stricter than others.

When you see your cash and credit tightening up, make whatever immediate, drastic changes in your operations you need to stop the flow of blood. (See DANGER SIGNS—TROUBLE AHEAD; TURN-AROUND OPERATIONS.)

To continue operating, you must first meet your payroll and pay payroll taxes. Beyond that, pay or satisfy those vendors who can put you out of business—telephone, electricity, utilities, critical materials and merchandise, landlord, note payments, and others. Make a convincing, documented plan to pay off your creditors. If you can't do it yourself, get your accountant to write up a reasonable payment plan.

Take this plan to your largest, strictest, most important creditors first. If you get their agreement, most smaller creditors will also agree. You must disclose your entire plan to all creditors and obtain their agreement. One possible plan is to ask for a moratorium on back payments and promise cash on delivery from now on plus a certain percentage of past-due amounts each month. Since this is about what a bankruptcy court allows, if your creditors believe they will get it from you without lawyers' fees, they may agree. This plan assumes that 100 percent of back debts will eventually be paid.

Your creditors don't really want to take over your business or want you out of business. They just want payment for what they've already done and would love to have you as a continuing, paying customer. Commit yourself and your team to performing as promised.

Legal Arrangement with Creditors

This doesn't happen overnight. It usually happens in larger companies, with larger dollar amounts and more creditors who are difficult to treat individually. It's done after you've been behind in payments to many creditors for a long time, and after you've negotiated individually with your largest creditors.

This sort of arrangement involves lawyers as well as desperate creditors who think they'll get more this way than if you claim bankruptcy. Lawyers draw up formal agreements, which all creditors voluntarily sign. Many states don't require court proceedings or approval.

This is practically the same as bankruptcy without a trustee or formal committees of creditors and stockholders. Some or all creditors agree to accept less than the total amount due them. However, administrative fees are smaller, so creditors may get more this way, which is their incentive to agree. Your past credit reputation and credibility are important in getting their agreement. Any amount of debt that is forgiven becomes taxable income to your company.

Voluntary Liquidation

If you decide to quit, and if your company still has a net worth, you can probably sell the company or the assets and pay off all or most of the debts. In some instances, the assets (sold singly or all together) may be worth more than the operating company. Real estate and old but serviceable equipment may be valuable. A last-in, first-out (LIFO) inventory

G

237

may be on the books at a ridiculously low figure. A fire sale at your cost may liquidate a large portion of your inventory.

Collect accounts receivable and pay off all the debts you can. Notes you've signed require a special sequence of payments, particularly when you start to sell or liquidate assets.

To liquidate equipment and fixed assets, consider an auction. To get top dollar, call in professionals who specialize in your type of equipment or merchandise. Their fee is high, but it still usually leaves more money in your pocket.

Cleaning, identifying, and technically describing everything for an auction is expensive. The auctioneers may combine your property or equipment with that of similar clients to draw a bigger crowd. An auction gets all your cash at once.

Decide before you start whether to go with professionals or to do it yourself. If you're a good salesperson and are so inclined, you can do almost the same thing yourself over a longer period. The best, most desirable items go first. Discount the dogs and undesirable pieces, or finally throw or give them away.

Either way, equipment or inventory dealers or professional junk men will make you lump-sum offers for everything before your liquidation or auction. Their total cash offer will be maybe 50 percent of the estimated auction proceeds, but you skip a lot of expense, headaches, and waiting. If you sell directly to them, they may then conduct their own profitable auction.

Involuntary Liquidation

If you continue to go downhill, are unable to make the required turnaround, and have one large secured creditor (usually a bank) that has the mortgage on all your assets, that creditor may foreclose and acquire control of your assets. The IRS may padlock your door for nonpayment and have its own auction.

These actions are usually a last-resort effort to collect by a large or preferred creditor. They don't want to operate your business; they only want to get paid. Involuntary owners of your assets would rather sell everything in a lump sum than go through the hassle of an auction with equipment they know nothing about. Technically, any excess amount received beyond paying your indebtedness, plus administrative, foreclosing, and liquidating expenses, should be paid back to you. Don't expect anything.

Bankruptcy

Bankruptcy is a federal proceeding intended to forgive your debts and give you a second chance. All other actions mentioned above are controlled by state laws. Although your debts will be legally forgiven and you have the right to go back into business, economic reality considerably limits your opportunities. Lenders remember or discover by a credit check that the last person to loan you money didn't get paid. New lenders are reluctant to take the same chance.

Don't go bankrupt if you can possibly avoid it. It's better to slowly liquidate and fade away, leaving bills to be paid later.

G

238

Fading away leaves a less specific, less permanent record, so it's easier to start over if you want to.

Capitalism without bankruptcy would be like Christianity without Hell.

—Frank Borman

Bankruptcy isn't a do-it-yourself game. You're in lawyer territory, because the amount of paperwork is staggering. The disruption to your business operations and managerial control is tremendous. You may lose control of your business if the judge considers your management incompetent or not totally cooperative with legal procedures and requirements.

It isn't against the law to go broke, but it is against the law to cheat while you're going broke. As cash runs low and it becomes apparent that not all creditors can be paid, management decides which creditors to pay. After formal bankruptcy papers are filed, the judge has the right to go back 90 days (12 months for "insiders") and require the return of monies paid to any party or reverse any preference payments considered unfair.

Bankruptcy law recognizes that employees and jobs are important and allows a waiting period to work out operations if that seems reasonable. Everyone loses something in a bankruptcy. Customers receive no more products. Employees receive no wages or benefits. Investors lose some or all of their capital investment, and suppliers can no longer sell their product. As long as there's a reasonable chance of recovery, it's to everyone's advantage to keep a business running rather than to liquidate and shut it down. The key word is "reasonable."

Unfortunately, none of these options are pleasant. If you're faced with this undesirable situation, read *The Save Your Business Book,* by John Goldhammer (New York: Lexington Books, an imprint of Macmillan, 1993).

G

239

Getting Out—How to Harvest the Fruits of Your Labor

AT SOME POINT IN AGE, desire, maturity, or lifestyle, you'll shift your thinking from wealth accumulation to wealth preservation: "Never mind getting more from this operation—just let me keep what I've got." This usually happens to people in their mid-50s. It may happen sooner or later for any number of reasons—health, satisfaction, family, peaked-out market, boredom, fear of the future, or wanting to retire or travel.

The following is a brief discussion of your options if your company is profitable and if getting out is a harvest of the beneficial results of your efforts. If the results haven't been good, and if you just want out on the basis of "Never mind the cheese, just get me out of the trap," see GETTING OUT—HOW TO ESCAPE THIS MESS.

This subject deserves a book of its own and multiple visits with professionals from several disciplines. Like getting married, getting out of the company that has been your life's work is something you'll do only once. Also like marriage, it's one of the most important things you may ever do, but you won't do it often enough to become an expert on all the complicated choices you'll have to make. You'll need legal, accounting, financial, tax, and managerial judgment and skills, all focused on your one-of-a-kind, probably once-in-a-lifetime transaction.

Because the process is so complicated, these paragraphs hit only the highest of the high points for each option.

Hire a Manager or a Team to Run It

If you want a manager to run the company while you run and play—still drawing full compensation and benefits, of course—think again. It's seldom satisfactory over a long period, even if you provide ownership and incentives to the most honest and conscientious managers you can find. (See ENTREPRENEURS' AND INVESTORS' IMPOSSIBLE DREAMS.) When you mentally and emotionally leave the company, it drifts into ways you won't like. You'll be dissatisfied with the results, or maybe lose the company to other management with less than full compensation to yourself.

If you even try this, you need golden handcuffs for the managers, strong incentives, and a clear understanding of your options and problems.

Let the Kids Run It

The important questions are these: Do you have one or more family members almost as dedicated to running it as you've been? Have you carefully planned and trained these persons to perform the CEO's job? Can they, will they, carry on your vision?

Fortunate and unusual is the entrepreneur whose next generation is dedicated, motivated, and capable. The second generation has the best chance. Conventional wisdom, with which I concur, is that business families go from shirtsleeves to prosperity to shirtsleeves in three generations. The third generation is the most likely to lose the family business. (See FAMILY BUSINESSES.) In-laws are family too, and sometimes they're more capable, but they don't always remain in-laws.

For the last several years, I've spent a large part of my consulting time straightening out family businesses that began to function poorly because of deficiencies in personality and capability of family members in management. Business problems would be easy to solve with normal

240

business judgment, but when family name and ego take over, financial losses usually occur.

Selling all or part to the kids is a sound business procedure. It's good for the kids to buy the company rather than getting it for free, but the tax and estate-tax situation becomes complicated and detrimental. Before you do it, explore these considerations thoroughly with competent tax counsel.

Sell It to the Employees

The biggest problem here is capable management, with control in the hands of preferably one person or, at most, a few. If you're satisfied with that, the rest is easy. Employees don't think like an owner, and they're not willing to risk everything like an entrepreneur. Who will guarantee the bank notes? Will the bank accept that guarantee?

Employees are always interested in taking over the company they've worked for. An employee stock option plan (ESOP) provides tax incentives for employees, owners, and banks to finance partial employee ownership. (See EMPLOYEE STOCK OPTION PLAN (ESOP).) For partial ownership (less than controlling interest), it works. For majority ownership and control, it doesn't. Management by committee doesn't work. Who will make the hard-nosed, unpopular choices?

A prospective client who had no children told me he wished to form an ESOP and turn his company over to his top five employees. Over lunch he explained the planning and meetings with lawyers and employees he had gone through during the last year to accomplish this plan. I pointed out to him that none of these employees could or would personally sign the bank notes needed to finance the inventory, nor was any one employee capable or desirous of running the show. The $12 lunch was the only fee I got for keeping his company out of this trouble.

Two brothers ran a fine retail store for many years. On the death of the first brother, the other sold the store for no down payment to a group of long-time employees, who obviously knew the business. The employees raised their salaries and never made a payment on principal. Two years later, the surviving brother took the company back to restore it to good financial health.

If you insist on selling to employees, don't sell control to more than a few. Satisfy yourself that one of the few can and will do the solo act of risking and managing. That employee should obviously have the lion's share of the stock.

Remember, all sales are taxable events. Part of your sales price goes to Uncle Sam.

Sell to an Outsider

There's a time for planting and a time for harvesting. The times for planting are the idea and survival stages, and as far as you want to go into the growth stage. The time for harvesting is when you've successfully grown a crop. It may be time to stop and smell the roses instead of running past them. It may be time to enjoy the fruits of your labor, before the failure of your physical strength and health handicaps you. What good will it do you to make more money if you can't enjoy it?

This is more of an emotional decision than a business decision. You—the entrepreneur who built the company—feel as though you're selling one of your children and a lifestyle as well; the purchaser is an investor with other good uses for his money. No wonder so many arguments occur over price.

Preparing the company for sale can take two or three years. Clean up sweetheart rental and usage deals. Get nonproductive relatives off the payroll. Stop excessive or unusual fringe benefits. Provide at least two years of full audits by a reputable firm. Run your accounting operations the way an unrelated third party would. Report your profits. Pay all your taxes.

Sell into a rising market. The purchaser must anticipate unlimited growth for the foreseeable future. If you're making a profit, sell multiples of earnings and determine the price accordingly. If you aren't profitable, sell the assets for their appraised value to someone who can use them to make a profit.

What's the sale price? Considerably less than you want. (See VALUATION—WHAT IS YOUR BUSINESS WORTH?) To negotiate the sale, get a professional, not necessarily a lawyer or accountant, to buffer the horrible things the purchaser will say about your company to drive the price down. Expect to be insulted about deficiencies in the way you've run the company and by the price first offered. Brokers

are unregulated and can be bad news, but good ones with an established reputation can be a tremendous help. Talk in confidence with your banker, your accountant, your lawyer, or other good friends.

Someone must prepare the sales package, much like an elaborate business plan. This is expensive and time consuming. If you can do it or have in-house people do it, so much the better. If a broker does it, the broker will want up-front money in case of no sale.

Prospective buyers may be (1) competitors who usually expect to pay the lowest possible price, (2) strategic buyers who want to combine your operation with theirs, and (3) investors or others trying to invest money profitably, who probably know very little about your business.

Get help on the sale-purchase contract. Not every lawyer knows this specialty field. The buyer wants to buy assets only, leaving you with known and unknown liabilities. You prefer to sell stock, which transfers liabilities and assets. Do you want cash or stock? There's a big difference. Get a good tax person who's familiar with the purchase and sale of companies. Negotiate reasonably.

Get a sample of the employment contract the purchaser wants you to sign, because you'll continue to be involved in company operations for one to three years. You are the purchaser's insurance policy. Who will you report to? Will you have to move? Your whole lifestyle will change. You'll no longer be the boss and be free to do as you wish. The new owners may ask for your advice but probably won't take it. They have their own plans for running the company or they wouldn't have bought it.

After the sale, don't rush to do anything with your cash except collect interest. You'll have many newfound friends. For most entrepreneurs, investing and managing money is harder than making it, and lots less fun.

You'll have no trouble finding books on selling your business. One I recommend is *Getting Out: A Step-by-Step Guide to Selling a Business or Professional Practice,* by Lawrence W. Tuller (Blue Ridge Summit, Pa.: Tab Books, an imprint of Liberty Hall Press, 1990).

Plan for Your Death

If you've been told to expect death due to a terminal illness or a lingering problem, make plans. If death is unexpected, and you haven't already prepared, it's too late. But if you have a good, motivated management team, it can do remarkably well for a period of many months while the new owner or owners try to figure out what to do. Most entrepreneurs leave everything they have to their spouse, who usually doesn't have the experience to run the business.

As soon as you're out of the survival stage, make a will that provides not only for your family but for what you want to happen to the business. If you expect it to stay prosperous and in the family, arrange for management control by putting voting stock in the right hands. Take care of inactive family members by giving them value but not voting control.

If the new principal owner isn't dedicated or experienced, that person should sell to someone as quickly as possible. Time usually works against a leaderless company.

If you make no will, state laws make one for you. In Texas, they are called laws of descent and distribution. Other states have similar laws with different names. These laws provide that, if you die without a valid will directing otherwise, your estate, which includes your company, will go to your heirs and relatives in specific proportions, depending on who your survivors are. It's the state's guess as to what you want done, and this guess may or may not fit your desires.

In addition to your will, dictate a cassette tape, replaced or updated every year or two, containing your personal advice to your executor (probably your spouse or offspring), revealing what you want him to do and how to proceed. Deliver it to your executor so it is sure to be found and used. Include such personal advice as "Don't trust _____. Call _____ and take his advice about such-and-such. Get out of _____ as fast as you can. All my assets are listed, and all active files can be found _____." The executor's problems are knowing what the assets are, finding them, and doing what your will or his or her prudent judgment requires.

Such off-the-record advice to your trusted executor doesn't have the force of law, but it's invaluable for effectively carrying out your wishes. I've been an executor several times. I could have saved much worry and money if the deceased

243

could only have answered a few questions, such as why he did certain things, where I could get reliable opinions or information, and where certain documents or assets were.

These transfers of ownership and control have tax consequences. Bring your tax specialist into the planning stage early on. Remember, if it doesn't make good economic sense to take a certain course of action, don't do it just because it saves taxes.

Getting People to Stretch to Their Full Ability

FEW PEOPLE, including you and me, ever develop to their full potential. Usually the reason is lack of effort. Sometimes it's lack of incentive. Some people think it's lack of education or opportunity, or lack of being "discovered." However, in America today, anyone who wants an education badly enough can get it. Opportunities are usually luck that follows hard work, and discovery usually happens after you've prepared yourself and demonstrated your ability to perform.

It's as difficult to keep a first-class individual in a third-rate job as it is to keep a third-class individual in a first-rate job.

Many companies don't encourage employees to think of new ways to do things, try new methods, or accept new assignments. Without such encouragement, most employees don't stretch to their full ability or seek anything new and different. The principal reason is fear of failure and its consequences.

Within your organization, employees must have a certain comfort level to feel secure enough to take on new, possibly strange jobs where there is a likelihood of failure. Setting this comfort level provides a sense of security and inner strength and establishes the environment for success.

Much real talent is buried within many individuals. Given the opportunity to shine, ambitious workers respond. Encourage critical and creative thought by being a good listener. Recognize that senior management, including yourself, cannot possibly think of all the good ideas. Employees must be confident that they can comment and suggest without fear of the consequences.

Give employees and managers more challenges, education, responsibilities, encouragement, and opportunities. Most of the time you'll be surprised at the favorable results. Occasionally you'll both be disappointed.

When an employee fails to perform in a new and larger responsibility, recognize the problem and discuss it. If the right level of openness and mutual confidence prevails, you can gracefully return the employee to her old job or move her to a new one where she can do a good job. This way, you won't lose a trained, semi-skilled employee. If the only way out of a failed attempt at a higher job is termination and shame, you'll lose good, capable people. Both of you will be happier if face saving and reacceptance at the old level is an acceptable alternative within your company.

> *When people set their own goals, they usually achieve them.*

Encourage employees to improve their job-related skills and knowledge. Send them to seminars or schools. Encourage them to get education or knowledge that you cannot provide. (See EMPLOYEE EDUCATION POLICY.)

245

Giving Out Financial Statements

DUN & BRADSTREET AND OTHER credit agencies frequently ask for copies of your latest financial statements. My advice is don't give them to outsiders.

Give financial statements to your bank and other companies that lend you money on signed notes; otherwise, they won't lend you money. Report taxable earnings to the IRS. All these institutions keep your financial statements confidential.

Your open-account creditors are entitled to know how you pay your bills. Give them a list of several of your largest suppliers they can call for a credit check. If they don't like what you tell them or what they get, their remedy is to ship no more goods on credit. Legally, they can't require you to furnish complete financial statements.

Because your early financial statements are universally bad, you do yourself more harm than good by releasing actual numbers. The people who are asking know that the statements probably look bad. You're better off to leave them in doubt as to how bad.

Go as Far as You Can by Yourself

IF YOU'RE LIKE EVERY OTHER entrepreneur I've ever known, you'd like to continue to own 100 percent of the company you built. And you'd like the company to become as large as General Motors. Reality being what it is, this has never happened and probably never will. But if you're like most entrepreneurs, you'll fight tenaciously to hold onto the largest percentage of your company's equity you can possibly manage.

Along the way toward utopia, you need all your skills plus others' skills plus more money. Each additional person you invite to join as equity owner should be someone who will make a vital contribution. Each will want and earn a slice of the pie. The pie is better and bigger because of each of their contributions.

The further you go by yourself, and the more of your plan you solidly accomplish, the better the deal you can make when you trade for equity. Why pay or trade with someone else to do what you can do yourself? Your strength at the bargaining table is based on what you've already accomplished, which lends more credibility to your future plans.

Your dream—the entrepreneur's dream—always starts as pie in the sky. Much shrinkage occurs as this sky pie becomes pie on the table. Time is a factor. If you make a deal now that considerably reduces your interest but gives the enterprise a real boost, you may be better off several years from now than you would be by sweating slow progress all the way.

This decision comes down to your managerial judgment and style. Will short-term sacrifice produce long-term gain? Is it better to have a large slice of a small pie or a small slice of a large pie? Only you can decide.

Well done is better than well said.

—Ben Franklin

Go to the Other Person's Office

WHEN YOU HAVE SOMETHING TO SAY to another manager or employee, go to her office or work station. If you drop in unannounced, as if strolling by, you'll set an informal atmosphere that flatters the person without frightening her.

You are in complete control. You can chose the subjects to be discussed. You can either encourage or discourage conversation about other subjects. The other party feels the confidence of being on her own turf. It saves time—you can leave whenever you want to.

Summoning someone to your office is formal and scary. Do this only when you need total privacy or when the subject matter requires this kind of atmosphere.

Goal Setting

GOAL SETTING IS THE PROCESS of identifying short-term future objectives and then focusing energy and attention toward their accomplishment. These action guidelines ensure that efforts aren't wasted on unimportant activities.

When you set goals, set deadlines for yourself. This makes you feel the need to complete the activity and helps you learn to accept imperfection. It accomplishes things. It also builds more stress.

Organized efforts to reach goals work wonders in business and personal life. Neither an army nor a sports team would expect to win without identifying ultimate goals as well as the intermediate steps necessary to get there. It's especially important for ambitious individuals and small, struggling companies that need focus and direction.

If you want to get ahead and achieve personal happiness and growth, establish personal goals to improve your capabilities, work habits, and education. New Year's resolutions are a form of goal setting, frequently with tongue in cheek and without real commitment to their accomplishment.

To be most effective, write your personal goals. Writing them forces you to think; the sequence, logic, and rationale of their accomplishment become clearer if you commit them to paper. Writing also gives your goals a sense of importance and permanence and marks a time of decision.

Many people think about goals, but finding the mental discipline to identify them and plan action to accomplish them is difficult. Many of us are mentally somewhat lazy. Thinking about goals is beneficial, but not nearly so beneficial as writing them down. Most beneficial of all is to have your management team identify company goals and make solid commitments to solving them.

Goal setting is the lowest level of your company's planning process. It must be directed by your company's mission statement, which must be in harmony with your vision. Short-term goals can be agreed upon and placed in writing more readily than a mission statement. Fewer than one company in ten has a written mission statement. Fewer than one in a hundred has a written vision.

247

A common mistake in setting company goals is for the boss to decide what the goals are to be and announce them to employees. Everyone folds his arms, says sure, and returns to what he was doing before the interruption. When employees don't participate in setting goals, they aren't committed to accomplishing them. They need to participate in the entire process or management will wind up talking to itself.

Write the steps to achieve each goal along with a timetable and deadline you can review periodically. Make the goals specific and quantifiable so you can measure progress. In addition, write down obstacles you believe you must overcome to reach the goal and how you propose to overcome them. This act alone can simplify your life.

When the problems you must overcome to reach an objective are nebulous, they seem bigger than they really are. We are all afraid of the unknown; imagination can make it seem worse than it actually is. Reducing the future to something known and recognized is a significant step. Writing your goals increases your confidence and decreases your fear. Seeing them on paper with ways to overcome them makes them less formidable.

Those who do not set goals are destined to work for those who do.

Don't select goals that are too high. When you see that you can't reach them, your effort will drop off, and the whole process will become a waste of time. Your goals must be within the capability of your resources.

Goal setting can be a powerful tool. Excellent books, especially for individual goal setting, have been written. (See BOOKS—INSPIRATIONAL BOOKS WORTH READING.)

Going Public or Initial Public Offering (IPO)

WHEN THE FINANCIAL PRESSURE to find growth funds gets stronger, you and your team may be tempted to seek anonymous outside stockholders who will furnish large amounts of money for growth and not really want to take active control of your company.

Solving this problem with only one or more prospective lenders or investors is called a private placement, because the debt or equity is privately placed with a few investors.

When you make this decision, evaluate how much your ego is pushing you. Being founder and principal owner of a publicly held company is heady stuff—at first blush. Believe me, there are many large thorns on this rose bush.

Bringing this offering to a large number of prospective stockholders takes expense and effort as well as the approval of the Securities and Exchange Commission (SEC) if you come under federal statutes. At the least, you need approval from your state agency charged with protecting the investing public. You're definitely in lawyer and Big 6 accounting firm territory with an initial public offering (IPO), whether large or small.

The minimum expense for accountants, lawyers, printing, and fees for an IPO is $100,000 or more. How much more isn't proportional to the amount raised, so if you go for it, go for the biggest amount of money you can reasonably use. Brokerage fees are on top of that.

If such a move is in your future, start getting ready about three years early. Get some outsiders on your board of directors, clean up your sweetheart deals with owners and insiders, and get full audits by a major accounting firm for three years.

Following such an offering, prepare to live in a fish bowl with no financial secrets. Prepare to defend your performance results and policies by comparison with industry standards. And prepare to live with both eyes fixed on quarterly earnings and your price/earnings ratio.

You're no longer the complete master of your business. To meet short-term demands of shareholders, you may compromise on quality. But if you cut product quality by eliminating some operations or materials, you default in your position as guardian of quality.

Employees and insiders are good as shareholders; you continue to deal with informed and understanding people. When you're responsible to outside shareholders with limited knowledge of your business (or sometimes any business), you may waste a lot of time explaining why you did or did not do things.

Shareholders invest for three reasons only—security, dividends, and growth. They are unsentimental and not interested in relationships with the work force, cleanliness of the workplace, or costs of raw materials. They want increased dividends and higher market prices for their stock. They are willing for your desires, direction, and business operating standards to give way to their priorities.

You learn to win by losing.

This isn't a situation most entrepreneurs enjoy. Consider selling the company and starting over with some (but not all) of the money you will receive.

Golden Rule

YOUR BUSINESS LIFE must recognize two golden rules.

The biblical commandment "Do unto others as you would have them do unto you" should control your policies toward customers, employees, friends, and family. This sound policy builds long-lasting relationships and a solid business.

The business world has a second golden rule: "He who has the gold makes the rules." This is true whether the person with the gold is your customer, your investor, your partner, your banker, or yourself. The key question is "Whose money is being spent?" That person has the winning hand.

G

250

*If you take care
of the business,
the business will
take care of you.*

The second golden rule doesn't have the force of a biblical commandment, but it unquestionably reflects strong economic reality.

Government Agencies—Dealing With

IF YOU'RE APPLYING TO a government agency for literature, information, services, or benefits, go there yourself. You can evaluate the situation and answer all the required questions.

If you receive a government questionnaire, call your CPA or outside accountant and ask whether other companies are required to furnish this information. Your accountant can tell you why the government wants this information and what your penalties would be for not complying. You may find that the information

you furnish amounts to an admission that you've violated a government regulation you weren't aware of. Usually, you have little to gain by answering a nonmandatory questionnaire.

Call the agency that sent the questionnaire (a phone number is usually given) and ask why they want this information. Your company name may have come up on the wrong list, or they may have misunderstood what kind of business you're in. Be sure you're in the category or business they think you are in, and find out whether there are penalties for not furnishing the information they're asking you to supply.

When a government examiner or field agent knocks on your door, it usually means trouble. The agent isn't there to congratulate you or thank you for doing something noble. Instruct your receptionist not to answer questions and to ask for a business card. Your receptionist should make small talk—weather talk—with the agent and give no information except the name of the company.

If the agent is from the IRS, you know what he wants. If the agent represents the Occupational Safety and Health Administration (OSHA), Equal Employment Opportunity Commission (EEOC), Americans with Disabilities Act (ADA), Wage and Hours Administration, Environmental Protection Agency (EPA), or any of several other agencies, he is probably there because of a complaint or an alleged violation of regulations. A disgruntled current or former employee may have filed a complaint. Your name seldom comes up on a random checklist.

The smartest way to handle this is to avoid being the first person in your company to deal with the agent. Why? Because from you the agent will expect detailed knowledge and an immediate decision. Until you know more, you won't know what decision to make.

Let someone else, someone with a pleasant personality and a medium level of authority, meet as a fact finder with the agent in the reception room. Train your secretary or a trusted intelligent employee to be prepared for such a visit. This person should ask questions while answering the agent's questions with a noncommittal "I don't know." Anyone the agent specifically asks to talk to is "out of the office this morning." This employee will be less hostile than you might be and can develop a good relationship with the agent that will be helpful later on.

Your employee can always claim ignorance of company policies or facts while gathering information you should know. She should admit nothing and sign nothing; she shouldn't volunteer information the agent doesn't already have. One thing you want to find out is what the agent already knows.

Your employee should ask these questions: Why are you here? Have we done something wrong? Are we in trouble? Is there a complaint or are there charges of a violation against us? What is the charge or alleged violation? Who filed the complaint? May I have a copy? Do you have a warrant to search for something specific?

Your employee should terminate the interview in the reception room, without a plant tour, and say that she will check into the matter and that the appropriate official will get in touch at a later date.

With the IRS, always deal through your accountant or attorney. Don't talk to them yourself; without realizing it, you may stick your foot in your mouth. You can sign the final papers without ever having personal contact with the IRS. Never volunteer information or furnish any documents not specifically approved by your counsel.

251

Your position with these agencies must be that it's your intention to observe the law and comply, if and when you can determine what the law is and what all the facts are. If you don't like what you're hearing, tell the agent you must confirm with your lawyer or accountant what he is telling you before you can agree or accept anything. Get copies of papers the agent wants you to sign so you can get a professional opinion before you sign.

Surely you've heard that the two biggest lies in the business world are "The check is in the mail" and "I'm from the government. I'm here to help you." It hasn't always been thus.

When I started in business in the 1950s, we didn't feel that the government was looking over our shoulders trying to find ways to make business difficult. I remember when the political argument was "Does the federal government have the authority to do this, since all rights not constitutionally granted to the federal government are reserved to the states or individuals?" Perhaps the political changes happening as this book is written will lighten some of the load on small businesses. (See POLITICS OF SMALL BUSINESS.)

I cannot close without saying something good about our government. The Small Business Administration and the Service Corps of Retired Executives (SCORE) do great things for small businesses, including providing financial assistance to companies too weak to qualify for bank loans.

Good luck.

Government Regulations You Should Be Familiar With

WHEN YOU START YOUR BUSINESS, you're probably not aware of the multitude of ways that federal and state requirements will interfere with the ways you'd like to operate.

Unless you learned about these things while you worked for a similar firm, one of the best ways to find the regulations that will most affect you is to ask an accountant familiar with small businesses such as yours. She can tell you which problems you're most likely to run afoul of.

I hope my brief discussion here is useful to warn you and prompt you to find more detailed information elsewhere. This discussion covers only federal laws, which are applicable in all states. An excellent discussion for entrepreneurs about the mine field of your state and most federal regulations is *Starting and Operating a Business in [Your State],* by Michael D. Jenkins and the Entrepreneurial Group of Ernst & Young (Grants Pass, Ore.: Oasis Press). This series of books now has a volume for each of the 50 states. They're rewritten serially; none is over a few years old.

The government agency that enforces any given law will help you understand and comply by sending free literature and explanations of the law. Most entrepreneurs don't have time to ask or study such things until a complaint is filed.

The agencies will still help. Call and tell them you're a small company trying to comply with the law and ask them to please send information so you can comply. Taxpayers pay people to answer your questions and help with problems as long as your intentions are honorable. You don't always need a lawyer.

You do need a federal employer identification number (EIN). This serves the same purpose as a social security number for your business. You will use it on every federal government report. Your state will probably assign you an identification number to use in corresponding with and reporting to them.

The following are some of the laws that will affect you, and the threshold number of employees where you become subject to each, as of 1995. As you add employees, you'll become subject to more government regulations. The theory is that you'll also have more money, resources, and knowledge to handle the increased reporting problems and financial load required.

These are guidelines only. Don't assume that the employment thresholds given below are automatic exemptions. You may be subject to a particular regulation because:

- Every time Congress meets, it passes new laws and changes old ones. The trend is to make old laws applicable to fewer employees.

- Most of these laws have multiple sections or areas of coverage. Some sections apply with different numbers of employees.

- This is only the briefest mention of complex legislation. Details cannot be included here. This is intended as a partial education and warning.

When this book went to press, these federal laws applied if you had the following numbers of employees or more.

None: Lone, Self-Employed Person
The Internal Revenue Service (IRS) requires you to file income tax returns and quarterly estimates of income taxes due during the current year. If you're a proprietorship, report business activities on Schedule C of your individual 1040 return. If you form a partnership or corporation, you'll file a different return and pay a different tax rate.

Your state probably has sales and use taxes that apply to all sales to final consumers. Check with your nearest state collection or reporting office for reporting forms and requirements or see Michael Jenkins' book referred to earlier in this section.

One or More Employees
Withhold income taxes and social security taxes (FICA) from employees' wages from

the first paycheck you issue. Pay the company's FICA portion until your employee reaches the required wage level. Monthly or quarterly returns, accompanied by money, become a real pain, but you must learn to live with it. Do this as long as you have employees.

In most states, report and pay both federal and state unemployment taxes, as well as workers' compensation insurance.

There's no simple way to tell at what point your business is subject to one or more federal or state laws relating to minimum wage, overtime, and child labor. The federal Fair Labor Standards Act (FLSA) includes employee compensation requirements in terms of minimum wage and overtime. Assume that it starts with the first employee. Contact the local wage-and-hour office. Some applicable state laws may be more stringent than federal laws.

Two or More Employees
The Equal Pay Act of 1963 affects almost all employers with two or more employees. It requires equal pay for women and men doing similar work.

Ten or More Employees
The Emergency Planning and Community Right to Know Act of 1986 requires you to report toxic chemicals used in manufacturing and processing.

Eleven or More Employees
The Occupational Safety and Health Act of 1970 (OSHA) applies. Some suggest that this regulatory monster does little

good for workers' safety but costs the economy billions of dollars. The required reporting, record keeping, and sign posting is a nuisance even if your workplace is safe. When you have 11 or more employees, you are subject to arbitrary inspections. Some record keeping and reporting requirements for OSHA start with your first employee.

Fifteen or More Employees
The Civil Rights Act of 1964 applies. It prohibits discrimination based on race, sex, religion, national origin, or disability in employment practices and is the legal basis for quotas and affirmative action. The Equal Employment Opportunity Commission (EEOC) enforces the law. Sexual harassment charges are filed under Title VII. The act doesn't specifically refer to sexual harassment, but the courts and EEOC have long interpreted it to include this form of discrimination.

The Americans with Disabilities Act of 1990 (ADA) is a sweeping, vaguely written act that gives rise to more lawsuits against businesses every year. Originally, it applied to companies with 25 or more employees. During the first year under the law, there were 16,000 complaints and 24,000 alleged job bias cases. The act is being phased in over several years, but the threshold number of employees has been lowered to 15. Title I may require modifying facilities, restructuring work schedules, or transferring qualified disabled workers to vacant positions. The hiring process is restricted by limitations on medical screening of applicants. You can't reject an applicant with an elevated risk of an on-the-job injury or with an existing medical injury that might be aggravated by the demands of the job. The law bans questions on an employment application or during a job interview concerning the applicant's physical or mental condition. Medical exams are still allowed but are greatly restricted.

Twenty or More Employees
The Age Discrimination in Employment Act of 1967 prohibits discrimination in hiring or firing on account of age if a person is 40 years old or more. This act was originally passed to prevent mandatory retirement at age 65, but the age for discrimination was later lowered to 40.

The Older Workers' Benefit Protection Act of 1990 brought employee benefits, pensions, and early retirement incentives under the Age Discrimination in Employment Act.

Fifty or More Employees
The Worker Adjustment and Retraining Notification Act of 1988 (WARN) applies if you lay off either 50 or more employees or one-third of your work force in a 30-day period. This law, passed over President Reagan's veto, requires you to give 60 days' written notice of large-scale layoffs or plant closings.

The Family and Medical Leave Act of 1993 requires employers to offer employees 12 weeks of unpaid leave for the employee's serious illness, after the birth or adoption of a child, or to care for a seriously ill child, spouse, or parent. The employer must also guarantee that the employee will be able to return to the same job or a comparable position after taking such leave.

One Hundred or More Employees
The Employee Retirement Income Security Act of 1974 (ERISA) requires that, if you provide fringe benefits such as group insurance (other than workers' compensation) or other employee welfare plan benefits such as pension or profit sharing, you must comply with ERISA. Compliance isn't simple. Benefit plans include health insurance, long-term disability, group term life insurance, and accidental death insurance plans. Prepare a summary plan description (SPD) to inform all employees covered by any welfare plan you sponsor.

If you're going to sin, sin against God, not the bureaucracy. God will forgive you, but the bureaucracy won't.

—Admiral Hyman G. Rickover

This listing is an oversimplification of complex legal issues. Although incomplete, it's intended to warn you that the more employees you have, the more government regulates the way you conduct business. There are many ways of determining the number of employees, such as the number for a given period during a calendar year, and laws change. Consult with your attorney, accountant, or relevant government agency to see whether a specific law applies to you.

Don't let these regulations scare you— they're just additional hills to climb. Other entrepreneurs have successfully dealt with them. Your outside accountant and the books mentioned above concerning laws in your state are your best sources of early, informal information about regulations and how to avoid trouble. If your company is small, you're not yet a target for fierce enforcement; that honor awaits you after you grow and succeed.

Growing Too Fast—Dangers Of

256

A BUSINESS ANTICIPATING FAST GROWTH should also anticipate financial danger. As sales rapidly increase, liquidity goes down. Many businesses go belly-up during or after a large expansion program because they commit excessive funds before they receive anticipated income. When sales and/or profits aren't forthcoming, newly created financial obligations are difficult or impossible to meet. Examples of dangerous financial obligations are investing too much in inventory without proven resales, making too large an investment in real estate, or financing an advertising campaign that doesn't result in expected sales volume.

The most painful part of growing is the need for more resources, which translates into the need for more money. You'll need it for more working capital (larger inventory, larger accounts receivable) and for more fixed assets to increase productive capacity (machinery, office space, larger building). Part of the money you require will come from vendors in the normal course of operations, but if profits from your increased sales are inadequate to furnish the growth capital you need for the increased volume, look for more money from lenders, partners, or investors to finance your prosperity.

To calculate the resources you need for each additional $100,000 of sales, use your latest annual balance sheet and earnings statement. Use the net sales volume as 100.000 percent (carried to three decimal places). Express all amounts on both the earnings statement and the balance sheet as percentages of net sales. Change the decimal point to a comma and exchange the percent sign for a dollar sign, and you have financial statements that show all assets, liabilities, and costs required for an annual net sales volume of $100,000. These are the amounts you must add to your present financial statements to handle another $100,000 of sales, assuming that the pattern of your operations remains the same.

The footing of total assets on the balance sheet shows the amount of additional assets you'll need to support each additional $100,000 of sales volume. Liability amounts show how much you will need to borrow from your open-account creditors or your lenders by virtue of increased volume. The increase in equity shows the amount you must provide from earnings during the year to avoid going more deeply into debt. Make up a deficiency in the equity section by borrowing, increased investment, or sale of stock.

Think about getting rich slowly.

This calculation assumes that the basic pattern of your operation is stable and that the percentages of assets to sales won't change much. This is normally a valid assumption, except possibly concerning fixed assets. Fixed assets are usually acquired with major financial steps rather than with smooth growth relative to size, such as occurs with accounts receivable and inventory.

Rapid growth can hide internal operating inefficiencies that may not show up

until the growth slows. Rapid growth sometimes stretches the company's internal structure and people almost to the breaking point. Stress and strain during such a growth phase can be extreme. Organizational complexity increases and communication decreases.

The worst thing that can occur is a fast increase in sales volume with a decreasing gross profit margin. The compound effect is to increase your need for capital while decreasing your ability to earn it. You'll be in deep trouble.

If you genuinely have runaway sales—if you have a product or service that is so attractive that customer demand outruns your capacity to supply it—quickly call for professional help. This can be a lucky learning experience, but you may not have time to learn on your own. Get professional production engineers, financial consultants, scheduling or servicing people, or marketing professionals who can help you meet demand profitably while you learn. Don't fumble this once-in-a-lifetime opportunity, and don't be ashamed to ask for expert help.

Make certain that your sales prices contain adequate gross margins, or your company can become committed to runaway low-margin products that can't finance their own growth. The preferred solution for too-rapid sales growth is to raise prices. This will control growth and make you more profitable at the same time. (See EXCESS CAPACITY; SALES PER EMPLOYEE)

Handshake Deals

I DON'T KNOW WHO IS TO BLAME for the demise of this long-standing custom, but it is certainly dead. After a long relationship with some individuals, you may feel comfortable enough to depend upon a word and a handshake, but these days it's exceptional.

Good understandings make good friends. Misunderstandings start when the unexpected happens, and one side thinks it should be handled one way and the other side thinks it should be handled a different way.

258

In the courthouse, a little bit of faded ink is better than the sharpest memory.

You can't afford a lawyer waiting beside a hotline or on your payroll. Consider the following procedures whenever the magnitude or nature of the agreement justifies it.

1. To avoid future misunderstandings, make your oral agreements as precise as possible. State what isn't included and/or covered and what isn't expected to be done as well as what is. If quality or specifications are important, include details. State when and how to conclude or terminate the understanding. If you're contemplating payment of dollars, state what's to be delivered and when, and when the dollars are due.

2. The day of the oral agreement, or the following day without fail, write a confirming letter to the other party expressing as clearly and completely as possible the deal as you understand it. Send two identical copies of the letter, both signed by you. The opening sentence should state, "This letter is to confirm the agreement we have made on _____ (date) concerning _____." State what each of you is supposed to do and when. Do this before you begin to perform your part of the agreement.

   Close by stating, "If you agree that this letter correctly expresses our understanding, please sign both copies and send the second copy back to me. If you do not agree, please make corrections on these pages and initial them, or promptly send me two signed copies of a letter that you think does express our agreement."

   Tell the other person you'll start to perform as soon as you receive the signed letter, or within perhaps five business days if no objections or discrepancies are reported back to you. Such a clear understanding, signed by both parties, with any changes initialed by both, is a legal contract enforceable almost everywhere. If you get no written answer, telephone to get an oral agreement and again request the signed copy.

Even if the other party doesn't sign the confirmation, your position is very strong for two reasons:

1. You asked the other party to notify you promptly if she didn't agree so that the agreement could be corrected and properly expressed in writing. If the person doesn't notify you, silence implies consent.

2. If the person fails to complain after you start to perform your part of the agreement, she has implicitly accepted the terms of the offer by accepting your performance.

In this way, you'll smoke out early misunderstandings and lay a firm foundation for future action. Your position is considerably stronger than the swearing match that results nowadays from some handshake deals.

259

Health—Yours

WHEN YOU'RE YOUNG, you consider your body indestructible—until an accident or the major failure of some part reveals the fallacy. As you grow older, you'll discover that the mind can make a contract the body cannot fulfill. To preserve your body, use common sense and moderation in whatever you do. Spend time in recreation and family enjoyment.

One side benefit of being boss is the opportunity to schedule your own vacations. You can choose several small ones or one long one. After stressful times, a long weekend for R&R is worth years of life. A tired mind is much more likely to make a mistake than a fresh, rested one.

After 40, spend time and effort (sweat) in the care and maintenance of your own physical plant. Hippocrates, the Father of Medicine, noted, "That which is used develops; that which is not used withers away." Any intelligent manager spends time and money making certain that the company's physical assets are maintained in top operating condition. Your own body deserves no less.

Choose recreation that you find fun and mentally relaxing as well as mildly physically demanding. When you're depressed or moody, 30 minutes of mildly strenuous physical exercise of any sort will improve your outlook and lift your spirits, and you'll find the next problem easier to tackle.

You need a full measure of health to successfully complete your plans.

Hiring Good People

NEXT TO MARKETING DECISIONS, people choices are the most important decisions you'll make. The ability to pick the right people is a definite talent. Improve your skill by observing and dealing with the many characters who will come through your doors. A helpful book is *Hiring the Best: A Manager's Guide to Effective Interviewing,* by Martin Yate (Holbrook, Mass.: Bob Adams, 1994). Yate discusses the entire hiring process, including placing want ads.

H
260

In your start-up company, your employees are the company. Good employees make good impressions without a lot of guidance. Inexperienced or incompetent employees consume your precious time in day-to-day management and damage control. Bad employees can cost you everything. In a start-up, every employee is a first-string player. You can afford no one sitting on the bench.

Gauging technical competence and knowledge is usually the easiest part of hiring. It's harder to estimate each candidate's attitude, work habits, potential for personal growth, versatility performing related tasks, and ability to become more comfortable and productive within your organization as time passes.

Search for team players you think will make dependable, steady contributions toward company goals. High motivation is as precious as talent. Screen out the less highly motivated and discard phonies. Think about possible layoffs; don't hire anyone who isn't necessary. Make sure you're comfortable with the people you hire because you'll be working closely with them either technically or financially. (See QUESTIONS FOR INTERVIEWING PROSPECTIVE EMPLOYEES.)

Ask applicants to fill out your application form, even if they have a résumé (it may have been prepared by others). You want the information and the applicant's signature on your form, which should include permission for you to verify all data and to discharge the employee if incorrect information is given, no matter when it's discovered. The applicant's signature should also waive objections for present or future drug tests, with discharge for refusal, and recognize that employment is at the will of the employer. Include permission to check on previous employment history, credit rating, and legal and criminal history. Ask for a current home address as well as the last address before that. The application form should include all the information you want that you're legally entitled to ask.

Most states allow testing for attitude and personality. Look for acceptable validated tests. All states allow testing for job-related skills and capacity. A physical exam sometimes may not be required until after a job offer, which may be made contingent upon passing an acceptable physical and drug test.

During your interview, encouraging candidates to speak is more important than making them listen to you for any length of time. At the close of the interview, make sure applicants get a chance to ask questions about the company in general or the position in particular. Ask them to tell you something about themselves. Get permission to check references from candidates you're most interested in. (See QUESTIONS TO ASK WHEN CHECKING REFERENCES.) If you're seriously considering the candidate, set up a final interview with the employee who will become the candidate's immediate supervisor.

Candidates come from several sources: friendly inquiry, friends of present or past employees, employment agencies, outplacement firms, or ads placed in trade publications or newspapers. If you're hiring to fill a senior position, promote someone from within if possible.

> *Whether the next employee hired in your department becomes your assistant, your equal, or your boss depends on how well you do this job.*

Employment agencies are a mixed bag. Some specialize in only one industry or skill, such as office workers or truck drivers. Agencies where the applicant pays the fee have as their only incentive to get as many applicants as possible on somebody's payroll, and they'll send you every applicant who can find your address, often without doing the pre-screening needed to save your time.

Agencies that expect the employer to pay the fee (anywhere from 10 to 25 percent of one year's salary) want to please you. They screen more selectively and waste less of your time.

A dependable employment agency's strength should be selecting the applicants most suitable for your needs through testing and interviewing. You can do everything they're doing unless they earn their fee by saving your time.

261

If you don't mind spending a lot of time interviewing, run an ad in the most widely read local newspaper. Describe your position in as much detail as possible. Request résumés and cover letters that include salary or pay and an outline of the candidate's skills most applicable to this job. The cover letter in the reply is usually written by the applicant and is a good indication of the person's thinking.

The newspaper can supply a blind box number that will keep you from being annoyed by a lot of telephone inquiries. Consider giving a fax number. Discourage phone calls from applicants until you're down to the last 10 to 15 candidates.

In normal times, you'll receive many résumés. Either you or a delegated person can weed out the obviously over- or under-qualified. Short telephone interviews to clarify omitted or unclear items or pay information will further narrow the field of candidates. In-depth phone interviews by you, the supervisor, or a knowledgeable employee may save further time. Finally, call in for interviews those most likely to fit your situation.

As a consultant, I've seen résumés submitted by people who were fired by a previous employer who was also a client. I was astounded to read all the great things they accomplished while employed there. Being fired was never mentioned.

Government agencies maintain employment offices at no cost to either employer or employee. The quality of candidates varies widely. Generally, applicants for professional positions don't apply through a government agency. Forty Plus is a national organization with chapters in large cities that helps managerial employees over 40 find a new job or make a career change.

Your principal input to this hiring process is your judgment of character and fit within your organization. Delegate the time-consuming activities in this process to others.

How Are You Doing Compared with Industry Standards?

SINCE COMPETITORS DON'T EXCHANGE confidential financial information, you will have difficulty comparing your performance with others in your industry. Fortunately, general yardsticks are available to measure yourself against.

If you give a bank or credit agency your financial statements, they quickly compare your performance with similar firms in your industry. The principal source of this information is Robert Morris Associates (One Liberty Place, Philadelphia, PA 19103), commonly called RMA. Their annual publication, *RMA Annual Statement Studies,* summarizes financial data gathered from credit sources during the preceding year.

Information is acquired and classified as follows. Each reporting bank or credit agency removes names and other individual identification from financial statements they receive, but identifies them by the federal government's Standard Industrial Classification system (SIC numbers). Your four-digit SIC number appears at the top of the first page of your federal tax return.

Basic classifications are manufacturing, wholesaling, retailing, services, agriculture, contractors, and other. All government business statistics are classified into these same groupings.

To make such diverse financial statements comparable, they are reduced to what is called *common-size* or *common-denominator* financial statements. For balance sheets, *total assets* is considered 100 percent, and all subdivisions of assets appear as a percentage of that total. For operating statements, *net sales* is considered 100 percent. The breakdown into gross profit, operating expenses, operating profit, and so on, appears as percentages of net sales. Only broad groupings of assets and expenses can be provided.

Within each SIC classification included (about 450), you must find the one that most nearly describes your principal business operations. Reporting businesses are further classified by size of total assets from small to large in six size groupings. All common and necessary operating ratios are computed and shown.

To show industry trends, comparable summary information for the last five years is included. The same information is also shown sorted by sales volume from small to large in five categories. All information in each classification is spread across two facing pages.

For people unfamiliar with financial statements and ratios, the annual book contains definitions and detailed explanations of all the data, as well as how to compute liquidity, debt coverage, leverage, profit, and operating ratios. The explanations are interesting and educational. I recommend them to you if you are unfamiliar with such things.

Your banker will probably let you look at a current copy of *RMA Annual Statement Studies,* or you may order a copy yourself from the publisher. Your local library probably has one. It's neither secret nor restricted.

Your comparisons will be valid only after you've been in business long enough for your operations to stabilize. The ratios that swing wildly during your survival stage obviously aren't stable enough for significant comparisons.

To make your comparison (the way your bank or credit source will), do the following:

1. From your tax return or the index and descriptions of each industry, select the SIC number that most nearly describes your operation. Find this page in the RMA book. Find the column where companies have total assets comparable to yours. The percentages in this column, representing averages from the number of reporting companies indicated, are the numbers you're going to compare your operations with. In the accompanying illustration (figure 5), the RMA percentages appear in column 4.

2. Regroup items on your most recent annual financial statements into the same summary groupings used by the RMA reports, and total each group. Round off everything to the nearest $1,000. Because of rounding, your totals may miss adding with complete precision in the last digit. Your amounts are shown in column 1.

3. Convert your balance sheet to percentages by dividing each group total by your total assets. Round to the

Your Financial Statements

(Dollar figures in thousands)

	(1) Actual dollars	(2) Your dollars distributed according to RMA percentages	(3) Your dollars as percent
BALANCE SHEET			
ASSETS			
Cash and cash items	$ 10	$ 90	1.0%
Trade accounts receivable	247	361	23.5%
Inventories	495	231	47.2%
Other current assets			
Total current assets	$ 752	$ 691	71.7%
Fixed assets—net	290	293	27.6%
Intangible assets		4	
Other noncurrent assets	7	61	0.7%
Total assets	$1,049	$1,049	100.0%
LIABILITIES			
Notes pay—short term	$ 61	$ 111	5.8%
Current maturities L/T/D		31	
Trade payables	253	147	24.1%
Income taxes payable	23	16	2.2%
Other current liabilities		43	
Total current liabilities	$ 337	$ 348	32.1%
Long-term debt	467	152	44.5%
Deferred taxes		6	
Other noncurrent liabilities		43	
Net worth	245	500	23.4%
Total liabilites	$1,049	$1,049	100.0%
EARNINGS STATEMENT			
Net sales	$1,614	$1,614	100.0%
Cost of goods sold	1,092	1,052	67.7%
Gross profit or margin	$ 522	$ 562	32.3%
Operating expenses	383	489	23.7%
Operating profit	$ 139	$ 71	8.6%
All other expenses	50	27	3.1%
Profit before taxes	$ 89	$ 44	5.5%

Figure 5. Use of Common-Denominator Financial Statements

Your Financial Forecasts
(Dollar figures in thousands)

(4) Percent from RMA	(5) All per- centages of net sales	(6) For $2,000 sales	(7) For $3,000 sales	(8) For $4,000 sales
8.6%	.6%	$ 12	$ 18	$ 24
34.4%	15.3%	306	459	612
22.0%	30.7%	614	921	1228
0.9%				
65.9%	46.6%	$ 932	$1,398	$1,864
27.9%	18.0%	360	540	720
0.4%				
5.8%	.4%	8	12	16
100.0%	65.0%	$1,300	$1,950	$2,600
10.6%	3.8%	$ 76	$ 114	$ 152
3.0%				
14.0%	15.7%	314	471	628
1.5%	1.4%	28	42	56
4.1%				
33.2%	20.9%	$ 418	$ 627	$ 836
14.5%	28.9%	578	867	1156
.6%				
4.1%				
47.6%	15.2%	304	456	608
100.0%	65.0%	$1,300	$1,950	$2,600
100.0%	100.0%	$2,000	$3,000	$4,000
65.2%	67.7%	1,354	2,031	2,708
34.8%	32.3%	$ 646	$ 969	$1,292
30.3%	23.7%	474	711	948
4.4%	8.6%	$ 172	$ 258	$ 344
1.7%	3.1%	62	90	124
2.7%	5.5%	$ 110	$ 165	$ 220

Figure 5. Continued

nearest one-tenth of one percent. The total of percentages should be 100.0, give or take a tenth. This has been done in column 3.

4. Convert your earnings statement to percentages by dividing each group total by your net sales. I have added a line for cost of goods sold. Additions and subtractions from bottom to top should total within 0.1 of 100.0 percent. This is also shown in column 3. Notice that the bottom number is profit before taxes—there's no meaningful way to average income taxes.

266

Your financial statements are now converted to percentage or common-denominator form. Compare your percentages in columns 3 and 4 with the national average percentages.

To make your comparison in terms of dollars rather than percentages, do this, as shown in figure 5, column 2:

1. Multiply the RMA average percentages (column 4) for each category by your total assets (column 1). This converts these RMA percentages to your amount of dollars, redistributing your assets on the RMA percentages. The result is in column 2.

2. Do the same thing with your operating statement by using RMA percentages times your actual net sales. Put these numbers alongside the operating-statement figures.

3. By comparing column 1 (your actual dollars) with column 2 (your total dollars redistributed by RMA averages), you can see where your operation differs from the national averages in terms of dollars.

On a separate sheet (or at the bottom of column 4), list the RMA liquidity and operating ratios. Compute the comparable ones from column 1 to see what your actual ratios are. Are you doing better than the national averages, or worse?

Do you want a quick and dirty financial model of your company that will show your future financial statements at any given future sales level? Convert your balance-sheet amounts to percentages of your own net sales, not percentages of total assets, by dividing balance-sheet amounts in column 1 by net sales in column 1. This has been done in column 5.

Your total assets are usually about 35 to 65 percent of your net annual sales, depending upon how asset intensive your business is and how rapidly your working capital turns over.

When you go through this process, you'll have a complete financial model of your company, as it now operates, in terms of percentage of net sales. You can then apply these percentages to any given sales volume and see your financial future. Figure 5 multiplies these percentages in column 6 by $2,000,000 sales volume; those in column 7 by $3,000,000, and those in column 8 by $4,000,000.

This financial model assumes that

your operation is stable, that your ratios and relationships vary within narrow limits, and that the financial pattern of the future will be like the base year. The results will be accurate if inventory turnover rates, as well as accounts receivable and payable turnover rates, remain about the same. Generally these things are true of growth-stage companies.

Have you ever noticed that the harder you work, the luckier you get?

Test this assumption if you have data for over three years of operations. Reduce those years to common-denominator percentages. Then compare all years' percentages and ratios.

Use this set of annual financial statements (expressed in percentages of net annual sales) as a simple financial model of your company. It shows the percentage of net sales dollars required to support any sales volume you choose to call 100 percent.

The biggest question you want answered is: "Can we finance a sales volume of $_____? If so, by what year?" The model will show short-term liabilities plus long-term liabilities plus equity. You must provide this total amount of financing for your future sales volume. It's immaterial (except for interest payments) what proportion of this total is short term, long term, or equity. The longer you have to build up equity (compute this amount), the less you have to borrow. If you can't earn enough, try selling stock. But that total amount must be provided from one of those three sources, or your operating ratios must drastically improve. Run your loan ratios and see how much you can borrow. The rest must be earned or raised by selling equity.

Then all you have to do is figure out how to sell that much or how you want to finance that kind of volume.

Human Resources Department

YOU WON'T HAVE A FULL-TIME human resources (HR) person until you're large enough to do a lot of hiring. But as soon as you have your first employee, begin to keep records. The number of records required for each employee and the information to go in them has increased enormously in the last 10 years.

You're going to be interviewing, hiring, and firing your first 20 or more employees yourself, so you must be familiar with government requirements. Sooner or later you can assign an employee with an interest in people to do the HR work and keep the files, in addition to other assignments.

Because of so many detailed requirements, this job isn't for an untrained person. As soon as you've selected your HR person, send her to a seminar or training session and encourage her to join an association of HR people. Subscribe to magazines or periodicals for further education. Buy some books on the subject.

You'll also need a highly qualified outside consultant who can answer questions, give advice, and hold your HR person's hand as you cope with your first Equal Employment Opportunity Commission (EEOC) complaint that the company wrongfully failed to hire or wrongfully discharged someone.

Unfortunately, you're more likely to be involved in a legal proceeding for these reasons than in any other type of lawsuit, except maybe a traffic ticket. (See HIRING GOOD PEOPLE; FIRING PEOPLE— AVOIDING FUTURE TROUBLE.) Fortunately, because of necessity and demand, many qualified consultants and firms are available. If you are in a large enough town to have the choice of several professionals, interview them and ask about their training and credentials. This profession is a new one; certification and skill levels haven't really been worked out.

All government requirements protect the employee, but you can make sure the application contains provisions in your favor, such as authorizing you to verify all statements and to require a preem-

ployment physical exam and lawful (according to your state) current or future drug tests. It should also include the applicant's understanding that he may be discharged if any statements in the application are found to be untrue, no matter when the discovery is made.

Procedures and requirements for hiring and firing are too numerous to present here, but most of your rights and obligations begin with the application for employment and the hiring of the successful applicant. Get an approved application form from every employee, including the good friend you hired first. "Approved" means that the application complies with current government regulations and contains all the waivers listed in HIRING GOOD PEOPLE.

You can dream, create, design, and build the most wonderful place in the world, but it requires people to make the dream a reality.

—Walt Disney

Standard HR forms are available in large office-supply firms. Get a healthy supply. Record changes in pay, job title, and number of dependents. Record reprimands or other disciplinary actions, injuries, and requests. Place them in each employee's personnel file.

Every company has two
organizational structures:
the formal one
on the charts;
the other is the
living relationship of
the men and women
in the organization.

—Harold Geneen

If you have the right HR person, she will easily gain the confidence of your employees. This person should roam your premises enough to be seen by every employee at least twice a week and have opportunities for brief but friendly conversations with employees. This person is really your safety valve, giving any disgruntled employee a chance to voice a complaint to a higher company official.

The HR person should be diplomatic enough to explain company policies without admitting mistakes or saying anything detrimental about the company. She should take any serious or repeated complaint to the proper supervisor, again diplomatically, to avoid crossing lines of authority or causing resentment against the complainer.

In addition to keeping all the files, the HR person or department is usually responsible for scheduling or recording vacations and training, and for working with the incentive or bonus program, suggestion system, administration of health insurance, 401k savings plans, and individual retirement accounts (IRAs). Although not really related, safety training is frequently assigned to the HR department.

The HR person or department usually reports to the senior administrative officer in the company or sometimes directly to the president. Maintaining employee morale, motivation, and enthusiasm is the CEO's job. A good HR person can do great things to help accomplish this.

For small companies, the HR Press (Box 28, Fredonia, NY 14063) handles a complete line of software and books for human resources management and employee training.

269

Incubators for Start-up Businesses

THE OBJECTIVE OF INCUBATORS is to help start-up and emerging enterprises beat the high odds against business success. They're designed and operated to help entrepreneurs hatch their fledgling ideas into thriving businesses. Most incubators have a success ratio of about 80 percent, far above that of new businesses in general. One of their functions is sometimes to dissuade or discourage budding entrepreneurs who aren't yet ready or whose idea isn't yet fully thought out or economically sound.

In this country, there are about 500 incubators of all types, principally in large cities. Most are nonprofit organizations, affiliated with or sponsored by city, county, or state government or an educational institution. A small number are privately owned, operated for profit. They're designed specifically for start-up and survival-stage businesses. They aren't restricted to companies that use high technology; they're suitable for almost any business but retail operations or medium or heavy manufacturing. Some incubators have waiting lists.

An incubator has facilities to provide lower-than-market-price administrative offices, warehouse or light manufacturing space, and shared business services. Another valuable ingredient is counseling by business people. Counseling may be classroom instruction, informal discussions by peer groups (which could start your own CEO roundtable), or one-on-one conferences between the director or counselor and the individual entrepreneur.

Counseling can be the most important part of the program at the incubator, although reduced-price facilities help ease survival-stage financial problems. The individuals of the Service Corps of Retired Executives (SCORE), who office with the Small Business Administration, give free advice and counseling to start-up operations but provide no working facilities. (See SERVICE CORPS OF RETIRED EXECUTIVES (SCORE).)

Some incubators are merely industrial parks with a few shared services but little counseling or financial assistance. Talk to other tenants as well as management to be sure the incubator provides the services you want.

If you move into an incubator, you'll be one of 10 to 20 or more businesses using the facilities in common and paying your share of expenses—copy machine, telephone answering service, receptionist, fax machine, typing, secretarial service, computers, conference rooms, business reference libraries, a coffee bar, and shipping, mailing, and receiving rooms.

Once your business is on its feet and running with several employees, the incubator expects you to get quarters elsewhere while it makes room for another start-up business. The time you're allowed to remain varies among incubators but ranges up to three years. By that time you should be on your feet and able to cope with real-world rent and expenses.

To find an incubator near you, contact the National Business Incubation Association, 20 East Circle Drive, Suite #190, Athens, OH 45701-3751, 614-593-4331.

Indispensable Person

IN A SURVIVAL-STAGE COMPANY, the founder is indispensable. If he dies or quits, the company usually goes under.

Work your way out of this situation as fast as you can. You could become injured or develop a long illness. You want your company to survive and grow, if possible, or at least to become salable. Preparing qualified back-up people is what big businesses call depth in management, but growth-stage companies cannot afford enough chiefs to have any spares.

Here lies a man who knew how to enlist into his service people better than himself.

—Andrew Carnegie

This means that you must build a team of cross-trained, skilled employees. Designate who will be in charge and arrange as best you can for succession and handling of authority in your absence. You may want to split your assignments to two trusted employees, one to take care of financial matters (check signing), the other to run operations.

Some insecure employees try to make themselves indispensable by hoarding important information. They might be the only ones who know how to perform an essential operation and be reluctant to share or train anyone else. Train other employees or work your way out of these situations as quickly as you can.

In the early days of computers, one of my clients discharged an employee. The next day the former employee reappeared and told his boss, "You can't fire me, I'm the only person who can run the computer." The boss asked what the company would have done if the employee had been killed in an automobile accident. "Then you'd have to get somebody else." The boss replied, "We're going to play like you died." (See "OR ELSE".)

I

271

Insolvency and Going Broke

EXPECT TO FIGHT FOR A LARGER CASH bank account for the rest of your business life, especially if your company is growing. If you're operating profitably, you may be able to keep your cash ahead of the growing demands for more assets.

Being insolvent is technically not the same as going broke, but in the short term, most creditors aren't interested in the fine points of the difference. Insolvency is the first step along the way to going broke.

Your company is solvent or liquid if it has cash on hand. You are insolvent if you're unable to pay your bills because you lack available cash funds, even though you may have plenty of nonliquid assets. Technically, you go broke when your liabilities exceed your assets, thereby producing a negative net worth. Liquidating the company at this point still won't pay all the creditors, much less leave anything for stockholders.

Every month that your company operates at a loss, the amount of that loss will be missing from your available cash almost immediately. If losses continue, they will sooner or later wipe out your net worth, at which point your liabilities exceed your assets and you've gone broke. (See GETTING OUT—HOW TO ESCAPE THIS FINANCIAL MESS.)

Make sure that periods of insolvency are short and temporary. Temporary insolvency can happen because you bought too much machinery or inventory, or because payroll, taxes, or note payments have a stronger claim on available cash than open-account creditors. There could be any number of reasons why there's not enough cash, but the result is the same. Cash management and cash forecasting are crucial to avoid insolvency.

A liquid asset is one you can quickly convert into cash. Liquid assets usually mean current accounts receivable, marketable stocks and bonds, or quickly salable inventory. Liquid assets don't include real estate, machinery and equipment, furniture and fixtures, uncollectible accounts receivable, or old, slow-moving inventory. If your customers don't pay your accounts receivable when they should, you can't pay accounts payable when you should.

The cutting edge is also the bleeding edge.

Going broke is no fun. It's tragic. It usually happens slowly while management does everything it can to pull a rabbit out of the hat and keep the company going. The fight is to buy time while you try to find more cash or identify the operating problem and work on solutions.

Since you can't pay all creditors, the question is which ones to pay. Your final choice comes down to this: "If you can't put me out of business immediately, you don't get paid." In the survival stage of my business, I used this policy for almost a year.

The worst insolvencies occur when, in a short-lived boom or near the end of one, you obligate yourself for purchase note payments that you can't make during a market downturn. This is always the danger in expansion.

Many companies go broke from overexpansion, expansion at the wrong time, or taking such a large forward step that their established base cannot financially support it in bad times. In that event, your objective is to stay in business until the general economy gets better or until you can figure out a way to make your own situation better.

Insurance

INSURANCE IS AN ESSENTIAL SERVICE, a necessary cost of doing business. What kinds and how much do you need? How much can you afford? The basic managerial decision for each type of coverage is whether to take a small, known loss today (the cost of the premium) in order to be reimbursed for a larger loss that might or might not occur during the policy period. No one policy or premium covers all risks. Each policy covers only the specific risks described in the insurance contract.

You need some insurance for your own peace of mind. People who lend you money require insurance to be certain that your property loss won't lead to their loss. State or federal law requires employee-related insurance.

But you can't afford all the insurance necessary to insure yourself against all possible losses. The risk you took when you went into business can't be covered by insurance; you take some risks just by getting out of bed every morning. Balance your present insurance cost against possible future losses. You can't always guess correctly. Losses are never expected or planned for. In the survival stage, you can afford only the coverage required by law and by mortgages—losses that could put you out of business if they occurred.

Any insurance agent will make an insurance survey for you at no charge and recommend policies and coverages she thinks you should have. Get a second opinion, too; another agent will make somewhat different recommendations. The size of the deductible, as well as endorsements that add or limit certain expensive risks, can considerably reduce your premium costs.

After your surveys, select only one local agent to handle your fire and casualty insurance needs, since you want

I

273

maximum responsibility for your insurance to rest with one individual. A general agent can't handle some specialized types of insurance, such as health and hospitalization.

Insurance required by state or federal law includes unemployment insurance and workers' compensation for injuries on the job. Automobile and other liability insurance may also be required.

Banks or mortgage lenders require that you insure them against loss or damage to the mortgaged property. This usually means fire, theft, windstorm, flood, and other casualty or comprehensive coverage. They require that their name be included as an insured party in the policy and that copies of notices, such as expirations and cancellations, be sent to them.

Other insurance is usually optional. If some insurable risk threatens the life of your business, cover it. Generally, coverages are for loss of value to owned assets (equipment, fixtures, inventory, trucks, automobiles, and so forth) or liabilities that your activities or employees create in the course of their employment. These include coverage for fire, windstorm, flood, theft, burglary, robbery, embezzlement, employee dishonesty, fidelity bonds, performance bonds, product liability, vehicle damage, and other possibilities.

After you and your agent decide what risks to cover, choose the company or policy that charges the least for the greatest coverage and smallest deductible. You want flexibility to tailor the policy to meet your particular needs by inserting or deducting desired provisions. As far as possible, avoid overlapping coverage.

Liability insurance and the need to provide for it have changed radically in recent years. Seek experienced guidance. Employee health insurance policies and requirements are in such a state of legal and political flux right now that no comment made in this book can be reliable. Consult with your insurance agent; but remember that liability and health insurance is a specialty field that the fire and casualty insurance person doesn't handle and knows nothing about.

Business interruption insurance is nice to talk about but is generally too expensive for small companies. Business-related life insurance on the life of the owner-manager or other key employees is in the same category.

Practice risk assessment and reduction by installing fire alarms, sprinkler systems, and safety equipment. To reduce your need for insurance, transfer the risk of damage to someone else whenever you can by the terms of your purchase or sales contract. Progressive insurance companies, agents, and your lawyer can help you do this. It's particularly important if you work extensively with contracts, operating instructions, warranties, or written documentation in your business.

Always notify your insurance agent as soon as a loss occurs, orally at first, then by written confirmation. Include details. Make sure you can document the loss for reimbursement purposes by keeping careful accounting records, inventory listings, police reports, employment applications, notices, photographs, and so forth, stored offsite to prevent destruction by the same fire.

File reports for employee-related insurance. Fight every claim against you that's unjustified under your state laws. Future premiums will reflect your past losses and claims.

When you have a loss, an insurance adjuster will visit you with a settlement proposal. The amount of partial loss is always difficult to ascertain and agree on. If a major amount is involved, consider consulting a professional in this field before you settle.

There aren't too many books on insurance, but a suitable one is *The Buyer's Guide to Business Insurance,* by Don Bury and Larry Heischman (Grant's Pass, Ore.: Oasis Press/PSI Research, 1994).

Intangible Assets—Capitalization Of

THESE EXPENDITURES INCLUDE organization expense (legal and professional fees and costs to get the company legally up and running), patents, copyrights, research and development costs, design costs, good will, customer lists, and so forth.

Intangible assets may or may not be listed on a balance sheet. They may or may not have future value. They may or may not be salable. If they're on the balance sheet, they're listed near the bottom, under other assets or intangible assets.

They may be listed on the balance sheet only when they've been paid for with identifiable cash payments. To appraise a "customer list" or "going business value" or "good will" that hasn't been purchased by identifiable cash payments is an amateurish attempt to sprinkle perfume on your balance sheet to make it smell better.

Deciding whether to capitalize these expenditures on the balance sheet or charge them off against current income is a managerial choice that must comply with Generally Accepted Accounting Principles (GAAP). That decision does not, however, have to conform to IRS rules for deducting such expenditures on tax returns. The IRS doesn't have to obey GAAP rules, even though you do.

When these expenditures are capitalized, they must be amortized or written off by monthly charges over the period of their expected value. Patents, for example, have a statutory life of 20 years from date of application.

Even though your already poor operating statements will look worse, it's best to realistically charge off these expenses as you pay them rather than capitalizing them now to be amortized later against future income. Since capitalizing these expenses makes current profits look better, small companies are sorely tempted to do so.

Bankers, creditors, investors, and shareholders are always highly suspicious of intangible assets recorded on your financial statements, even though you bought and paid for something you think will ultimately produce income for the company. Practice has shown that you often pay for an expensive education called experience. Bankers and investors mentally deduct the total of intangible assets from your net worth to produce what's called *tangible net worth,* a more realistic appraisal of the company.

Instead of worrying about the realistic value of intangible assets, spend more time worrying about intangible liabilities, presently unknown or not yet recorded on your balance sheet.

Integrity

WRITTEN LAW IS THE MINIMUM moral standard of ethics acceptable in a Judeo-Christian society. However, people may obey all written laws but still have no credibility or integrity. Most people outside of prison have broken no criminal laws, but that doesn't mean they are honest or have integrity.

Having integrity means doing the things that earn the trust of your family, friends, employees, and customers. Integrity must be demonstrated and consistently performed at the top of the organization; it must be obvious in the corporate culture. It mustn't be a veneer, or employees and customers will soon see through it.

The best tests of integrity that I know are your answers to the following questions: "After an oral agreement with this person, do I feel confident that I can turn my back and know that he will do exactly as stated, and in no way take advantage of my inattention?" "Has everything this person told me in the past turned out to be completely true, with no explanations or half-truths?" "Have this person's actions conformed to his statements?" "When doubtful questions occur, is she reasonable in resolving them?"

Do the right thing, because it is the right thing to do.

—Harry Truman

Interest Rates

THE GAME OF BORROWED FINANCING means borrowing at a low rate and using the money to earn a higher rate. This difference strengthens your company. Most years I was in business, I continually borrowed at 6 to 8 percent, but I earned a 20 percent return.

Earned rate of return is a function of your entrepreneurial and managerial skill. The rate at which you borrow is almost, but not totally, beyond your control. Banking is competitive; you can find variations in quoted rates as much as 1½ percent. Frequent jumping around for small rate variations is self-defeating because your banking relationship involves confidence and credibility. In 24 years, I changed banks three times.

Your loan will be quoted as 1½ to 3 percent above prime, depending on the bank's assessment of the risk involved in loaning to you. Prime rate is the rate charged to the most creditworthy companies. Inquire to clarify the definition of "prime." New York City prime? *Wall Street Journal* prime? Prime established by your individual bank? Another definition? Prime will probably be as established by your individual bank for its local use. Your local bank probably has no Fortune 500 customers to lend to. It never used to happen, but nowadays bank competition sometimes results in loans to highly qualified local companies at below-prime rates.

If you're satisfied that you're getting a reasonable deal, sign your name and then work like hell. Other choices are to find another bank, do without the money, or cancel your growth project. Personal endorsements are required of all survival-stage and almost all growth-stage companies.

When inflation raises interest rates, this game plan won't work. My first home mortgage was at 4½ percent. During the Carter administration, prime interest rates reached 21½ percent. I cried, paid my loan down as far as I could, and paid interest on the rest.

Internal Controls

"INTERNAL CONTROLS" ARE ACCOUNTING buzzwords for the procedures and policies you have set up your company to prevent dishonesty, theft, and embezzlement.

One of the most basic rules is to separate two closely related parts of a procedure or transaction so that two people would have to agree or collude to commit and cover up any dishonesty. For example, the employee who reconciles the bank statements each month shouldn't handle deposits or make up checks.

Here are other examples of good internal control procedures.

Cash

- Serially number all checks, purchase orders, and sales invoices.

- Endorse checks for deposit only. Don't presign blank checks.

- Prepare bank reconciliations promptly each month.

Accounts Payable

- Separate approval of invoices from payment. Verify delivery ticket and price before issuing checks for those invoices.

- Clearly cancel or perforate invoices that have been paid so they cannot be processed again.

Accounts Receivable

- Separate recording the sale from the charge to the customer's account.

- Separate collecting money for sales or credit from posting the credit to the sales or customer's account.

- Require multiple signatures on checks signed by anyone other than yourself, especially those with large dollar amounts.

- Immediately investigate customer complaints of unfilled orders.

- Require managerial approval for unusual discounts or bad debt charge-offs.

- Be suspicious of any unusual activity in an inactive account.

General

- Assign one employee to prepare the payroll and another to issue the checks.

- Require that employees responsible for keeping records take periodic vacations so that a temporary replacement may uncover irregularities.

- Put TV cameras in the storage area to guard against employee theft.

- Require supervisor approval for all time cards or overtime hours to be paid.

- Separate the physical handling of an asset and the record keeping for it.

The type of business you're in may have special problems, such as loss of inventory, that require special procedures. Your accountant will recommend many fraud-preventing procedures. Your annual audit, if you have one, should include a private letter to management that discusses and recommends internal control procedures, along with other significant accounting matters. (See DISHONESTY, THEFT, AND EMBEZZLEMENT.)

Internal Revenue Service (IRS) Is a Preferred Creditor

UNLESS YOU DO ALL YOUR BUSINESS on a cash basis, you'll quickly learn your rights and obligations as both creditor and debtor. You can't avoid being both. You're the debtor to your bank, your suppliers, your employees (in the period between paychecks), possibly your investors, and a host of other people. You're the creditor to your customers and others who owe you money.

Payroll checks are sacred to your employees and mustn't be late. Bank-note payments are an obligation on a written note; if you expect to borrow money in the future, these payments must be paid on time, regardless.

When business is bad and cash is tight, the easiest way to ease the pain is to defer paying your open account creditors for a short time. If the time gets too long, some will complain. Decide which ones to pay first and whether to make partial payments or total. Over time, you'll learn to handle this problem well. You'll learn which creditors will wait and work with you, and which won't.

One who won't work with you is the IRS. Once it knows you're not paying promptly, as required by law, it has the power to levy (seize) the funds in your bank account, padlock your doors without notice, and take immediate possession of all your assets. That means you can be out of business in less than an hour.

The IRS has creditor's rights and collection methods no one else has. Since the government depends upon collecting taxes for its continued solvency, it has provided for itself, by law, certain rights and collection procedures that put its claims above all others, including payroll and the owner.

Play by the rules. You'll sleep better at night.

Don't consider payroll taxes an open-account payable that can be deferred a little while longer if necessary. These taxes, part of the payroll process, must be paid along with the payroll. The IRS does not view this money as yours. It's your employees' money, the same as their payroll, because you deducted most of it from their paychecks as withholding and FICA taxes. As trustee for the government, you possess this money only long enough to transmit it with the proper tax report form to your bank as required by law.

The tremendous volume of paper and cash that goes to banks and to the IRS makes it difficult for them to immediately detect that you've missed one or more payments, but within a short time the

I

279

IRS's computer system will pinpoint you as a late or nondepositor. It will react with vigor, and maybe with the powers and actions described above. Although it usually notifies you by letter, demanding immediate payment, it claims it's not required to do so, because you are responsible for knowing the law.

The moral of the story is this: Pay withholding and FICA taxes to your depository at the same time you make the payroll.

Required quarterly deposits on federal income taxes don't get the IRS as excited as payroll taxes do, but almost. These funds aren't trusteed funds. IRS enforcement powers are the same, but they're usually more lenient and understanding. Occasionally, they will even negotiate the amount due and terms of payment on income taxes.

They have power to examine your records and require proof that no other person or creditor has. For suggestions on how to deal with IRS agents, see GOVERNMENT AGENCIES—DEALING WITH.

One of the surest ways to get the IRS snooping through your financial records is to be late, incomplete, or in violation of their reporting rules. Don't try to use the business to shelter personal expenses, such as paying and deducting as business expenses any significant personal bills, putting personal servants or family members on the company payroll, taking company assets for personal use, or failing to report income. It's painful when you're caught, and it sets a horrible example for employees.

Except under unusual circumstances, even when you win a fight with the IRS, you lose. Be wary of trying.

Inventory

IF YOUR BUSINESS HAS NO INVENTORY, you are blessed. Examples are service businesses, direct-selling operations, intellectual property, consulting, and computer programming.

More accounting sins are committed in the name of inventory than any other asset on the balance sheet. Inventory causes more accounting arguments, because no one can say with precision exactly what an inventory is worth.

If you're in construction, manufacturing, wholesaling, or retailing, your largest single asset is probably your inventory. Managing it better is worth time and money. Management rewards are decreased financial requirements (make more sales from less inventory), less building space required for smaller inventory, better customer service with fresh material and latest styles or models, and less loss from theft or deterioration.

The other side of the coin is that you can't do business from an empty store. Generally, the larger the inventory, the higher the sales volume. Trying to keep old, unsalable merchandise out of your inventory and making every inventory dollar do the work of $1.25 is a never-ending struggle for management.

When you set up your accounting system, a significant decision is which inventory valuation method to use. The same inventory valued by two different methods may give answers differing by as much as 15 percent. Use a valuation method accepted by the IRS for your tax return. Independent CPAs and bankers accept the same methods. If you change methods, you must usually get IRS permission. When you select a valuation method, your objective is to match a cost dollar to a sales dollar for your operating statement, and to place a value on the inventory on hand for balance-sheet purposes.

Valuation is difficult because as purchase prices fluctuate or manufacturing costs vary, every replacement of additional units may be acquired at a different price from the last units received. Following are the more common methods:

- FIFO (First In, First Out) assumes that the first units acquired are the first units sold. This method gives a valuation similar to a moving average value. This is the old, conservative method.

- LIFO (Last In, First Out) matches the cost of most recently purchased

units against current sales, reflecting a current gross margin. The inventory valuation remains low, retaining the cost of the first units ever purchased. LIFO has tax-saving benefits in times of rising prices because it reports lower profits.

- FISH is an apocryphal reference to "First In, Still Here"—true in many inventories but not an accepted method. FINO is also apocryphal—"First In, Never Out"—an item or a price you never want to run out of.

- AVERAGE COST averages the value per unit for all units on hand every time a new receipt or acquisition occurs. That new average value is used for all sales until the next addition.

- STANDARD COST is a cost you develop or compute for a product you make over and over. Use this cost for all transactions, even though actual cost may vary slightly. You always have a variance account for variations from your standard cost. This is common in processing and high-volume manufacturing industries.

- ACTUAL COST is the only method that gives you a true indication of your gross profit on each job if no two jobs are alike. This is used in construction and most service industries.

- RETAIL METHOD tracks the selling prices of all inventory items. The cost

I
281

of what's still on hand is calculated from the total selling prices of all items on hand by a complicated series of calculations involving markups and markdowns by department and departmental gross margin percentages.

Specific industries have developed valuation methods and practices suitable for properly reporting their income. Your accountant will footnote the method you use on your audited balance sheet. At least once each year, it's customary to take a physical inventory to determine the quantity of each item on hand. Compare this actual amount with the recorded and calculated quantities on hand to determine the annual inventory error.

When it's your own money, you tend to spend it more wisely.

Good inventory management requires that you know how many of each item have been sold during a given period, how many are on order, when they're expected, how long before future deliveries a replacement order must be placed, and

what the economical order quantity is. (If you buy the same item from two vendors, you have other problems.) Examine the quality of merchandise you receive; if the ratio of returns to purchases is unfavorable, seek a new supplier. Calculate carrying and ordering costs, economical order quantity, and reorder points.

To conserve cash, consider quantity discounts on purchases, invoice payment terms and how to defer payment, and freight charges. Negotiate with vendors to obtain tighter delivery schedules and slower payment terms. Systematically return excess inventory to suppliers if your industry allows it. Find a way to identify old, slow-moving inventory items. Discard or fire sale slow-moving products to reduce carrying costs and improve turnover. Keep your inventory alive, fresh, and churning.

Forecast changes in purchase prices of inventory items. If you expect prices to rise, add inventory. If you can purchase replacements at a lower price, reduce inventory. Be careful to guard against inventory buildup.

Today, it's almost inconceivable that any sizable inventory could be managed without a computer. Sophisticated bar coding is a fast source of accurate inventory information. Specialized software programs manage specific business inventories. In small retail operations, these systems will almost totally manage your inventory by what you sell, including placing orders for replacement merchandise.

Invisible Wall of Management

THE INVISIBLE WALL IS A PSYCHOLOGICAL barrier that prevents some entrepreneurs from growing their companies to a size at which they cannot control everything directly.

Learn to multiply yourself, to get agreed-upon work done by others.

In the survival stage, supervision is direct. The entrepreneur hires everybody, knows everybody, is in the center of all activities directing them, and makes all the decisions. As business increases, more worker hours are needed. The entrepreneur hires a few more people; they all work a few more hours. At this small stage, a driving, controlling owner makes all the decisions and sees that everything gets done properly. But her obsessive drive and need for control (the very things that make her a good entrepreneur!) are the time bombs that keep her from taking the next step.

With further increases in business and employees, operations reach the point where 24 hours a day isn't enough for the entrepreneur to do or to supervise everything that must be done. A growing gap may exist between what's been planned and what actually happens. Decisions don't get made. Problems don't get solved, and customers get unhappy.

Growth stops. Although the entrepreneur does all that personally can be done, frustration sets in. The entrepreneur may be dissatisfied and depressed about the business without being able to pinpoint why. She has run into the invisible wall of management, which can stop further growth.

When the need for a manager becomes apparent, the one-person operator experiences stress and anxiety. Can the other person be trusted? Will this person steal from the company? Will he apply the same standard to the job the owner has? (Probably not; this person isn't the owner.) Frequently, these psychological difficulties are major stumbling blocks.

When pressed to hire a skilled professional manager, some entrepreneurs reluctantly do so but circumscribe that person's duties or authority so that failure is built in. When failure occurs, the entrepreneur tells herself and everyone else, "I tried a professional manager, and it just didn't work—I've got to do it all myself."

Of course, nothing says the business has to grow any larger. If you're at this point—if financial status and your ego

I

283

are satisfied—use earnings to pay off all debts, and enjoy. This could be the life of independence and ease you wanted.

Most likely, you desire further growth and financial strength. Fortunately, this wall is neither impenetrable nor unavoidable. But you've got to identify it as the root problem causing inefficiencies, confusion, and lost opportunities.

You can raise or move the invisible wall if you develop additional knowledge and skills. When you recognize it, it's no longer invisible. Attend seminars, short courses, graduate schools, read books, join CEO roundtables. Your mentor, if you have one, will spot the problem before you do.

Entrepreneurs who prepare for this problem pass over it with stronger operations both before and after the size-level change that stops those who are unprepared.

Prevention is the same as the cure, except that it begins before the problem

> *Unless you're going to be a violinist or a safecracker, your success will probably depend upon other people.*
>
> —William McGowan

becomes severe. Start early to multiply yourself through others you've selected, trained, and motivated. In the survival stage, just one or two trusted supervisors are all you need to keep things going smoothly. Don't try to do it all, even if you can.

I

Kiting Checks

DON'T DO IT. This practice is more dangerous than walking a soapy tightwire in a rainstorm.

If you don't know what it is, I'll not give you any additional information.

Know Your Cost of Doing Business

YOUR ACCOUNTING SYSTEM MUST MATCH a cost-to-produce amount to each invoice or income-producing transaction. You must be able to know and analyze the margin produced by subtracting the cost of goods sold from the invoice amount.

The cost of goods sold includes direct costs required to produce the product or service (basically raw materials and labor) plus the indirect costs of production only, such as shop or sales-floor supervision, warehousing, transporting, inspecting, receiving and shipping, marking, painting, overtime and vacation expenses, general supplies, and the rent and utilities for the production area.

These indirect production costs, called *burden* or *shop overhead,* have to be allocated to other, direct production costs to get total cost of goods sold. (See MARGIN, GROSS MARGIN, OR MARKUP.)

If you don't know which sales are profitable, you may be just swapping dollars on parts of your sales volume. In that case, an increase in volume may do you more harm than good if it's in low-profit or money-losing items.

A retired CPA told me that in retrospect he got more satisfaction, and his clients got more help, from the cost-accounting systems he had installed than from any other aspect of his accounting practice. To me, it's inconceivable that a business with more than a few employees doesn't have a rudimentary but dependable way to determine the margin on each transaction. But very few do.

Some accounting systems never provide more detail about your cost of doing business than subtracting total production cost from total sales revenues at the end of the accounting period. This system won't work for long unless either you have such a high margin that the slop from fat transactions more than covers the slim ones, or you have dumb competitors who also have no cost-accounting system. If your smart competitor has good knowledge of his cost of doing business, he will undercut your price where the margin is great enough and leave you with all the unprofitable business.

If you make advanced estimates and must bid or quote jobs, you need a system

K

285

for comparing the cost of the finished job to the originally estimated cost. You never hit it exactly (unexpected things go wrong on all jobs), but to keep your estimating procedures as sharp as possible, continually compare the actual cost to the estimated cost so your next bid will be as accurate as you can make it.

In cost accounting, the biggest room for error and the most arguments come from allocation of indirect production expenses. Discuss these things with your internal and external accountant and everyone responsible for cost control and estimating within your business. Through such discussions, everyone involved will have a clear idea of what expenses are included in what budget number, and how best to control them.

If you don't know what the cost is on each income-producing transaction, you can use the standing joke that "we lose a little on every sale, but we make it up on volume."

Knowing When to Quit or Change

IT TAKES A HIGHER LEVEL of managerial skill to know when to get out of a deal than to know when to get in. Every deal is a good deal when you go into it; if you don't think so, you don't go into it.

Give the new project or policy a thorough trial. Don't quit too soon. Only after operations and experience have shown problems will you begin to have questions. Can you fix the problems? How much time and money will it take? After you fix them, will your business be profitable? How long will it take to hit breakeven? Should you abandon the project? What can you salvage? How can you back out gracefully?

Managerial ego always plays a major part in these decisions, because it's embarrassing to admit that what you thought was good and great when you started you now know was a partial or complete mistake. The ego or the pride that keeps you from recognizing the mistake will cost you even more money if you continue to support a losing project.

It's easier on your ego and on your pocketbook to admit little mistakes than to admit big ones.

Knowing Which Expenses to Cut

SUCCESS OR FAILURE DEPENDS ON YOUR choice of expenses.

Your total expenses are limited by your total sales income, plus what you invest or borrow. In order to survive long term, you must spend less than you take in.

What are the choices that will effectively run the business but not exceed your spending limits? Do you pay higher or lower salaries? Do you buy more materials and supplies or less? Do you buy more or less insurance? Do you pay more or less rent? Do you buy Cadillacs or Chevrolets? Do you buy the best or the cheapest?

Evaluate the results of dollars spent toward accomplishing your goals, because there are never enough dollars to do everything you want. Do you cut advertising? Do you cut product quality? Do you buy cheaper materials? Do you cut on front or appearance items?

For as long as you stay in business, you'll lie awake nights thinking about this question: "How can we decrease costs without decreasing quality or service?" Usually, whenever you cut time, you're also cutting expenses. The low-cost producer of a quality product will be the winner in all capitalist competitions.

You or a manager with incentives must know the cost to the company of each operation, person, and service furnished to the customer or incurred by your business. And if sales drop by 30 percent and you're surrounded by good friends and employees who have worked hard, the survival of the business may depend on what you or your incentive managers know about where expenses can and cannot be acceptably cut.

Here's where you earn your pay. Your commitment to the survival of the whole business exceeds your commitment to any single individual or group.

Your judgment comes from experience. Make the best decisions you can and don't hesitate to change them if you find you're wrong. (See YOU ARE THE SOLE GUARDIAN OF THE BOTTOM LINE.)

You don't become a good pilot by sailing only smooth waters. You're the seaman in charge of the lifeboat. If you try to save too many people in one small boat, it will sink and you'll lose the boat and all on board. You must decide how many and which ones are to be saved.

After you go through several downturns or major changes in your market, you will have had your trial by fire and will be a confident and capable manager.

It isn't fun and it isn't easy, but at times, survival depends on your decisions and your actions.

287

Labor Unions

IF YOU TREAT YOUR EMPLOYEES RIGHT, they'll have no need or incentive to join a labor union. You certainly don't want one.

Since the turn of this century, labor unions have been a powerful force for good in this country. During the early days of the Industrial Revolution, labor abuses existed which made the struggle worthwhile. Their formation and rise was accompanied by strife and bloodshed, but strong unions helped eliminate Industrial Revolution abuses such as child labor, long working hours with no overtime pay, unhealthy working conditions, and management's exploitation of labor.

During the 1930s, Franklin Roosevelt formed a strong Democratic political coalition based on labor unions and minorities. New laws favored unions' organization and growth. They gained membership and political power. They influenced many laws to improve working conditions.

Now, laws and government regulations require and enforce compliance of what labor unions fought for. Today in the United States, few workers are mistreated and working conditions are generally good, so unions have steadily lost their appeal to workers.

However, union leaders still fight for many of the same things they fought for 50 years ago. Just as industrial management gets out of step with changing markets, so has union management gotten out of step with the workers they serve and the workplace environment.

Union senior management are still working on their old theory: "More pay for less work. Create more jobs by limiting what each craft can do." Until this policy is changed to "More productivity, therefore more pay," union managers damage themselves and the American economy. They're sending American jobs overseas.

Management and labor can work together so both are more productive and have better lives. But labor unions' top management must change, the same way IBM, Sears, and General Motors top management has changed, because markets and social conditions have changed. Younger workers no longer feel that they get value received for their union dues, so they no longer join.

Treat employees with fairness, understanding, dignity, and compassion. Reward their productive efforts. Have an up-to-date employee policy manual that you adhere to, including a written grievance procedure. Keep communication open between senior management and all employees. If you do these things, you probably won't need to worry about labor union troubles.

I strongly recommend that you have a written employee policy manual as soon as possible, about the time you have 10 or more hourly floor employees. At an advanced stage, my employee policy manual totaled about 25 pages and included a written grievance procedure. (See EM-PLOYEE POLICY MANUAL OR HANDBOOK.)

Every entrepreneur I know thinks dealing with a union will be harmful to business. If labor unions are active or prevalent in your industry, take time to read some books or go to a seminar on the subject. You'll be surprised at how the cards are stacked against you. Dealing with unions is a highly developed and specialized area of the law.

If you suspect a union organization drive, call the most experienced, special-ized labor consultant or lawyer you can

find to help you avoid what you consider illogical or unjust pitfalls. Respond with speed, vigor, and specialized knowledge. Even with the best and most honorable intentions to treat your employees fairly, you can unknowingly get your company into deep trouble if you don't know the rules you must play by. The rules are so pro-union that they'll make you mad, but they're still the law.

Your best course of action is to get employees so involved in the business that a union has no appeal. The union will then look like it's taking money out of their pockets instead of putting money in.

Lawyers and CPAs Compared

LAWYERS AND CPAS ARE VERY DIFFERENT in both their professional positions and their approaches to problems.

Your lawyer is openly, unashamedly, wholeheartedly, and without question on your side. She has no responsibility to others, except as required by common courtesy, morals, the law, and canons of ethics. Your lawyer is your advocate and should fight like crazy to get maximum advantage for your side, no matter how it hurts the other side.

Your lawyer is an expert who uses her expertise to help only you. Your fee assures her loyalty to you alone. Any hint of loyalty to anyone else involved, either in the present dispute or on some prior occasion, is a possible conflict of interest

that the lawyer must disclose and explain to you.

In a court case, your lawyer will seek to get everything she can for you and leave nothing, not even dignity, for your opponent. Balancing equities is the responsibility of judge and jury, not of your trial lawyer. This isn't the basis for a good business deal, which requires a totally different legal approach. Many lawyers can't shift mental gears from the "I win, you lose" approach at the court-house to the "I win something; you win something, too" approach necessary at the negotiating table.

A good business lawyer knows that the client's best interests are served if she helps the client make a reasonable deal with manageable business risks and known liabilities.

The lawyer's function in the proposed deal is to raise all the warning flags, both orange and red, about problems that her knowledge and experience indicate might happen. You must evaluate the business risk of each eventuality and decide whether or not to accept it.

Don't ask your lawyer for a business decision. The answer is often unworkable because it's too one-sided. Let your lawyer tell you what's legal after you've used your business judgment about what's fair and how much risk is prudent.

The CPA is also an expert, but he uses that expertise to examine in detail your accounting practices and procedures. You then want the impartial CPA to tell your creditors and the world, "I've examined this company's financial statements, and they correctly represent the company's financial position for the period under review."

The CPA isn't entirely on your side against the world. The CPA is more like a referee who knows the rules of the game for everyone. He makes certain that you are representing your company's financial position fairly to the rest of the world, even though you're the only one paying his fee.

You're paying the CPA to use his expertise to look at your financial statements, then use his credibility to tell others your financial statements are correct. If the CPA can't do this, if his examination shows that your financial statements are incorrect or not in compliance with Gen-

erally Accepted Accounting Principles (GAAP), the CPA will discuss the matter only with you. If you and the CPA can't agree on a presentation of your numbers that will meet the professionally set standards, then the CPA must publish no report with his name on it, or must withdraw from the engagement.

An accountant sees everything either totally white or totally black. You have either a debit or a credit. You either add or subtract, with no in-between. A lawyer sees so many shades of gray between black and white that it's difficult to know exactly where the line of justice should be drawn. That's what juries are for.

The accountant is professionally trained never to overstate anything. He takes the conservative approach and accepts only confirmed, provable, and written factual evidence. This way the CPA's credibility also helps you. If your lawyer uses the same criteria, get a different lawyer.

Accountants spend their entire professional lives working with different aspects of business. Most lawyers, except the occasional corporation or business lawyer, spend their professional lives working on concepts that don't relate to running a business. They certainly know that potential liabilities exist, but they usually can't evaluate the business risk involved.

CPAs can't work on contingent fees, because correctness and fairness aren't for sale. Such payment methods would influence their judgment. The best lawyers, however, frequently work on a contingent fee; that's their incentive to do the best job they can.

Lawyers are valuable because they unashamedly get everything they can for you. CPAs are valuable because they have the financial expertise and enough independence that an outsider will take their opinion to corroborate your evaluation of the financial conditions inside your company.

Lawyers—Selecting and Hiring

RECOMMENDATIONS FROM FRIENDS and trusted business associates are still the best way to select a lawyer you'll be happy with. Ask your mentor or your CEO roundtable colleagues to suggest a business lawyer they're satisfied with. Your banker, insurance person, or other trusted business associates can also give you candidates to check out.

You want someone with broad-based business experience to handle you while you grow, but someone hungry enough to be flexible on fees because she wants your business. Large firms aren't interested in your small business, but the lone practitioner is frequently unable either to handle the range of problems you will encounter or to turn out the necessary work quickly.

Look for the mid-size firm with from three to ten lawyers. Seek a business specialist within the firm. See this person when you think trouble is brewing; don't wait until it's a crisis. Don't shop fees on the basis of hourly charges. The $250/ hour specialist may do you a lot more good than a $150/hour uneducated generalist.

Interview more than one lawyer candidate. Find out who has imagination and initiative and who seems to fit with your ethics and temperament. Don't pay for prestige.

Make an appointment with each candidate. Say that you're interested in an exploratory meeting to discuss handling your problem and that you want to locate competent, professional help. Don't hesitate to ask whether there will be a charge for this preliminary meeting. Most professionals will say no

You should feel comfortable with your lawyer because you're going to work together in a significant relationship. The closer the association, the more likely you are to get beneficial results and the happier the relationship will be.

Ask what the firm or individual specializes in, or what clients she typically serves. Describe your situation enough to be sure she doesn't handle competitors you object to. Explore possible conflicts of interest. Conflict of interest means that a lawyer cannot represent two people at the same time who have opposing interests to even a slight degree.

L

291

Good questions in your evaluation interview are these: What percentage of your practice is devoted to business problems like mine? Will you be the attorney working on my case? What choices do I have to resolve my current legal problem? What will this cost me? Look out for lawyers who are evasive and rambling when you ask specific questions.

Don't hesitate to talk about fees; you need to understand how you're going to be charged—by the hour, flat fee, or contingent fee. The lawyer can't quote the exact number of hours your work will take, but she will tell you that similar matters generally take either approximately so many hours or some estimated fee.

Contingent fees are suitable in some cases. They run from 10 to 20 percent on collecting debts to 33 percent (sometimes 50 percent) on other contingent matters. This percentage depends on who's paying the ongoing expenses of the lawsuit and on the amount and certainty of recovery.

Suit the payment method to the particular case. Use less expensive firm members for less demanding issues or parts of the work. Get specific hourly rates for partners, associates, or paralegals. Get an itemized statement each month. Try to set a date by which your work should be completed. Don't agree to a retainer based on calendar dates.

When you ask, "How can I accomplish my purpose legally?" your lawyer probably can't tell you, any more than your doctor can tell you "How can I keep well?" Expect that most of your lawyer's advice will be negative. When you suggest a course of action, your lawyer will talk about liabilities, reasons it may not work, terrible things that might happen, or problems that may develop if you do it. A lawyer's worst fear is that a client will come back later and ask, "Why didn't you tell me this could happen?"

Lawyers who negotiate business deals have a different attitude from trial attorneys. A trial attorney will attempt to get a winner-take-all verdict—everything for you and nothing for your opponent. A business lawyer tries to negotiate a fair deal, getting for you what you want and need and giving the other party what he wants and needs. The lawyer who tries to get everything for you and nothing for the other side is a deal breaker, not a deal maker.

It takes a certain maturity and attitude in a lawyer to realize that he can best serve clients by helping them make the deal they want rather than insisting they take zero risk. A lawyer's real function is to advise you of risks and business dangers you might incur and to flash yellow or red warning lights on certain courses of action. Then you must decide whether or not you wish to take that risk or make that deal. You don't have to take the lawyer's advice.

Only a few lawyers are creative enough to tell you it can't be done your way, but you can reach the same objective by a different legal path. These are the lawyers you should seek. The lawyer you wish to hire to represent your business interests usually has a completely different background from the lawyer who handles your will, or the lawyer who handles your divorce, or a trial lawyer.

The knowledge you want your lawyer to have doesn't come from law school. Look for business wisdom, experience, and sophistication. Your lawyer should be a soothing presence in the background of your business life, available for routine legal matters and occasional crises.

Layoffs or Reductions in Force (RIF)

THESE ARE THE TIMES that try men's souls. If firing one person is a gut-wrenching occasion, a layoff or reduction in force is your worst nightmare. There's no easy way to fire people.

The last thing you want is such bad economic conditions that a layoff or reduction in force (RIF, as the British call it) is necessary to preserve solvency or possibly even the business. Usually, economic downturns occur rapidly. Growth and recovery come more slowly. Holding on too long to no-longer-needed employees or expenses seriously damages a business financially.

Recognize and deal with reality, no matter how unpleasant it may be.

Prime candidates for termination are the nonperformers who should have been fired in the first place, those who are otherwise troublesome in normal times, and those whose jobs aren't essential to serving customers. Examine all levels—executives, managers, supervisors, and production workers. If you lay off only hourly paid workers with no reduction in office workers or supervisors, you'll end up with an unbalanced operation and disgruntled employees.

When you have to lay people off, do it all at one time if you can. This traumatic event, painful to all concerned, is best done only once, so recovery and readjustment can quickly begin. Cutting off the dog's tail with one big chop is much less painful than cutting off several pieces a little at a time—and it accomplishes the same thing.

Lists of suggested layoff candidates that you ask other managers for should be in their own handwriting, with no copies shown to anyone else. Write out the final list yourself. Anything typewritten or in a computer is too easily compromised. Premature revelation of the plan or the individuals slotted for the layoff by a subordinate employee can create a very delicate situation.

Following the layoff, rebuild the confidence of those remaining. They need reassurance that the next cut won't get them. If you must reduce your force, it's better to cut too deeply with one cut and then hire some employees back than to need another round of cuts. Rehiring people laid off or hiring new people builds confidence. However, additional small layoffs destroy confidence and lead to slowdowns to preserve what little work there may be.

If further cuts are necessary after the first cutback, consider putting remaining employees, including executives, on reduced hours, or think about an across-the-board reduction in pay. Cut everyone's hours or offer part-time jobs to groups of full-time employees. This keeps trained, experienced workers by giving them some income rather than dropping their paycheck to zero, and the company maintains a ready reservoir of good employees for the time when business improves.

During these times, keep your employees informed as to what's going on. Tell them what they can do to help. Give them pep talks. Tell them the truth. There will be more than enough rumors anyway.

Lead Time for Managers' Thinking

THE MORE SENIOR THE MANAGER, the further ahead he or she is capable of thinking, planning, and managing, and the more that skill is required. In small companies, usually only the entrepreneur possesses vision, the most far-seeing form of thinking and planning.

High-level planning is like an army moving through the woods. People in the front line can see and manage only the problems within their immediate vision. Somewhere behind this line, supervisors or middle managers look at maps, manage supplies and resources, and plan where to go and whether to go faster or slower to comply with their orders. In the very back, the general orders people to climb trees or sends out airplanes to see what's coming, determines where to concentrate resources, and decides in what direction the army should move next.

Good managers see problems coming and solve them while they are small, before they get close and become crises.

Clerical people and bookkeepers look only backward. They can't do tomorrow's work today or get ahead by recording tomorrow's transactions, checks, or cash deposits. Many junior managers or accountants look only at the numbers, and not at the causes or meanings or how they can influence the numbers.

The battle is tomorrow. As a manager, you should know that some numbers are large and getting larger, and you should know why. Other numbers are getting smaller. You or someone or something else is making them smaller. Do you know why? Do you know what should be done about it?

Skills required at each level of management are proportional to how far into the future an individual's capabilities and talents allow her to make plans and direct actions toward goals.

Leadership in Your Business

YOUR BUSINESS LIFE WILL BE SIMPLER and your organization will run more smoothly if you act as a leader rather than as a boss. If you're the owner, you are the boss, and everyone knows it. But accomplishing your purposes by leadership rather than by just issuing orders greases the wheels of progress immeasurably.

Entrepreneurship and leadership are not exactly the same, although the entrepreneur is clearly in a position of leadership. Leadership must have a readily recognizable objective shared with followers. All must know where they are going. Einstein was an intellectual leader, but he was followed by no armies or groups of cheering people.

The first quality a leader must have is a guiding vision, a clear idea of what he wants to do. All leaders have a strongly defined sense of purpose. Where people are aligned behind a leader with a clearly defined vision or purpose, a powerful organization exists. In his great *Essay on History,* Thomas Carlyle wrote, "History is the essence of innumerable biographies."

Military leadership and business leadership aren't the same for two principal reasons. First, successful military leadership is measured in part by minimum loss of life. Failure occurs when the cost in lives is too great to accomplish the mission. No more lives can be created by successful accomplishment. Individuals get no benefits except continued survival. No profit motive exists as when gain or loss in dollars is measured. The dollar cost to successfully invade Europe or take the next hill is never calculated or part of the commander's evaluation.

Second, the concept of teamwork is different in military and business leadership. The difference is dictatorship versus participative teamwork. In the military, no intelligent opinions or input is expected or requested from privates whose lives are at risk. No criticism, new ideas, or evaluation of alternate plans from subordinates is tolerated. In business, where the only risk is dollars, intelligent input from people closest to the problem is encouraged and weighed in the final decision. The principle of looking out for #1 keeps all participants focused on the objective, especially when all share in the profits or lack thereof. In both cases, when the leader makes a final decision, enthusiastic compliance with that decision is required.

Leadership is a transfer of motivation—getting people to do things because they want to, not because they have to. Leadership transfers the initiative to individuals so things don't stop when the leader isn't around.

The leader must have self-confidence. Others won't follow a leader who is not confident. Leadership doesn't require a thick carpet in a large office, a rich lifestyle, or impressive surroundings. Charisma isn't the same as leadership; charisma alone isn't enough. It isn't even essential, but it's usually present.

Oral and written communication skills are essential. The leader must have an objective and must clearly communicate it to his or her followers. The leader must clearly define the problem as well as the solution. Just saying "trust me" is ineffective, unless trust has been built up over a period of time.

If a person's only objective is building her own ego, this person isn't a leader but an egomaniac. Leadership isn't a person-

L

296

ality cult that smothers subordinate leaders. When a dominant person builds a cult of personality, and then something happens to that person, the leaderless group falls apart.

> *True leaders inspire people to do great things and, when the work is done, their people proudly say, "We did it ourselves."*
>
> —Lao-Tzu

A strong, dominant personality may accomplish some of the purposes of leadership, but domination and leadership aren't the same. Domination is a master-servant relationship, not a leader-follower relationship.

Leadership plays a big part in management team building. In any unorganized group, a leader emerges within a short time and a supportive team structure develops. People instinctively recognize and follow a leader. If you proclaim, "I am your leader, follow me," none will follow if they don't have confidence.

Leadership requires admitting mistakes. Your people know when mistakes are made. You know, too—so admit them, at least to your close followers and staff.

Are leaders born or made? Certainly some are born, but leadership can be an acquired talent. Everyone can improve his leadership skills by working and practicing. Leadership has responsibilities. You're a role model for the culture you want to create. Your inner values will be adopted by the organization. Followers are more likely to do as you do, not as you say.

How do you become a leader? How do you become a better leader? People will follow you when you respect their human dignity and individuality and concern yourself with their welfare. Continuous feedback must occur—the continuous exchange of information and mutual support between you and the group. If you give them your concern, they will give you theirs. The intensity of concern from the top down should be greater than the intensity of concern from the bottom up.

Treat people as individuals. Respect their personalities and opinions. Give public praise and recognition; keep criticism constructive and private. Do not belittle anyone at any time—it does nothing for your stature as a leader. When problems arise, recognize them: "We have a problem. How can we solve it?" not "You made a mistake. Here's what you should have done." Always treat everyone with common courtesy.

The leader must build several layers of subordinate leaders. One of the missions of leadership is to replace yourself. Build an organization that can survive without you with the same high morale and the same objectives. Training other leaders is one of the main jobs of leadership. Bring out the best in people under you.

Cultivate your own style. You are unique; don't try to be someone you're not or take on a style that doesn't fit you. The number-one responsibility of leadership is to generate a clear and shared vision for the company and secure others' commitment to the vigorous pursuit of that vision. No matter what your style, you must perform this function. The forces you need for leadership are ambition and drive, competence and expertise, integrity and moral fabric.

Use the business to make great people; don't use people to make a great business. What employees want most from their leaders is direction, meaning, inspiration, trust, and hope.

> ## *You manage things; you lead people.*
>
> **—Admiral Grace Hopper**

A good book on business leadership applicable to the small business is *Flight of the Buffalo,* by James A. Belasco and Ralph C. Stayer (New York: Warner Books, 1993).

Lean and Mean

DURING THE SURVIVAL STAGE, your operation is by necessity lean and mean. Everyone on the team is a productive player on the field. No one sits on the bench. Everyone earns her spot on the team with every paycheck.

In the growth stage, after prosperity has arrived, it's easy to add little luxuries and hire helpful, smiling people who don't work as hard as you had to "back when." This is particularly true of indirect workers or supervisors, who make helpful noises but contribute less than a necessary share of productive labor for the common good. With production workers, you can readily see who does his share and who doesn't. An extra employee in an overhead or service department can't be measured by such a direct yardstick.

In good times, when the living is easy, your tendency will be to allow fixed expenses and unnecessary people or functions to become institutionalized. When the inevitable downturn occurs, cutting off these expenses and people is slow and painful. Better never to have hired them in the first place. Downsize and reengineer as you go along—then you won't be forced to do it by economic necessity.

The management practices that can cure a troubled company could have kept it well.

The purpose of this book is to help you and your team run the company as a lean, mean, money-making machine during both good times and bad. This means better service and less expensive products for your customers, more compensation and bonuses split among fewer, happier, higher-performing people, and more profits to put into growth, new products, or services.

This is easier said than done, but it's your smartest way to run the company.

L

298

Listening

His thoughts were slow;
His words were few,
And seldom made to glisten.
Always welcomed wherever he went:
You should have heard him <u>listen</u>.

—Author unknown

LEARN TO KEEP YOUR MOUTH SHUT and listen.

Listening is as vital a part of communication as talking. It's one of your most important managerial skills. When you listen, someone communicates with you on a two-way street. Careful listening is flattery.

If you talk, you repeat what you already know. If you listen, you learn.

—Chinese fortune cookie

Listen to your customers all day, every day. They'll give you ideas to improve your products and your service. If you listen to enough of them and generalize their answers, they'll tell you how to run your business to please them.

Listen to your employees without messing up discipline or the chain of command. They'll tell you how to make things cheaper, easier, and faster. They'll tell you what's going on in your company.

Listen to your managers for the same reasons. The person closest to the problem has intelligent suggestions about how to solve it. If you listen with interest and intensity, the speaker will tell you more. If you listen with boredom and as a duty, she will tell you very little.

For many people, just getting thoughts, problems, or feelings off their chests by talking to the boss is enough to make them feel better, even if there's little you can do about it. The fact that you cared enough to listen is important and appreciated. Don't swear at the messenger when you're told something you don't want to hear.

When the conversation or meeting is over, summarize specific commitments made or not made, as well as actions either of you is to take in the future. This helps keep misunderstandings to a minimum. What one person says and what the other hears are often different.

Once I listened sympathetically to an employee's reasons for a pay raise without giving a definite answer. After the passage of some time, the same employee, apparently assuming that silence meant agreement, reminded me that I had promised him a raise. It was an embarrassing situation. (See COMPLAINTS FROM EMPLOYEES; COMPLAINTS FROM CUSTOMERS.)

Listening doesn't diminish your leadership. Listening enhances it.

L

299

Litigation

WHEN YOU OR THE COMPANY gets charged with an offense or involved in civil litigation, although the question usually concerns business, many business people throw up their hands and let lawyers take charge.

If you find yourself involved in legal proceedings, let your lawyer know that you expect to participate in settling your business problem, even though you may rely heavily on legal professionals for certain kinds of help or to defend yourself. Alternatively, tell your lawyer that you prefer to negotiate and settle the differences rather than litigate. If he balks at this, consider changing lawyers.

If you're the aggrieved party, don't file any legal papers until you've tried personally contacting and discussing a settlement with owners or decision makers on the other side. Courthouse action should be the last resort, not the first choice. However, you may wish to discuss legal rights and procedures with your lawyer early or partway through the negotiations.

If you're defending yourself against a charge by or through a government agency, you can always go directly to the agency to discuss the matter, but be careful not to make any damaging admissions. Agency employees will tell you what action or settlement is customary and give you the information and forms you need. Ask the agency for names of firms and individuals who practice before them; this type of practice is called *administrative law,* a specialized area of civil law. In some cases, an engineer or other professional person may be a better representative than a lawyer. Be sure to ask how much time you have to file your written answer or affidavits.

If you've been served with court papers as defendant in a civil lawsuit, you need immediate legal assistance. If you let a few weeks go by without responding, you may forfeit your right to defend yourself.

If you or your company is the defendant, let your representatives or lawyers work alone at the first meeting to discuss a settlement. Arrange to be present at future meetings if you can keep your composure. If you feel that time is being wasted on immaterial or insignificant issues, bring the subject back to practical economics. Limit the meeting time, which is easier to do if business people are present and in control.

Become acquainted with opposing lawyers and the parties they represent. They are really the ones you must eventually fight or settle with. Remain willing to listen. Don't believe you already know all the facts or the complete situation as your opponent sees it. Be as objective and reasonable as you can in understanding the rules, as well as the thinking, knowledge, objectives, and possible settlement position of the other side.

300

Your objectives and the lawyer's may be different. In court, a lawyer's objective is to win everything for the client and leave nothing for the opponent, and the lawyer wants a commensurate fee. That same attitude at the negotiating table is sure to kill a pending deal.

> *Find out what the other side really wants. Find a way to give that, or part of it, while you also get what you want.*

If you think you can make a fair settlement directly with your adversary (not his lawyer), by all means call and ask for one or more private, face-to-face meetings. If each of you brings a lawyer, that makes four—and the problems are that much bigger. Such a meeting is premature until each of you has a complete understanding of the other's facts, position, feelings, and settlement options.

Make sure you advise your opponent that these discussions are for settlement purposes only, and therefore that nothing said in these meetings can be used against you in the trial if the settlement breaks down. Don't introduce any new facts or issues. Immediately convey to your lawyer the results of all such contacts and discussions.

You're looking for the lowest-cost solution, even if it means humbly paying off your opponent. Pride is an expensive luxury. Lawyers love clients who'll fight for principle and pay as they fight. You'll save legal fees if you and your employees do all the grunt work and gather all the data. Tell your accountants to get all the necessary numbers together.

The lawyer's code of ethics dictates that one lawyer may not talk directly to the other lawyer's client unless the other lawyer is present. You don't have to observe that rule. You may talk directly to the opposing businessperson whenever it's to your advantage to do so.

You both probably want to settle the matter with the least amount of pain, time, and money. Two reasonable people can often resolve their business differences to their mutual satisfaction without much help or interference from lawyers.

Discuss a fair settlement. Negotiate without arguing. Ask the other person to state the minimum she might settle for; state the same for yourself. See how far apart you are and if differences can be settled. If you can agree, write it down, and both of you sign it. Tell your lawyers to make it legal. You both must think you've gotten something—fairness and equity with honor. Find incentives for working together, not for cutting throats.

If you don't reach a settlement, you're back to paying your lawyer to talk to the other person's lawyer. Agree to mediation or arbitration, if you think that's faster or less expensive. (See ARBITRATION AND ALTERNATE DISPUTE RESOLUTION (ADR).)

301

Loan Agreement

BY THE TIME YOU RECEIVE MONEY from any bank or lender, you will probably have negotiated and signed three documents:

1. A *promissory note*—your legal promise that you will pay the loan back to the lender according to the agreed terms, with interest.

2. The *loan agreement*—frequently a complicated document requiring negotiations and several drafts as it goes back and forth between attorneys. This sets out the terms and conditions by which you agree to operate the company as long as you have the loan.

3. A *chattel mortgage* (covering personal property) or *mortgage* (for real property)—describes and locates the mortgaged property you have pledged as collateral for the loan. This document legally creates a security interest in specific property and provides for foreclosure and sale of the property for the benefit of the lender if the debt is not paid. This document must be recorded in the appropriate state or county records to give public notice of the existence of the mortgage.

The law generally prescribes the form of the promissory note and the mortgage.

The loan agreement must be customized for your individual situation. All its provisions are negotiable. Don't accept the lender's statement that the agreement is standard or boiler plate. For example, it's to your advantage to render the fewest routine financial reports because of the trouble and expense involved.

In the loan agreement, the lender requires you to run your business in a businesslike manner. The lender wants to be routinely or immediately informed of potential operating problems that threaten either the collateral or your ability to repay.

The loan agreement usually contains both affirmative and negative covenants. Affirmative covenants state that you *will* do certain things, such as maintain a certain current ratio or other liquidity ratios. A standard affirmative covenant requires you to have adequate fire and casualty insurance and to furnish this proof to the lender. The lender requires notification from the insurance company if premiums aren't paid.

An affirmative covenant may require you to furnish certain financial reports, such as aged accounts payable or aged accounts receivable. Another might require you or your accountant to certify that during the period in question there have been no financial happenings contrary to the agreement or adverse to your ability to repay.

Negative covenants state that you will *not* do certain things without the lender's approval, such as lease or buy additional equipment, raise salaries above a certain level, or pay out dividends. Normally, negative covenants do not permit you to obtain financing from any other source without notifying the lender and obtaining consent. Negative covenants may also stipulate that your net worth may not fall below a certain dollar amount.

The longer the term of the loan, the more restrictive the covenants. The general purpose of most of these covenants is to keep the borrower in a safe operating position to repay the loan.

The loan agreement always contains a section called "Events of Default," which specifies certain situations that may cause the loan to mature or come due in full immediately. These events are failure to pay interest or amortization within a specified period, perhaps the termination of a lease, loss of patent or other valuable property, or death of the owner. Either failing to live up to an affirmative covenant or violating a negative covenant

defaults the loan, which makes the entire balance due immediately.

Although the lender always has the option to foreclose the loan for any default, he will usually avoid foreclosing if he can. To prevent trouble, ask for a signed waiver of his right to foreclose each time you report a known violation.

Never sign an important loan agreement without first showing the documents to an attorney who's had lots of business experience. For example, wherever the agreement states that the lender's consent is required, the attorney will try to add a statement in your favor that such consent shall not be unreasonably withheld. Try to have some borrower's covenants removed or reduced to give yourself more time or more freedom.

The loan agreement for factoring receivables or inventory is quite different from the bank loan agreement described here. (See TERMINATION OF AGREEMENTS.)

Negotiate terms that will be least burdensome to you without denying the lender the security he must have.

Lonely at the Top

Bullfight critics ranked in rows
Crowd the enormous stadium full.
But he's the only one who knows—
And he's the one who fights the bull.

—Domingo Ortega

BEING AN ENTREPRENEUR IS LONELIER than being a bullfighter—no one is watching but your employees and creditors.

Seen from your employees' and associates' perspective, you're supposed to know it all, make all decisions, and never be wrong. You can't discuss your uncertainties, fears, and failures with them.

Isolation comes with the territory. You'll spend a lot of time talking and communicating, but you'll have few opportunities to unburden yourself or get advice.

It's unwise to completely level with most of the people you deal with day to day. You can't complain to your customers or reveal your fears to employees. Expressing your doubts to suppliers spoils their trust in your resourcefulness and ability to pay. You can't discuss your problems with your bankers, or they'll get worried. Talking to your paid advisors is expensive. It's unfair to unload on your family and unrealistic to seek advice from friends employed by a different company.

So who can you talk to? Other entrepreneurs and small-business owners—at trade shows, at Chamber of Commerce business meetings, or anywhere. You aren't the only one with problems. There's comfort in knowing things could always be worse.

The best thing you can do is join a CEO roundtable, get a mentor, or form an advisory board. Choose whichever source of guidance and comfort makes you most comfortable at the moment. You'll wonder how you ever got along without at least one of them. (See CEO ROUNDTABLES OR PRESIDENTS' CLUBS; MENTORS AND MENTORING; ADVISORY DIRECTORS.)

304

Looking Out for #1

EVERYONE PRIMARILY LOOKS OUT FOR #1—himself. You'll have a difficult time in life or in business if you can't live with this basic fact of human nature.

If doing what you think is in your own best self-interest doesn't motivate you toward being in business for yourself, quit reading this book and get a job that you think *is* in your own best interest.

Your customers and your employees are doing what seems best to them in their own enlightened self-interest. You take care of yourself best by taking care of your customers and employees.

Make it in your customers' best interest (best quality, easiest, cheapest, and best service) to buy *your* products or services rather than your competitors'. When they buy from you, they must be convinced that they're looking after themselves.

Base your business environment on the genuine belief that while your employees look after your business, they also look after their own self-interest. They must believe themselves better off working for your company than anywhere else, or they won't work for you.

Your employees must feel that you're their vehicle for wealth and greatness over the long haul, and that they are yours. The best human relations are mutually self-serving. The extent of your concern for them is generally repaid in the degree of their loyalty to you. From this partnership of self-interest springs wealth for all and feelings of care and concern.

When your employees get an adverse decision or temporary setback, they must be convinced that, on balance, their own best interest still lies in looking after your best interest and that of your customers.

This, then, is the strength of teamwork. Employees' choices will be governed by value systems they learned at home, plus any incentives or motivation you provide. Use incentives to get your employees to do what you want them to do and what customers want them to do, because it's in their own best interest.

In the words of Adam Smith, the customer will pay you the lowest amount she can, not in excess of the amount paid to a competitor, to receive the product or service that brings her satisfaction. Your cost of providing this service must be low enough to attract the customer but also high enough above your cost that your company makes a profit on the transaction, or you won't be here next year to provide the service.

In communistic and socialistic societies, everyone is supposed to be working for the best interest of the state and every other citizen, not his own. Mikhail Gorbachev said that what was wrong with the communist system was that there was no incentive for the individual to do anything.

You can have everything in life you want if you can just help enough other people get what they want.

People following their individual freedoms and exercising property rights as their own best interest dictates are the basis of the capitalistic system, the free market economy, and the entrepreneurial incentives that drive you on.

After 50,000 generations, human nature isn't likely to change. Your employees, your customers, and you are all looking after #1. When you do so, your company will grow and profit by supplying a product or service of more value to your customers than the money they pay your company.

Losing-Money Operations

IF YOUR BUSINESS ISN'T MAKING MONEY, the capitalistic system is telling you one of two things: either you're not performing a needed service, or performing that service is costing you more than people will pay for it.

If your dollar volume is growing but you're not making money, you may be performing a valuable service but your costs are either too high or above what the market is willing to pay. You're inefficient at managing or producing the service or product. You're a high-cost producer. The low-cost producer ultimately wins in any market.

When you consistently lose money, shut off the blood flow as quickly as possible, drastically if necessary. Backward financial steps are never easy or pleasant, but sometimes you must take them.

If you're losing money because of a general downturn in the economy or in your segment of the market (affecting all your competitors as well), cut back quickly. My experience has been that markets turn down abruptly and fast,

and they grow back slowly over a much longer period. You can watch your net worth plummet dramatically if you don't reduce your expenses as your revenues decrease. Try to recover liquidity by selling inventory, which becomes less liquid in slow markets.

Review your operation to see where you can improve efficiency, see what operations or employees you no longer need, make operations more cost effective, or buy fewer materials cheaper. (See KNOWING WHICH EXPENSES TO CUT.) Your decisions after review can cause layoffs. (See LAYOFFS OR REDUCTIONS IN FORCE (RIF).)

Every month that you lose money, you grow financially weaker. Sooner or later you're out of cash and out of business. Do something about it before it gets that bad.

If you make a profit every month, even if some months it's just a small one, your company will slowly but steadily grow financially stronger. It's important to remember growing just a little stronger every month over a long time produces a strong, robust company.

Low-Cost Producer

YOUR CONTINUOUS BATTLE IS TO BE the low-cost producer of your service or product. If you're the low-cost producer, you

will win all the price wars. You'll win all the profit wars. You'll enjoy prosperity and growth.

This applies more directly to tangible products than to services. The advantage of a lower production cost, even if it's only slightly lower, deserves your constant attention and efforts. (See MARGIN, GROSS MARGIN, OR MARKUP.)

If your cost is substantially lower than the market average, say at least 20 percent less than your competitors', don't cut the market price by the same amount. You may not have the productive capacity to handle all the business at one time, even if you could get it, or the money to buy that many productive people or that much space or facilities.

If you engage in price competition, do it cautiously. Prices are always easier to cut than to increase. Competitors usually lower their prices to meet yours, so you will all continue to compete at the lower price level. Enjoy your locked-in profits for a while, until your facilities or production capacity is paid for. (See PRICING.)

You'll need those profits to pay for research and new equipment. Your competitors, who still use their old productivity or technology, will lose the production-cost battle to you. You can choose the speed and timing of your price cuts until they decide to pay to upgrade their technology to equal or exceed yours.

Luck

GENERAL GEORGE S. PATTON, who chose "Lucky" as the code name for his headquarters, said that good luck is merely an extension of hard work.

Anyone who is a failure will confirm that success is just a matter of luck.

Luck is where preparation and opportunity meet. Prepare, and the opportunity will come.

It took me over 10 years in a continuously falling market (the petroleum equipment market from 1957 to 1969) to reach an annual volume of $1,000,000. In 1970 the market started upward and our sales took off rapidly. I remarked several times that if someone had said, "Tom, you sure are lucky," I would have hit him in the mouth.

Management by Exception

MORE GROWTH-STAGE COMPANIES should adopt this effective big-business technique.

It can be used only after you have a good information system (IS) or accounting system in place with enough historical information to let you determine what you consider standard performance. Establish an acceptable "par for the course" budget or forecast, which is the performance you expect to happen. You must have this numerical yardstick to measure actual performance against.

The 80-20 rule tells you that 80 percent of the current numbers or accounts will be acceptably close to the par you've established but that 20 percent may be too high or too low. Don't worry about the 80 percent that are close to par—they're not problems.

The 20 percent that aren't close to par are the exceptions—the problems—that you need to investigate. Concentrate your managerial attention on these exceptions that don't conform to the expected pattern.

With little trouble, your computer can produce statements highlighting the current numbers that are outside the "don't worry" limits you've established. Save your time by working only on these exceptions.

When you're drowning in numbers, you need a system to separate the important few from the insignificant many.

Management—Definition and Priorities

MANAGEMENT IS THE ART of getting planned work done through others.

You can't have all the skills, knowledge, time, and money you need, so gather within your organization the needed resources and skills. Then organize and manage people to work toward the common goal.

That sounds simple, but thousands of books have been written about it. If you want to be more than a one-person company, you have to spend much of your time learning and practicing management. Learn to delegate and manage people, not things. A mechanic manages things.

Subjects that managers are concerned with are sometimes called the five M's of management: manpower, machines, methods, money, and materials. If you manage the manpower correctly, that will help you tremendously toward taking care of the others.

Priorities

Ivy Lee, an early-day efficiency expert, was told by Charles Schwab, the president of a small company called Bethlehem Steel, that he had 15 minutes to prove to Schwab that he could improve company operations. Lee told Schwab to write the six most important tasks he had to do tomorrow in order of priority, and to carry the list with him.

"Tomorrow morning, start on item one," he said, "and don't stop until it's finished. Then start on item two, and so on. Don't worry if you don't get beyond item one, because you've been working on the most important thing for your company. Revise your list as other things become more urgent or important, or as you finish them. This way you'll always be working on the most important things.

"Do this every working day. Then get your other managers to do the same. Try it as long as you wish. Then send me a check for what you think this advice is worth."

Several weeks later, Schwab sent a check for $25,000. This made Lee the highest-paid consultant of his day—$25,000 for fifteen minutes of advice.

This sound managerial principle assumes you've already defined your corporate goals, written your mission statement, and listed objectives or yardsticks to measure priorities by.

The favorite joke about long-term versus short-term goals is "When you're up to your ass in alligators, it's hard to concentrate on your most important job, which is to drain the swamp."

Everyone else will focus attention on whatever you consider important enough to focus your attention on. People learn what makes you smile and what brings a frown. Knowing that difference is what younger managers work on. Improvement comes when managerial focus lasts long enough to make permanent changes or improvements in basic procedures or attitudes.

309

> *The direction of a group is not determined by those who bring up the rear.*

If your managerial focus is too short and changes too often, the result is confusion and loss of confidence in management. Under these circumstances, people who don't want to change or don't like the new policy think they can delay long enough for the pressure to go away.

This is called the butterfly school of management. Today you get all excited about something and raise Cain to get it fixed. Tomorrow, as fixing just gets started, you find something else wrong and want that fixed. Flitting from problem to problem without permanently fixing any of them confuses and frustrates employees. They can neither predict nor please you. Most people want to please you if they can figure out what you want.

The butterfly-type manager is a good starter but a poor finisher.

Putting out fires is called management by crisis. Lack of long-range planning and good management means you'll spend all your time handling the latest short-term crisis. Don't confuse what's urgent with what's important.

Management—Democratic

MANAGEMENT IS NOT A DEMOCRATIC process. The only place for a binding democratic vote is in a genuine board of directors meeting, if you have them. Everywhere else, you must make the tough decisions and live with the results.

I definitely don't mean to close off communications or to be an autocratic manager. It's important to get input—ideas, discussion, and commitment—from everyone involved. It's equally important that people feel free to express opinions even when they know you don't agree. But when all the suggestions and recom-

mendations are in, the final decision is really yours.

Harry Truman had a sign on his desk: "The buck stops here." Location of final responsibility wasn't in doubt.

There's an apocryphal story about a cabinet meeting held by President Lincoln during the dark days of the Civil War. After listening to the opinions and advice of each cabinet member, Lincoln called for a vote. "Those in favor say aye." There was total silence. "Those opposed say no." All present voted no. Lincoln announced the result: "The ayes have it."

Management—Style and Ego

MANAGEMENT STYLE IS INDIVIDUAL. Under similar circumstances, different managers make different decisions because of their knowledge, education,

experience, value system, ego, or perception and evaluation of the problem.

All decisions are multiple choice. Almost every answer has elements of correctness and incorrectness. Different managers draw the line in different places, and your employees know it.

Someone else can manage your company. If you die, someone else will have to. That person's list of the ten biggest problems will probably contain six or seven problems you listed and three or four you didn't. That manager has different priorities and will spend her own and employees' time and effort doing different things in different proportions and with different emphasis.

But customers must be served at something above the survival level or your company will go out of business. This doesn't mean either of you were right or wrong. The difference is management style.

There are three basic ones:

1. *Autocratic*—giving orders and instructions without explaining why.

2. *Leadership*—explaining, motivating, and setting the example.

3. *Participative management* or *teamwork*—getting help and commitment by encouraging participation rather than insisting on an imposed solution.

Each style is appropriate and effective under different circumstances. In business, leadership and participative management are most effective and conducive to the motivation and teamwork necessary to grow a company. (See MANAGING PEOPLE—THEORY X AND THEORY Y.)

The real criterion is what course of action, as modified by opinions of employees and customers, will produce the greatest amount on the bottom line. Decisions that produce quick short-term profit to the detriment of long-term employee and customer relationships aren't productive.

Management culture is the embodiment of managerial attitudes and the company procedures that become rooted in that attitude. Your chosen way of doing business will imprint itself on all employees and survive within your company long after the original owners or builders are gone.

Ego

Everyone has an ego. Entrepreneurs and salesmen have big egos, high self-confidence, and high self-esteem. They must have these to withstand the rigors and trials of everyday business encounters with customers or employees. Some people are better than others at concealing and evaluating their own ego.

When ego gets in the way of a managerial decision, the result is often bad. Many deals have fallen through, not for lack of merit but because egos weren't satisfied, particularly those of the principals on opposite sides. Ego is never the expressed reason, but uninvolved observers and subordinates can tell.

In fact, your own ego may keep you from recognizing how your ego drives some of your decisions. It's difficult to "see ourselves as others see us." Ask your spouse or a trusted manager to point out decisions in which he or she thinks your ego overrides logic or merit.

The best executive is the one who has sense enough to pick good people to do what he wants done, and self-restraint enough to keep from meddling with them while they do it.

—Theodore Roosevelt

Ego is a powerful but not easily recognized factor in almost all entrepreneurial and managerial decisions. Ego makes you look at yourself rather than the problem. It often has a large influence on hiring, firing, and promotion decisions because these decisions are based on interaction between two egos.

One of the best ways I know to keep ego problems out of employee relations and managers' meetings is to focus on what's right rather than on who's right. By doing this, you keep the conversation and thinking centered on teamwork and actions toward the common goal, what's right for the team and the company. Decisions become less personal, and all share in accomplishing the goal.

When who's right becomes more important, egos get trampled and hurt. One person may briefly feel good as his suggestion wins approval, then dejected as a "better" one is brought forward. Finger pointing promotes personal conflict, hurt feelings, and a bad atmosphere for enthusiastic teamwork.

Managerial ego costs you when you stay in a money-losing deal because your ego won't let you admit that you made a mistake. When you start, you think every idea you act on is a good one.

Once you've begun, back your action with your best effort and give things a fair trial, but remember that not every idea proves to be a good one. When your ego won't let you cut your losses, it can be very expensive.

An example of an egotistical manager is the entrepreneur who insists that no one in the company but himself has good ideas. In my early career, I worked for such a person. The trusted "official family" recognized this. When we thought of something we agreed was beneficial, we conspired and took turns suggesting the improvement to him. He reacted as expected, giving many reasons why the idea wouldn't work. Ninety days later, he would propose it as his own idea, and the new policy or procedure would be put into effect.

I'm not saying an ego is bad. A strong ego, a high level of self-confidence and an optimistic attitude are essential for entrepreneurial success. I am saying you should recognize that your ego can cause you to make some bad business decisions.

Manager or Supervisor—Ideal

NOT EVERY ONE OF YOUR EMPLOYEES is ready or qualified to be a supervisor, but it's worth your time, effort, and money to select and train the best ones. The more people you have with in-depth managerial understanding and skill, the more smoothly your organization will run. Naming someone a manager doesn't automatically make that person a good supervisor.

An ideal manager should be consistent and fair with all employees. She is considerate of feelings, doesn't play favorites, and is neither unreasonable nor overly demanding. She sets a good personal example and builds enthusiasm among employees. Hard work and enthusiasm aren't the same as managerial skills, but they go a long way toward bridging the difference.

The ideal manager keeps an open door and listens attentively to employees, encouraging them to ask questions and to make their own decisions. She encourages initiative and new ideas, and is not argumentative. She does not think small.

A manager's job is to keep information flowing smoothly both up and down the chain of command, keep subordinates informed, and give clear instructions. A manager represents subordinates to her superior.

A supervisor keeps the chain of command intact and resists any tendencies he or other employees may have to jump to a higher level. A supervisor is interested in workers' progress as individuals. The good supervisor gives credit where credit is due by publicly seeking and praising people who make recognizable contributions.

The good supervisor has all-around knowledge of his trade, plans and organizes well, and is self-disciplined enough to accept and meet deadlines. The good supervisor continuously seeks to improve everyone's skills, including his own. He is honest and straightforward and has a sense of humor.

M

313

Spend more time running the business than you do running the office. You cannot make money running the office.

Employees prefer a supervisor they can be proud of, one they respect and trust. They want their supervisor to practice leadership and self-control, particularly under the pressure of an emergency, and to be consistent and predictable. Nobody likes to be led by a loser.

Supervising is easy in an established company when operations are smooth. It's the unexpected problem or crisis that brings out the leadership and courage of the seasoned manager.

The ultimate test of the manager or supervisor is the execution of the company's plan, the smoothness and enthusiasm with which he can move his section cooperatively forward. When you want to know if a supervisor is doing a good job, watch and listen to his subordinates.

Managerial Decisions—Judgment and Balance

314

FOR YEARS I KEPT a small balance scale on my desk as a reminder that everything I decided must be weighed against alternate choices and results. Balance advantages against disadvantages. Do the greatest good for the greatest number of either employees or customers, as you perceive it.

All managerial decisions are a matter of balancing perceived good results against perceived bad side effects. Every decision results from finding the balance point between several alternate decisions. In any decision, there are unknown and unmeasurable intangibles.

Different managers give these unquantifiable factors different values and arrive at different answers. No two entrepreneurs or managers will find the same balance point.

Experience has taught me that there is no one solution that is correct for all companies. One of the most interesting aspects of being a business consultant is observing and perhaps influencing the judgments and operations of different business owners. Where each puts her emphasis, which activity she spends the most time on, is revealing.

Few decisions are real no-brainers—either all white or all black. If they were, any monkey could decide. Expect disappointment and grumbling, in thought if not expressed, from some employees or customers following every significant managerial decision you make.

Your managerial balancing act comes down to judgment.

Judgment

At first, your judgment is based on intuition, emotion, and early business experience. Then later comes logic. Even later, an educated gut feeling tells you what to do. The older I get, the more confidence I have in my gut feelings, but by now my gut has been educated by years of experience.

There's no way to measure judgment, and there's almost no way to teach it. Judgment improves with knowledge and experience if you logically analyze results and don't make the same mistake twice.

Judging technical decisions is one of your most important managerial skills.

There's always a better way; you must constantly search for it. You can spend a lot of money chasing the wrong technological solution. Promoting people with the best judgment is more important than promoting people who are technically best qualified.

The most important decisions you make as owner-manager are probably marketing decisions (including the original idea you went into business with) and personnel decisions. In most cases, the latter are fundamentally more important to your business than technical or financial decisions.

The final judgment on any important matter must always be made by someone whose business life and fortune are on the line. Most likely, that person is you. Nevertheless, not only do you stand to gain or lose a major chunk of money by your decision, but so do the people you've chosen to help you run the company. Get input and ideas from your senior managers before you make these earth-shaking decisions.

Biting the Bullet
Even if you make each decision for the greatest good of the greatest number, your decision will pinch someone who's not in the greatest number, and you may be unpopular. But you're not trying to win a popularity contest; you're trying to run a successful business and win respect for your integrity and honest intentions to do what's right for the company and your employees, customers, associates, and suppliers.

Your managerial position for the tough decisions must be one that's morally correct, and one you can defend as a good business decision. Get all the facts you can, and once you're sure you're right, go ahead. The shoot-from-the-hip quick answer may not be correct after you gather more information and consider all the angles.

To do nothing is to have made a decision.

The question is this: If I do something that's good for this problem, what other problems am I creating or making worse? Morale? Cost? Cash? Employment? Customer acceptance?

Since you're the owner, you've got to bite the bullet and make final decisions in crucial, basic situations. Here are some of the toughest:

- Selecting or hiring senior managers. Do you choose the smartest and strongest you can find and afford, or do you select those who don't threaten your authority and knowledge?

- Expanding into a new market or bringing out a new product line. Is it the right time? Have you done your homework?

- Considering product quality or long-term goals versus short-term or temporary gains. Where do you compromise?

- Considering good and bad effects, as well as unexpected side effects, that flow from a decision. Are you shooting from the hip with inadequate information?

- Seeking or accepting help or advice from associates or a qualified outsider if you're unable to solve the problem. Is your ego in the way?

Knowing what to change and when is the epitome of managerial talent and judgment. These decisions determine how successful your business is and how much is left on your bottom line.

Managers' Meetings

WHEN YOUR COMPANY IS BIG ENOUGH that you hear "I don't know what's going on" complaints from managers, start to hold scheduled, formal management meetings. If you've created the right atmosphere, managers' meetings are one of your best opportunities for team building, updating reports, and keeping everyone informed about what's going on in other areas or departments.

Management meetings keep everyone working toward the same goals. Potential conflicts or misunderstandings are more easily avoided. In an atmosphere where there's genuine teamwork and motivated management, frequent and continuous communication between all levels of employees is a way of life.

Weekly managers' meetings are fairly customary, usually on Monday or Friday. I held mine on Fridays so more time could be spent over the weekend summarizing, thinking, and planning. This helped

everyone hit the ground running in the right direction Monday morning.

As soon as reliable financial information from the prior accounting period is available, discuss detailed financial and operational reporting in your meeting. Include comparisons with budgets and with the previous year. Timely reports and prompt meetings catch memories while they're still fresh enough to explain or understand what has happened.

Set an agenda for regular meetings that suits your situation. You could use each meeting for a short report on cash, followed by individual or departmental reports of activities or accomplishments. Or you might schedule one department to give a more detailed report of plans and accomplishments on a rotating basis.

Keep the meetings lively, interesting, and useful. With your highest-paid managers in that meeting, time is expensive, so keep things moving. If the department or division head cannot attend, he should send his best substitute. Don't waste the majority's time with unimportant things that concern only a few. If the format doesn't accomplish the purpose, change it. (See MEETINGS—IDEAL.)

If you prepare and pass out confidential written reports for discussion, gather and shred them after the meeting. Each department keeps its own files and information, so there's no need to build up duplicate files in all departments.

Input from everyone is important and needed. If possible, get everyone to agree on or at least understand priorities and objectives so all are pulling in the same direction. Stifling dissent and expressing strong differences of opinion are best done in private, if necessary.

You, the entrepreneur, make or silently approve all final decisions that are suggested by the manager giving the report. Afterwards, insist on and expect support from all. Then each manager will make individual decisions that contribute to overall company goals.

Managers—Selecting New Ones

PROMOTING DESERVING EMPLOYEES from within adds to morale and encourages individual growth. But if you need someone with new skills or greater technical knowledge than is available in house, hiring outsiders is the only way.

It is difficult for superior workers to do their best under mediocre managers.

Next to marketing decisions, the most important decisions you make for your company are the people you hire, retain, or promote to managerial positions. You, your company, and everyone working there will live with the results of your hiring decisions.

If your company is small, hiring an outsider as manager will cause resentment from old-timers who think one of them should have the job. However, you must make the decision that's best for the company. If the outsider really has the technical and people skills, she will win the respect of the group within 90 days. Employees will then accept the outsider and her instructions as well as the wisdom of your decision. If you've selected a phony or an incompetent family member, the resentment will linger or grow.

If you hire an outsider for a senior managerial position, in addition to checking references, educational accreditation, and professional accomplishments, pay $500 for a background check, credit check, and lawsuit check. Judging a person's ability to be effective at this level from three interviews or a résumé isn't satisfactory. If a person can't manage his own life or credit, why do you think he will do better managing yours?

If you promote your best manager from within and she fails at the new job, you not only have an operating problem but you've probably ruined your best manager. Other managers will have lost confidence in the promoted manager's abilities. Moving her back to her old job is a demotion. She will probably resign.

When you're selecting quality managers, look at the following characteristics. People who have more of them are more consistently successful at any job they undertake:

- Logical thinking
- Organization of time

- High energy level
- Getting along with people on three levels—superiors, peers, and subordinates
- Perception—sensitivity to others' thoughts and feelings

Complying with hiring laws is sometimes difficult. You must find someone compatible with your management style, approach to customers, attitude toward work, and other employees. Proceed slowly enough to check references and get to know the person thoroughly. Based on merit, hire or promote the person you think will be best for your company in the long term.

Every managerial position you seek to fill will require some degree of technical knowledge. The best technician isn't necessarily the best manager. Choose the candidate with the best people skills and best judgment over the candidate with the greatest technical knowledge.

Managing People—Theory X and Theory Y

THIS 30-YEAR-OLD THEORY is still the best and most concise description I've seen for opposing managerial assumptions and attitudes in dealing with employees. Douglas McGregor expressed these ideas in *The Human Side of Enterprise* (New York: McGraw-Hill, 1960).

Theory X

1. Employees are stupid, lazy, dishonest individuals who work only because they have to.

2. These employees are motivated by detailed rules, threats of punishment, penalties, commands, and "driving."

3. Management style is dictatorial, authoritarian, detailed, and penalty oriented—the "stick" approach.

Theory Y

1. Employees are intelligent, energetic, trustworthy individuals who want to do good work.

2. These employees are motivated by explaining objectives, setting goals with their participation, setting examples, and leading.

3. Management style is leadership, motivation, guidance, inspiration, rewards, and the "carrot" approach.

People who do things because they want to will accomplish a lot more than people who do things because they believe they have to.

> *The deepest principle in human nature is the craving to be appreciated.*
>
> —William James

319

Margin, Gross Margin, or Markup

PROFITS OR FINANCIAL GAINS you expect to make from your business start with the difference between what it costs you to buy or produce a product or service and what you can sell it for. For each individual transaction or sale, this is called *margin.*

Every successful entrepreneur I know maintains intense and constant scrutiny of his margin for each transaction—the most crucial information on the way to profits.

The total margin for all individual sales during the period shown on your financial statements is called *gross margin* or *gross profit.* Your operating state-

ment shows this number where the cost of goods sold is deducted from net sales.

This is the first important calculation of your earnings statement. Then, operating or fixed expenses (such as selling, general, and administrative expenses) are deducted from that number to show your operating profit. If your gross margin isn't large enough to cover those expenses, you'll show an operating loss.

Your break-even point is the sales volume that allows your gross margin to cover fixed expenses (sales, general, and administrative). Sales in excess of that amount will be profitable. If it costs you more to produce or buy a product than you can sell it for, you'll never break even until you can lower your cost or raise your selling price to produce a gross margin. (See PRICING.)

Covering your fixed expenses with a large percentage gross margin on a small sales volume is much better than using a large sales volume with a low percentage gross margin.

Gross margin is of basic significance in computing the amount of start-up capital required for any new venture. You should be able to provide, at or during start-up, enough capital to cover business operating expenses (general and administrative expenses, including your salary) until you reach the break-even point, where gross margin will equal these expenses.

The slimmer your gross margin percentage or amount, the less margin you have for mistakes. When you have a gross margin of only 15 percent, a small mistake can be fatal. If your gross margin is 40 percent, you can recover from lots of mistakes.

The margin is exactly the same number of dollars or amount that's called markup in some industries, but the percentage is computed using a different number as 100 percent.

The difference is whether you consider setting price or cost as your 100 percent reference point. If you sell something for $1.00 which has cost you $0.70, you have a *margin* of $0.30 or 30 percent of the $1.00 selling price.

If you buy something for $0.70, how much must you mark it up to produce a selling price of $1.00? Here you're speaking of the $0.70 cost as 100 percent. A *markup* of 42.9 percent on the 100 percent cost of $0.70 is required to arrive at the $1.00 selling price. This is computed by dividing $0.30 by the $0.70 cost.

Some people speak of a 30 percent markup on a product costing $0.70 and selling for $1.00. Both parties must understand what's considered 100 percent or there will be confusion.

Marketing

MARKETING AND SALES AREN'T THE SAME, although in a one-person sales force, there's little room to differentiate. Just as you are your own sales manager if you've appointed no one else, you are also your own marketing manager.

Marketing includes more than just selling. Marketing is the intentional creating and maintaining of customer relationships. This continuing process starts with understanding your market and your customers and includes anything that creates and maintains a favorable environment for sales.

Sales are individually made, usually with one salesperson talking to one customer and taking an order. Marketing is preparing all the programs, advertisements, attitudes, events, printed materials, and preliminaries that make the sales event happen smoothly and frequently. Marketing includes preparing point-of-sale materials, sales brochures, trade shows, promotions, packaging, pricing, and advertising.

Start your marketing plans even before you have invented or produced a final product or decided on your final business idea. There's no point in inventing, developing, or producing something you can't sell, unless it's for your own use. Many of your decisions in the developmental process should be controlled or influenced by your plans to find buyers. Unfortunately, that doesn't happen often enough.

Only a few products or services have truly universal appeal or use. Know your company's niche market or quickly find that segment of the larger market that it can profitably serve. You'll waste much sales effort and money if you don't know how to distribute product information economically to potential customers. Once you've identified your target market, concentrate on communications and activities that will bring you closer to actual sales.

All start-up companies are desperate for sales. The easiest course of action is to hire salespeople and send them out to do what they do best: sell. As the entrepreneur, you think they should know what to do. If they need help, brochures, price lists, or advertising, they'll ask for it. Maybe—or maybe not.

The real-life trick is to monitor sales results, quickly detect both favorable and unfavorable developments, and act immediately to adapt to new sales realities. Where and how are most new customers found? What features of your product or service cause them to buy from you?

If you don't do enough preliminary marketing thinking and planning, your company will move into its own market position and personality. If the company survives at all, it will ultimately follow the path of least resistance to find the most sales to the most customers. Many companies are gone because they ran out of money before the entrepreneur could find the most favorable market and identify the ideal customer profile.

Entrepreneurs frequently say, "We're short of cash," or "Our profit margins are too low." They seldom say, "I haven't clearly defined my market or my position in it." Positioning is a means of targeting marketing efforts to specific segments of the market that the company can uniquely serve.

Customers' buying habits and attitudes are strong. Getting customers to make major changes is tedious and expensive.

Look at your business from the outside in, through the customer's eyes, rather than from the inside out.

Marketing Plan

YOUR MARKETING PLAN IS THE MOST important part of your business plan, even more important than the financial section. It deserves to be carefully thought out and complete at the beginning. As you get larger, separate it from the overall business plan. It requires more frequent revision and change.

In achieving success, there's no substitute for having a written plan and tracking it to get results. Large companies operate with goals and comprehensive strategies, with prescribed step-by-step activities to achieve specific results.

Your mission statement contains a succinct description of your marketing plan in one to three sentences. Once you know your ideal customer's profile, figure out the shortest, most impressive and eco-

nomical way to present why he should buy your product rather than your competitor's.

Your plan includes your marketing concept—who you are, what you do for people, and how you can make it easier for people to do business with you. What need do you satisfy? What motivates your customer to buy your products rather than someone else's? What kind of business do you now have, and what kind of additional business do you want to get? What type of sales organization will best introduce your product and serve your target market?

Define your present customer base. Who accounts for the largest percentage of sales? The next largest? Knowing what the customer does with your product is an important part of your marketing knowledge. You must know how she uses it to know how to improve her use and satisfaction. If you know that, you can figure out how to serve her better.

Design a sales effort that will produce sales for your company in the marketing segment you identify. And remember, nothing turns out the way it's planned.

In the marketing plan, answer the following basic questions:

■ What is your overall market—local, nationwide, or worldwide? What economic or demographic features influence this market? What's the industry sales volume? Is it growing, declining, or remaining constant? How many competitors do you have? How big?

■ What kind and type of company or person is your ideal customer? What is your ideal customer's size, location, status, activities, and other distinguishing characteristics?

■ How do you reach this customer most easily and economically? What is your continuing program? What do you do first? What do you do next?

■ Why should this customer buy your product or service rather than your competitor's? What do you do uniquely and better than anyone else?

■ What price should you sell your product or service for? Why?

How does this compare to available competition?

■ What level of service or availability should you maintain? Is speed of service or location of products important? What should the warranty be?

■ What does the product cost to produce? What profit margin do you expect?

■ What are the strengths and weaknesses of your competitive situation? Who are your competitors? What other products or services compete for your customers' dollars?

■ What product or service changes or improvements should you consider?

Don't try to be all things to all people. Decide what not to sell. Maxim's doesn't sell hamburgers, McDonald's doesn't sell chateaubriand, but both are in the food business.

The best marketing approach differs drastically from industry to industry and within segments of an industry. The nature of the sales effort depends on how the marketplace for that industry and product works. It also depends on the company's strengths and weaknesses.

This example may show you an entrepreneur's path to marketing success. A brilliant engineer developed an economical method of adding a wear-resistant surface to large steel plates but had trouble marketing the finished product. One single specialty salesman traveling by car found enough customers to keep the company in business, but without much growth. The engineer made a deal to market the product through a local steel distributor who had 20 salesmen, an obvious improvement. Each of the salesmen put a few more pages into a voluminous catalog, but never mentioned it to customers because none knew anything about it, and new products are hard to sell. Total sales showed little improvement.

After another year, a deal was made with a national steel distributor with 150 salesmen. The result was the same, for the same reason. The lone specialty salesman sold just about as much as the national sales organization. The engineer concluded that he must build a specialized finished product using this abrasion-resistant product and market the finished product in a niche market. He chose a large refinery valve, the one that wore out most frequently and was hardest and most expensive to replace. Within several years he had practically cornered the world market for this refinery valve, and his prosperous company's sales volume had multiplied many times over. Same product—different marketing approach.

Your local bookstore has several books on marketing plans and how to research and write them. Remember, your business objective is to create customers. From serving them, you expect to create cash flow. That's all there is to it.

Introduce a new marketing strategy even when you have a good one. The market is constantly changing, and what worked best two years ago may not work now.

Mastermind Advisory Group

UNLESS YOU HAVE A CORPORATION, you don't need a formal board of directors, but experienced, outside opinions are frequently helpful.

For wisdom, guidance, or just a sympathetic ear, you need an informal, mastermind group (similar to a focus group) of three to seven people, trusted friends whose business judgment you respect and with whom you can freely discuss your most serious problems. They must feel free to express helpful opinions, including constructive criticism, on what they think is best for you.

You don't ever need these people to meet as a group. Plan a meal or a drink in an atmosphere where you have time for an unhurried, serious conversation, and present your problem to each as a friend.

Each person will have a different attitude and a different emphasis on various facets of the problem. Each will ask different questions. And each will suggest solutions from the viewpoint of his own experience. Every time you present the problem to a different person, you'll understand it better yourself. At some point, your solution will become clear.

Happiness is having dreams. Success is making those dreams come true.

Meeting the Payroll

NOT FEELING THE RECURRING PRESSURE to have cash on hand to meet the payroll is one of the business experiences that separates departmental managers of large businesses from entrepreneurial owners.

Meeting the payroll is the most compelling, recurring crisis you'll face. Paychecks that bounce or are late create an insurmountable obstacle to management credibility. Most creditors will usually wait a few more days, but your employees' families expect that check on payday to buy groceries, pay the rent, and take care of clothing and household bills. It must not be late.

Similarly, your check to commission salespeople and independent contractors is their paycheck. Their families as well as their smooth-running financial relationships depend upon the same dependable, prompt delivery. Wives (and sometimes husbands) frequently come early on payday to pick up their spouse's check for urgent bills.

If checks are unavoidably late or temporarily no good, put an extra $20 in each paycheck when it does arrive. This will work only once, however.

Whatever planning is required to have enough cash in the bank to meet the payroll, do it.

Meetings—Ideal

THE MAIN PURPOSE OF ANY MEETING should be to get simultaneous input of ideas from multiple sources, to reach agreement or understanding on specific problems or procedures, to give information to everyone at the same time or from the same source so there is less chance of any misunderstanding, or to strengthen teamwork and commitment as all agree to work for the same goal. But if there isn't any clear or urgent need, don't have a meeting just because it's Wednesday morning.

In some large companies, meetings can become a practical alternative to work. People who either hate to make decisions or would rather talk about work than do it can fill many business hours with pointless meetings; almost any subject will do. You might surprise yourself at the cash cost of a meeting if you multiply the hourly wages of all who attend by the number of hours they were present.

Keeping these meetings productive is more likely if an agenda (including adjournment time) is prepared and circulated prior to the meeting. Electronic mail (e-mail) makes some meetings unnecessary if your company is big enough to have a computer network. Complete minutes of proceedings usually get in the way, but you should confirm decisions or actions with brief memos for clarity.

The following steps are necessary to have an ideal meeting:

1. Decide on a specific purpose or purposes for the meeting.

2. Write an agenda that covers all the necessary subjects to accomplish those purposes.

3. Personally notify anyone who is to have a prominent part in the meeting or who is expected to present anything. Rearrange the schedule if necessary.

4. Send a notice to all who are to attend. Give date, time, place, and purpose of the meeting. List those who are requested to attend and ask to be notified if they cannot. Include the agenda if appropriate.

5. Send reports or materials to be read or understood before the meeting.

6. Be sure you have everything you need for the meeting (i.e., enough copies of reports, graphs, and printed material). Be sure the meeting room is ready with chairs, paper, felt-tip markers and drawing board, flip charts, or whatever else you need.

7. Start on time. Keep it short. Keep the discussion on track and on the subject so you can accomplish the stated purposes.

8. Appoint people or agree exactly who will be responsible for taking any action. Agree on a date by which each step or item is to be accomplished.

9. Follow up within 48 hours with necessary confirmations or other information.

The above steps are for an internal meeting attended by employees of your company. Meetings with outsiders (such as customers, bankers, or financial people) don't usually generate the same notices or preparation. However, you'll have more productive and satisfactory meetings if you prepare for them in much the same way.

When you travel to another city to attend a decision-making meeting, meet first at supper to discuss the problems affecting any decisions that must be made. Use the night for analysis and thinking, and meet again at breakfast to finalize things.

Tired minds make tired choices.

Buying a meal is the cheapest way to get a person's undivided attention. Breakfast meetings are best. (Lunches are good, too, but supper is marginal.) At a breakfast meeting, everyone's mind is fresh. Yours is the first problem of the day, and the attitude is "Let's get this one solved so we can get on with the rest." Alcohol is never mentioned. You can concentrate on the problem without the interruptions of phone calls or other business activities.

Mentors and Mentoring

YOU PROBABLY HAVE A BUSINESS ROLE model—a previous boss, friend, relative, or parent whose course of action and demeanor you've always admired. At decisive moments, you've patterned yourself after this person, consciously or unconsciously.

A mentor is a real-life role model, usually an older person, who provides sympathy and understanding and helps you improve personally and in your business career. Your business mentor will hold you accountable for performing according to your plan.

Business has become so complex that your learning curve takes longer, but you're under pressure to learn faster because market cycles are getting shorter. A mentor can hasten success by keeping you focused on profits and helping you avoid costly mistakes that she is already familiar with.

Many small business owners are good enough salespeople to have experienced a good measure of success with the top line, which is sales volume. The mentor focuses heavily on the bottom line, on ways to help you increase your profitability and develop the managerial skills of all your managers.

Many mentors call themselves "profit mentors" because they keep you focused on your profit objectives. Profit mentors should cost you nothing because they should make you more money than you pay them. Aim to get your investment back with big dividends that keep coming for the rest of your managerial life. Your biggest cost should be your committed time and cooperation.

Consulting is a short-term relationship with limited objectives. The mentor relationship is a lasting alliance with repeated, regular sessions with your chosen mentor, focusing on you and your business. Every week or two this regular relationship puts you on the spot, spurring you to perform according to your stated plans.

The average person learns from his own mistakes, while the genius learns from the mistakes of others.

The mentor who can be of most help is one with many years of experience as entrepreneur, CEO, or department or division manager with a larger company. This person should have had to make financial and personnel decisions, then live with or correct mistakes, including her own, when they were discovered. You want experience, maturity, fresh viewpoints, and familiarity with your operations. You're looking for battle scars from the same kinds of battles you're fighting.

A mentor is on your team as an instructor, a companion, and a coach, not as a player. She will help you improve your management skills, not take control. A mentor is a counselor, experienced team member, confidential sounding board when you need one, supporter and motivator, partner and trusted friend. The mentor is a guru who gives honest advice without fear of offending you.

The mentor helps you choose your purpose, mission, vision, and goals. The mentor helps you develop business plans and organization charts, establish sales forecasts and budgets, and develop policy manuals. A mentor speaks straight and isn't a yes-person. A mentor asks tough questions and holds you accountable for results. A mentor takes a personal interest in you and your business success. Your success is her success.

When you find the mentor in whom you have confidence, establish a formal relationship, probably involving money, as well as a definite time to meet. Unless a mentor is a relative or very good friend, you'll get what you pay for.

You both need a clear understanding about hours and fees. Set clear goals for the relationship and the business. Weekly meetings at a regular time provide the best continuity. The relationship can be terminated any time you feel it isn't producing the desired results.

Working with a CEO mentor is like having your own in-house MBA program. The mentor should review financial statements and problems with you and help you decide on appropriate remedies. If you desire, the mentor may attend major policy meetings with employees, shareholders, banks, and suppliers.

The mentor is around the company often enough to be accepted by employees and management as part of the team, not as an outsider, so they're more likely to reveal their true opinions and thoughts. They'll speak to her more freely and frequently hold problems until she arrives. Much of the usual cost of educating a consultant is spread over a long-term relationship with a mentor.

Go out of your way to make sure your senior employees know the mentor personally. If all they see is the mentor going straight into your office for a two- to three-hour closed-door conference, the only result of which appears to be your quoting new ideas or emphasizing some pet project, your employees will consider the mentor an enemy.

The mentor should be considered a member of your management team. It's in your best interest for the mentor to spend time in private conversation with senior managers. They should feel free to discuss their problems. The mentor should attend some special or routine management meetings to assess these managers and their reactions to you, and to catch the flavor of your management style.

If the mentor doesn't establish a confidential, team-member relationship with your managers, they will suggest cutting out the mentor when you discuss cost cutting during the next business downturn.

What terminates the mentoring relationship? It's not a cut-and-dried decision. After one to two years, you've picked the mentor's brains and gotten most of the benefit of her knowledge and experience, depending upon your stage of development and how much advanced knowledge and wisdom she has to impart to you. After this, you may feel inclined to pick another brain, or you may feel that you can do what you need by yourself. By this time you should be experienced enough to select another mentor who is compatible with your ideas, ambitions, and plans—you may have arrived at the stage where you don't need a mentor.

Later, after you succeed and retire or change your circumstances, you can become a mentor for some inexperienced entrepreneur.

329

Mission Statement

YOUR MISSION STATEMENT is a carefully expressed written statement that tells your new and continuing employees and the world exactly what you went into business to do. It's like your Ten Commandments.

Your vision concerns the company you're trying to build and the market you're trying to serve. As your business grows, your philosophy of business emerges and becomes apparent to your employees and customers, even if you don't write it down. The mission statement must be compatible with this. Your goals are individual stepping stones toward accomplishing the agreed-upon mission.

The mission statement should contain key words and phrases that describe precisely what you're trying to do for your customers. It should help focus the company's efforts on those areas that promise the greatest return. It should clarify the mission for employees and inspire them toward its accomplishment.

In its simplest form, your mission statement should contain three things:

1. what you do, especially what is unique or advantageous about it;

2. whom you do it for, particularly what customers are most likely to buy from you; and

3. why customers should buy from you, which includes what you do better than anyone else.

A deadline for its accomplishment makes your mission statement a specific goal.

The owner or top manager generally writes the first draft, but in roundtable groups it should be submitted and discussed with everyone in the company. The process of trying to get associates to consciously agree on the purpose of the enterprise is often difficult and almost always revealing. People with widely varying motives can be brought together where common purposes and motivation can be agreed upon.

When decisions are made strictly on bottom-line arithmetic, people get crunched along with the numbers.

Involve as many employees as you can in formulating your mission statement. Expect and accept changes and clarification. Avoid platitudes; strive for reality and relevance; "The customer is always right" and "We're going to be the best" aren't what you're searching for. Keep the mission statement short and to the point, but make it complete. Leave out extraneous matters, including religion. A million slogans are floating around out there, but a clear, concise, meaningful statement is hard to get.

There will be many battles over what the mission statement should and should not include, but the final draft should be acceptable to everyone. Work on it in conference with the managers who will commit to and live by it. You want it to be clearly understood by managers, employ-ees, suppliers, and customers—and to inspire and motivate them.

Once it's in writing, give it to your customers, your employees, and anyone else who will stand still and listen. Make a large plaque of it, and hang it in your reception room or near the checkout stand. Periodically, whenever market conditions or your operations require, revise it to reflect what you're doing now or moving toward doing.

An ideal example of a mission statement that is short, direct, and motivating is the old Avis slogan: "We try harder."

Mistakes—Admitting Them

UNTIL YOU DECIDE TO QUIT your business, you're going to make mistakes—some large, some small, none fatal (you hope). Be realistic enough and honest enough with yourself to recognize your own mistakes and failures as well as the shortcomings of your company. You must be able to differentiate your dreams of the future from the realities of the past and present.

Nothing goes onward and upward without interruption. A simple change of circumstance or overreaching can create problems. Don't be afraid of "two steps forward, one step back." A backward step helps regain equilibrium and a solid base for those next two steps forward. As they say in boxing, winning consists of getting up one more time than you're knocked down.

Save your humble pie for when you're dining alone, if you wish, but unless you're completely honest with yourself, you won't grow in wisdom, stature, and managerial skill. You will too quickly reach your level of incompetence.

Face reality squarely enough to admit mistakes to yourself and, on occasion, to others. Don't let a large or insecure ego get in the way of progress or profits while you stubbornly let your small original mistake grow into a new, larger one. You're fooling yourself if you think that none of your customers (or employees) have noticed your errors.

> ### *The only way to make no mistakes is to do nothing.*

It helps morale and sets a good tone for teamwork if, on proper occasions with individuals or before a group, you sometimes admit that you made a mistake when you made that decision last month or took that action last year. Follow this admission with what you're now doing to correct the situation.

Honest confession is good for the soul (yours and your company's) and will so surprise your associates that you'll get lots of cooperation and help. They'll be less afraid to admit their own mistakes.

Make little mistakes first—try little things or run a pilot model. Don't bet the farm on anything you haven't proven.

Money vs. Time

WHICH DO YOU HAVE THE MOST OF—time or money? And is time working for you or against you? Time is always a factor in your decision-making process.

Many of your managerial decisions will be based on your answers to the above questions. With lots of time, you can arrange a better deal, find substitutes, get more training or information, gather more money, or work your way around an obstacle. With lots of money, you can solve problems now by hiring experts or buying whatever you need.

In the survival stage and much of the growth stage, you'll probably have more time than money. You'll substitute learning time or planning time for money in many actions. For example, in your deci-sions on new or used equipment or fixtures, you might choose affordable older equipment even though it's slower and not as productive.

In late growth stage and all of the big-business stage, you'll have more money than time. In this lovely state of affairs, buy new equipment specifically suited to your situation rather than almost-right used equipment.

When you expand your floor space or capacity, the money-versus-time question becomes the real decision point. How much of tomorrow's need or capacity can you afford to provide with today's dollars? Buying now for future needs really puts your managerial judgment of money versus time to the test.

Mutually Profitable

UNLESS BOTH SIDES PROFIT from a deal, it won't last. A one-sided deal, even if signed and agreed upon, will not endure.

A fair handshake deal between two well-intentioned people is better than a one-sided deal with a person whose real intention is to beat you out of something. A 30-page contract can't cover all the contingencies and survive if the underlying intent isn't there. The party who lacks the intent will find a reason or a way to end the relationship.

It's better to make a decent deal with an honorable person than it is to make a very favorable deal with a son of a bitch.

M

333

Name—Choice Of

BEFORE YOU COMMIT YOURSELF to printing literature or publicly marketing any business name or name change, be careful that you're not infringing on someone else's legally established name or trademark. A search of county, state, and federal records for this purpose isn't expensive, and it can save you major expenses later, maybe even a lawsuit.

The best choice for a company name is something short, simple, and descriptive of your business. It should be a name that's easy for prospective customers to remember and associate immediately with either the type of business you're in or something distinctive about it.

N

334

Once you've established a name and used it long enough to have acquired some favorable customer recognition, for heaven's sake, don't change it. One of the worst things a new owner of an established, successful company can do is to change the name to something customers don't recognize. It may be good for your ego, but it will confuse your customers and employees.

On the other hand, you may have a good business reason to change the name of your own or an acquired company. It may have a poor reputation, a name that conjures up more bad feelings than good. If so, change the name to emphasize that there's new management, a different company, or a major change. How much you want to emphasize that this was "for-merly Such-and-Such Company" depends on how much residual good will there is. You may want people to think it's a brand-new company and to forget about the old one.

If you want to change the name of a successful operation, do it gradually as you reprint your signs, literature, and sales material. At first, use both names: "Old Name, a Division of _____," "affiliated with _____," or "formerly _____." During the first six months to a year, print the new name in smaller type than the old. For the second step, either make both names the same size or make the new name larger if it has established favorable customer recognition. After two years or so, use only the new name and drop the old. This way you can gradually use up all the materials printed with the old name and replace them with your new name.

Pride is a commitment and an attitude that separates excellence from mediocrity.

If you find that you're innocently infringing on someone else's name or trademark, you can usually avoid an expensive lawsuit by agreeing to change over a specified period. After several years of using the initials of one of my new companies, I was notified that they were also the initials of one of the largest companies in England. Their trademark, using these initials, was registered in Washington, and their legal department was prepared to insist that I cease and desist using same. I didn't have the money to fight and would probably have lost anyway. They

agreed to the above procedure.

Of course, your marketing name has little or nothing to do with the name on your corporate charter or other legal papers. You or your lawyer can file "doing business as" (DBA) papers or whatever is required in your state to operate under an assumed name. All my comments here are directed toward the more important concepts of customer recognition and reaction rather than legal names.

Negotiating

LEARN TO NEGOTIATE WITH IMAGINATION, confidence, understanding, and apparent reluctance. Well-developed negotiating skills are essential for small-business owners because they make so many one-of-a-kind deals. Every time you hire someone, you negotiate payment and performance terms. Every new vendor has different terms and conditions.

Other than small, packaged retail items, few things have a fixed price with only one set of terms and conditions. In fact, you can cut corners or gain additional concessions from any major transaction by negotiation. Learn to negotiate concessions or guarantees for yourself. Learn to deal with them when the other party wants them from you.

Even if you're anxious to make the deal, don't show it. Appear reluctant; you'll get more concessions. Never say yes

too quickly. When the other party mentions price for the first time, visibly flinch or hesitate. Use facial expressions or body language to indicate disbelief or disappointment. The first offer is always worse than the final quotation. Always try to get at least one concession from the other side for every concession you make.

Silence is one of the best negotiating tactics you can use. When the opposition pauses, expecting you to comment or counteroffer, remain silent. After a pause, your opponent may offer more concessions because you didn't respond to the previous offer. The one who wants the deal the most is the one who breaks the silence.

In important negotiations to buy a company, a failure of communication within my own company cost me dearly. I had made my almost-final offer and was awaiting a response. Hearing nothing after two days, I called on the company owner in person and improved my offer by an additional 6 percent. He replied, "I called yesterday to tell you we accepted your offer, but if you want to sweeten the deal some more, we'll still take it." The slip notifying me of his phone call hadn't reached my desk. (It was still one of the best deals I ever made. We increased the company's sales by a factor of 15 over the next 10 years.)

Usually, when negotiations are completed and a contract is ready for signatures, the deal goes through with no further problems. However, some people or ethnic groups never consider the negotiation process ended. Oral understandings don't always get into the final papers, or a question that you consider settled gets reopened later. Some people continue to negotiate extra concessions, including last-minute, handwritten changes in final documents, until the last dollars are exchanged.

When you're in an involved, multi-part negotiation, agree in the beginning that no early, partial understandings are binding until all items are totally negotiated and agreed. You may give away something on an early, minor point that you may not wish to concede in light of later changes.

You get not what you deserve, but what you negotiate.

Negotiating well is an essential skill. It's an interesting exercise in human nature—and it's rewarding, too. A good reference is *You Can Negotiate Anything,* by Herb Cohen (Secaucus, N.J.: Citadel Press, 1991). Listening to tapes is also a good way to develop this skill.

N

336

Niche Markets

WHAT YOU'RE LOOKING FOR IS A NICHE in some market that you can fill better or faster than anyone else. Find a niche for a specialized product or service with a potential volume too small to attract and hold the large companies but fine for your small company. Serving a particular market niche better than any other company becomes the unique reason for your economic existence.

Small companies have these advantages in filling niche markets:

■ Your reaction or delivery time can be faster. From the large company, requested material comes on the next regular shipment, or after the delays of processing through three departments, getting approval from others, or fitting into the schedule. You can process this information faster and serve the customer better.

■ You can supply customized products or services, or you can modify products or services quickly, easily, and in smaller quantities to suit special or limited individual needs. The large company has standardized models, colors, sizes, quantities, and procedures. Variations either cannot be delivered at all or only at excessive cost or delay. You can supply models or items that are in too little demand, too small in volume, or too specialized to be economically manufactured and delivered by the large company.

■ You can make it easier for customers to get what they want by doing business with you than by dealing with the big boys. Everyone likes to take the path of least resistance; make it the path to your door. You may be more convenient geographically; you may offer one-stop shopping or one-source responsibility for multiple services or products, or specialize by offering a larger variety of a few chosen items than is available in other places. You cannot be everything to everyone, so specialize.

■ You can provide more personal service with a smile and attention to customers' individual needs. Deliver at night or at the back door or with other needed items. Customize even the paperwork to meet customers' requirements. Make the customer feel wanted and appreciated. Large companies find this difficult to do.

By the time you've filled one niche market, you'll probably have found another that's similar or related. Such finds are your expansion opportunities. If you find enough of these niches and build a big enough company, some smart, young entrepreneurs will find niches in your market that your company has become too big and too slow to service properly.

N

337

Businesses planned for service are apt to succeed. Businesses planned for profit are apt to fail.

—Nicholas M. Butler

Non-Compete Agreements

IF SPECIAL TECHNICAL KNOWLEDGE or valuable information is proprietary and significant to your business, consider having key employees who know and use the information execute non-compete agreements as allowed by your state law. Discuss with your lawyer how you can legally protect your information from disclosure or prevent employees from using it to compete with you after they've left.

To show that you consider the information valuable and proprietary, you will have to demonstrate the procedures or safeguards you routinely use within the company to keep unauthorized persons from finding or knowing the information. (See TRADE SECRETS.) For example, mark all drawings or technical descriptions "confidential." Documents, equipment, or the areas where they are used should be kept under lock and key to control access and use. No checklist can guarantee success, but you must demonstrate genuine efforts to keep the information secret from all but authorized employees with the need to know.

Enforcing such agreements is difficult because courts are reluctant to deprive anyone of the right to make a living. Essential to your success is for the court to find that the information is unusual, proprietary, and not readily available elsewhere, and that the agreement is reasonable in its future limitations in both time and geographic location.

The time limit might be from one to three years after termination of employment. The geographical limits might be within 5 or 150 miles of your location, within the same county, or within the same state, depending upon the nature of your business and its customers. A limitation on solicitation of business from your customers is hardest to enforce.

Have your lawyer draw up an agreement between the company and each employee you expect to be bound by such an agreement; usually this includes only key technical or managerial people. The best time to get it signed is when the employee is hired. Discuss and explain it as part of the hiring process. Keep signed copies in a safe place.

Ask your lawyer what's necessary to make a binding contract with employees who already work for the company. The content and wording of the agreement are important. You want their agreement that they will not disclose the information to others, including other employees, who have no need to know. You want them not to become owners, managers, or employees of competing firms within the time and space limits of the agreement.

There's value in getting signed agreements even when your lawyer tells you enforcement is doubtful. Most people are honest and will observe the moral obligation they've agreed to, especially if they think it's fair and reasonable.

N

338

Opinion Differences among Managers

YOU WANT ASSOCIATES AND MANAGERS to be innovative, independent thinkers. This means they won't always agree with you or with each other.

Two equally dedicated managers can come to opposite conclusions based on their evaluations of the same facts or circumstances. In most instances, they're equally sincere in trying to do what's best for the company. But business problems have so many facets that deciding which are crucial becomes a matter of opinion based on personal or business background or experience.

Encourage your managers to express constructive ideas and solutions to problems. Stop or discourage destructive criticism or personal attacks. When problems arise, use your sense of humor and peacemaking skills to maintain a calm atmosphere and keep the proceedings moving toward less personal, less violent discussion. Explain that even a good plan must give way to a better.

If you and I agree all the time, one of us is unnecessary.

All final decisions are up to you. That's where the buck stops. After you've considered everything, thanked everyone for his input, and made your choice, expect all to fall into line and give their best efforts to go forward. If team spirit doesn't prevail almost all the time, you may have a player who should be on a different team.

O
339

"Or Else"

ANYONE WHO DELIVERS THIS ULTIMATUM to you should be prepared to accept "or else." If it's spoken by a valuable employee or manager, remind her of this and give her a chance to reconsider before you accept her offer.

The reason is obvious. If you're not willing to take the "or else" option, you hand the other person a ready-made weapon to get whatever she wants for the remainder of your relationship.

Don't make yourself uncomfortable or your company unmanageable by giving associates or employees this power. To keep future relationships on an even footing, 99 times out of 100 you'll have to accept the "or else." If there's an urgent reason why you can't do without this employee right now, work your way into an acceptable alternate solution as quickly as possible, then act appropriately. (See INDISPENSABLE PERSON.)

Organization Charts and Operating Structures

IN THE SURVIVAL STAGE, all employees—including you—are so busy working they don't have much time to plan. You hold few or no staff meetings because everyone knows what's going on. Everyone is on a first-name basis. You don't have an organization chart, and you don't need one. You delegate very little—you just do it. Management is a one-person show for one happy family of workers.

Even if it's just one person, every business operation requires the basic functions of sales, production, and minimum administration. Depending upon the nature of your business, you may also need engineering, design, research, and other specialized functions as you grow. Each function will expand into more people and ultimately into departments.

The entire purpose of your operation must be oriented toward better customer service. Continued growth means new management approaches, adopted not in a sudden shift to brand-new methods but in an evolutionary process.

If you can sense the need for these changes and implement them without psychological hang-ups or disruption of the company's daily efficiency, you'll move successfully from one phase to the next.

If you can't deal with the changes, you'll find your company stuck at a certain level because of your late decisions, inefficiencies, and unintentional neglect.

As the operation grows and becomes more complex, organizational structure appears and management practices begin to evolve; delegation becomes functional specialization. Functions form into groups, such as production, sales, inspection, and shipping. These or others may become one-person departments, or one person may have responsibility for several significant functions, none large enough to require full time.

Your enterprise becomes the sum of these parts. Coordination and control take the form of added information systems, reporting mechanisms, and more frequent planning and performance reviews. Operations require meetings, memos, policies, and procedure manuals, many of which you never dreamed of when you started.

A growing organization must be flexible. Organize it the way it wants to work—the simplest way. As it gets larger, it loses flexibility but gains focus and controllability.

340

The earliest specialized requirement is probably sales. The sales department will expand to include marketing, advertising, possibly inside and outside sales, specialized product sales or territories, and sales administration. If you're in a retail operation, sales will be your largest department.

The next specialized requirement is production. Your reputation may bring in the first business, and your ability to deliver quality may create satisfied customers. If you want your business to grow beyond your own productivity, you'll have to turn work over to trained assistants. The worst thing you can do is decide to do more work yourself rather than take time to train others. This mistake limits your company to the productivity and supervisory capability of one foreman—you.

The production department eventually grows into shifts, and specialized departments—scheduling, inspecting, purchasing, shipping and receiving—each with foremen and supervisors who coordinate production and push products out the door to customers. If you're in construction, manufacturing, or distribution, production will be your largest department. If you're in a repair or service operation, every person who produces also works with customers in a unique way.

Your organization must fit your operations. Organize to serve customers. If this means the shipping department is the largest department you've got, and the smartest person you've got is running the shipping department, so be it. Make that person a vice president.

With every additional person, managerial problems and administrative burdens grow. It won't be long before you have at least one person who only shuffles papers and talks on the phone to suppliers and customers. To keep everyone paid and money flowing, an accounting department is born. Then comes insurance, sales and income taxes, accounts receivable and payable, government and financial reports, and dealing with lenders.

Whether you like it or not, you'll have to study financial statements and other performance reports more frequently. This requires organization within the accounting department. Early on, you've probably purchased a computer system. If your business has grown out of the survival stage and you still insist on using gut feelings to measure financial conditions, you're probably headed for oblivion.

The need for more reports and information leads to an information system (IS). Accounting leads to finance and administration, 401(k), human resources, and myriad other things. Specialized essential functions, such as complaints, design, engineering, safety, quotations, research, transportation, and so forth, must be performed by someone.

By the time you reach the growth stage, the organization has changed two or three times. The quantity of everything increases—more people, more shipments, more dollars. Make an organization chart. Your organization has a direct effect on maintaining profitability. Until you put out an organization chart, people think they report directly to the boss, and they do.

341

When you're small, when you're actively involved in day-to-day activities, your priorities are no mystery to the employees. They can see what you pay attention to and direct their efforts accordingly. But when you become distant from daily operations, and other managers become intermediate links in the communication and instruction chain, priorities can become confused. The result can be employees who think they're doing the right thing while you wonder, "What's wrong with communication around here?"

To achieve managerial focus, you'll have to share financial information previously known only to you. The shared reporting and management control system takes the place of your daily presence. It cements agreement on priorities, on methods of measuring results, and on levels of planned performance. If your company is to grow, managers must grow in knowledge and performance.

When you conduct and dominate a meeting, you hear only what you say yourself. What managers think is more important, but you hear what they think only when you're silent and they're talking. Efficiency comes from catching minor problems that occur between the divisions and working out solutions.

Things don't make successes, people do. Your job is to be alert to common-sense indications that the company has grown into a stage requiring modifications in management or organization. Management is progress from one phase to the next. It's a moving target; each

phase requires the development of a different approach involving your managerial style, the company structure, managers' stages of development, and the efficiency of the reporting and control systems. The process of adopting new methods must start at the top. Don't procrastinate, and don't duck the decisions.

Organize your operation the way the system wants to work to satisfy customers. Don't force it into a preconceived, textbook pattern.

What I have described here is building a growing company as you go along, not reengineering an older company. In reengineering, an organization reviews its existing structure, management systems, and strategy, discarding the pieces that don't add value and reassembling what's left into core business processes that are customer driven, fast, and efficient. If the company is organized and managed correctly and continuously, reengineering should not be necessary.

A good analysis of this problem is found in *The Cost-Effective Organization: How to Create It, How to Maintain It,* by James K. Hickel (Lakewood, Colo.: Glenbridge Publishing, 1993).

Overhead or Burden—Allocation Of

THIS IS THE MOST CONTROVERSIAL, least exact part of the accounting process. It's the largest reason that the question "What does it cost us to produce and deliver this product or service?" cannot be answered with greater precision. If it weren't for this problem, accounting would be a more exact science.

The *direct costs* of any job are easy to identify—raw materials, hours spent by employees on specific jobs, or costs related to a specific job, invoice, or transaction.

However, every business also has general expenses difficult to relate to a specific job, called *indirect expenses, overhead,* or *burden.* These include rent, truck expense, cleanup expense, clerical and office salaries, supervisory expenses, inspection and quality control expenses, safety, insurance, advertising, and marketing expenses. These important expenses are difficult to control in total and difficult to reasonably allocate to specific jobs or activities.

The usual allocation methods are

- estimated percentage of direct labor dollars

- estimated amount per direct labor hour

- estimated amount per machine hour or crew, truck, or cost-center hour

- estimated amount per dollar of sales or per transaction

Your objective should be to apply or absorb between 90 and 100 percent of actual overhead or burden during any six-month period. Overabsorbed burden, which creates false earnings, shouldn't happen more than two months per year; otherwise your burden rate is too high. Verify this calculation often enough to ensure reasonable accuracy.

You'll have some interesting theoretical discussions about which is the most nearly correct method of applying overhead, none of which can be absolutely proven. Discuss with your managerial team and with your accountant the most realistic and reasonable way to allocate these expenses to accurately reflect your costs and operations.

A company that was entering a very profitable year had a smart accountant who recommended that the company drop its manufacturing burden rate early in the year from 1.75 to 1.35 times direct labor, thereby charging more overhead expenses directly to earnings rather than keeping them in inventory valuation of finished goods. This would lower the company's reported profits by $200,000, and the accountant thought he could make a reasonable case for the change, acceptable to outside CPAs and the IRS.

Whatever you decide, make certain all who use the information understand what is included in allocations to each account.

O

343

Owner's Privileges

ONE OF YOUR MAIN PRIVILEGES as the owner is to write your own job description. In a real one-person company, you start with all the jobs. If you had a job description, it would be "Do everything!"

With each additional employee you hire, you have a chance to get rid of the jobs or everyday responsibilities you don't want. Keep the vital ones, those you're good at, the ones you like. Gradually assign others to other department heads, departments, or employees. If you don't, you'll hit the 24-hour limit of your ability to work, and maybe the invisible wall of management as well.

You've got to have an atmosphere where people can make mistakes. If we're not making mistakes, we're not getting anywhere.

—Gordon Forward

In this way, you establish and change your organization chart. Designing and filling it out allows you to select your teammates. Since you'll probably choose people with compatible philosophies, attitudes, and work habits, this can make life very pleasant and work a joy—until you have to fire one of them. If you can't do that when you need to, your business will suffer.

You get to set your own pay, both base pay and incentives. (See ENTREPRENEURS SET THEIR OWN WAGES.) Know what the business can afford, which may not be what you'd like to have. Know what range of executive pay is appropriate and where your pay fits in with that of your managers; check with members of your CEO roundtable. (See RELATIVE PAY FOR CORPORATE OFFICERS.)

My wife once asked me when I was going to cut back on my work hours. She reminded me that when I was an employee I had told her I went to work early and came home late to impress the boss, and when I became an owner I did it to set an example for the employees.

You set your own hours and working conditions. You get whatever office you want, furnished any way you want it. Self-discipline requires that you be reasonable, accomplish all you can, and see that others do the same.

At one time I had surgery that left control of my right arm weakened. I took up tennis for therapy and really enjoyed the physical conditioning and mental relaxation it provided. But I always felt guilty leaving the office at 4:00 P.M. for a tennis match. At my CEO roundtable, another entrepreneur explained why he always played in the middle of the day: no one questioned where he was going when he left during business hours, and he was always present at opening and closing time. I had ready access to indoor tennis courts, so I followed his advice.

You also set your vacation schedule. The business comes first, but it's not difficult to combine business with pleasure by finding recreational opportunities near business contacts. Frequent long weekends or vacations every quarter gave me more meaningful rest and relaxation than one long vacation every year.

Owner's privileges don't include the right to abuse them. You set the example; don't think it won't be followed. If you cheat or neglect your duties, you signal approval to employees who may be tempted to do the same. What you do speaks so loudly that no one will hear what you say. (See PERSONAL EXPENSES CHARGED TO THE COMPANY.)

Since no one tells you what to do, you must have enough self-discipline to do what's best for your business even when you might enjoy being greedy, selfish, or lazy instead.

From all this, you must learn that the real boss is the customer. You'll probably never hear customers complain about any of these things, but they can indicate their disapproval by disappearing. If you set the wrong examples or send the wrong messages to your employees, your customers will surely see the end result and act accordingly.

Part-Time Management for Small Business

THIS REFERS TO THE CEO, not to other employees or professionals who may be assisting him. No small business succeeds without one dedicated, knowledgeable, and authoritative person being in charge and present almost all the time. Normally this is the entrepreneur, the person who has the most at risk. For temporary periods of illness, vacation, and travel, the momentum will keep the company going, but not for long.

Owning a start-up or small company is a full-time job if you expect it to grow and prosper. You can work part time to get started and ease the initial financial load, but your objective must be to work at it full time as soon as possible.

Four young people, each with a full-time job, planned to open and run a physical fitness facility that they were certain would succeed. Each had some degree of talent or knowledge to contribute; ownership and profits were to be split four ways. When it became obvious that no one planned to quit his or her job and run the new venture full time, I told them it had no chance of success. After two more meetings, they agreed. I think they were saved from considerable financial loss and heartache.

Being a part-time manager of an entrepreneurial business is like being a little bit pregnant. If you're considering hiring a manager to do your work, see ENTREPRENEURS' AND INVENTORS' IMPOSSIBLE DREAMS.

Partners—Choice Of

THERE ARE ONLY TWO GOOD REASONS for taking on a partner or partners—you need their money or you need their management. Your objective is to get both with the fewest partners. Be sure you have a sound business reason for taking on a partner, not just because that person is your friend, relative, neighbor, or former business associate.

This discussion concerns partners as co-owners of a business partnership, not a corporation. If associates are merely employees, they can be just as valuable and contribute just as much, but your business and legal relationships will be different.

Taking a business partner isn't too different from taking a marriage partner. You'll probably spend more waking hours per week and communicate more at your office than at home. If things don't work, ending the business relationship may be as difficult and as emotionally and financially draining as ending a marriage.

Money alone isn't the motivator behind most small business partnerships. Joint effort, "two heads are better than one," is the stronger reason. Once you have a partner, you're no longer working only for yourself. You and your partner are accountable to each other. Your partner can influence or control the decisions you want to make. When you have partners, it's never quite your own business.

Collectively, partners have undisputed control of the business. Designate or recognize someone as the controlling partner—if not overall, at least in specific areas of responsibility. A 50-50 partnership becomes a standoff, with no one able to cast the deciding vote, when there's a dispute or misunderstanding.

When you take on partners, you become accountable to them just as they're accountable to you. Each of you is an agent of the business and of the other partners. Third parties can sue you for your partner's business actions. All partners should guarantee all notes and obligations that any partner personally guarantees. Remember to do this if your partners come on board after the note is already guaranteed.

Choose a partner whose technological strengths and areas of expertise differ from yours. Your areas of greatest skill should cover her areas of ignorance. If you're both strong in the same area, the partnership won't go smoothly; you'll argue over methods and procedures within areas of your common expertise.

Synergy is created when partners achieve jointly what they could never accomplish individually. One partner may be the idea person and the other the doer who puts the plan into action. One may be the optimist and the other the realist. And some partnerships fall into the old good guy-bad guy routine. It's more than just management—it's body chemistry. The right partner can be a powerful help for your business.

Agree on how, and how much, income you'll take out of the business. Certain disaster awaits you if your partner thinks you reneged on your obligation to make him money. Another strain can come when adversity or a cash shortage strikes. Not everyone reacts the same way. You may not know how your partner will react. He may not know how you'll react.

Establish clear individual responsibilities. The business works best when each person has specific jobs and does them; two people often disagree and argue when they try to do the same task. Be sure you both have the same sense of motivation. Discuss your goals; put them in writing. Agree on business ethics and procedures as well as on a mission statement and common objectives for the firm.

A certain amount of chemistry and a lot of communication are necessary. Do you get along together? Can you openly discuss business and generate new ideas and plans? Do you have mutual trust? No partnership can survive without it.

At least once a week, discuss the business. Each of you must be open and express your feelings; there can be no secrets between business partners. Resolve minor feuds and irritations as soon as you recognize them. Unsaid things create conflicts. Unsaid things that fester and grow worse in one person's imagination create the deepest conflicts.

Watch out for side deals, hidden profits, and conflicts of interest. If either of you is involved in deals with others that remotely touch on your partnership, bring them into the open and discuss them before you start.

You don't want a partner who has different feelings about working than you do. If she wants to make a high current income and you want to plow earnings back into the business, you'll have problems. Frustration occurs when one partner works hard while the other plays golf. Full time for one partner and part time for the other won't work. Decide in advance on outside work and unshared outside investments that require time—work time not devoted to the common business.

Find a lawyer to help you write a partnership agreement. The courts are full of people litigating oral agreements. Memory can be conveniently inaccurate when partnership litigation occurs. Some go into partnerships because it seems best at the time, but times change. Your partnership agreement must have written into it a means for dissolving the partnership. How and when can one partner buy the other out? A partner's death or disability should terminate the partnership. Being in business with the surviving spouse is never the same.

Your partner's lifestyle or personality traits are more likely to cause a business split than lack of money or managerial competence. Your partner's personality, or yours, may change over the years. What you originally thought was an excellent working relationship may be a poor fit several years later.

The only person who automatically qualifies as a partner in your venture is your spouse. That's usually an informal partnership at home and, at times, in the business. On the plus side, two brains are better than one if both are committed to the business.

But your spouse as a permanent active partner usually adds more problems than solutions. Over the years, it involves too much togetherness and brings more opportunities for conflict than for harmony. Disagreements over how to raise the kids and spend the household budget involve less conflict than deciding whether to expand to new markets or fire certain employees.

Family members as partners are usually more harmful than helpful. When dealing with blood relatives, relationships and emotions can interfere with good business judgment. In most cases, families survive a business conflict or disaster, but the business may not survive.

Although everyone knows a few business partnerships that last a lifetime harmoniously, there are drawbacks and pitfalls. Almost none last into the second generation or beyond.

If you want to be the entrepreneur who calls all the shots, forget partners.

Partnership—Doing Business As

UNDER THE UNIFORM PARTNERSHIP ACT, adopted by most states, each partner has the right to share in the management and conduct of the business, share in the profits, receive indemnification for or return of payments made on behalf of the partnership, receive interest on advances made to the business, have access to the books and records of the partnership, and have a formal accounting of partnership affairs.

Each partner's obligations include the following:

- Contributing money toward recovery when the partnership sustains a loss

- Working for the partnership without guaranteed pay in the customary sense but rather for a share of the profits

- Submitting to majority vote or arbitration when differences arise about the conduct of affairs

- Giving other partners any information known personally about partnership affairs

- Accounting to the partnership for all profits coming from any partnership transaction or from the use of partnership property

A limited partnership allows one or more partners to limit their liability to the extent of the amount of money they've invested in the business. They can't be active in the business; their partnership contribution must be either cash or tangible property, not services. Otherwise they're assumed to be a general partner.

The limited partner's function is to put up money and share in the profits or losses, but not to share in certain liabilities if the business fails. State laws govern these transactions.

Limited partnerships aren't common in operating businesses. If you're operating as a limited partnership, comply with the laws of your state, most of which require a written partnership agreement. Otherwise, all partners are general partners.

A new business form known as a limited liability partnership is now legal in a few states. This hybrid is usually taxed as a partnership, but affords the owners limited liability like a corporation. Check with your lawyer for the rules in your state. (See CORPORATION, PARTNERSHIP, OR PROPRIETORSHIP—FORMS FOR DOING BUSINESS.)

Past-Due Accounts—Collecting

THE ONLY THING WORSE than having no sales is having sales you can't collect for. "No sales" cost you only your overhead or fixed costs; bad debts cost overhead plus product or service cost. Such losses offset a large volume of what should be profitable sales to arrive at break-even.

The best way to prevent bad-debt losses is to have a consistent policy of encouraging and monitoring collection, as well as a good procedure for granting credit in the first place. (See CREDIT—GRANTING AND MANAGING.) Your policy should prevent salespeople's selling to customers who aren't creditworthy or to delinquent accounts. Check a prospective customer's credit before you accept or ship the order.

Send invoices either with the shipment or as soon as possible thereafter. Mail statements to customers the day after the close of the billing period. Bill large sales immediately. If possible, invoice customers when you process the order rather than when you ship. Bill for services on an interim basis. Keep careful watch on receivables that aren't current. But keep in mind that an excessively restrictive credit policy can lead to lost sales. As always, you are seeking the proper balance between two requirements.

Don't consider your company well managed unless you have a consistent policy and procedure to spotlight past-due accounts as well as a detailed, phased

collection procedure, starting a few days after the due date. The older the debt, the less chance you have to collect it.

Few people enjoy asking for money, but if you don't insist that your customers keep current, it's your own fault. Get the right person to do collections; not everybody is suited for it.

Since you want salespeople to be friendly and to be welcomed by customers, asking them to conduct hard-nosed collection calls may be inappropriate. In some industries, salespersons routinely do collection follow-ups; in others, they don't. In either case, salespeople must understand company credit policies so they don't waste time calling on prospects who have poor credit.

Don't be afraid that if you demand payment on time you'll lose customers or business. You've probably lost them anyway, so waiting longer just prolongs your agony and increases your cost. Make sure customers know your clear, written credit policy. You can still make exceptions, but if customers don't know your rules, you can't expect them to comply.

If you've allowed an old customer delinquency before, it's worth special attention to get him to conform to your new policy. If you lose the customer, make special efforts to win him back.

Use credit terms and procedures customary in your industry. Here is a suggested set of phased collection steps:

1. Deliver the invoice with the merchandise or service, or as promptly as possible. Clearly state payment terms on the invoice. Your customer can't start processing until she receives the bill.

2. Send a statement at the end of the month. Clearly indicate past-due invoices. Repeat your invoice terms.

3. A few days after the due date, or at whatever time your grace-period policy may set, send a copy of the current statement with invoices marked "Past Due."

4. One or two weeks after that, send your first letter or make your first phone call. Letters are less threatening and more easily ignored, but phone calls are more effective.

5. After the close of the next accounting period, mark the statement "Urgent" or "Perhaps you've overlooked this." Start a series of ever more threatening letters or make more phone calls. Keep collection letters or phone calls simple and to the point. Don't apologize for asking to be paid. The goal of the phone calls is to get promises of specific dates and amounts. Take notes. Computer software is available to track every customer contact. You can enter every conversation and commitment.

6. If you receive no payment, make a follow-up call within the specified interval. Refer to the conversation in which the commitment to pay was made. Follow the phone call with a letter expressing thanks for the specific promise, and repeat the promise. The employee who calls should be thoroughly familiar with the account and its history and should ask to speak with someone who has the authority to make the payment. The employee should demand payment in a nonapologetic voice in accordance with the invoice terms. If the amount involved or the relationship with the customer justifies it, an appropriate officer or person from your company should visit the customer.

P

351

7. If you don't receive satisfactory payment, notify the customer that she is on credit hold and must pay cash for all future purchases. You may even require cash for current shipments plus an additional percentage to be applied to old invoices.

8. Ask the customer to sign a note with specific payment terms, perhaps with other security, to evidence the indebtedness. It's easier to get results at the courthouse when you're suing on a note than when you have an open account.

9. If the account is such that you can file a lien, do so before the statute of limitations expires. As a matter of policy, never allow time limitations to pass without filing a proper lien. Set up a system to monitor this.

10. As a last resort, offer a discount as high as 25 or 30 percent if the customer will pay the old bill. Discuss proper payment on future business.

11. Either turn the claim over to a collection agency or lawyer, or try to barter or offset the claim in some other way.

Once you put these policies into effect, customers will know what to expect when they don't pay their bills. There may be some resentment at first, but if you're considerate and businesslike, this will eventually evaporate. Consistency creates a strong position for countering the customer's excuses and requests for extra time. It's easy to say "I'm sorry, but these policies are for all our customers, without exception. We think they are fair, and we have to stick with them."

View collecting debts as a business transaction, not as an emotional experience.

352

Patents

IF YOUR BUSINESS IDEA IS PATENTABLE, by all means go for it. It adds engineering prestige to your product and may scare off some competitors. But don't consider it your insurance policy for guaranteed success in the marketplace.

If people invest in or have a patent, they often think they'll have no competition, that wealth and fame are assured. But merely having "Patent pending" on your product may not help you get a head start toward market position. More markets are conquered by following the military advice of General Nathan Bedford Forrest—"Get there firstest with the mostest"—than by trying to prevent competition with a patent.

Don't spend extra time searching desperately for a patentable idea if your entrepreneurial idea is something else. My guess is that less than 5 percent of the U.S. gross domestic product is dependent on active patents, and fewer than 10 percent of all patents issued have real marketplace value.

From my experience, a large number of satisfied customers will put more money in your pocket than most patents. I've seen both sides of patent litigation, and I'm co-inventor of a totally worthless patent. We should have spent our money on marketing.

Getting a United States patent takes from two and one-half to five years and can cost $10,000 or more, spread over successive steps in the process. The U.S. Patent Office issues United States patents.

If you make your patentable device available to the public either in an oral or written description or by offering it for sale, selling it, or publicly using it, you must file a patent application within one year or you won't be able to obtain a U.S. patent. An idea cannot be patented, but a mechanism, device, process, or improvement to accomplish an idea can.

Although you can take some early steps by yourself to save money in the patent process, if you have an important patentable device, it's essential to get a patent lawyer quickly.

Start by using words and drawings to describe your invention to your patent lawyer. He will then have a professional search made to see if it has ever been patented. The search may take from 10 days to a month; the average cost is about $1,000. You'll get back the patent history of everything that's close, together with a patentability opinion.

If search results are satisfactory, the lawyer will prepare your application, requesting the broadest possible coverage, and file it with the patent office. You may make as many claims with as many variations as you wish.

When describing your claims, less language is stronger. However, each additional element you include in your claim increases your chance of getting a patent because it narrows the coverage of your claim.

The confidential application will be examined by the patent office to be sure it's new, useful, and nonobvious. Expect your first application to be rejected as unpatentable because of other patents or for reasons that will be disclosed in the rejection. Respond to rejections by narrowing the coverage claimed to eliminate conflicts with prior patents. If your first application is not rejected, your original claims of coverage could possibly have been broader.

Several rounds of rejection and revision of your application are usually necessary to clarify and obtain the broadest possible coverage that doesn't infringe. Each additional rejection and response takes from three to six months, sometimes longer, and costs several thousand dollars in legal fees.

If you persist and narrow your claims enough, you will receive notice of allowance and issuance of a patent. If issued, the patent is made public by the patent office. If a patent isn't issued, no public disclosure is made, and you (the inventor) may still rely on the trade secrecy of the invention to protect it from being copied. (See TRADE SECRETS.)

Applications are filed by, and patents issued to, individuals and companies. A patent or application by an individual may be assigned at any time to a company; such a transfer often accompanies the original application. Specific ownership of the patent is significant. Both employees and consultants working on any developmental project should be bound by contract to transfer to the company any

P

353

inventions, patents, know-how, or trade secrets that result from their work. (See NON-COMPETE AGREEMENT.)

During the life of your patent (20 years from filing date), you'll have the exclusive right to make, use, offer for sale, or sell in the U.S. all devices, and practice all methods, that contain all the elements found in any one claim of your patent as issued. You must notify others of the existence of your patent by marking "Patented" on each product or the container in which it is sold.

The way around an existing patent is to accomplish the same purpose with a substantially different apparatus or method. The elimination of just one element (literally and equivalently) of those listed in a claim in the patent, or the use of a device previously patented but now expired, will not infringe the claim of the other patent.

Foreign countries, under international patent treaties, will accept a patent application filed within one year after you file your application in the United States and allow you to claim the filing date of the U.S. patent as the effective date of the foreign patent application. The financial requirement for each foreign country in which you wish to register is similar to that in the U.S.

Pension and Profit-Sharing Plans

THE PRINCIPAL REASON ANY COMPANY makes annual contributions to a pension fund is to encourage employees to work for that company for a lifetime, then to retire on a pension. If employees aren't going to work for the company for a lifetime, or at least for a very long time, the company is less responsible and less concerned with employee retirement plans.

When Congress passed the Employee Retirement Income Security Act (ERISA) in 1974, it failed to understand those simple motivating principles. The number of pension plans and the amount of money contributed to pension funds has steadily declined since then. Additional legislation has made qualified and tax-exempt pension plans even more burdensome and unattractive for small companies.

You must share earnings with employees and give them incentives, including incentives to keep working for the company for a long time, but government-qualified pension and profit-sharing plans aren't the way for small companies to do it. If you don't believe this, call a local pension consultant. For pension purposes, encourage and contribute to 401(k) plans for your employees.

Percentage of Earnings Compared with Percentage of Equity

LEGALLY, THESE ARE TWO DIFFERENT things, although they may have equivalent motivational value in shaping your relationships with business associates.

You should and must give incentives and rewards to managers whose daily decisions and efforts influence company earnings. The usual thinking is "You can have X percent of the company." However, until you're certain that these are the people you wish to be in the business bed with for a long time, propose instead, "You can have X percent of annual earnings." Consider clarifying that to "after taxes."

Setting up this incentive is easiest. No purchase or sale is required. It's easy to put the agreement in writing with the help of a business lawyer. The agreement should specify when payment is due and that the company's financial statements or tax returns, as prepared by inside or outside accountants, are considered final. Terminating employment for any reason terminates the agreement. Include a provision for pro rata determination of earnings in the first and last years unless employment happens to hit year-end. (See BONUS AND INCENTIVE PLANS.)

A percentage of the earnings or income stream keeps the manager's attention focused and rewards him annually (or more often) for the company's perfor-

mance results. If the relationship is terminated, the bonus stops. There are usually no long-term repercussions.

Legally, a percentage of equity or stock is different, even though it's thought of in the same way by many employees and usually has the same motivational effect. When stock is transferred or sold, money or value changes hands, and a relationship somewhat like a business marriage is created. Terminating the relationship requires new agreements, money payments, and messy and unpleasant negotiations—unless you've executed a buy-sell agreement as explained in BUY-SELL AGREEMENTS WITH OTHER SHAREHOLDERS. (See also EMPLOYEES AS STOCKHOLDERS.)

Don't guarantee anyone a fixed percentage of the company. Instead, sell a fixed number of shares, which you describe as "at this time X percent of outstanding shares." If and when you sell more new stock to the next manager included in the plan, the older employee's number of shares remains the same, but her percentage of total ownership decreases. Explain this so there will be no misunderstandings or hard feelings when it happens. To maintain corporate flexibility, you have no simple way to guarantee that a fixed number of shares will always equal a fixed percentage of total outstanding shares.

355

Without a buy-sell agreement, getting this stock back is a mixed bag—sometimes easy, sometimes impossible. If you don't want outside or inactive stockholders, execute a buy-sell agreement with each individual shareholder.

Persistence

CALVIN COOLIDGE SAID, "Nothing in the world can take the place of persistence. Talent will not; nothing is more common than unsuccessful men with talent. Genius will not; unrewarded genius is almost a proverb. Education will not; the world is full of educated derelicts. Persistence and determination alone are omnipotent."

P

356

The race goes not always to the swift, but to those who keep on running.

Personal Expenses Charged to the Company

IT'S SO EASY TO CHARGE PERSONAL expenses to the company that some entrepreneurs can't resist the temptation. It sometimes goes as far as putting household employees or servants on the payroll, buying automobiles driven by family members, paying for social and personal memberships or activities with no business relationship, and uncounted other expenses.

Since you're the boss, none of your employees will tell you that you can't do this, although you would probably tell other employees that they can't. Enough semibusiness expenses mix with semipersonal enjoyment that no owner, including me, can claim to be totally conscientious about differentiating between business and personal expenses to the penny. But if you cheat, you send the message to others that they may also cheat.

Of course, the IRS has detailed rules about mixing business and pleasure. If you go too far, you'll have an embarrassing and expensive confrontation. Your accountant should ask you to either personally okay questionable expenditures as business expenses or charge them to your personal account receivable for future reimbursement to the company.

Outside auditors search diligently for such items and will call your attention to anything they think is out of line. If they tell you they can't defend some expenses to the IRS with a straight face or in good conscience, you've gone too far. If your only explanation is "I didn't think you would catch me," you've gone way too far.

What you do speaks so loudly that I cannot hear what you say.

Personal Guarantees or Endorsements on Debt

FOR YOUR OWN OR YOUR BUSINESS indebtedness, you don't have much choice—sign and then work like hell to pay the note. If you hesitate, the banker's comment will be "If you don't believe this is a good loan, why should *I* believe it?"

Know thyself. You'll be a better entrepreneur.

Until you get to the big-business stage, expect to personally endorse all company obligations, or you probably won't be able to borrow the money. Endorsing means you may have to pay from whatever personal resources you have if the company cannot pay. From the day I started to the day I sold my business, I don't remember ever having a note at a bank, except a real estate loan, that I didn't personally endorse.

After you've had some degree of business success and built up a good credit rating, you're certain to have a struggling friend with poorer credit ask you to endorse her note. Banks or finance companies have complete credit information and means of evaluating risks. They no doubt have good reason for refusing to extend credit to your friend without the endorsement or guarantee of stronger financial backing.

After having paid off four such notes (I was a slow learner with a soft heart), my advice to you is to state this: "As a matter of policy, I don't endorse any notes except my own and my close family members."

When you need someone to endorse your notes, find someone who hasn't read this book.

Planning

THE ONE WHO'S BEST PREPARED WINS. That means the one who has planned best. The more complete your planning, and the earlier you do it, the better the progress of your enterprise.

Critically analyze and change your plans, at least annually, or when events indicate that your plan isn't working. Give new ideas or activities a fair trial period, then readjust. Plan ahead or fall behind.

Think your way through it as well as you can. The one who starts nothing until all objections are met will never start anything. Eliminate all the unnecessary chances you can. Then accept the risks you have to.

Plan your work, and work your plan. An old military maxim also applies to business: A poor plan well executed is better than an excellent plan poorly executed.

People don't plan to fail. They just fail to plan.

No matter how carefully you plan, things won't work out the way you expect them to. Murphy's Law states that whatever can happen will happen. Mrs. Murphy's Law states that it will happen when you can least afford it. (See STRATEGIC OR LONG-RANGE PLANNING.)

Politics of Small Business

YOU MAY NOT LIKE or even be interested in politics, but if you're in business, government laws and regulations directly affect you. Your best interest lies in constant awareness of political happenings and government policies that affect small business. Give of your time and money to produce a political result you think is favorable.

Join the National Federation of Independent Business (NFIB, 600 Maryland Ave. SW, Suite 700, Washington, DC 20024, 800-NFIB-NOW), and other groups that politically support small business. If you're a woman business owner, join the National Association of Women Business Owners (NAWBO, 1413 K Street NW, #637, Washington, DC 20005, 301-608-2590). These groups are politically active in the interests of their members. Join your trade association. It may have a political function.

Growing a small business means that you start with nothing, create a new business, furnish products and services to willing customers, create jobs, and pay taxes. This is one of the opportunities of the capitalistic system. At least one person may get rich during this process, usually the entrepreneur.

This basic reality seems to have escaped many politicians and government economists. The present political climate loves employees but doesn't like employers. It promotes warfare between them and between rich and poor rather than cooperation, individual responsibility, and opportunity. Wealth has become such a dirty word in recent years that the income tax system has been openly used to redistribute wealth from those who earned it to those who did not, a concept that would astound our Founding Fathers. Small business owners should encourage capital accumulation for small business. When we punish productive citizens and thrift and encourage unproductive citizens and idleness, we hinder progress.

It's inevitable that as government power expands, individual freedoms will contract. Some politicians seem unable to understand this simple truth about human nature: That which is subsidized or encouraged by government grants of money will grow and increase as free people change their activities to obtain the free benefits. That which is taxed or burdened by the government is discouraged and will decrease as free people change their activities and seek ways to avoid the burden.

Key building blocks to maintain the values on which this country is founded are the family unit, education, a capitalistic economy, and religious freedom. The family unit, where children are raised by capable, adult parents, is the basic building block of society and the educator of future generations. Anything that weakens or harms that structure weakens the whole of society.

Support the community and civic organizations where you live and where you work, even if that means two different groups.

Give time and money to the politicians and causes of your choice, those you think will benefit small businesses and strong families. Your children and grandchildren will be better off if you spend some of your time and money being politically active for causes you believe in.

Prayer

PRAYER IS A MEANS OF SEEKING divine guidance, inspiration, and comfort in times of trouble. It's a well-accepted technique for managing both your business and your private life. It's a means of giving thanks when things have gone well.

Your business life and your home life have a place for a power greater than yourself. You can receive guidance and comfort by doing everything you possibly can and then seeking additional help by prayer. The work ethic teaches that the Lord helps those who help themselves.

If you're not familiar with it, give it a try.

We pray for miracles,
but we work for results.

—Peter Drucker

360

Preparation

THE BEST-PREPARED PERSON USUALLY wins. This is true not only in business but in all other walks of life.

What the fool does in
the end, the wise man
does in the beginning.

Prepare for your meeting. Prepare for the conference with your banker. Prepare for the call on your customer. Off the top of my head, I can think of nothing that you want to accomplish that you won't do better, faster, and more effectively if you prepare thoroughly.

Preparation includes learning, thinking, and planning. It includes objectives, agendas, lists of things to do, and timetables. It also includes coordinating people, materials, and information, and the detailed planning to reach objectives.

It's hard enough to hit a target when you know what you're shooting at. If you haven't identified your objective and prepared to accomplish it, your chances of getting there are poor.

President's Daily/Weekly Report

YOU MUST WATCH YOUR BUSINESS'S VITAL signs—the numbers that tell you how healthy and well-functioning your business is. This report is your early warning system, continually monitoring your selected vital signs. You need a report like this daily, semiweekly, or weekly to be sure that you stay on top of the most important things in your business, that no unpleasant surprises are sneaking up on you.

Monthly financial statements, which give you 12 accurate readings per year, don't come often enough to keep you fully informed about the state, direction, and progress of your business. You need more frequent, accurate, comparative information on events and status. The next monthly statement may be too late.

Make the report as formal or informal as you and your accountant want to. For many years, I used a green accounting pad with lines, columns, and penciled-in numbers. I used one line for each item of information I wanted, and one column for each reporting period, with the date at the top. The current sheet with filled-in columns was on top in a folder with the last few months' information available for quick reference directly beneath. We kept two to three months of data in the folder.

If you want a printed report, set up a computer spreadsheet with multiple lines and columns. Drop the oldest column and pick up the new one each time you print

and distribute the report. Keep as many columns on the report as you consider important to spot trends up or down.

How often you choose to monitor your business data depends on how rapidly your business is moving and how thirsty you are for information. If your business moves rapidly or you're in crisis, you may want information daily. In other businesses or times, semiweekly or weekly may be adequate. In growth-stage companies, managers may want or need some or all of your information, along with other departmental information, in a report for themselves.

Designate a specific person to furnish accurate data for each line of the report. This person should be responsible for keeping the original information, summarizing it, and sending it to the general ledger. If accurate current information is available, use it. If not, memo amounts are acceptable if calculated from current, proven, accurate data plus the most accurate addition and subtraction amounts available to bring it up to date.

Every amount used should reconcile back to the most recent general ledger amount. Correct errors when the next general ledger report comes out. You'll soon know whether you can depend upon the interim numbers.

The advantage of the report is that you can readily compare the current amount with recent amounts in adjoining columns. Search for up or down trends—warnings that something's changing or proof that all's going well.

Listed below, for possible inclusion in your report, are the vital signs needed for a complete business check. You don't need them all. Putting too much information in this report can confuse and overload you rather than helping you stay on top of the vital signs you need.

Since this report is all done in memo form, you can frequently change it. Start with cash, payroll, accounts receivable, and sales. After a few months, you can add anything that you and other managers consider significant. Experiment with what's comfortable and vital, but insist that the numbers be on the report at a specified time and be as accurate as possible.

- *Cash* is and always will be your most important concern. Every business defect ultimately shows up as a cash shortage. A positive cash flow is essential for making the payroll, paying bills and taxes, meeting note payments, and generating growth money. You need to know the bank balance at close of business yesterday, plus expected income and outgo in the next days or weeks as reported in the following sections. It takes several lines on your report to project expectations to a relevant date. Your question is "How much cash do I have today, and how much will I have in the near future?" (See CASH TRACKING AND FORECASTING.)

- *Payroll* requires cash on hand on payday. Include payroll taxes in this amount. Ideally, you need accrued payroll by week, number of people, and a breakdown to tell you how much is overtime pay and how much is straight-time pay. If it's significant, you may wish to segregate vacation pay or other unearned pay because only a certain amount of this payroll money is productive. How much detail is available and significant to you depends upon you and your business. The question you're answering is "Will there be enough cash to cover payroll and payroll taxes on payday?"

- *Accounts receivable* as of yesterday, or some portion of it, will become cash flow in the immediate future. Monitor both total receivables and the length of time certain accounts have been owed to you. With a computer, it's a simple matter for someone to run off an aging report. You want your average days outstanding to be where you expect it. This may take several lines. Your questions are "How much do customers owe me? How much will be collected in the next few days? Are there old accounts I should worry about?"

- *Sales* are one step ahead of accounts receivable in the working-capital turnover cycle. Yesterday's sales are today's current accounts receivable. Total month-to-date sales indicate how much you're going to have in accounts receivable and how much

P

362

you're going to have in cash. Year-to-date sales tell you whether you're ahead of or behind your projections. You may need to break this down by major categories, major product lines, geographical regions, or salespersons. If lead time between orders booked and final invoice is long in your business, orders booked or productive hours billed may be a faster indicator of future income than invoices, which always bunch up at month-end. When this is the case, the total backlog, or total orders on hand but not yet completed and shipped, is important. Your questions are "Are sales on, ahead of, or behind budget or expectations? Must we cut back on expenses because of poor sales?"

■ *Accounts payable* is where most of your available money goes. To protect your credit rating, stay aware of the current amount of accounts payable and the average age of your payables. You may wish to segregate inventory purchases from other business expenses, and you may need to include accruals for materials received or ordered but not yet billed. Your question is "Will I be able to pay my bills as expected and promised?"

■ *Bank-note payments* must be included in your cash requirements. The total amount of indebtedness that you owe the bank, the total amount due within one year, and any payments due within the next 90 days, broken down by principal and

interest, are significant. Your question is "Will I have the money to make my note payment?"

■ *Tax payments* of sales taxes, ad valorem taxes, or income taxes should be listed if they're coming due within the time frame you're concerned about.

■ *Open orders for capital goods* shows cash required to pay for incoming equipment or assets. These items usually require big lumps of cash upon delivery. Be prepared.

■ *Line of credit,* if your financing is arranged in this manner, shows the amount of the commitment, the amount drawn against it, and the available amount you can currently draw. The question is "How much cushion in my present credit line can I draw on immediately, if I need it?"

■ *Inventory* management and control may be crucial. At least weekly, verify the inventory level and its division into major departments or product categories. Your question is "Is my inventory about right in relation to my sales?"

■ *Gross profit margin* is readily available only in some businesses. If you can tell what your gross profit margin is on sales volume, monitor that. If possible, break it down for different locations, product lines, and items.

Insist that this information be in a report on your desk by a certain time. Minor inaccuracies are preferable to late

P

363

or delayed data, but make corrections as soon as you are aware. Late information is what you've got right now with monthly financial statements.

You need the simplest form that can give you the information you need. This information is pointed toward control of cash in particular and your business in general, so you can quickly do something if trouble develops. Leave off pennies. As the numbers get bigger, leave off two or three zeros; it's easier to keep track of shorter, simpler numbers.

Price War

NEVER BE THE ONE TO START A PRICE WAR. Don't participate in one if you can possibly avoid it. Even the company with the lowest prices can't get 100 percent of the available business.

A price war can hurt you, your company, and your market for years to come because customers focus on price rather than on value or benefits. Cutting prices only invites your competitor to match your cuts, which means both of you compete at a lower profit margin. Look at what's happened to the airline industry in the last several years.

Getting prices down is easy. Getting them back up is difficult. Federal anti-trust laws prevent collusion or even discussions between competitors to fix prices or lessen competition. If you're at a trade show or other gathering where agreements concerning prices are mentioned, find an excuse to leave immediately. Don't stay and listen.

If you get into a price war, being the low-cost producer will help you. The low-cost producer almost always wins. Look for ways to cut costs. If you can figure out what part of your products or services customers don't want and eliminate those (along with their accompanying costs), you've helped yourself.

There is hardly anything in the world that some men cannot make a little worse and sell a little cheaper.

—John Ruskin

You can't immediately or quickly offset lower prices with higher volume. If your gross profit margin is 30 percent, you need more than a 9 percent increase in total sales volume to offset a 3 percent decrease in price. Before you start or join the price war, calculate how much you will have to increase your volume to keep the same bottom line.

Your real goal is to find a way to differentiate your product from the products suffering the price cut. Focus on the special features of your niche products, their quality and utility, and on your competitive advantage. Sell those features as a justification for your price differential.

Temporary price cuts targeted at a specific market or customer or to move excessive inventory generally don't start a price war. If you're careful, your competitor won't start a price war through misreading your moves.

If you're going to lose volume, be sure you're losing it only on price and not on quality, delivery, or attitude. Cut your quality or delivery only after careful analysis of the effect on your customers.

Continue to call on and stay in touch with customers you lose because of price. Make it easy for them to return when prices or other factors change.

Set a bottom-number sales price below which you would prefer to lose the sale. Tell your customers if they want to buy on price alone, to buy from X, the lowest-priced supplier. If X is selling below its cost, then the more volume X gets, the more it's draining its resources.

Your break-even point is the sales volume you must have in order for your gross margin to cover all fixed expenses. Keep this number in your head constantly so you know when you can breathe easy during the month. (See BREAK-EVEN POINT; MARGIN, GROSS MARGIN, OR MARKUP.)

A price cut is like an atomic bomb— you can use it only once, and the fallout may hurt you as much as your enemy.

Prices—Cutting

WHEN CUSTOMERS REQUEST A PRICE concession, ask, "If I meet this price cut, will I get the order?" If they don't say yes, don't do it. They may only want you to cut your price so they can shop for a cut from another competitor. Asking this question avoids their trap. Wait for their next call to find out the lowest price you must quote to get their business. Then, if you know your cost of doing business, you can decide whether or not you want this business.

The bitterness of poor quality lingers long after the sweetness of low price is gone.

Consider whether this is a long-term contract or just one order. The Robinson-Patman Act of 1936 requires that you sell at the same price and terms to all customers similarly situated. This act doesn't apply to repairs, no two of which are exactly alike.

Evaluate whether cutting price on the item will anger other customers. Those who have already paid the higher price may ask for refunds, then repurchase at the lower price.

Cutting prices is easy. Raising them again is always difficult.

Pricing

P

366

SALE PRICES ARE SOME OF THE MOST important decisions your company must make. Closely supervise pricing decisions. Continuously monitor or review them in light of costs and the competition.

Your pricing objective is to sell at the price that will yield the greatest gross profit or gross margin from your operations. A higher price would drive your customers to a competitor; a lower price would reduce your margin per transaction to give a lower total gross margin or gross profit. (See MARGIN, GROSS MARGIN, OR MARKUP.)

To develop your market position, decide which product-quality and service level you want to appeal to. For example, consider automobiles, a large, competitive market. Mercedes, Lexus, and Cadillac are priced at the top of the line, but their prices are beyond the reach of the mass market. If you go for volume, the largest dollar volume is always in the middle of the market price scale. Some low-end cars will always be sold, even with lower quality and fewer features, because some buyers won't or can't pay more than the lowest price.

The best-selling products or services are those that are perceived to be slightly above average in quality and features at an average price. Fewer dollars usually change hands at the top and bottom of the price range.

Whichever segment of the market you choose, the price must be acceptable to the consumer as a satisfactory measure of value received. The price must also return to you enough to cover all reasonable costs and provide some excess for growth and improvement.

Customer demand, production cost, and cost to sell or market are the three elements that most strongly influence all pricing decisions. Offer something different or better than your competition or customers will have no reason to switch to you. Your advantage may be better distribution, faster delivery, reliability, friendliness, or service.

Management's job is to provide products or services at a profit to all, including the customer. The salesperson's job is to produce sales at prices established by management. Never let the sales department or an individual salesperson set prices to customers without your approval or that of a manager who's fully aware of costs and profits and who personally participates in a profit-sharing program. Anybody can give products and services away or get orders for the lowest-priced product available. It takes a salesperson to present your product and its benefits and sell it for a price that yields a profit to both seller and buyer.

The only time salespeople should be allowed to establish their own selling price is when the company will receive a fixed amount on the transaction. If salespeople want to cut their commission, or get more by selling for a higher price, that's usually all right. But if they're on straight commission (say 10 percent), for every $1 they give up by cutting the price, you give up $9. On those terms, the company can lose money fast while salespeople still make something.

Most small companies use one of three pricing methods: competitive pricing, cost-based pricing, and what the market will bear (supply-and-demand balance).

Competitive Pricing

Competition for customers' dollars, whether it's for a similar, related product or even unrelated products or services, determines small-company pricing.

If similar products or close substitutes are on the market, let their sales and prices be an indication to you. If the prod-

uct allows, test-market in a limited market or area and try to determine the demand-price curve.

What do others sell a comparable product for? Are you going to meet the market or buy temporary or permanent volume by selling for less than the competition? Is a premium price justified in consumers' minds because you offer something unique, easier to use, or easier to get?

Be a price follower in your market when your company is small, when your product or service is difficult to differentiate from others, when a few large competitors dominate your industry, or when you don't know enough about your market to feel secure as the price leader. If your market search is successful, you will find a small niche where larger margins are possible because of lower competition.

Cost-Based Pricing

Customers don't really care what it costs you to produce or obtain the product. Your cost only establishes a minimum below which you can't sell your product, make money, or stay in business over the long term. Decide how to be the low-cost producer and keep an adequate gross margin. Your principal objective must be to sell at a price that returns all costs with enough left over to make a profit and to put something back into growth. Know your exact cost and mark it up.

If each of your products or services is one of a kind, with each bid or contract for a designed or customized item, find the markup formula that allows you to supervise the job, live up to your warranty, make a profit, and still be the low bidder. Learn to choose your customers, select the jobs you'll bid, and identify those where your chosen specialty or uniqueness gives you an advantage. If your customers come to you because of some special quality and not because you charge less than your competitors, consider raising your prices.

Except for a cost-plus job or one based on actual time and materials (the basis for many repair and service operations), you can't determine your selling price solely on what it costs you to produce the product or service.

What the Market Will Bear (Supply-and-Demand Balance)

The strongest single factor determining the price at which you can profitably sell a product or service is the competitive market and what customers will pay for your product. Survey the demand and the supply available to satisfy it. Your ability to supply is usually 60 to 85 percent of your capacity. Is there sufficient demand for you to sell that much at competitive prices?

Pricing is a process of balancing how much can be sold against the unit selling price. Know what all the costs are—selling, administrative, shipping, delivery, purchasing, and packaging. Place your value price somewhere between your cost and the sales price that will produce the greatest net profit. This balances the gross margin, sales volume, and capital employed in the inventory and receivables to handle that sales volume.

You can never know exactly what the demand for a new product will be, but if you have samples and ask enough customers, you can estimate it. Carefully select the customers you're going to ask. Their answers will be dependable only if they themselves are friendly, honest, intelligent, and have excellent knowledge of both the market and competitive products or services.

If you want to attract customers in the high end of the market using a high price, make *skimming* your pricing strategy. This is particularly suitable when you have a new product and little or no effective competition. You may have to reduce your price later when you have competition, but for now you can skim the high price on the front end to recover your developmental cost.

There's no point in asking your customers whether they will pay a higher price. They'll probably tell you no and scurry around trying to find an alternate source. I recall one well-established valve manufacturing firm that sent an elaborate, technical questionnaire to existing customers asking them to name the features they'd like to have in a new valve. After tabulating the replies, the company carefully designed and built the desired valve. It was a complete flop. When they put all the features customers requested into one valve, they couldn't keep the price competitive with specialized valves, customized for special uses, that were available at lower prices.

If you want to penetrate an existing market, you may have to use a low-pricing strategy to get into that market. This is known as "buying" market share, because you pay your entry fee with lost profits on lower prices. Some customers will try your product simply because your price is lowest. Carefully explain that this price is an introductory offer, or your product can develop the reputation of being cheap and of lower quality. After you've achieved name recognition and volume, raise the price to more competitive levels. Small increases are easier for customers to swallow than large ones.

> *There is a difference between the best that money can buy and the best value for the dollar. Knowing which is most important to the customer is crucial.*

If your sales volume isn't satisfactory, the first option is to lower your prices and accept less profit per unit with the expectation of greater volume. Next, you could differentiate your product from your competitors' by emphasizing service, performance, delivery time, financing arrangements, quality, or another feature important to your customer.

If you sell from a catalog with list prices and discounts to distributors, change discounts often so they won't be perceived as permanent. Otherwise future price increases will be difficult.

Your pricing strategy must also react when a competitor comes out with a new product or service or with a price that's substantially different from yours. Continually think of ways to lower your costs so that you can sustain a lower price than your competitor.

Your last option is to drop the product completely if you can't make money at it. This is a tough decision to make, but sometimes it's the wisest course. (See KNOWING WHEN TO QUIT OR CHANGE; MISTAKES—ADMITTING THEM.)

In your pricing policies, be aware of the Robinson-Patman Act of 1936, which deals with price discrimination. This act prohibits you from selling the same product at different prices to customers engaged in interstate commerce where your acts have a tendency to injure competition. If the products are different, if there are cost differences, or if you lower the price for everyone because of changing market conditions, quantities purchased, or other payment terms, different product prices are acceptable. If you're in doubt about selling identical products for different prices, check with your attorney.

When you change your price, you'll become acutely aware of the sensitivity of your customers to raised or lowered prices. Observe your industry and your competitors. Keep your finger on the pulse of the market.

You can walk away from sales you don't want. In the final analysis, the bottom line (profit) counts more than the top line (sales), even though there is no bottom line without a large top line. If you're obsessed with the top line, you're likely to be a chronic loser because you'll have insufficient margins to cover all your expenses.

Product and Business Life Cycles

NOTHING GOES ON FOREVER—not your business, not any product, not your youthful vigor or even your life. Whenever you launch a new company, product, or service, you'll see it start, grow, and then reach a plateau of volume or acceptance. If you stay long enough, you'll see competition come in or market alternatives develop.

Ultimately, what you created will fade or fall and be replaced by something newer or better. In a rapidly changing industry like computers, the whole product cycle can be less than two years.

If you plot sales volume against time on a graph, the result is shaped like a bell and is called a *bell curve* (see figure 6). The embryonic or introductory stage starts from zero and curves upward through time. The growth stage shows market acceptance and recognition and has a steep upward slope like the front side of the bell. The rounding off at the top, called *maturity* or *plateau,* indicates that the market has become saturated or competition has developed. The down slope on the far side, curving slowly back to zero again, is *aging* or *decay* as sales decline and cease.

If you consider only the first two-thirds of the complete bell curve, you see a somewhat straightened letter S. This S curve goes up, reaches its maximum, then starts downward at a more gentle slope. Although it goes down more slowly than it went up, it will ultimately go all the way back to zero.

There is a unique bell curve for each company, product, or service within a company. To keep the overall company growth curve going up, continue to introduce new products or services, or enter new markets, thus combining the continuous new growth up-slopes of additional S curves.

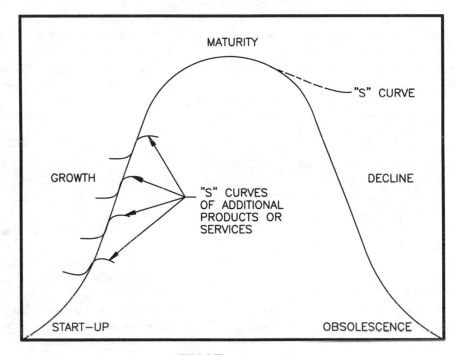

Figure 6. Bell Curve and S Curves

Profits

PROFIT ISN'T A DIRTY WORD. Profit is the reward for efficiency and effectiveness.

Your operation must say this to your customers: "We want you to buy our product or service for a price we both think it's worth." The price you both think it's worth must be high enough to enable you to make a reasonable profit, which you will use to make your business grow.

Whenever your bottom line is red, your company grows weaker. Whenever your bottom line is black, you grow stronger. Over a long period, the difference it makes can be tremendous. No business can last long without profits.

Promoters

P

372

PROMOTERS PUT A DREAM on the road to reality. They have a valid place in our capitalistic economy and provide some businesses with a starting platform no one else can provide.

Vision and salesmanship are necessary to start a large operation. Promoters have vision and are good salespeople. Typically, they recruit a lot of people to make a joint effort on their projects. As a general rule, however, promoters aren't good business managers.

For this reason, and the fact that their dreams and promises can't be verified, promoters scare bankers, and they usually end up dealing with investors. But some large, successful businesses today wouldn't be providing jobs and customer services if it weren't for some promotor's successful efforts.

Economically, it's best if they promote, collect their promotion fee, and then get out of the way so stable, realistic business managers (who could never have raised the money or put all the pieces together) can run the company.

I don't know of a single book on training a promoter, finding a promoter, or how to become a successful promoter. It requires a born or self-developed skill and temperament.

The point at which a promoter crosses the line and becomes a con man is difficult to define. It sometimes takes a long time for a con man to become apparent. (See CON MEN.)

Push Decisions Down

START AS EARLY AS POSSIBLE in your organization to push decision-making responsibility down to the lowest-level person who can intelligently make that decision. It breaks up the one-person-makes-all-the-decisions preference of many entrepreneurs and starts the habit and culture of delegating responsibility. The inability to turn loose of authority and decision making is the downfall of many entrepreneurs who would like to see their companies grow larger. (See INVISIBLE WALL OF MANAGEMENT.)

Pushing decisions down trains middle and lower managers in responsibility and decision making. The result is better, faster service because decisions are made closer to the problems, closer to employees who can do something about them. (See GETTING PEOPLE TO STRETCH TO THEIR FULL ABILITY.)

Decisions must be made at the lowest possible level for management at the top to retain its effectiveness.

P

373

It also keeps a lot of things off your desk, freeing your thinking and planning time for more important concerns.

Quality, Features, and Value

QUALITY AND VALUE ARE NOT THE SAME. *Quality* is the absence of defects, or the closest thing to that. Quality may also mean the greatest purity, the best performance, the most beautiful workmanship, the best taste, the greatest construction, the finest handiwork. Higher quality is always available for more money, until you reach the finest product or service money can buy. But few of these are sold. The absence of defects costs top dollar, but that's not the same as value.

Features include color, size, performance, capability—characteristics that add utility, usefulness, or enjoyment to the product or service. Some features may add greatly to the cost, some very little.

Value is the customers' perception that they receive more-than-adequate quality and features for the dollars they spend. Customers always try to get the best value. They may want the least expensive product in its field that will serve their purpose, or they may want the most features, knowing that they'll probably pay more money.

Few people would claim that a Ford is as high in quality as a Cadillac. But it will travel just as far, just as fast, for less money, so many people consider a Ford an excellent value. More people buy Fords than Cadillacs. Other customers see the balance of qualities and features they want and are willing to pay for in a Dodge, a Toyota, or a Volkswagen.

It's not cheaper things
that we want
to possess
but expensive things
that cost
a lot less.

Value is a measure of the amount of desired quality and features per dollar spent. Customers have their own perception of value. Your judgment of the combination of features and quality that the greatest number of customers in your target market will perceive as value is the core of your marketing decisions. These are some of the most significant decisions your management team will make.

Q

374

Questions for Interviewing Prospective Employees

THE MOST COMMON METHOD OF FINDING and hiring the employees you want is through personal interviews. Many laws and regulations have been passed in the last 10 years aimed at eliminating discrimination in the workplace, including discrimination affecting hiring procedures.

These laws prevent discrimination by prohibiting the employer from asking questions concerning age, race, national origin, religion, sex, disability, marital status, workers' compensation claims, health-related matters, or sexual preference. The best test for allowable questions is this: Is the question necessary to determine the candidate's ability to satisfactorily discharge job responsibilities?

Some states are more restrictive than others, but you can usually test for attitude and personality. Look for a validated test that serves your purpose. You can always test for job-related skills or capacity to perform. You may not require a physical exam until after a job offer. These days, you must be more sophisticated and perceptive during the interview in order to select employees you think will fit in with your organization.

The following are suggested questions to probe applicants' attitudes and ability to get along with their fellow employees:

- "If you found your ideal job, what would it be?"

- "If you're searching for a job, you're certainly considering other employment. Why do you think you'd like this job?"

- "Why do you think you're qualified for this job?" (Be careful of overqualified people. They're either looking at your job as a temporary spot until they can find something better, or they have a personal problem, such as drinking or indebtedness, that will cause you problems also. They could also represent a test of your employment practices by social pressure groups, government agencies, or unions.)

- "What gave you the greatest sense of accomplishment on your last jobs? What did you hate to do and put off as long as you could?"

- "What problem or procedure caused you the greatest trouble or frustration on your last job? What occupied most of your time? What occupied the second-greatest amount of your time?"

- "What three things did you like best about your last job? What three things did you like least?"

- "Did you feel you were mistreated in your last job? By whom? How?"

375

- "Did you have any employee conflicts or confrontations on your last job? Were they with your supervisor or a fellow employee?"

- "Why did you leave your last job? The job before that?"

- "What were the good things and the bad things about your immediate supervisor on your last job? On the job before that?"

- "What personality traits in a boss annoy you the most?"

- "What kind of employees did your last company seem to hire and retain? Did you fit in and feel comfortable with them? What made you feel uncomfortable? How well did you get along with people on your last job?" (Since human nature doesn't change, the prospective employee will be inclined to get along with people the same way on your job.)

- "Describe your strong points as an employee. Describe your weak points."

- "What stands out for you as the most interesting task or project you've handled in your job history?"

- "Describe a boss or co-worker with whom you had a superior working relationship."

- "What are your self-improvement goals? What progress have you made on them during the last year (quarter or month)?"

- "What job do you expect (or desire) to be doing five years from now? Ten years from now?"

- "When I call your last employer for a reference on what kind of employee you were, what is he or she going to tell me?" (This answer is frequently more revealing than the actual conversation with the employer.)

- "What do you find most challenging about the job I've described? What do you find most interesting? Least interesting?"

- "If you're as smart as the person we're looking for, you're just as curious and particular about whom you go to work for as we are about whom we hire. What questions about our company (or this job) may I answer for you?"

Be sure to investigate any gaps in the applicant's employment history as well as unusual descriptions or explanations. These could reveal a prison term or a time the applicant wants to hide for some reason.

Two final questions can be revealing: "Why should I hire you to be a member of my team rather than any of the other applicants who have been here?" and "What is the one reason why I should not hire you?"

None of these questions examine technical ability, knowledge, or capability to perform the specific job for which you are hiring. You must satisfy yourself as to these capabilities by other means.

Questions to Ask When Checking References

IN TODAY'S LITIGIOUS SOCIETY, an employer can easily be sued for slander for making allegedly derogatory remarks about a former employee that prevent her from getting another job. The employer you're asking as a reference must therefore be very careful what he says, even if the employee was caught red-handed doing something outrageous, illegal, or dishonest.

Where are the corporate entrepreneurs? The answer is: there are none.

—Harold Geneen

Exercise the same caution yourself when someone calls to check references for one of your former employees. Even though the truth is a perfect defense against the former employee's allegations, proving it can be difficult and expensive. What can be proven in a court of law and what you know is true are two different things.

For each company the applicant lists on the application, ask for the department and name of the applicant's imme-

diate supervisor. If you can, talk directly with that supervisor, who knew the applicant best, rather than someone in the HR department who will just read part of the applicant's files to you.

When you check by phone with the applicant's former employers, they will frequently verify only name, dates of employment, job title, and possibly maximum pay. After listening to all the good things about the individual, ask the following:

"Please tell me specifically about this person's duties and areas of responsibility within your company. I know what my company's job involves, and your information will help me tell whether this person is qualified for our position." Follow up by asking specifically about performance of a specific task or important duty of the job you're hiring for.

"Everyone has both strengths and weaknesses. You've told me this person's greatest strengths. What were her greatest weaknesses?"

Final question: "Would you rehire her? In a job with more or less responsibility? At a higher or lower wage scale?"

When you're being questioned about one of your former employees by a prospective employer, ask, "What do you want him to do?" If the new job description doesn't correspond to yours, you can plead ignorance with no offense and no risk of a lawsuit for defamation.

Q

377

Quick Decisions—Shoot from the Hip

SNAP DECISIONS CONCERNING MAJOR problems can be made only by people who, because of intense study over a period of years, have readily available enough background information and current facts to know what to do now in a rapidly changing situation. These people are usually commodities traders, emergency-room doctors, or battlefield commanders.

Snap answers to questions for routine or unimportant items are expected and expeditious. You're indecisive if you can't make those.

In senior management, few things change that rapidly or require that sort of decision making. Seldom are all facts known or all side effects obvious enough to make off-the-cuff decisions on significant policy matters.

If someone suddenly presents you with a problem that has long-term effects, don't rush to judgment. Gather the facts. Consider all the angles. Whom or what will it help? Whom or what will it hurt? What will it cost? Is time working for you or against you? Ask others for opinions. Consider all alternatives and all secondary or side effects.

Schedule business trips that involve major decisions as overnight trips. Before you go, do all the research and be as familiar with background information as you can. Afternoon arrival gives you time for discussions during or after business

on the day of your arrival. After the meeting and alone overnight, you'll have time to think and check on questionable information. The following morning, you have time for clarification and more discussions or more questions before making your decision.

Just as doctors must correctly diagnose the problem before they prescribe corrective medication and treatment, you must identify problems and consider alternative consequences of solving them. Without keeping your long-range goals in view as a backdrop, many of your short-term decisions may be wrong.

Usually, the decision you're seeking addresses this question: Within the short-term limitations on my actions, what should I do now that will contribute most to my long-range goals?

The action sequence of "Ready! Fire! Aim!" will get you into more trouble than delaying an important decision for careful consideration.

Raise Your Level of Incompetence

THE PETER PRINCIPLE (originally expressed by Dr. Lawrence J. Peter) states that we all rise to our level of incompetence. Unfortunately, it's true, whether you're an employee, a manager, or self-employed. If you're self-employed, your incompetence holds back the entire organization underneath you.

Fortunately, such limits aren't permanent unless you allow them to be. You can improve your skills and knowledge if you're willing to work or attend seminars. Consult talented people; persuade them to join your efforts so limits for the whole organization can be raised. Read books like this one. (See BOOKS—BUSINESS AND MANAGERIAL BOOKS WORTH READING.)

> *Whatever you can do or dream you can—begin it. Boldness has genius, power, and magic in it.*
>
> —Goethe

Your formal education may be over, but your informal education started at commencement. You should attend two or more seminars on subjects of your choice each year you're in business. Getting away for a few days while you get concentrated information and education on your most pressing problem will increase your business knowledge and confidence. Some of your best information will come during discussions with fellow students during the break periods.

You're in deep trouble if your attitude is "I know it all. I built this company with what I already know, and I don't need to change." You've reached the upper limit at your present skill level if your opinion is "There's my way or the highway." It's great for your ego, but it's bad for your business.

When you reach your level of incompetence, your business suffers. I had a client once whose 15-year-old business, of which he was 90 percent owner, couldn't seem to grow larger. Volume bounced from $10,000,000 to $14,000,000, with a spotty profit record. He wouldn't hire high-quality people who might question or threaten him. He wouldn't delegate enough authority to get jobs done, and he wouldn't give recognition, praise, or bonuses to others for doing well. It became obvious that my client had reached his level of incompetence as a manager, although the level was rather high. It was difficult to be his consultant; a consultant cannot survive by recommending that clients commit suicide. I did recommend that he sell the company. He didn't. Now the company is gone.

R

379

Length of tenure alone doesn't prove competence. No one can fire the boss, so just because you've been there a long time and survived longer than everyone else doesn't necessarily mean that your level of competence is superior, that you've kept up with current technology, or that

you haven't become just plain lazy. Being alive doesn't mean healthy growth.

You must constantly improve yourself, or you and your business will stagnate. Push your level of incompetence ever higher by increasing your business knowledge and education.

Relative Pay for Corporate Officers

380

IN MOST COMPANIES, the best-paying job is the chief executive officer (CEO), which is also the top administrative post in the company. In some companies, the top-paying position is the chief marketing person. In a few others, it's a financial person. In some small companies, the highest paycheck sometimes goes to a chief technical person, but as companies get larger, administrative types who understand marketing tend to take over the top spot.

After you've gotten large enough to have a full complement of corporate officers and helpers, your pattern of executive pay will probably look something like the following: if you consider the CEO's salary as 100 percent, the second highest paid officer averages generally about 70 percent, the third highest paid gets about 60 percent, and the fourth highest is paid about 55 percent. Others range downward from there, either in defined pay

grades or groups of similarly situated managers.

These numbers show relationships based solely on merit and performance, undistorted by shareholdings, partnership equalities, family relationships, or sacred cows.

In smaller companies, of course, the entrepreneur sets her own wages. Others are paid the best compromise between what the company can afford and what the entrepreneur thinks they're worth. There are always special situations that the owner thinks justify payments to some that others consider a gift rather than earnings.

All pay scales are relative, but these are general guidelines. Some associates will be dissatisfied with their pay, no matter how hard you try to do what you think is fair. You will never have an employee who considers himself overpaid, including yourself.

Results vs. Activity

ACTIVITY IS NEITHER A RESULT NOR AN objective. You must understand the difference. Many employees and managers try to impress themselves and others with busywork or make-work. They shuffle papers, make phone calls, attend meetings, use computers, or rush to and fro carrying things or delivering papers.

The customer wants and pays for results. Managers set certain objectives, intermediate goals, or targets that are measurable and that contribute toward the results the customer will pay for.

Activity is the responsibility of the individual and her immediate boss or supervisor. Supposedly, the individual's activities contribute to objectives or required results, but a surprising amount of the time activities only give that appearance. You should be able to recognize false activity.

What you're searching for is maximum results or progress toward an objective with minimum activity. If you reach the result or the objective with zero activity—hurrah! Don't even try to measure activity.

Don't tell me how hard you worked. Tell me how much you got done.

—James J. Ling

In your job descriptions, budgets, and memos delegating responsibilities to managers, don't describe or list any activities—specify only the objectives to be achieved. Quantify results or objectives as much as possible and establish time lines. You can then monitor progress.

R

381

Retirement

IF YOU'RE TEMPERAMENTALLY SUITED to be an entrepreneur, you aren't suited for retirement. You've spent a lifetime taking charge of your life, and you can't easily change those habits. Once your business is gone, if you're a real workaholic, you're going to start wondering what to do with yourself. You'll need something to throw yourself into and work at. If you have a favorite sport that keeps you active—golf, tennis, bowling, hiking—your physical and mental health will be better.

You'll need something more than retirement because you're going to catch up on your reading, loafing, resting, love-making, family, and kids pretty quick. You're going to look for things to do. You might get more involved in civic, church, cultural, charitable, political, hobby, entertainment, or educational activities.

Getting your life and your dollars to run out at the same time is a real challenge.

My advice is don't go back into a different business that requires your active management, although this is sometimes very tempting to entrepreneurs. (See SECOND OR UNRELATED BUSINESSES.)

If you retire, you quickly learn that money is easier to make than to keep. Many people who start out well-to-do from employment or ownership at some mature time in their life dissipate large portions of their wealth before they die.

Most entrepreneurs have been too busy making money to have learned how to handle it wisely. The best book I know of is *Wealth: An Owner's Manual,* by Michael Stolper (New York: Harper Business, 1992). The younger you are, the more important this book is to you, because you have time for the compounding effect of wealth building.

I was present at a meeting of successful entrepreneurs of advancing age who were discussing the ideal retirement. The consensus was that in order to retire worry-free, you need a fully paid-for principal residence you're pleased with. It would be nice also to have a second home or vacation home, also fully paid for. This gives you a change of pace and scenery. Adjust your lifestyle so you can live on a 10 percent return from whatever additional funds you may have. Then you won't have to drain your principal, and you can live forever without worry.

If the funds you've accumulated or received from liquidating the results of your lifetime of work are sizable, consider using professional money managers—not brokers. If your pile is big enough, divide it into two to four pieces and contract each piece to a different money manager of your choice for one year. Monitor and compare their performance. Take money away from the one who's doing most poorly. Either give it to the one who's doing best or find another money manager. This way you're diversifying by having a team of managers and constantly comparing one against the other.

You might become the equivalent of a local Silver Fox Advisor (see SILVER FOX ADVISORS), mentor of small-business CEOs, or help others trying to follow in your footsteps. At a recent Silver Fox Christmas party, the wife of a newly retired member said she was still trying to figure out what to do with four times as much husband and half as much pay as she used to have.

Return on Investment (ROI)

DIVIDE PROFIT BY TOTAL INVESTMENT to determine the percentage of return on the investment. Business owners and financial people frequently use the rate of return on investment (ROI) as a measure of profitability. Usage varies as to what specific items from the financial statement are used as measures of profit and investment.

Profit is usually considered profit after taxes. Since S corporations and limited liability corporations (LLCs) don't pay taxes or show them on financial statements, they usually use net operating profit. To get a comparable after-tax number, they deduct maximum personal income tax from operating profit.

Investment, as used in the formula, could mean the total assets employed (the largest number on the balance sheet—at the bottom) or only the equity that is the shareholders' investment. The percentage answer will, of course, show less return on total assets than on the shareholders' investments. Outsiders ordinarily use return on total assets to evaluate the effectiveness of management. Insiders and stockholders usually use return on equity, which is the investment they're interested in.

> *QIS—Quality, Integrity, Service. You'll never go wrong if you build your business on this foundation.*

As an investor or as an owner, you usually compute ROI based on cash-on-cash. Never mind what you borrowed; the interest you paid was deducted from profits as an expense. Your concern is that you wrote a check for so much cash, and that you got or will get so much cash or value in return. To determine cash-on-cash ROI, divide the cash you invested by the return in cash (or cash equivalent) you will get.

R
383

Risk vs. Reward

EVERY BUSINESS DECISION YOU'LL MAKE for the rest of your life is based on your conscious or unconscious evaluation of disadvantages versus advantages. This boils down to risk versus reward.

There's always risk, including the risk in doing nothing. Time passes, even while you procrastinate. To do nothing is to make a decision. The evaluation comes down to deciding whether time is working for or against you.

Wherever there's an opportunity for gain, there's also an opportunity for loss—guaranteed. Anyone who tells you, "You can't lose on this," is lying. If the primary aim of the captain were to preserve his ship, he would never leave port. But there is risk in staying tied up at the pier as well—anything from bankruptcy to hurricanes.

R

384

———

Opportunity always involves some risk. You cannot steal second base and keep your foot on first.

———

The reward or advantage may be only the least of several evils, but there is almost always some advantage to be gained or retained in making one choice over another. Your background for deciding includes your experience, education, emotional strength, status, your financial position, the company's financial position, and your sensitivity to the feelings of others.

Learn to evaluate the business risk of every decision. For every important decision, make up a decision sheet listing advantages on one side and disadvantages on the other. Weigh the consequences. Try to assign a dollar value, either at present or over the next year, to each possible outcome.

Many risks or rewards are intangible and can't be quantified or expressed in hard dollar numbers. List them anyway. Weigh them in the decision-making process. Consider the side effects or unintended effects on all or specific employees and customers.

By making one choice, you preclude making others. When you walk through one door, other doors close.

Sacred Cows

LIKE THE SACRED COWS OF INDIA, there are often people, ideas, products, or procedures within an older organization that are exempt from receiving criticism or doing productive work because the boss or a sub-boss protects them.

If they're people, they may be family members. They may be old employees, old friends, or relatives who hold their position for some reason other than competence and productivity. Criticizing them or recommending their discharge may even be cause for firing the employee raising the question.

If the sacred cows are procedures, products, or attitudes, they were probably begun with high hopes by some senior boss. When time and performance prove them wrong and no longer productive,

they should be changed or axed. But pride, ego, family relationships, or refusal to admit that a mistake was made in the first place can keep some sacred cows alive for a long time.

Get rid of them. If they're people, pay them off or retire them if you can afford it. Keeping them within an organization of people trying to work and please customers is like dragging an anchor.

Have no sacred cows in your business, including yourself.

S

385

Sales Analysis

IT'S IMPOSSIBLE TO ANALYZE your sales too thoroughly. You want to find out where your customers and sales are coming from and why, so you can go out and get a lot more just like them.

Record into your database all the information you can. Supplement information at time of sale by adding the customer's name, address, or type of business if you know it. You might have different data-

bases that can be related to each other to tell you everything you want to know. Today's computer programs can easily make these associations.

Answer these questions about your sales and your customers: Are most of your sales to large companies or small? To men or women? To rich or poor? To young or old? To new or repeat customers? Do they buy more or less the next time?

How did they find your company? What brought them to your door? Do they buy one item or many? Where are their homes or locations? What area or neighborhood has the most customers?

Additional information that doesn't appear on the sales ticket or sales order must come from remarks picked up by your salespeople. Find your most fertile areas for sales growth and go after them. Do your customers answer newspaper ads? Magazine ads? Radio advertising? Direct mail? How can you reach future ideal customers fastest at least expense?

Every time your salespeople talk with actual or potential customers, they're making a market survey. If they're alert, they can generalize for you or perhaps give you specific numbers and details. Do customers want additional products? Do they buy one item from you because you have other, similar items? What do they like best about your product? What do they like least? What do they like least about your service or performance? What do they like most? What do they like best about your competitor?

Internally, your accounting or sales administrative people should continually analyze sales. What's your most profitable product? Least profitable? Who are your most profitable customers? Most profitable salespersons? Departments?

In addition to analyzing all your sales, you need a way to look at potential sales in your market. Find demographic statistics or lists of all firms or customers who might use your services. Also, find a way to estimate the total market for your products or services and your market share, either overall or by product line.

Often your industry's trade association or a governmental agency has such statistics. If you keep looking, you'll find a way to gauge the size of the total market and what your current share is.

Continually analyzing your sales and your total market will keep you on top of your present business and point the way to go in the future.

Sales Calls

EVEN IF YOU'RE NOT A GOOD SALESPERSON yourself, make sales calls with your salespeople and take your business card that identifies you as president. You'll learn a lot, and your customers will be flattered. Not many company presidents line up outside their doors. They'll retain your card with your phone number and, if something goes wrong, will feel free to call you.

When you tell your salespeople you want to go along on some of their calls, they'll take you to companies and good customers who know them well. They know the friendly reception they get will make an impression on you.

Rather than leave it up to your salespeople, however, make a list of customers or companies you want to see for whatever reason, and insist upon seeing them. Go where they haven't ordered from you lately, or go where they've never ordered from you. You'll learn from their reactions and comments, and you can tell how well they've been covered by your salespeople in the past.

> *There ain't hardly no business what comes in that ain't been gone out after.*
>
> —G.O.K.

When salespeople call on existing and new customers at their business locations, the golden hours are from 9 to 4 on Tuesday, Wednesday, and Thursday. Monday afternoons and Friday mornings are also good times. At other hours, customers are too busy looking after routine business chores to give a salesperson an unhurried welcome.

If your salesperson can get 4 meaningful customer calls each on Tuesday, Wednesday, and Thursday, and 2 each on Monday and Friday, that's 16 successful calls per week. To get 16 successful calls, the salesperson must try to make at least 25.

Some quick arithmetic—dividing your cost for one salesperson's salary, car, expense account, and fringe benefits by 16 calls per week—will give you a scary number for the cost of each effective sales call. However, taking one or more customers to lunch every day brings more opportunities for good will and sales presentations and is well worth the small additional cost of the meals.

No salesperson should be in the office doing administrative or paperwork during the golden hours when customers are available and receptive. Off-hours and times when customers don't want to be interrupted are the times for office housekeeping, reports, planning, and internal matters. With today's excellent communications—electronic, graphical, and voice many companies are doing away completely with salespeople's offices.

For small companies, detailed sales call reports generally aren't productive. Salespeople hate them. You probably don't have time to read or analyze them, anyway. Usually, the better the salesperson, the poorer the paperwork. Customers' orders are the best call reports you can get.

Every sales call is a market-research interview. You can find out what potential customers are interested in—what brings them to the edge of their chairs—and what puts them to sleep. Often they'll make comments about your competitors or their alternatives to your services that can guide your expansion plans.

Follow your market closely. If you see a competitor doing well, analyze why.

Sales Managers

SOMEONE MUST PERFORM THE FUNCTION of sales or marketing manager. If you haven't appointed someone else, you're it.

Unless you have only one salesperson, don't make your best salesman or saleswoman the sales manager. The ability to be best at point of sale in personal conversation with the customer and the ability to select and direct a group of salespeople are two very different skills.

A super salesperson is someone from the home office with authority to cut the price.

Sales managers must be coaches and team players. They must encourage, teach, and speak well of other salespeople. They must unselfishly share or forego commissions, rewards, and glory. They must select and train salespeople, and they must settle misunderstandings fairly about territories, accounts, orders, commissions, cars, expense accounts, offices, and company policies. Sales managers must be perceived by salespeople as fair, impartial, honest, supportive, and inspirational. (See SALESPEOPLE.)

If you've made your best salesperson your sales manager and find him unsatisfactory in that position, try to save that person as an employee. Make it easy to sell in a different territory, department, or situation, and save the person's pride and confidence.

Sales or Income Stream

SALES ARE THE SINE QUA NON of any business. You compete for sales in a free market economy where the customer can choose whether to use and pay for your services or someone else's. Until you've built up an income stream from sales that more than covers your fixed and variable costs, you're not destined to survive in business very long.

When you start in business, expand, or enter a new market, go for the income stream as fast as you can. The more quickly you produce income, the less your cash requirement will be. If you can produce cash income from advance deposits before you have to furnish the product, you've decreased your cash requirements even further.

As soon as you can, sell whatever you've produced of acceptable quality. Don't wait to start selling until you have the complete product line, or absolutely the best models of your product, or the latest improvements. But always make certain that your quality is good, or you'll ruin your reputation for quality before you ever get off the ground.

If you are the one-in-ten entrepreneur whose area of expertise is sales, count your blessings. Hiring good administrators while you do the selling is easier than hiring good salespeople while you look after production or administration.

If you're not a natural-born salesperson, study salesmanship and go to seminars or sales courses. Even if you detest it, go with your salespeople to call on customers at least two days a month. That won't really keep you in touch with your market, but it will help.

Money management and the production of an income stream is what you're in business for. Until the income stream covers all expenses, you don't have discretionary income. Allocating resources or money isn't possible.

> *When you're out of quality, you're out of business.*
>
> —Zig Ziglar

Sales per Employee

IT'S IMPOLITE TO ASK COMPETITORS or even good entrepreneurial friends what their sales volume is. However, they'll gladly answer your question about their total number of full-time employees. They might as well tell you sales volume because you can figure it out by simple arithmetic.

When you divide your total annual sales volume by the total number of full-time employees, the result is the amount of annual sales per employee. Your competitors probably have almost the same sales per employee as you do, so multiplying their number of employees times your sales-per-employee number will give you their approximate sales volume. This is true because similar competitive businesses usually have similar operating ratios. (See HOW ARE YOU DOING COMPARED WITH INDUSTRY STANDARDS?)

Here's the technically correct way to find your number of full-time employees. First, find the number of full-time employees on the last payroll of each month (all payrolls—weekly, biweekly, semimonthly, and monthly). Then use the average of the 12 monthly numbers.

Even if your business is seasonal or if you ended the year with more employees than you started with, this gives you the equivalent number of employees that produced and sold the annual sales volume.

Another significance of this number is that your sales must increase by the same amount before you can justify hiring another employee. Of course a production worker, a salesperson, a clerk, and a manager don't do the same work or make the same paycheck, but after you leave the survival stage the averages and proportions remain about the same.

Your objective always is to get sales per employee as high as you possibly can. This means maximum productivity per employee, maximum margin per sales dollar, and maximum gross and net profits to be shared by those productive people.

Sales per employee varies with the type of business. Service businesses, with few expensive assets and no inventory, have the lowest sales per employee. If your average employee makes $30,000 per year (total annual payroll as reported on your federal payroll tax returns divided by number of employees as computed above), annual sales of $100,000 per employee is probably adequate.

For businesses with large investments in assets and inventories per employee, such as automobiles, steel, refineries, and chemical plants, annual sales per employee can easily be in excess of $1,000,000. Compaq Computer increased its sales per employee from $305,000 in 1991 to $716,000 in 1993, a tremendous increase in such a short time.

Applying this yardstick to your business will help your future planning.

Salesmanship

THE BEST DEFINITION OF SALESMANSHIP is helping prospects adopt your predetermined conclusion in such a way that they think it's their own.

Two novitiates for the priesthood shared a room during the long training and meditation period. Both were smokers and found the long, silent prayer sessions difficult to bear without a cigarette. One volunteered to ask the priest about smoking and asked, "Father, is it all right if we smoke while we pray?" The father

replied, "Heavens no, my son! That would be sacrilege and irreverent." After a month went by, the other novitiate said he would try to get permission to smoke. He asked, "Father, is it all right if we pray while we smoke?" The reply was immediate. "Certainly, my son. It is proper to pray at any time."

Moral: Spend learning and preparation time considering how you're going to present things.

Sales courses tell you there are two

reasons why people don't buy your products or services—one is the reason they tell you, the other is the real reason. Analyze your own buying decisions: What are your own reasons for not buying? What do you tell others?

Take one or more courses in selling; every large city has several available. Send every salesperson you've got to suitable sales training or refresher courses.

Many books and audiotapes are also available from any good bookstore. The best book I know for selling continues to be Dale Carnegie's *How to Win Friends*

and Influence People (New York: Simon and Schuster, 1936). The 1994 edition, also published by Simon and Schuster, is available at your local bookshop.

> ## Nothing happens until somebody sells something.
>
> **—Red Motley**

Salesmanship—Levels Of

IN A VERY REAL SENSE, all people in the company are its salespeople. When they deal with any outsider, by phone or in person, they make an impression on someone who is now or might become a customer. Discussed here are people whose primary assignment is to talk to potential or actual customers, and the sales talent they should exhibit.

Service people are the company's representatives who either service and sell to the final customer or repair and install, frequently at the customer's location. Within the customer's organization, everyone knows who they are, what company they represent and its reputation, and what their products are.

Properly trained service people use opportunities to keep people thinking about the company and its products. They spread the word whenever a new product or service is introduced, but only to customers who are already using company products. These people should grease the wheels of progress and leave a good impression wherever they go, but they don't make big waves or directly generate new customers.

Order takers or inside salespeople take orders over the phone or talk to customers who walk in the door. They don't need the same sales skills as outside or cold-call salespeople. Order takers know models and stock on hand. They know how to handle people well and have a good follow-up procedure. Everyone they talk to already knows your company and your general line of products and just needs assistance to get the right model, color, and delivery, and maybe a slight push to make the final decision to buy.

Salespeople make waves. They make something happen where nothing happened before. They ring new doorbells, talk to new people, and convert new customers from their present buying habits to the habit of buying from your company.

Advertising helps, but salespeople persuade others to act. They put strangers at ease quickly. They know their product, get an order for it, and move on. Good salespeople want the full commission and full credit for what they do. They aren't necessarily good team players. (See SALESPEOPLE.)

Sales managers must be unselfish and must encourage others to grow and accomplish things. They're team players, more concerned about the team than themselves. They must be able to select, hire, plan, organize, coach, and direct salespeople. It's a mistake to make your best salesperson your sales manager. (See SALES MANAGERS.)

These are the sales levels usually found within a company. At some point, however, you'll probably meet two additional levels of sales talent.

Promoters put a dream on the road to reality. At start-up, they're selling an intangible that they hope to make into a tangible operation. They visualize. They imagine how a nonexistent company or product can become a reality if people are motivated and resources are assembled.

Often, they're poor managers, but they usually want to remain on board as senior managers after the project is launched; after all, it's their baby. This leads to trouble. Someone else who's a better manager but a poorer promoter can probably run it better, handle people better, and make it grow, but that someone would probably never have been able to start the dream. (See PROMOTERS.)

The *con man* is a genius at making a salable product out of blue sky. His intangible product remains intangible. It takes a very talented salesperson to do this. (See CON MEN.)

S

392

Salespeople

IN OUR ECONOMIC SYSTEM, salespeople are a special breed. If you're a salesperson and also an entrepreneur, you're blessed with more than a normal share of talents.

For every person who can successfully market or sell something, there are at least five who can successfully manufacture or produce it. Although mediocre talents can be improved by training, less than 3 percent of the general population are suited by psychology and temperament to be really good at selling.

Salespeople must be able to have doors slammed in their faces three times in the morning and still face prospect number four in the afternoon with an optimistic smile. This isn't for everyone.

No two salespeople sell alike. It's difficult to generalize about their personal characteristics. They must have high self-confidence and self-esteem. They're often selfish and egotistical. They don't always speak well of other salespeople and dislike schedules and paperwork. They frequently have a high sex drive. Many don't handle their own money well. By the nature of the job, many salespeople spend most of their time away from the company and operate autonomously with heavy requirements for good personal organization and initiative.

As an owner, don't ignore or fail to participate in the sales effort because you're not comfortable with it or don't understand it. No one else has the drive for the success of the company that you do. No one else has the financial or personal investment. If you don't emphasize customers and sales, no one else will. If you're inattentive, half-hearted, or vague, the sales effort and possibly the whole company will sink.

Learn all you can about salesmanship, your market, and your customers. You can't know too much. Lack of such knowledge is the greatest weakness of many technically oriented entrepreneurs.

Most important is the quality of the people you hire to do your selling. Hiring the right person with the right skills and experience is the best thing you can do.

If you select the wrong people, no amount of training or managing will help them make it.

Hiring good salespeople is difficult because most people trying to get sales jobs can make a good impression in their employment interview regardless of how poorly they may do over long-term employment. Ideally, try to choose people who have been successful at selling for other companies that have a similar market or sell to similar customers. Hiring high achievers in the first place is generally better than washing out the losers after wasting training time and money.

Once you hire them, don't hesitate to let them spend two weeks in house learning about the company and its people, the technology and the product, the company's policies, and the competition. Then let them work under whoever will be their immediate supervisor for a while. Finally, let them accompany one of your experienced salespeople until you're sure they can make proper presentations on their own. After that, set up periodic personal conversations with them for reports, discussions, and performance reviews.

You must motivate some people. But for salespeople, hire already motivated people and make sure you don't demotivate them. Money isn't their only motivator; ego is also involved. Pay them adequately, but feed their egos. My sales manager always drove a better car than I did. Contests and awards are good motivators, but they become demotivators if the same person wins all the time.

S

393

Write a policy about what you will accept on expense accounts—which items are acceptable, specific amounts, and total amounts. Spending too much on expense accounts isn't good, but spending too little or leaving the impression of being cheap is worse.

Never let a customer's problems go unsolved.

Different markets and customer situations require different kinds of selling. The way to sell to retail customers isn't the way to sell used cars, industrial supplies, electronic equipment, magazines, medical services, airplane parts, or life insurance. Know your customers and your market. Select salespeople suitable to the task.

Your salespeople should see themselves as problem solvers for customers, not as vendors of your merchandise. Success is measured not only by dollar volume but by customer satisfaction as well. It takes a mix of optimism and persistence. The best salesperson I know gives the customer a feeling that he's on the customer's side, trying to get the most for the customer's money from this big company he works for.

The nature of your customers and their buying habits determines what kind of salespeople will do best for you. Your best salesperson may sell five times as much as your poorest salesperson. I know of no proven test that will help you tell the difference before hiring.

Your objective is to know the candidates as well as possible. I suggest multiple prehiring interviews under different circumstances and with different in-house people—one in a social atmosphere, one in a technical atmosphere, one where the potential salesperson is the only stranger.

Once you have a good salesperson, get that one to help you find another.

S

394

Salespeople's License

EVERYONE HAS HEARD THE COMMENT that salespeople have a license to bend the truth or to exaggerate some to make a sale. I don't agree.

I *do* agree that salespeople's jobs are to sell products or services. Without enthusiasm and belief in their product, salespeople cannot present it sincerely and convincingly. They must have confidence in it themselves, or they can't expect others to have the confidence to buy. Generally, people buy things from people with whom they feel empathy, and they buy from people they like and respect.

Salespeople's license gives them the right and obligation to put their best foot forward, so to speak, and to emphasize all the good things about their products. They don't have to mention the weaknesses, but if customers ask questions or make comparisons, salespeople's license doesn't allow lying about or misrepresenting anything.

If you ever expect to sell anything to one of these customers again, sincerity is more likely to get an invitation to return than any degree of high-pressure selling. Almost all customers resent high-pressure selling. It often produces negative results.

I once asked a real estate salesman for an opinion about the effect of a restrictive city ordinance on the property he was presenting to me. He replied, "Mr. Gillis, you've got to understand that I'm trying to sell this property. To get a fair answer to that question, you should ask someone else." I respected him for it.

Always tell the truth, but don't always be telling it.

Satisfied Customers = Job Security for All

IN THE COMPANY, everyone's real boss is the customer.

As long as you satisfy your present customers and get more, you won't have layoffs for lack of work. If you don't satisfy your customers and your business volume goes down, some people will lose jobs because there's less customer demand for their work.

Allow enough customers to become dissatisfied and you will lose your job and your company, too.

To remind everyone of this fact, a successful entrepreneur I know has printed on every pay envelope, "This money is sent to you by satisfied customers who chose our products rather than those of competitors."

Say No to Some Business

LEARN TO SAY NO TO SOME BUSINESS. Specifically, learn to say no to business that's related but beyond the scope of

your chosen market where you can effectively compete. For example, Kmart doesn't sell diamond rings, and Neiman

Marcus doesn't sell paper towels. You can't be all things to all people.

You must also learn to say no to what really *is* your chosen business when you think you may not get properly paid for it. Since your profit margin is probably less than 10 percent, a $1 sale you don't collect for will equal your total net profit on an additional $10 of sales. Those aren't good gambling odds. Credit and collection policies and procedures need your careful attention.

Other business you don't want is from customers who demand that, in order to get their business, you must not do business with their competitors. This happens only in some industries and usually with new, small suppliers. Don't tolerate it. Tell them if they wish to discuss contracting for the total output of your facility, you can discuss that. But don't allow a customer to tell you which other customers you can do business with.

Another time to say no is when the price gets too low for you to handle the business profitably. (See PRICES—CUTTING; PRICE WARS.) This brings up other considerations, such as your production cost, your workload, your need to hold good employees, and your need to get business from that customer.

When you cannot or choose not to fill customers' orders, you'll leave a good feeling and an open door for future business if you tell customers where they can get what they want. Smile, thank them for coming to you first, explain why you can't fill their order, and tell them where they're most likely to find what they want. You'll get the first phone call or visit next time.

Saying No to Customers and Employees

SOMETIMES "NO" SHOULD BE FIRM, instantaneous, and on the spot. Sometimes "No" should be slow, its effect on others carefully considered and explained.

In either event, deliver your decision firmly. Close the matter without leaving room for false hopes that you'll reconsider. Be diplomatic. Indicate that you want to go forward from here.

If you've said no to customers, you wish to keep their good will and respect. Tell them the reason for your decision.

Let them know you want to keep their long-term business on a fair and equitable basis. If you've said no to employees, you want to keep them motivated and working as part of your team. You want them to know that you're reasonable, fair, and honest.

It isn't easy. You'll get impossible demands from people who frequently see only their own side of the problem. Employees usually request more pay, privileges, or status symbols. Customers usually want more discounts, better terms, or special consideration. They're both requesting improvements in their situation at your company's expense. If you grant these requests, they will decrease your bottom line. That's your decision. But employees or customers usually won't think of your side until you diplomatically explain it.

Of course, times to say yes come along. You'll recognize them. They're easy. Saying no is what's hard. (See LOOKING OUT FOR #1; YOU ARE THE SOLE GUARDIAN OF THE BOTTOM LINE.)

Second or Unrelated Business

YOU CANNOT SERVE AS FULL-TIME CAPTAIN of two ships at sea at the same time. If you organize yourself and your team, you can be captain of larger ships with related departments and different cargo, but you can actively manage only one ship headed for one destination at one time. A few people can manage more than one business, but the number is small.

In this book I talk about businesses that require your active management day in and day out. This doesn't apply to occasional real estate, stocks, or joint ventures that don't require your personal time and attention constantly. Nor does it apply to your time and service in social, civic, athletic, charitable, or other non-financial groups.

For your business to succeed, you must immerse yourself in the intricate, day-to-day operating details. Knowing what's important and mastering the necessary skills requires an apprenticeship that may take years. Don't divert your limited time and attention to another business until the one you have is large and well-organized enough to run almost without your supervision. At that point, you're a passive investor, not an entrepreneur or active manager.

Resist the temptation to diversify to other kinds of businesses. I've seen many people who didn't resist, and who lost their shirts as a result. Stick to your core business. Stick to what you know how to do. To diversify, link up with exceptional people who are already proven masters of the new field you're entering.

Making money is easier and more fun than keeping and managing it.

A second, unrelated business is what you're tempted to get into after you've sold or left your first successful business.

At that point, you have a proven record (in one field only), probably some available money, plus business attitudes and work habits that impel you to get involved in another business you can actively manage.

Observation of former clients and friends has shown me that second businesses requiring active management are usually disasters. A switch to a completely new business requires another apprenticeship of many years. Also, your tendency is to try to get too big too fast because big financing is available—from your own bank account, of course. You can make big mistakes.

If you're going to do this, start small. Learn the right ways like you did in your first business. Watch the business closely and carefully monitor expansion. My experience has included my own hard work in a money-losing cattle ranching operation, which I loved doing but knew nothing about.

There's a limit to how many separate businesses you can master in a lifetime. Mastering a business generally takes years. Many highly accomplished men and women succeed at only one.

It's better to make passive investments with people who have proven success in their field, but that isn't easy either.

S

398

Secret Deals with Customers

A SECRET DEAL WON'T STAY SECRET very long. You'll make one customer temporarily happy and others mad when they find out about it.

> *Most things depend on*
> *the satisfaction*
> *of others.*

On your pricing policy, list quantity discounts any qualifying customer can take advantage of. A secret and special deal for Customer A will become known to Customer X when an employee changes jobs from Customer A to Customer X. Then you're in trouble. If your policies and practices can't stand the light of day, either change them or don't make secret deals, because they'll see the light of day sooner or later. Many discriminatory pricing practices are also against the law.

Whatever you give or tell a customer, you may as well give or tell your competitors, because the customer will quote your information to your competitors while trying to get a better deal.

Seed Money or Start-up Financing

I KNOW OF NO EXCEPTIONS to the basic rule that the entrepreneur has to contribute all or a sizable portion of the seed money invested in the business. Some of it must be taken from family income and living expenses. If you're going to grow this financial beanstalk reaching to the sky, which you own and control, you must plant and water the seed with your own money.

Set aside enough money to support yourself and your family for at least one year above and beyond your business needs; 18 months is better. In some states, you can borrow against life insurance or against equity you've built up in your home.

When you run out of funds, find other investors willing to bet on you or with you. You're searching for investors willing to risk capital on an unproven business deal. They may be family members, friends, or financially successful people who rely more on you as someone they know and trust than on the unknown merits of the business venture. These investors must be willing to invest capital in a business deal that a venture capitalist would consider too risky. They're hard to find. Entrepreneurs often take on partners solely for the capital they contribute.

The outside investor knows that when business goes sour, walking away from it is easy unless you've made a sizable investment of your own money. Until you have a profitable business performance record, banks and financial institutions will lend you money only on valuable collateral or hard assets.

Your education or technical background isn't adequate loan collateral. I was approached by three Ph.D.s working for three separate industrial rehabilitation firms who wanted to start their own business together. They thought their educational investment should be all they needed. Since they were professionally qualified, they couldn't understand why the bank wouldn't loan them 100 percent of their start-up money.

A Small Business Administration study proved the preponderance of owner financing for small businesses. They found the following breakdown of the sources of initial capital:

S

399

52.5%	owner's cash
11.6%	loans from family or friends
8.1%	previous ownership of required assets/fixtures
15.7%	loans from financial institutions
6.0%	credit from suppliers
6.1%	all other sources

I wish I could tell you there's an easier way to get seed money for your start-up, but I can't. The difficulty of getting the down payment on a business is one of the capitalistic system's ways of separating dreamers from doers, of weeding out those without enough fire in the belly to make a business go. I have never known an entrepreneur who did not think lack of capital was holding him back.

Sense of Humor

A SENSE OF HUMOR is an important part of managing people. If you don't have much of one, don't frown on or discourage another manager who does.

S

400

Mirth has strength in it.

The ability to loosen up a tense meeting with levity is a real contribution to smooth relationships. This doesn't mean telling jokes; an offhand remark or meta-phor is all that's needed. At a tense moment, making an absurd comparison or poking fun at some sacred cow, or your-self, can keep tempers and feelings from flaring and can avoid permanent psycho-logical scarring.

How many smiles are there around your office? How much laughter is there in your organization? Happy people smile and laugh, even when they're working hard. It adds to camaraderie and team spirit. A happy ship makes the journey seem shorter. After a meeting that includes tension or conflict, always try to end on a pleasant, upbeat note.

Service Corps of Retired Executives (SCORE)

SCORE IS A NATIONAL ORGANIZATION that is a good source of free information and help for wannabe and start-up entre-preneurs. The Small Business Adminis-tration (SBA) furnishes its offices, litera-ture, and other instructional materials. You don't have to apply to the SBA to get help or information from SCORE. There are about 13,000 SCORE members.

The individual counseling and group seminars SCORE provides give a general overview of what it takes to start a busi-ness. There's no charge for most of these services, and no appointment is neces-sary. Some workshops and literature have a nominal charge to cover expenses.

In addition to counseling, SCORE has programs for training, education, and advice. Publications are available on many business subjects as well as specialized programs for women business owners and minorities. SCORE's reference library contains information about business planning, marketing, operations, and financial analysis.

SCORE volunteers are generally retired men and women whose business backgrounds include managerial experience in every technology and type of business imaginable. They try to match an applicant with one or more people who've had experience in a field or business similar to the applicant's. They freely share managerial knowledge and technical expertise with prospective and active owner-managers. SCORE volunteers can help you write business plans, show you sample plans, and give computerized assistance.

The approach is generally one-on-one, although a team of counselors might help you. All information you furnish to SCORE is confidential and won't be disclosed to outsiders.

To find the nearest SCORE facility, call 1-800-U-ASK-SBA, the Washington, D.C., SBA switchboard.

S

401

Sex in the Workplace

BOYS WILL BE BOYS and girls will be girls. That won't change just because you're trying to run a business. And statistically, many married couples meet their spouses in a business-related setting.

But your purpose is business and serving customers, not running a dating service or social club. Your legitimate concerns include anything that hurts or interferes with business, plus any personal activities that occur during business hours, on business premises, or that use business resources or facilities. You must be certain that the entire climate in the workplace is businesslike, without favoritism or subtle flirting games.

Real or imagined sexual harassment is a serious problem. Employers have a legal obligation to provide a workplace free of harassment and unwelcome sexual advances for all employees. In this sensitive area, accusations and legal actions can be disruptive and disagreeable for all concerned. Stakes are high and getting higher. Everyone has rights—the employee, the harasser, and the company. These rights are frequently in conflict.

State prominently in your employee handbook—if possible, on the first page—that you are an equal opportunity employer. This means that you do not discriminate because of race, color, religion, sex, disability, or national origin in recruiting, selecting, training, compensating, promoting, transferring, laying off, recalling, terminating, or providing facilities or any other program.

Also, state that the company doesn't permit or tolerate any form of sexual discrimination or harassment. Request that any employee who feels that he or she has been discriminated against or harassed contact a supervisor or the Human Resources Department. State that an employee guilty of discrimination or harassment is subject to disciplinary action up to and including discharge.

Get the employee's signature to acknowledge receipt of the handbook. Permanently post on your official bulletin board the government's Equal Employment Opportunity Commission notice.

The scope of the problem was described in a survey by Norma Fritz published in *Personnel Magazine* (February 1989). It stated that 42 percent of complaints included teasing, jokes, or other remarks; touching, leaning over, or cornering caused 26 percent of complaints; pressure for sexual favors, 17 percent; pressure for dates, 12 percent. Only one percent included actual or attempted physical contact. The same survey noted that 36 percent of the complaints were made about immediate supervisors, 26 percent about other people in power in the workplace, and 32 percent about co-worker behavior.

The two basic elements constituting harassment are that unwelcome conduct occurs and that the conduct is sexual in nature. Since the conduct usually happens when two people are alone together, and since they usually tell conflicting stories, the truth is difficult to establish.

The employer is responsible for employee conduct, whether or not the employer is aware of the harassment. Every complaint or hint of complaint must be promptly and thoroughly investigated to determine the facts. Such things are unpleasant for everyone and must be handled carefully, discreetly, and confidentially.

---

*I*nsist on the policy of
the wise old Indian chief:
Don't crap too near
the wigwam.

One time, I received a series of worried phone calls from a senior manager's wife who insisted that someone at the business was breaking up her marriage. She wanted her husband assigned to different duties. I honestly told her that I was unaware of any such activities and that as long as the performance of business was not affected, my rights to question and interfere were limited. After several months, I gave her husband time off and arranged for both of them to use my vacation home. I sent her money for sexy lingerie and encouraged her to have a romantic week.

Not long after, an attractive office worker burst into my office, dissolved into tears, and asked for a few days off to solve distressing personal problems. After calming her, I repeatedly asked if there was any way I could help. Free legal advice to employees was a fringe benefit of the company, but she refused to give any details. She insisted through tears that she needed no money, only time off. Finally, I handed her a large bill, telling her that I knew of no emergency problem that would be harmed by extra funds. She could consider it a loan and pay me back later, if she wished.

Only later did I find out that I was innocently supporting both sides of this office romance. The worst part was that several months afterward a trusted shop employee told me that the rumor going around at the time was that I was having an affair with this attractive employee. A crying woman going in and out of my office provided the only evidence needed for the office rumor mill to jump to conclusions.

Defamation is the publication to a third person of a false statement that tends to harm the reputation or good name of another. Sexual matters always involve someone's good name and reputation. All three parties—the employee, the harasser, and the company—have rights regarding their own defamation.

This should be enough to persuade you not to take sexual harassment lightly. A good book on the subject is *Sexual Harassment in the Workplace,* by Ellen J. Wagner (New York: AMACOM, a division of the American Management Association, 1992).

Sharing Financial Information with Employees

ONE THING YOU SHOULD AVOID publishing or advertising is certain internal information, such as managerial pay scales and executive salaries. And although you don't want to distribute detailed operating statements to the whole world, your managers can't do their jobs properly without detailed performance statements. If you have them on a bonus or incentive compensation, they must have reports and numbers to make the decisions that will increase their incentive.

Anything you do at your business will sooner or later be seen by at least a few people you'd prefer to keep it away from. If your employees are as smart as you want them to be, they'll make intelligent guesses about anything you try to hide from them. And the company rumor mill will make less intelligent guesses. Live so you won't be embarrassed when such things are more widely known.

Sometimes information is embarrassing when it reveals your own mistakes or others', but the overall effect is still healthy. It's better to err on the side of giving too much information to trusted employees than too little.

Give managers enough information to do their jobs effectively. If you're doing *your* job, you have nothing to hide from associates whom you expect to be whole-heartedly on your team.

The ultimate in disclosure of financial operations and use of such information for management and team-building purposes is described in *Open-Book Management: The Coming Business Revolution,* by John Case (New York: Harper Business, 1995).

Of course I can keep a secret. It's just the people I tell it to who cannot.

Silver Fox Advisors

THE SILVER FOX ADVISORS (SFA) are a group of semiretired successful entrepreneurs and former business executives in Houston who use their proven talent and experience to help established and newer, growing businesses. They're like successful graduates of a lifelong business school coming back to help newer undergraduates in real-life entrepreneurial situations.

The group started in 1986 when Houston was in a severe economic slump. Most large businesses were downsizing and small businesses were struggling. Ken McDowell, in his early 70s at the time, believed with others that there was enough proven business talent on tennis courts and golf courses every day to help these small businesses pull out of the slump, if these talented folks would just get organized. Putting such a group

together would give the members an opportunity to give back to the business community some of the knowledge and rewards they had gained over the years.

The idea was presented to two groups of friends. The name "Silver Fox Advisors" was chosen. Joe Bond, a lawyer member, got the corporate charter, and Mark Neilsen, a former Metromedia executive, got letterhead, business cards, and a brochure. I wasn't a founding member but joined the following year.

Although the members had supposedly retired from their businesses, none really wanted to quit totally, nor did they want to work 40-hour weeks. They wanted to keep in touch with and help growing businesses, although they had no guidelines or business plan. None of the members, all former owners or senior executives, had shrinking-violet personalities.

At first, we tried giving away advice and consulting services. (The membership application form includes an agreement to do some pro bono work.) We were quickly inundated with requests for more time than we were willing to take away from our retired status. We are all unrepentant capitalists, and we have now established the policy that the first interview is always free. Until we have some discussion, we don't know if we can help or which Silver Fox can be the most helpful. There's a fee for advice given after the first meeting; we feel that a client who's unwilling to pay is not likely to act on our advice. We continue to do quite a bit of selected pro bono work.

We limit membership to 25, not including up to 8 associate members and 5 advisory members, but try to keep as many business backgrounds and disciplines as possible represented. Eligibility for membership requires a background as principal owner of a successful small company or as a senior executive for a large company whose responsibilities included final, bottom-line decisions for a major division or department, as well as hiring and firing other managers. The work experience must include successful long-term executive management of diverse business problems and living with the financial and human results of one's decisions.

We reorganized as a nonprofit corporation to limit one person's liability for another's work. We meet twice a month, but communicate by phone and fax continually. The financial obligation of membership is an entry fee to cover printing costs, and a quarterly assessment to pay a pro rata share of office, phone, and executive secretary's expenses.

This structure allows each member to work as much or as little as he or she wishes. Members are responsible for finding their clients and making working arrangements, including setting fees, billing, and collecting those fees.

In general, we do little work with start-ups, but the Service Corp of Retired Executives (SCORE), which is affiliated with the SBA, specializes in this area. (See SERVICE CORPS OF RETIRED EXECUTIVES.) Most of our client businesses range in size from 5 to over 500 employees, with sales volumes from a few hundred thousand per year to over $200,000,000. The variety of operations and problems we encounter is without limit, as befits the imagination and dreams of our entrepreneurial clients.

For-fee activities of the group include consulting and acting as members of advisory boards. Some members have served as temporary CEOs or other senior executives for clients with short-term vacancies. The largest activity is mentoring. Many members serve as mentors for three to ten business owners and are on several official and unofficial advisory boards. (See MENTORS AND MENTORING)

A former chairman of SFA heads the program of the Greater Houston Partnership (Houston Chamber of Commerce) which has set up about 20 CEO roundtables. Many SFA members serve as

S

405

mentors for these groups. Our speaker's bureau furnishes speakers on business topics to any group requesting them.

We promote the free enterprise system and work with educational, governmental, and other organizations that share this goal. We have assisted the State of Texas Department of Commerce in evaluating business applicants for state aid funds. Some members serve as part-time professors and work with students at the University of Houston Center for Entrepreneurship and Innovation. The organization does not raise money, nor is it a source of money for investment or speculation. Every large city and lots of small ones would benefit from such a group. (See CEO ROUNDTABLES OR PRESIDENTS' CLUBS.)

Small Business Administration and SBA Loans

THE SMALL BUSINESS ADMINISTRATION, a division of the U.S. Treasury Department created in 1953, has offices in all large cities. This federal agency promotes the growth of small businesses.

Although most small companies deal with it only as a source of capital, the SBA also provides help other than money. One valuable service is advice and help by the Service Corp of Retired Executives (SCORE), who have offices in the SBA facility. (See SERVICE CORP OF RETIRED EXEUCTIVES (SCORE).) This group of mostly retired executives and managers donates time and experience, offering management and technical assistance free to start-up and growing businesses. These individuals receive no compensation other than minimal out-of-pocket expenses.

To be eligible for assistance from the SBA, you must meet its definition of small business, which depends on the nature of your business and your industry, measured by number of employees and dollar sales volume. The SBA doesn't compete with banks or make direct loans to businesses. Rather, it guarantees up to 80 percent of the amount of selected, previously approved loans made by banks to companies that meet their qualifications.

However, the SBA also guarantees this percentage of loans that the bank normally wouldn't make—loans to start-up businesses, loans with maturities of up to seven years, and loans to companies that marginally fail to meet equity and collateral requirements. The bank then makes and services the loan but has less at risk because of the SBA guarantee.

Not all banks handle SBA-guaranteed loans, but some specialize in them. Inquire at your bank or get a list of participating lenders from the SBA. Some application forms require as much as many as 150 pages of information. You can fill them out yourself, but they're so detailed that most businesses use professional firms or packagers. They charge a fee, but because they're more familiar with the requirements and procedures, they save you time and energy.

> *To open a business
> is easy; to keep it open
> is difficult.*
>
> —Chinese Proverb

The packager's primary function is to complete the contents and structure of your loan package so it may be presented to commercial lenders in the most favorable light. The SBA keeps a list of qualified packagers. Be sure to discuss their fees before you agree to use them.

The time it takes to process your loan depends on how thoroughly you've completed your application and how long it takes to get the bank's approval and the SBA's. Some complain that red tape and paperwork slow the process.

SBA-guaranteed loans are usually collateralized by everything in sight: real property, receivables, inventory, equipment, stock, personal guarantees, and possibly assets personally owned by the managers. Any individual who owns over 20 percent of the stock must personally guarantee the loan. The loan document contains covenants and restrictions because the lenders still look to the borrowing company as the party primarily responsible for repaying the loan.

After being in business for almost 10 years, I overexpanded. I bought too much new machinery and incurred too many expenses. Then I was rewarded by a market downturn rather than the sales and profits I expected. My banker got scared, but he helped me get an SBA loan. Almost three years later, he felt secure enough to loan me enough money both to pay off the SBA and to expand by buying the assets of another small company.

S
407

Socializing with Customers

WHETHER YOUR BUSINESS FRIENDS ARE also your social friends depends upon your temperament, your spouse's temperament, and the nature of your business. There's no hard-and-fast rule.

If socializing either alone or with spouses helps your business, and if everyone is comfortable, fine. If it doesn't directly help or if it makes some people uncomfortable, don't stir up trouble. In some businesses, you can't avoid socializing; in others, avoiding it is best.

Gambling with customers is strictly a no-no.

Socializing with Employees

WITHIN YOUR BUSINESS, encourage open communication and feelings of warmth, friendship, and trust. If you feel you can do this better by going out to dinner, playing golf, going on a hunting trip, or having a business breakfast with your employee or employees, do it.

Whether to include spouses should be a comfort judgment. If you feel that it helps, by all means include them. The employee's spouse probably has a greater influence on the behavior of the employee than you do. Company picnics, Christmas parties, and plant open houses frequently promote better relations between employees and management.

Don't do it if you don't feel it will create a better business atmosphere. Some managers feel that if they get too close to employees and their families it becomes more difficult to discipline them or fire them. They don't want to know the kids who depend on that paycheck.

I can give you no specific advice on this question. Your own experience and reactions are your best guide.

Speed of Response Time—Your Biggest Future Opportunity

SPEED OF RESPONSE time is the next quality yardstick in better meeting your customer's needs. Time-based competition is emerging as the next strategic business battleground.

Time is linked to everything your customer wants—quality, delivery, lead time, price, and service. It's nothing new. Time is common to all core business processes. Eliminating internal delays requires that your departments and people have simultaneous access to the same accurate information and use it to build an efficient system to give you a competitive advantage.

Forty years ago, businesses often accomplished their goals through cost-based strategies by being the low-cost producer. During the '70s, economic value to the customer was emphasized. During the '80s, the shift was to quality of product and zero defects.

Now the leading edge of competition is moving to a time-based strategy. Being successful now requires more than just quality products with a low cost. Almost every company still in business has a reasonably successful quality-improvement program and more intense focus on giving customers what they want.

Computers and information systems (IS) are the heart of the movement toward speedier service. Computers have been both the cause and the result of present trends toward fewer middle managers, whose traditional function has been to gather information about problems, handle the small ones, and pass larger ones upward to the next managerial level. With improved IS and networks, information now flows faster and more freely to senior managers, and decisions return faster. With middle managers gone, fewer people and delays get in the way.

The principles of just-in-time inventory, short-time material transfer, computer-aided design and manufacturing (CAD/CAM), and faster estimating procedures have dramatically cut manufacturing procedure time. The significant time now is total time from customer request to delivery, not hours of machine time (including waiting and scheduling between different operations). Total time involves time in the sales department, customer service, production control, manufacturing, inspecting, accounting, and delivering.

In some of the largest, most progressive industrial plants, customers use electronic data interchange (EDI). When the industrial plant customer contracts with chosen suppliers for goods or services, the industrial customer's IS communicates with the supplier's IS to place the inquiry, receive price and delivery information, and place the order. After delivery has been confirmed, the supplier renders its invoice by EDI and payment is transferred to its bank account. All this is done without any paperwork moving between the customer and the supplier—only electronic signals, leaving electronic audit trails at both companies. More plants and progressive suppliers hook up to this system each year. Bar coding for product recognition speeds this process.

> *The customer is king. There is only one boss—the customer—and he can fire anyone in the company from the chairman on down, by spending his money somewhere else.*
>
> —Sam Walton

S

409

Your management challenge is to cut in half the time needed to accomplish each task, then cut it in half again. This means cutting or eliminating paperwork processing time, planning and managerial time, and delay time routing paper copies. Your team must microanalyze the flow of information, paper, and material to find and eliminate waiting time and queue time.

A light manufacturer of customized products used to take a week to respond to a customer request for a quotation. The company now quotes price and delivery in half a day or less because required information is readily available in the database—availability of engineering and materials, manufacturing time, shop load, and delivery schedule. If the order is received, its entry into the system starts the required actions, including issuing final shipping instructions, delivery ticket, and invoice.

If you want to be ahead of customers' demands, talk with your management team about implementing such a program in your company. It's a long-term program that will affect every department and every procedure. It will take years of cooperative effort, original thought, and creative approaches. It will transform your company.

Improvement in time management demands the same commitment of the owner and senior management as total quality. You need management commitment even more than you need computer hardware and software. It becomes something of a religion.

Management must provide continuous personal involvement and leadership and not delegate the task to the quality control department. The goal is continuous improvement, not immediate improvement.

Stock Options as Incentives

FOR SENIOR MANAGERS AND ASSOCIATES who respond to long-term incentives, stock options can be an inexpensive extra incentive. Normally, stock options aren't effective for motivating lower managers or employees with a short-term time horizon; for these people, a bonus or percentage of current profits works best. Most lower managers and employees never expect or intend to invest in company stock anyway.

In a growth-stage company, growth capital usually comes only from earned income with no sale, equity refinancing, or recapitalization of the company in the foreseeable future. Any of the latter three events usually triggers sudden, substantial growth in stock value and stock options. Stock options granted prior to or under those circumstances can be very motivating.

Discuss your plans to use stock options with your tax advisor, because IRS rules on recognition of gain seem strange to most people. You might grant options hoping to help an associate, only to find that he may have to recognize gain in value and pay taxes based on an event that yields no cash with which to pay the taxes. This isn't the intended result.

Granting the option, which must be done by resolution of the board of directors after an independent appraisal of fair market value, costs the company very little and, if done at the present fair market value of the stock, costs the employee nothing.

A stock-option incentive is a bet on the future. The duration of the option and all terms and conditions concerning its exercise must be included in the board's resolution. If future events increase the stock value and provide a cash-sale event, the option can be exercised at the lower, original option price and immediately resold at the higher sale price. The individual then pays taxes on the gain at short-term gain rates and keeps the rest of the gain.

Phantom stock can be used in lieu of actual stock. This gives the employee all the financial benefits and incentives of genuine stock ownership without diluting existing ownership or requiring the issuing of actual certificates. If you get good tax advice and do it carefully, this provides the identical incentive value and financial rewards to the employee. (See EMPLOYEES AS STOCKHOLDERS.)

Strategic or Long-Range Planning

IF YOUR OBJECTIVE is only to look after yourself and your family until you die, then you don't need to worry about having a vision, creating a corporate culture, training other people, or creating anything of long-term value. But your thinking and planning should include these things if you're building for the future, for your family and kids, for other families or customers, or for a longer-term goal.

In the survival stage, your long-range plan is merely to survive your mistakes while you figure out how to pay bills and get more customers. You'll continuously change as you do whatever is necessary to stay in business and do a job you can collect for.

Thinking about long-range planning starts somewhere in the growth stage when you've reached a degree of stability and consistent operation that you can use reasonably to forecast your short-term future. But thinking about the future and making a written forecast, which I strongly encourage you to do, isn't the same as strategic planning.

This is really an extension of your business plan into the future, based on deliberate thought and planning. If you haven't written your business plan, do that first, then start planning where you want to be in the distant future.

Strategic planning starts with the future, not the past. It concentrates on what position you wish to occupy in the future, then works backward to the present to identify actions you must take now to get there.

In its barest essentials, strategic planning requires detailed consideration of three questions:

1. Where do you want to be in 5 years? Or 10, or 20?

2. Where are you now?

3. What should you do now to make certain that you arrive at your goal in 5 years? Or 10, or 20?

Detailed consideration of these three questions requires the deepest thinking and soul searching that you, your managers, and your advisors have probably ever done. Prepare everyone for this subject with advance questions and outlines. Then go to an uninterrupted weekend retreat or business session dedicated solely to this subject. If neither you nor a significant member of your team has ever conducted anything like this before, you should probably get professional help the first time or two. Maybe your mentor or a member of your advisory board can guide you and the group to logical, reasonable procedures and conclusions.

When you think about where you want to be in five years, consider what you think will be the state of the market at that time, changes in government regulations that may affect the market, possible advances in technology and in the economy, and the competitive situation (including international influences). This is the most difficult part of the whole process.

Where you are now includes an honest assessment of present strengths and weaknesses in each of your strategic business units. If you have only one major product line going to only one market, you have only one strategic business unit. How do your customers perceive your company and its operation? What are their unmet needs and future requirements? What are your strengths and weaknesses relative to your competitors? What should you do about them?

After you finish thinking about the first two questions, deciding what to do now becomes a problem of allocating available resources—people, skills, money, and assets—toward your prioritized goals.

If you are planning for one year, grow rice. If you are planning for 20 years, grow trees. If you are planning for 50 years, grow men.

—Chinese Proverb

The first results of this process may not be apparent until after four to ten formal management team meetings, not to mention many informal discussions with less than the whole group. The result isn't just a more accurate picture of the future but better decisions and preparations for the future. (See FORECASTING AND FINANCIAL MODEL BUILDING.)

Stress

MOST ENTREPRENEURS THRIVE ON STRESS. It becomes a way of life.

If you don't thrive on it, you're in the wrong business. The intestinal fortitude and strong desire for independence and control that got you into business push you to act and succeed.

Stress is a normal way of life for the whole human race, and has been since the days of the caveman. There are degrees of stress, but you can't lead a normal life without considerable stress over money, relationships, beliefs, and desires. Don't fight stress—it's normal. Learn to control and use it. Don't let it control you.

Although they're under greater stress, usually self-imposed, entrepreneurs have better health, live longer, and usually live happier than other segments of the population. The stress of juggling several important balls in the air stimulates their imagination and effort.

A kite rises against the wind rather than with it.

In order to live with and enjoy the stressful life you've chosen, take care of your body, take care of your family, and take care of your spiritual and physical well being. Don't be afraid to let others help you or give you advice.

S

413

Subconscious Mind for Problem Solving

AT TIMES SERIOUS PROBLEMS seem to defy solution. Psychology recognizes that the subconscious mind doesn't sleep, but continues to work on problems properly presented to it. Intense mental concentration and emotional commitment toward finding a solution are the keys to using this powerful tool.

First, thoroughly review in your mind the main problem and all its aspects. Consider everything that bears on the problem, directly or indirectly, short term or long term, while you consciously search for a solution. Consider and evaluate every solution you can think of. For clarity and logic, write your statement of the problem and your evaluation of possible solutions.

If no acceptable solution comes to you, work on other problems. Return to this problem later and thoroughly reconsider any new solutions or possibilities that may have occurred to you. If this repeated mental churning of all parts of the problem doesn't produce a satisfactory answer, then consciously turn the problem over to your subconscious mind while you direct your attention to other things.

Sooner or later, when you least expect it, an answer or new solution will occur to you. You'll recognize it immediately as the best solution for all parts of the root problem. Then you can decide on a course of action. You'll wonder why you hadn't thought of this solution before. This is your subconscious mind speaking to you in a creative way.

Success

SUCCESS IS A JOURNEY, not a destination. Of course, you'll pass milestones of success as you complete a program, win a prize, or accomplish an objective; but passing one milestone doesn't mean you've passed them all. Enjoy the success you've achieved. Tomorrow is another day with new challenges and opportunities.

Success is measured by happiness, pride, and self-respect, as well as accomplishment and money. Successful people are willing to learn, to try again or try something new, and to accept the reality that no one wins or loses all the time. If your life hasn't had a few failures, you haven't tried very much.

The Declaration of Independence guarantees you life, liberty, and the pursuit of happiness. You have no guarantee of ever finding happiness, or having once found it, keeping it. But you have the right to keep pursuing it.

Success is steady growth and increased market penetration. You're suc-ceeding if you've paid your bills, grown in mental stature and understanding, raised your family, and helped others accomplish the greatest things they are capable of. You're succeeding if you have a wholesome relationship with your spouse, your children, your employees, your customers, and your vendors.

The difference between a successful person and others is not a lack of strength, not a lack of knowledge, but rather a lack of will.

—Vincent J. Lombardi

If you've created a company, jobs, and customer satisfaction where none were before, you're succeeding. If you serve as a role model for others, you're succeeding.

You don't have to become the richest person in the neighborhood or as big as General Motors to be a success.

Sweat Equity

EQUITY IS THE PORTION OF THE BUSINESS that belongs to the owners. In a corporation, it's represented by shares of stock issued to the owners, usually in return for money invested.

The ability to learn faster than your competition may be the only sustainable competitive advantage

—Arie P. DeGeus

If the entrepreneur or inventor who is the principal actor and full-time manager of the business doesn't have hard cash to purchase the agreed share of a joint venture, she will be promised a share as an incentive to work hard—to "sweat"—for the common good.

All such agreements should be fully understood and put into writing before any substantial amount of work is done. Failure to do so will lead to serious misunderstandings and hard feelings that can wreck the enterprise.

Every successful entrepreneur has a tremendous amount of emotional sweat equity that she has put into the business. Generally, it can be turned into money only by selling the business, or part of it, to others for cash.

S

415

Team Building for the Entire Company

UNLESS YOU PLAN TO DOMINATE everything in your company and make all decisions, work at team building. You want all your employees to feel they're members of a winning team, and you want your managers to help build, educate, and coach that team.

It won't happen by accident. Concentrate on your managerial team first; then include more and more people.

Everyone in your organization is unique and looks at things from a perspective shaped by his own background and experience, including age, race, religion, sex, geographical upbringing, education, and training. If you clearly communicate your company's goals and objectives, you'll be able to pull these different people together and motivate them to pursue common goals. That's what team building is all about.

> *Coming together is a beginning; keeping together is progress; working together is success.*
>
> —Henry Ford

The team and the vision must be more important than any individual. The players must feel that they're part of something greater than themselves, which inspires them to participate selflessly. Trust and communication between team members and their leaders are the foundation of team building.

Effective teamwork requires leadership and delegating skills. You're not leading if you do all the work. If delegating authority and responsibility doesn't come easily to you, attend a seminar or workshop on team building. If your managers aren't team players, send them to a seminar, talk to them yourself, or get rid of them if you have to. I've seen a vice president fired who was a very intelligent manager but whose handling of his people kept them so upset that teamwork did not exist and personnel turnover was excessive. After his departure, the team worked smoothly and set new performance records.

Whether you act as a leader or as a boss determines your management style. There's no real question about who's the boss, but if you're also a good team leader, more will be accomplished by happier people.

Participative management and *open-book management* are rapidly growing concepts that point in the same direction as the older phrase *team building*. They include setting goals, frequently and completely communicating those goals, and

T

416

comparing results. Positive results must be rewarded and negative results openly discussed.

The team-building links between knowledge, leadership, and communication can be illustrated by the professional quarterback who says in the huddle, "We really need to win this game. Let's score a touchdown on the next play." The players respond, "We're with you. What's the play?" The quarterback answers, "How long have you guys been on this team? You're supposed to know all the plays, especially what I want done in this situation. What are you being paid for? You guys are supposed to be professionals and I want performance. You should know what we need to do to win this game."

Many owners don't effectively communicate the game plan. Worse yet, many don't even have a game plan.

An informed team pursuing a clear vision can win the day and the war. It's worth your effort to be their leader. (See LEADERSHIP IN YOUR BUSINESS)

This subject is important. I recommend two books describing detailed examples of team building: *The New Partnership,* by Tom Melohn (Essex Junction, Vermont: Omneo, an imprint of Oliver Wright Publications, 1994), and *Open-Book Management: The Coming Business Revolution,* by John Case (New York: Harper Business, a division of Harper Collins, 1995).

T

417

Technicians as Managers

YOU MIGHT NATURALLY THINK that the best automobile mechanic should open her own shop or that the best computer programmer should start and manage a software company of his own. Outstanding technological skill is important, but that alone isn't enough to start and grow a company.

In addition to having technological skills, an entrepreneur must manage people and money. Without these two skills, the best technical skills can't keep the business going. When managerial skills are lacking, the operation usually stays quite small, within the skill level of the technician, or it gets taken over by some-

one with better people and financial skills.

For example, the Heisman Trophy is awarded each year to the outstanding college football player of the year. How many Heisman Trophy winners can you name who have become well-known coaches or team owners? How many Pulitzer Prize winners have gone on to manage or own newspapers or publishing houses? How many Nobel Prize winners in any technical field have risen to the top as owners or managers of companies using their technology?

Unless your service to customers is totally self-contained (such as service provided by some doctors, programmers, researchers, writers, or lone practitioners), you have to get along with other people who'll help you. The sine qua non is dedication and hard work, serving customers, and managing people and money.

Recently a skilled technician presented his ideas to prospective investors and was repeatedly asked how he intended to market his new process. He kept replying that his technology was a great improvement, superior to anything now known. He couldn't explain who his logical customer would be or who would write him or his company a check for this new process. Needless to say, he got no financial backing.

Technicians see development as a continuing process. They frequently stress the need for further research and development prior to production. True, development must never cease, but at some practical point the design must be frozen and production started to get an income stream flowing. Only the U.S. government, researching for military purposes,

can meet unlimited technical research payrolls without effectively marketing a product that produces profits.

T

418

Just being a technological expert or innovator doesn't make you good at business.

Because the entrepreneur or manager must get everyone pulling in the same direction, it is fundamentally important that he be able to get along with people. John D. Rockefeller said that he would pay more money for the skill of getting along with people than for any other skill. For the entrepreneur, people skills and managerial skills are more important than outstanding technological skills.

Temporary or Part-Time Employees

COMPANIES ONCE DEPENDED ON temporary employees only to fill in for sick or vacationing employees. Now they're discovering that using temps gives more flexibility than a traditional, permanent work force. Use of temps allows the company to work peak periods as needed without the penalty of idle full-time employees when business is light.

Temporary work is somewhat like self-employment. Temporary workers can always quit if they don't like it. And if they're placed in the right jobs, they can serve productively.

Use of temps is more prevalent as government regulations cause more problems with hiring and firing traditional employees. With temps, legal problems in hiring and laying off are almost non-existent. For these reasons, growth in the use of temps has been astronomical.

If you're not certain that a situation is suitable for a permanent job, using temps is not only justified but recommended. You can acquire them with almost no notice and let them go when they're no longer needed without worrying about discrimination lawsuits or severance packages. Neither party has a long-term commitment.

Temporary jobs used to be ordinary jobs with low-level skills. Now, anyone from a floor sweeper to a skilled computer technician to a vice president is available from temp agencies. Many good employees seeking full-time employment take temp jobs because they provide income between permanent jobs, additional work experience, and a risk-free way for both employee and employer to see if their situations fit.

Generally, temps are not part-time employees. They want to work full 8-hour days or 40-hour weeks, but they may be employed only until a particular project or catch-up job is completed.

Read the agency contract you sign when you hire the temp. Contracts aren't yet standardized, and government regulation is in a state of flux. Laws can change rapidly, but at present, part-time workers don't have to be covered by all the fringe benefits you must provide to full-time employees. Your contract probably provides that you may return or reject unqualified employees. Some contracts specify that if you hire a temporary employee, you owe a fee to the agency.

There appears to be little resentment or few problems between regular employees and temporaries as long as skill levels, pay, and working conditions are similar. This means that the temporary agency that provides full benefits, including hospitalization to its employees, is going to charge about the same fees you're paying your regular employees, possibly slightly more. The advantage is freedom from government regulation and the risk of being sued for wrongful discharge.

T

419

Termination of Agreements

NOTHING LASTS FOREVER. Good things come to an end just like bad things. Expect change and prepare for it.

Most people assume that whatever is happening now will continue for at least the foreseeable future. Starting and continuing anything establishes a pattern that people take as an implied promise of continuation without interruption or change. When an adverse change is necessary because of unforeseen events, people resent it and lose confidence.

> *Just as good fences make good neighbors, good understandings make good friends. You know immediately which side of the fence the problem is on.*

T

420

My legal training and business experience have taught me to look realistically at the possibility of change or termination and to make the most logical provisions I can up front before I make a commitment. The application to written agreements is obvious. The unwritten, sometimes unspoken, understandings of others can result in hard feelings and disappointments.

A good way to handle the problem is to use an automatic review date of six months or say that you'll take another look at the situation at the end of the year. If a review date is planned and understood in advance, resentment toward required change is less likely.

Beware of automatic renewal clauses in written agreements. Beware also of the requirement that written notice of termination must be delivered more than 30 days before the expiration date or renewal is automatic. It's better to provide for automatic termination unless specifically renewed.

On the pleasant occasion of forming a partnership or signing an employment agreement, thinking about termination may be painful, but this is the best time to do it. During negotiations, talk about making some provision for accident, death, or dissolution.

Test Runs, Trial Balloons, or Pilot Models

TEST BEFORE YOU INVEST. Build a pilot model, run a market test for acceptance, or run field trials for performance. Test everything you can before you make a heavy financial commitment. Something unforeseen just might go wrong.

Make small mistakes first. This applies to expensive marketing efforts and production changes; extensive, expensive inventory purchases; or anything else that involves a significant new step and significant money. Until you prove quality and performance by actual tests in small, affordable increments in your customer's environment, don't make major commitments.

Self-delusion is too easy. You must have the imagination to visualize great things and the optimism to believe they can come true. However, making a big bet on blind faith in unproven opinions is a recipe for certain disaster. Don't say, "I know it's right because my instincts and knowledge tell me it is." It must be right because you've proven it with a test run or sample tryout.

Don't bet the farm on anything you haven't proven.

"That's Not My Job"

REPRIMAND OR FIRE THE PERSON you hear saying this to anybody—either a customer or another employee. This answer is guaranteed to stop the conversation and create resentment.

If you are not serving the customer, you'd better be serving another employee who is.

It's every employee's job, as well as common courtesy, to serve customers and to help other employees serve customers. Any employee who doesn't know how to solve a customer's problem can at least send the customer to a supervisor or to someone who does know. A fellow employee's questions deserve an answer or directions to where the answer can be found.

A soft answer turns away wrath. A friendly answer creates good will. You want your company to be easy to do business with. A pleasant, friendly, and helpful answer certainly starts things in the right direction.

T

421

Time Management

I'VE TRIED EVERY TIME MANAGEMENT method and system known to man. None of them exactly fit my lifestyle, memory, or work habits. You don't *have* time.

You *take* time to do what's important to you, the things highest on your list of business and personal priorities.

Everyone from the pope to the president has the same 24 hours per day you have. Sleep takes about 8 hours. Many people spend about 8 hours at productive work that will produce a better family, a better product, or a better society. This 8 hours of work is usually accompanied by a paycheck.

What you do with the remaining 8 hours of your 24 determines where you will spend your life on the social and financial scale. You spend 3 to 4 of the 8 hours eating, driving, dressing, talking, and socializing. The remaining 4 hours is the only discretionary time you have. You might enjoy sports, exercise, or physical conditioning, or you might spend your off time reading, maintaining your house or car, traveling, or being a couch potato.

Conflicts between family and business will occur. Sometimes you'll resolve them in favor of the business, other times in favor of the family. You need balance, relaxation, and laughter. You need quality time and caring time with your family and children. Pay attention when they send you signals of loneliness and need.

Many entrepreneurs are workaholics or close to it. If you're lazy, quit now because you may not become a successful entrepreneur. If you're an entrepreneur, most of your discretionary four hours will go toward your business in some way— reading, attending meetings, cleaning up problems, or pursuing further education.

Schedule your time to meet your obligations and to be most productive. To do this, you must keep track of appoint-

T

422

ments, time commitments, phone numbers, and projects or problems you're working on now or planning to work on sooner or later.

Your time-management system should have a way to keep up with your long-term objectives. Emergencies requiring your immediate attention will arise, such as a general power failure or an employee accident. Urgencies of the moment sometimes outweigh long-term consequences.

> *I was so busy doing things I should have delegated, I didn't have time to manage.*
>
> **—Charles Percy**

Some systems would have you spend more time on planning and keeping score than on playing the game. These exercises miss the point. I seldom look backward to see what I did. My outlook and planning are all toward the future.

Family time is important. Religious time is important. Recreational time is important. Business time is important. Vacation time is important. Sleeping time is important. How important? You must decide.

Timely Financial Information

AT VARIOUS TIMES IN THIS BOOK, I've stressed the importance of timely financial information. Surveys of why small companies go broke frequently highlight lack of current financial information as one of the principal reasons.

On an initial interview in September, a prospective client informed me that he had just discovered he'd been losing money since the first of the year. He called me because he was afraid he was running out of cash. First, I told him he scared me to death because his financial statements were so far behind. Further, I couldn't be much help to him if I had to base my conclusions and suggestions on his oral statements about the current status of his business. He wasn't keeping score closely enough even to know that he was losing money, much less figure out why.

Telecommunications enables companies to move information rather than people.

If you don't insist on timely financial statements because you don't understand them, you can find several solutions. Ask your accountant to give you the most condensed financial statements she thinks you need in order to know what's happening in your business.

Ask also for a written narrative, with a title like "Comments on Accompanying Financial Statements," calling to your attention the three to ten most significant developments or changes shown by the statements. The report should be from ½ page to 1½ pages long, no more. Study it in your spare time. Educate yourself.

An owner of a medium-sized company who was principally a salesman told me he was embarrassed to have a long talk alone with his banker because he couldn't confidently answer the banker's questions. The written comments procedure mentioned above gave him the knowledge and confidence to handle his banking relationship.

Information described in PRESIDENT'S DAILY/WEEKLY REPORT will educate you about the most timely information you must pay attention to. Attending a seminar on accounting information for non-financial executives would also be of tremendous help.

It's difficult to play a heads-up game if the score card you're using is badly out of date.

T

423

Titles as Rewards and Incentives

A SMALL COMPANY USUALLY has more titles than money. Titles mean nothing as far as performance goes. They do have meaning in terms of ego, appreciation from the boss, and apparent authority to outsiders, friends, and neighbors. At little financial cost to the company, you can reward some of your people with the ego boost that comes from a title.

There's a definite downside to overdoing this. Firing a vice president is more difficult and could be more damaging financially than firing a supervisor. Some lawyer may ask you why you once thought this person's performance was good enough for promotion to vice president if you now think this person is so bad he has to be fired. You may owe damages.

T

424

> *Any problem will go wherever it finds a solution, regardless of your organization chart.*

Another drawback is the managers-don't-get-their-hands-dirty syndrome. The moment you appoint some people foremen, lead men, or production managers, their hands go into their pockets. A men-

tal block develops about touching any equipment or showing or physically helping a production worker in any way. Finally, taking away a title is much worse than bestowing one. Coordinator is an easier title to change than manager.

As entrepreneur, you don't have to be president, but it's customary. Since you can define your own job, you might be the best salesperson or the best engineer, but call yourself president for prestige or because you like it. Name yourself president and sweep the floor if you wish. Or take the title of chief engineer and keep a screwdriver and pliers in your hand all day long, but hire a good general manager. Design your organization chart and duty assignments to reflect the way you want to work.

Give yourself whatever title you want, but if you don't ensure that managerial functions are performed, you'll soon have nothing to manage. Your business won't operate unless someone functions as chief administrator, sales manager, head of the technical side, and the production manager who kicks products out the door to satisfied customers. The functions and production that the business needs to have performed are crucial. What you call them doesn't matter.

There are many incentives and rewards for employees that do not involve bonuses or large amounts of money. *1001 Ways to Reward Employees: Money Isn't*

Everything, by Bob Nelson (New York: Workman Publishing Co., 1994) suggests many ways to provide recognition and encourage enthusiasm and productivity without too much money.

When you do small things well, the larger things that need doing will find you. If you have the idea and the guts, titles mean nothing.

Trade and Professional Associations

JOIN AND PARTICIPATE in your trade association and other business organizations. You and your competitors have much in common that you can discuss and work on for your mutual benefit, even though you would secretly be pleased at any misfortune that might befall them.

Don't use trade association meetings to hold discussions of pricing or other concerns that would violate the antitrust laws; the consequences can be very serious. If any conversation turns toward restraint of trade or swapping information on bids or pricing, promptly and politely look for the nearest exit.

Encourage and pay for memberships, meetings, and seminars in professional or technical societies for your managers. It's important to the company and to you for them to keep their knowledge and professional standing current. The stature of your company will grow as the number of industry and technical leaders in your company increases.

T

425

Trade Secrets

TRADE SECRETS are a company's proprietary knowledge that gives it an advantage in the marketplace. A *trade secret* might be defined as any useful business information your competitors don't have: a process, unpatented invention, engineering technique, formula, or customer list. Not included is anything that's standard practice in the industry, or any knowledge possessed by or known to skilled workers throughout the industry.

Trade secrets are covered by individual state laws, not by federal law as patents are. Different states define them differently, but most state laws protect secrets not generally known to competitors only when the company takes consistent and definite actions to identify and protect its secrets and to prevent unauthorized disclosure.

If you're going to try to enforce your rights concerning your trade secrets, you must prove the steps you've taken to keep them secret, including steps to keep unauthorized people within your own company from knowing. For example, are your drawings, quotations, and written materials stamped or marked "Confidential"? Do you keep these papers or perform this function in a restricted and secure area? Do you lock the documents up at night? Do your employees know that this information is confidential? Do unauthorized employees not know or have access to this information?

Allow access to only those persons who need to know the secrets to perform their jobs and who are bound by a secrecy agreement. Store materials containing company secrets in a safe place, including overnight storage. Destroy them when they're no longer needed so they cannot be leaked.

If you have employees or consultants who deal with these secrets, get them to sign a confidentiality agreement at time of employment. It should cover the period of employment, as well as afterward. (See CONFIDENTIALITY AGREEMENTS; NON-COMPETE AGREEMENTS.)

Defending your trade secrets means you're trying to protect your usage or process by secrecy rather than by disclosing the information in a patent and invoking patent protection. Trade secrets frequently aren't patentable. If others discover these secrets by reverse engineering or develop the same information on their own, they can't be stopped from using the knowledge.

Training Employees and Managers

AS YOUR BUSINESS GROWS, it surpasses your ability to know more about everything in the business than anyone else. Even if you can do everything at first, you can't do everything forever at the higher volume of the future. The growing operation at some point will exceed your personal ability to control it.

If you fail to recognize this, you'll retreat into doing what you know best or like best, thereby abdicating the role of owner-manager, including holding everyone accountable for achieving results by teamwork.

Entrepreneurs are essentially doers; they don't see themselves as teachers. They act to achieve goals. They often fail to realize that by training or building knowledge and capability into others they're really accomplishing goals for themselves. Being simply a role model isn't enough.

Learning and training should go on continually for everybody in the operation. Insist upon it for yourself as well as present and future managers. Help employees learn more that will improve your business. Provide books and trade information and encourage them to learn elsewhere, too. Every company that uses technology should maintain a library of technical books for employees to use.

The company that stays on the leading edge of knowledge and performance in its industry will continuously grow.

Let managers and employees know that you expect increases in their knowledge, skills, and performance levels so they'll grow as the company grows, and that those who don't will be left behind. I used to tell my employees, "Whether the next person hired is your assistant, your equal, or your boss depends upon how fast you grow."

Plenty of training is available outside your company, even if you have no time or opportunity within the company. (See EMPLOYEE EDUCATION POLICY; TRADE AND PROFESSIONAL ASSOCIATIONS.) If you have enough people to justify the training, such as a computer software course that everyone needs, find an instructor to come to your facility.

Running your own company is a joyful lifetime of on-the-job training. This should be true not only for you but for your managerial associates as well and for all employees who hope to become managers someday.

T
427

Trial Period for New Employees

BECAUSE OF TODAY'S EXCESSIVE government regulation of the employment and discharge process, it's important that you make a regular employment commitment only to employees who have survived your selection process and a trial working period. You can never be 100 percent certain that a new employee will fit, but actual experience on the job is a better test than any amount of interviewing or testing.

New employees can remain on their best behavior and give false impressions of long-term attitudes and work habits for as long as three months. You want to find out how they'll perform after they quit trying to impress you and their fellow workers. If you can, make your trial period at least six months; if they can hold out that long, they're probably good for the long run.

Another good way to observe work on a trial basis is to hire temporary employees from an employment agency, who don't expect long-term employment. If they work out well, then you can offer them regular employment. (See TEMPORARY OR PART-TIME EMPLOYEES.)

On your employment application, include permission to check all information and references and an agreement that employment is on a trial basis for the first six months (or the longest period allowed in your state). Your health insurance, unemployment insurance, and other company benefits shouldn't start until after such a period. At any time during the trial period, you should be able to terminate the employee without explanation or documentation. Check the laws in your state to be certain you're in compliance. (See HIRING GOOD PEOPLE.)

If you have reason to question the long-term performance or capability of an employee before the end of the trial period, invoke this right and terminate employment.

Turnaround Operations

WHEN YOU'RE HEADED in the wrong direction—that is, going broke—you need to turn your company around and head for profits again.

If you stay lean and mean and react quickly to changes in your market, costs, and operations, including downturns as well as market opportunities, you're doing your own turnaround a little at a time. If you keep your company focused on profits, you won't need to take drastic turnaround measures.

Among the indicators of a sick company are chronic shortage of cash, consistent loss of money, customers leaving, and dispirited, unenthusiastic employees.

First, realize that problems can be solved and that you're the one to do it. If you don't, others can, but if they do, you lose control of your company, perhaps permanently. To start the turnaround, you must be willing to rethink and reexamine the company's basic business theory. You've got to stop saying, "I know," and start saying, "I'll find out."

Get advice. Get help from a mentor, business friend, consultant, or your own employees, without letting pride get in the way. Most successful turnarounds are based on new thinking, which comes from either new management or some outside source. Ask new questions and get new answers, or you won't be able to turn your business around.

Show that you're taking charge. Figure out what areas of your business are losing money. Perhaps company resources are invested in the wrong things, or people, knowledge, and money are committed to operations or projects that should be stopped or sharply curtailed, even if they're your personal favorites.

Find out what works and build on it. Even a sick company has islands of strength. Listen to your employees, customers, suppliers, and consultants. Try to improve attitudes and boost morale. Find something new, possibly dramatic, that you can sell, publicize, or change to get enthusiasm flowing again.

Make a cash plan and a crisis plan aimed at getting control of your cash and making it flow again. Monitor incoming funds and watch every penny that goes out. Pay only for things that keep your business doors open, such as payroll, utilities, essential suppliers, and payroll taxes. Once you've got cash controlled and working capital flowing, you've got a chance to solve other problems.

Raise new cash any way you can. Collect receivables; liquidate inventory or supplies; sell unnecessary assets, unused machinery, equipment, and cars. If you own real estate, sell it and lease it back.

To get additional financing from your bank or credit sources, you'll have to convince them of the following things:

■ Management knows the root causes of the company's problems and has corrected them.

■ The turnaround you've made is permanent or at least will continue into the foreseeable future.

■ Market demand for your products or services is strong, so steady or rising sales are expected to continue.

■ You have sufficient collateral for both the old and new loans.

At this time, a good business plan is mandatory.

In the short term, a turnaround usually means immediate cuts in the work force. Try to reduce costs, but the problem in the long run may be reengineering the operation. Unless overall company performance improves, you haven't made a turnaround.

Take employees into your confidence. Tell them what you're doing and build an enthusiastic team dedicated to saving the business. Give the workplace a facelift, even if it means rearranging and painting it yourself on weekends.

Don't be afraid to take a big step if one is indicated. You can't cross a chasm in two small jumps.

—Lloyd George

After years of success, your business is probably overstaffed. Focus everyone's attention on key tasks organized around the flow of work to satisfied customers and the flow of information. Make sure every job is necessary and that every employee is doing a job that needs to be done. Reevaluate every employee, including managers. Get rid of diversions and busywork. By performing better, reestablish credibility with your customers and suppliers. Reassure them of your commitment to quality.

T
430

> **The judgment to make good decisions is based on the experience of making bad decisions.**

With little time and money to turn around a difficult situation, a tough manager who took over a failing company called a meeting of all managers. He introduced himself and said, "If you're doing your job, I need your help, and I want you to stay and help me. If you're not doing your job, or if your job isn't necessary to the survival of this company, start looking for another job, and save us both a lot of trouble, because I *will* find out, and you *will* leave at that time."

Be aware, however, that neither lay-offs nor internal reengineering will restore an ailing company that makes an obsolete product or tries to service a declining market.

If your business keeps going downhill despite your heroic efforts, the basic theory you're in business for is probably obsolete. Executives in older companies take as gospel the assumptions on which a company was founded because, at first, they lead to success. They base their decisions, actions, and behavior on these assumptions. The longer these theories work, the more they become the foundation for the organization.

However, in today's rapidly changing technologies and markets, business theories become obsolete faster. Many executives are unwilling to accept that turning around the company requires fundamental change in these assumptions or in the senior management team.

Sick companies can and do get well again, but only if they change. Remember that stupidity has been defined as doing what you've always done and expecting different results.

A good book to get help from is *The Art of the Turnaround: How to Rescue Your Troubled Business from Creditors, Predators, and Competitors,* by Matthew L. Shuchman and Jerry S. White (New York: AMACOM, the American Management Association, 1995).

Urgency—Atmosphere Of

ONE OF THE SUREST SIGNS of a company that's going places is a sense of urgency on the part of the employees. It's in the air. You sense it as you walk through and observe people's actions and reactions to your being there.

It comes from everyone knowing what she's responsible for, and knowing that she won't have it finished by quitting time this afternoon. Hence the urgency—knowing there's more work to be done than can fit into the day. The urgency is to do as much as possible and to know as much as possible about the business and its customers. Such employees obviously have a sense of the company's mission and a vision of what the company is trying to achieve. They know that tomorrow will be the same.

People's facial expressions and interactions quickly tell you whether they're behaving this way because they're motivated and want to, or because they're driven to it by fear. Fear creates totally different body language and treatment of fellow employees.

Motivated people are alert and active. Their conversation is friendly as they exchange comments and greetings. They don't stand around in groups or crowd around the coffee machine or in the copy room except to pause while conducting urgent business. There's plenty of smiles and exchange of pleasant banter, brief stories about family, health, or a sports or social occasion, but not much wasted time. No one dawdles or stretches out work, because there's too much to be done.

> **Progress is like a wheelbarrow: nothing happens unless somebody pushes.**

When this atmosphere exists, the entrepreneur or owner has created it. The example and attitude trickle down from the top, like the vision and the policies that provide motivation. (See BOSS SETS THE EXAMPLE AND ATTITUDE.)

A universal sense of urgency is one of the surest signs I know for predicting success in an organization. If this is coupled with an atmosphere of genuine concern for customers, the final outcome can never be in doubt.

Vacations

TAKE VACATIONS, AND SEE THAT OTHERS DO, too. Tired minds make tired decisions. You need the best decisions from informed and refreshed minds. Vacations provide relaxation, change of pace, physical and mental renewal, and quality family time.

Vacation time also allows thinking time. Stand back from the trees and look at the forest. Ask yourself, "What if?" Come back with renewed vision and perhaps a revised mission.

As companies grant longer and more frequent holidays, and as economic pressure on the family grows, employees increasingly ask to convert earned vacation time to cash.

Company policies frequently provide three weeks of paid vacation (and sometimes four weeks) after so many years of service. Two consecutive weeks of vacation is really all a person needs to refresh himself and his family in body and spirit. It's usually all a family can afford if traveling and visiting are included.

From the company's viewpoint, enforced vacations for all employees serve two important purposes:

1. An employee's absence gives an immediate supervisor an excellent opportunity to accurately appraise the job effectiveness of the vacationing employee. When he is absent, do more things go wrong and go undone, or do things work more smoothly?

2. Your auditors will tell you to insist that all employees take vacation time as a means of uncovering embezzlement and other illegal activities. Evidence and activity records can be hidden by an employee who is present 100 percent of the time. Such schemes frequently come to light when a substitute performs the absent employee's job.

It's best for both the employee and the company to insist on one week, preferably two, of actual time off not subject to conversion to cash. Beyond that point, consider discretion and policy.

Include answers to the following questions in your vacation policy:

- What will happen to accumulated but unused vacation time?

- Must all earned vacation time be taken together, or can it be split into two or three leaves of absence?

- How far in advance must regular vacations be scheduled?

- What discretion do managers have in refusing or rearranging requested time if work loads or production needs are adversely affected?

- Can an employee use vacation time for emergency, sickness, funeral, or accident requirements without the usual advance request?

V

432

In your employee policy manual, coordinate your vacation policy with other policies concerning sick leave, family sick leave, maternity leave, funerals, jury duty, and hospitalization.

Valuation—What Is Your Business Worth?

IT'S WORTH LESS THAN YOU THINK, if you're the founder. If you think some rich fool is going to come along and pay an exorbitant price for your company, you're dreaming. Less than one company in two hundred is sold for the asking price, and that's because of an unusual buyer, an unusual match, or extraordinary timing.

You've achieved a great deal of satisfaction from your success in starting and growing the company. You've proved you can do it. You probably also think that your uniqueness and proven success justify a premium purchase price. This illusion is seldom shared by the purchaser, who is usually considering several alternative purchases and looking for the greatest value for the fewest dollars. As an outsider, the purchaser sees errors and shortcomings in your operation and organization that you haven't been aware of or haven't had the time or money to fix.

You always think the sales price should be higher because you're selling a lifestyle as the boss, with freedom to set your own schedule and job. The purchaser is investing in a company, weighing this against other investments, and doesn't want to purchase your lifestyle.

Dealing at arm's length with the first person who seriously negotiates with you about purchasing your business is humbling, eye-opening, and sometimes insulting. Trying to get you to lower your unstated price, the prospective purchaser will point out all the negative things about your company and the way you've conducted business. If the buyer disappears after you name your asking price (as seller, you must go first), it's because she doesn't want to hurt your feelings by stating what she thinks is a realistic counteroffer.

No one will really know what your business is worth until you sell it, thereby establishing proven value. Until that occurs, you can get estimates anytime you're willing to pay for them, but a good professional estimate will cost from $3,000 to $30,000, depending upon how much work is done outside your company. If you have an employee stock ownership plan (ESOP) or another agreement that requires annual appraisals by independent, outside appraisers, then you must have this done. Two professional appraisers working independently may differ by as much as 25 percent in their valuations.

Most valuations consider only internally recorded data, such as historical financial statements. Without spending a lot more money and going outside the company's records and operations, the valuation cannot take into account competition, nascent or potential market developments, customer surveys, your market share, market penetration and trends, general economic conditions, or possible developments outside your market that could drastically affect the company's future.

You or your accountant can make a quick and dirty valuation, based on internal financial history only, with software called Value Expert, published by Innovative Professional Software, Inc., of Englewood, Colorado. This program can be a template for Lotus or any of the common spreadsheets and requires an input of three to five years of financial data, including business ratios and graphs. There's no provision for external data. Use your judgment to input assumed interest rates, time-weighting, and other assumptions about growth and the future. If you use the software to its fullest, your result includes valuations calculated by eight different methods, most of which are mentioned below. The broad range of calculated values gives you a reasonable idea of your company's possible worth.

A good book on the subject is *How to Price a Business: A Guide for Buyers and Sellers,* by Raymond C. Miles (Englewood Cliffs, N.J.: Institute for Business Planning, 1987). If you're really serious, an expensive book used by many business appraisers is *Handbook of Small Business Valuation: Formulas and Rules of Thumb,* Third Edition, by Glenn Desmond (Llano, Calif.: Valuation Press, 1993), available from the Institute of Business Appraisers, Inc., Boynton Beach, Florida.

These are some of the attributes that are considered good in a company that's for sale, which therefore tend to increase the asking price:

- High compound growth rate in both sales and net worth for over three years

- Full audits by reputable firms for at least three years

- Detailed budgets and forecasts that have proven accurate in the past

- Depth in management

- An established, excellent market reputation

- Continuous new product development

- Staying current with applicable technology

The following characteristics are considered drawbacks, and therefore tend to decrease the offered price:

- A few large customers rather than many small ones

- No depth in management skills

- Bad location or other marketing disadvantage

- Slow, erratic growth rate

- A gross margin that is below the industry average

- Operating losses

- Poorly presented, late financial statements and internal operating statements

- No new products or technological advances in recent years

Every appraisal attempts to determine fair market value. *Fair market value* is the price that a buyer, willing but not forced to purchase, and a seller, willing but not forced to sell, would agree on, with both having full knowledge of all the facts. Professional evaluators always use several calculation methods and then summarize to state what they believe is the fair market value, in their opinion.

Formulas to establish the value for some businesses, especially service businesses, are generally accepted within the trade or industry. Such formulas are usually multiples of either sales, gross margin, cash flow, or asset values. The executive secretary of the trade association for any industry is a good place to inquire about such practices.

A service business is sometimes based on confidence in the business owner and personal relationships between the owner and clients or customers. The small amount of fixed assets involved may be inconsequential in the transaction. The basic question is "Can the relationship and earnings be transferred from the seller to the buyer?" Intangible and unmeasurable factors are the number and strength of competitors and how much the seller will help in the transition.

Three accepted approaches to valuation are the market-based approach, the asset-based approach, and the income-based approach. In the market-based approach, the valuator compares the subject business to comparable businesses for which market values have been established by recent sales. In an asset-based approach, individual business assets are valued and then added to estimate the total value of the business; intangible assets are usually ignored. The income-based approach considers the expected future earnings of the business, discounted to estimate their current value.

Other frequently used valuation methods are capitalization of earnings, comparable market value, replacement cost, liquidation value, multiple of earnings, multiple of cash flow, multiple of gross revenue, capitalization of excess earnings, discounted future earnings, and formulas based on book value.

If you wish to know how the IRS will value your business in your estate, get a copy of Revenue Ruling 59-60 from the nearest IRS office. IRS's approach and methods have been revised and litigated over many years and are binding on the government, unless your estate wants to litigate also.

435

Vendor Gifts to Your Employees

EVERYONE LIKES TO DO BUSINESS WITH friends. Favors, meals, gifts, and watching sports events together make for better friendships.

The basic question is when do such gifts and favors from salespersons to prospective purchasers go beyond cementing friendships and become preferential, influencing factors in what should be a business decision?

Anyone who makes buying decisions is often tempted to return a previous favor by showing preference. The more spending a person controls, the more frequent, valuable, and pressing the temptations become. Everyone is virtuous when there are no temptations, but since the beginnings of the human race, some people can't resist. I've had to fire three purchasing agents for mixing the company's best interests and their own pleasure or money.

Suspect possible kickbacks whenever you see isolated large expenditures without the time and documentation that usually go into making such purchases. Beware of large expenditures made in haste that short-cut usual procedures. There should be detailed specifications, several competitive bids, written proposals, and approvals or comments solicited from other employees or departments. Periodically review benefits received from long-term monthly contracts for services or supplies.

In some countries, under-the-counter payments are a way of life in finalizing business contracts. It's simple—no payment, no contract. In such societies, the problem becomes knowing which person or persons in the bureaucratic organization are the decision makers and therefore the ones to pay. Employing a local sales agent on a generous commission is the only way to do business in such a culture. Thank goodness that isn't true in this country.

Until your company gets quite large, maintain a close supervisory friendship with the person(s) authorized to spend company money. Have a personal talk concerning policy with each new person entrusted with buying decisions. Discuss in detail the conduct you consider correct and what you consider incorrect. Make it clear that you will tolerate nothing that's not clearly in the best interests of your company. Anything else is unfair to other employees who don't make spending decisions.

Have a firm understanding and policy, preferably in writing, as to what behavior or gifts are acceptable from vendors and what are not. The final comment or sentence should be "If there's any doubt, get permission from me in advance."

I finally decided to live with the following policy: Anything that you, your spouse, or other employees could witness or consume on the spot with the vendor,

V

436

or within a few hours, was acceptable as a friendship-building item. It had to be consumable or become a memory in a short time, not a permanent, expensive, or long-lasting reminder. This allowed coffee, meals, golf, and most sports or entertainment events. Tickets to events within a week and involving no travel expense (no long trips), where the vendor would not be present, were okay.

No tangible gifts with a value over $40 were allowed. This allowed pencils, cheap pens, pocket knives, inexpensive toiletries, desk pads, and so forth, but not golf clubs, TV sets, VCRs, furniture, clothes, barbecue pits, cosmetic kits, or anything of real, long-lasting value. Nothing was allowed on desks or on display with the vendor's name or advertis-

ing. Weekend hunting or fishing trips or special-event trips with vendors were allowed only with prior approval.

As an entrepreneur, you are on both sides of this gift question. You or your salespeople want to build friendships with customers who make buying decisions. And corruption exists on the customer's side as well. I once called on a potential buyer who was unfamiliar with my product. I handed him a sample and pitched it. He said I could sell a lot more if I just used the right kind of grease. The right kind of grease was two tickets to an expensive sports event, he said. I left without making the sale.

If you're in business long enough, you'll be disappointed in some of the people you've trusted. Good luck.

Vendors—Policy Toward

YOUR VENDORS ARE ESSENTIAL to your success. To them, you are the customer. While you're buying from them, you can see the value of quality, salesmanship, service, and dependability from the customer's side. Your interactions with suppliers should build friendly relationships.

True, they would love to sell you all they can. True, also, that people in your company must make buying decisions based on your company's own self-interests, regardless of friendships, gifts, or other favors. Pointing this out shouldn't be necessary. Acceptance of

these principles by both parties is the basis for a lasting and mutually profitable association.

Vendors should show you how to handle problems with their services or products when they arise. The good suppliers will try to earn your trust and turn you into a customer who doesn't chase prices.

If your vendors know their business, their salespeople can and will educate you concerning the latest developments and trends that affect your business and theirs. Most salespeople also carry industry gossip, opinions, and generalizations about your operations and those of other companies. You want to earn and have them carry away good opinions of your operation.

You need a dependable source of inventory, materials, and supplies. The right suppliers can help you keep your inventory investment at a minimum by supplying you in a timely fashion. *Just-in-time* is a modern procedure of computerized inventory control that delivers raw materials, supplies, or inventory to you just in time for you to use or deliver to your customer without tying up large amounts of your cash in idle inventory. EDI (electric data interchange) is becoming more common with large companies and making possible timely, paperless transactions.

As long as your company is small, you will personally select and know most of your vendors. As you get larger, this is one of the duties you'll probably assign to others. Just as you had your friends and favorite suppliers, so will others in your organization want to favor their friends with your company's business. Your vice presidents and your managers have friends they want to favor, too. (See VENDOR GIFTS TO YOUR EMPLOYEES.)

Because too many salespersons and too many sales calls can waste your company's time, you may need to require

appointments for vendors' visits or limit the days and times for drop-in sales calls. Decide whether you think you're getting service, education, and value instead of unnecessary interruptions from the sales calls that come into your business.

> *A friendship founded on business is better than a business founded on friendship.*
>
> —John D. Rockefeller

Your policy must be that, all other things being equal, doing business with friends is good, but a real friend wouldn't ask you to pay a premium to do business with him. You shouldn't expect a discount, but you shouldn't pay a premium either.

With principal suppliers, maintain friendly contacts at higher-than-salesperson level. Such contacts can help resolve problems with credit, deliveries, and quality.

Venture Capitalists

IF YOU AND A VENTURE CAPITALIST group successfully make an agreement, you are to be congratulated. Experienced, hard-nosed investors agree that your company has excellent prospects for the future. You're in for a fast ride together. Unless you have excellent prospects for fast growth, you don't make a deal with venture capitalists—but it's understood that you have to give up a large part of the equity in your company in return, usually a controlling interest, for the money and the ride.

Venture capitalists aren't business lenders like banks, who want only to get their money back and to feel secure while you're using it. Venture capitalists are a combination of lender, investor, and owner. On the downside, they want their money back, and on the upside, they want to ride the skyrocket to success with you and share financially in your burst of glory. They'll do everything they can to be certain that you're the skyrocket they seek. They're looking for *fast*, steady growth, not *slow*, steady growth.

Venture capital groups are as varied as banks and retail stores, with different objectives, policies, and selection criteria. Their financial goals often lead them to high-technology companies.

You've heard them referred to as "vulture capitalists," but there's no way you can be forced to sign their papers. Likewise, you can't force them to invest in your company on terms they don't accept. If you can work out a deal you both agree to, you'll have an exciting few years ahead of you.

What Venture Capitalists Look For
Venture capitalists look for a company with an established, excellent profit and growth record. Ideally, it's a company growing faster now than available bank and private financing allows. Venture

capitalists provide growth financing during the rapid-growth period and cash in when the public offering is made.

They usually invest someone else's money. Their objective is usually to obtain 30 percent or more annual return on their equity investment, and 20 percent or more per year on funds that they loan or guarantee. Not every company can demonstrate reasonable assurance of such future growth.

Because of the time and effort involved in detailed investigation, structuring, and negotiation of such a deal, as well as the legal and accounting costs involved, the minimum investment they consider worthwhile is $500,000, with $3,000,000 to $20,000,000 or more preferred. Making a successful deal takes an incredible amount of time and work on your part as well as theirs. You can both spend a great deal of front-end money and still have the deal fall through.

Venture capital fund managers are usually seasoned professionals who thoroughly investigate only the most promising opportunities. They're financial types who have more than a nodding acquaintance with numbers and financial statements, so they quickly eliminate over 90 percent of the proposals they review. Few of the remaining ones survive the intense scrutiny; fewer still become completed investments.

Because they're willing and able to invest large sums in small businesses, they're overrun with requests and proposals. Nine out of ten proposals are rejected out of hand because the applicant is not in a growth industry or an

439

industry understood by and acceptable to the venture capital group; or the applicant doesn't have an established growth record or doesn't believably present a business that can grow as desired; or the applicant doesn't have a management team that can handle such money and growth. The real key is the management team, as well as the venture capitalist's belief that this management, suitably financed and motivated, can produce the desired results.

Even after the most intense scrutiny during the selection process, of 10 typical deals made by venture capital firms, two will succeed as planned, four will be moderately successful, two will get the investors their money back, and two will go broke. The reason the venture capitalist needs a big return from some of them is to balance out those that don't make it.

High Rate of Return vs. Control of the Company

Venture capitalists are more interested in getting high rates of return on their investments than in taking control of companies. Their goal is to make a lot of money fast, liquidate it to cash, and get out within a few years. They're not operating managers looking for a job. They want large dollar returns by operating your company, not an emotionally satisfying lifestyle.

Venture capitalists usually aren't managers. They want you to have every incentive to succeed, because they're in the boat with you. They sink or swim when you do. They want control only as necessary to protect their investment, such as seats on the company's board of directors.

The venture capital firm's staff provide varying degrees of management assistance. Sometimes they're active, sometimes they want a consulting fee for this activity, and sometimes they want only an advisory role. The relationship is that of friend, advisor, and coach. They become partners, advisers, and participants, not just spectators. They're not your enemies.

Exit Strategy

Because the skyrocket ride that venture capitalists seek is short term (usually 3 to 7 years, certainly less than 10), they want to see a clear way to get their money out within that time frame before they put any money in. They know the growing business probably won't have the cash to buy them out.

Therefore, their exit strategy often involves taking the larger, fast-growing company public by selling stock. Since this is the first time the stock of that company has been offered to the general public, it's called an initial public offering (IPO).

How to Approach Venture Capitalists

First, remember that there's no shortage of investment opportunities for those who have the money to invest. Your offer has to compete with established high-yield offers backed by impressive credentials. If your idea is new or different, your problem is lack of a track record.

The whole process starts with a proposal that you prepare and present to the venture capitalists of your choice. They won't come looking for you.

The proposal must appear to be professionally prepared even if it isn't. The executive summary, no more than two pages long, is the most important part. If those two pages don't grab the reader's interest, she will go no further. A good proposal can easily take five months to prepare and cost over $5,000; the summary may be read and discarded in less than five minutes.

Your proposal must contain a complete marketing section, a description of the product or service and its distribution, complete information on your management team, and a detailed financial forecast for the venture capitalists' expected three-to-seven-year participation.

Also include in the forecast additional second or third tiers of financing, your usage of all these funds, and an exit strategy to buy the venture capitalists out.

If this sounds like the route you wish to go, an excellent book is *The Entrepreneur's Guide to Raising Venture Capital,* by Craig T. Norback and Greenberg Consulting (New York: Liberty Hall Press, an imprint of McGraw-Hill, 1991).

Vision

YOUR VISION REALLY HAS TWO dimensions—one for your personal life and one for your business. The two must be compatible. I encourage you to reduce them both to writing, but this discussion involves only the vision for your business.

Your idea for a product or service grows into your vision for the company you want to have and the reputation you want it to build. Your actions and policy decisions allow your employees and customers to read what they think is your vision, even if it is never written. Intentionally or not, your company builds an image that may or may not conform to your chosen vision.

The vision is the guiding light that keeps everything together and moving smoothly in the same direction. Driven by your idea, the vision includes major elements of the idea, your ego, and your dreams. Your vision provides guidelines to live by without end or time limit as you achieve intermediate goals and accomplish missions. As long as you remain with your company, the vision is never dead or static but grows and changes.

Where there is no vision, the people perish.

—Proverbs 29:18

Your business plan states how you'll implement your vision. Your mission statement expresses various parts of your vision. One part is to serve customers. Another part, frequently unexpressed, may be to build the biggest service company in your city, to own the largest chain of stores in your state, or to be a leader in your club, community, or church.

Vision includes corporate culture, marketing, goals, and images you build internally with employees and externally with customers. The vision is more nebulous than your business plan and less frequently written.

V

442

Strong corporate cultures, like strong family cultures, come from within, and they are built by individual leaders, not consultants.

—Craig R. Hickman

Articulate your vision to your associates. They must find it acceptable within their value systems and in their own best interests if they are to follow it wholeheartedly. If your vision is just to make yourself rich, that's not going to motivate a group of enthusiastic followers.

Your vision directs how your company plays the game and where it's going. If the visible result isn't acceptable to enough customers to keep it growing or to satisfy you, you'd better change something. You cannot change the wind, but you can change the set of your sails.

A change of direction will not happen quickly if you have a lot of people and assets. You can turn a rowboat around its center, but a battleship needs five miles of maneuvering room to turn itself around. Ideally, the keeper of the vision should continue with the company until it's well into the growth stage.

The older your company is, the more formalized and fully developed the vision is, because you and your management become committed to it. The vision—the dream—isn't transferable. The vision of a new owner or CEO will replace the old. The next generation, or the next president, will see a different vision. The product idea remains the same, but the vision does not.

A good book to help develop your vision is *Vision: How Leaders Develop It, Share It, and Sustain It,* by Joseph V. Quigley (New York: McGraw-Hill, 1993).

No one expressed a vision with greater eloquence or feeling than Martin Luther King Jr. It moved a generation to follow.

What Business Are You Really In?

IF YOU HAVE A WELL-THOUGHT-OUT, well-written business plan or mission statement, then you've already identified the main road you want to be on. If your purpose is hazy, if you don't know where you're going, you'll drift along and maybe find something interesting, maybe not.

If you feel uneasy about where you are, ask yourself, "Am I on the main road toward the objective I want to reach, or on a detour wasting my time, energy, and resources?" Then honestly ask yourself if pleasing your ego is more important than pleasing your pocketbook or your customers. If you're still not sure, ask a trusted friend or friends. (See ADVISORY DIRECTORS.)

Sometimes you can go some distance on a detour before you identify it as such. The older and larger your company, the easier one department can divert itself onto a side road. Quickly reverse this trend and get back on the main route.

The decisive question is usually one of these: Am I specializing in the business of making and selling a particular product? Or am I specializing in the business of serving a particular set of customers in my limited market?

> ### *Keep asking yourself, "What business am I really in?"*

Whether you're product oriented or customer oriented makes a tremendous difference to your business future. Products may go out of style or become obsolete. Customers may change their habits and tastes, but they're always there, buying something.

You can't be all things to all people. The more narrowly you focus on your niche market, the more successful you will become.

443

What If?

"WHAT IF?" QUESTIONS ARE HELPFUL in completely exploring any problem. They're a valuable tool for encouraging team building, getting feedback, employ- ing additional thinking, and searching for new ideas within your organization. Such questions, originally considered in the abstract, can become the basis for decisive action after being thoroughly considered and debugged by many minds working toward the same objective.

There's no way you personally can have all the ideas or foresee all the consequences of acting on an idea. In addition to your own musing while doing work that doesn't require your full attention, ask "what if?" questions of your associates and managers, either individually or in a management meeting. You'll stimulate their thinking as well as your own. Discussions and decisions reached this way are marvelous for building teamwork. "What if?" questions give everyone a chance to get into the act and give you a chance to evaluate the depth and imagination of your associates' thinking.

Don't ask just the simple questions; the difficult ones need serious consideration. What if we raise our prices? What if we lower prices on a specific line or model? What if we do something none of our competitors are doing? What if we do exactly as our competitors are doing? What if our prime supplier goes broke? What if our best customer goes broke? What if we sell directly to the consumer? What if we enter a new line of business? What if we change locations? What if we offer a cash discount? What if we do nothing? What if we do something radically different? What if our competitors do X, Y, or Z? What if the government changes the laws? What if our employees go on strike?

"What if?" questions are part of strategic planning. You must think outside the box that contains all the things you usually worry about. What if new technology made your process obsolete? What if global conflict developed? What if your basic material or product were unavailable because of flood, earthquake, or civil disturbance? What effect would instant, inexpensive, graphical communication have on your business? (See PLANNING; SPEED OF RESPONSE TIME.)

Once you've built a computerized financial model of your company that goes at least five years into the future, you can examine many courses of action with no financial pain. Of course, you must make a lot of assumptions concerning the unknowns you put into the model. (See FORECASTING AND FINANCIAL MODEL BUILDING.)

444

What's Left Over Is Yours

EVERY DREAMER, employee, or future entrepreneur wants to be the fortunate business owner who gets to keep the mountain of money left over after all bills are paid. "After all bills are paid" is the defining phrase. There's a flip side to this coin. If there isn't enough money to pay all the bills, where does the money come from to cover the shortage? Same place—your pocket—except it goes out, not in.

Even if money is left over this month or this year, you have obligations to pay back principal and interest money you borrowed to make lease improvements or purchase fixtures. You must be patient during years of hard work before the pot of gold is big enough for your share to make you rich.

Patience and farsightedness are also required to see that, if you've properly shared earnings with those who helped make them, there will be more for everyone further down the road. (See YOU ARE THE SOLE GUARDIAN OF THE BOTTOM LINE; ENTREPRENEURS SET THEIR OWN WAGES.)

Women-Owned Businesses (WOBs)

THE PERCENTAGE OF WOMEN-OWNED businesses (WOBS) in the United States increases every year. As a group, they're probably the fastest-growing segment of the economy in the '90s. The National Foundation for Women Business Owners and Dun & Bradstreet made a survey of WOB operations in 1994 that showed 7.7 million businesses earning $1.4 trillion in revenues. They employed 15.5 million people, which is one-third more than the worldwide employment of the Fortune 500 companies. The same survey confirmed the continuing difficulty of women business owners in trying to obtain credit and in not being taken seriously by some of their male counterparts.

Helen Hodges, owner since 1989 of Separation Systems Consultants, Inc., of Houston, and a national board member of the National Association of Women Business Owners (NAWBO), summarized for a recent meeting of the Silver Fox Advisors some of the characteristics of women business owners that she perceived as being different from those attitudes and operations of businesses operated by men:

445

- Many women business owners don't necessarily want to have a big business. A woman's self-worth or ego is not tied to the size of her business in the same way a man's seems to be. More important to her is being in control of her time and energy and making a contribution.

- All women entrepreneurs are overcommitted in terms of time. In addition to business pressures, they have families and parents and feel social pressures to network, gain personal support, and meet others like themselves. The net result is that many are overstressed and overextended.

- Many women business owners tend to be unaware of the give-and-take of the business world and the way some things get done—"the way the game is played." Unprepared by extensive business and financial backgrounds, they are naive when it comes to basic banking relationships, securing credit with vendors, business referrals, and negotiations.

■ Women entrepreneurs rely more on trust and intuitive personal relationships in how they do business. As a result, a violation of trust with a WOB is more difficult to repair whether the violator is an employee, a colleague, or a vendor.

■ Women business owners don't always understand driving a hard business deal or tough negotiations for final settlement. They sometimes take these hard dealings personally and have a difficult time later relating to those they dealt with unpleasantly. This appears to some women as perhaps a violation of trust.

■ Women are more patient than men, sometimes delaying dealing with obvious personnel problems, which may generate more loyalty among employees. They have more stick-to-itiveness, working longer and harder at solving some problems.

■ Women are accustomed to doing everything they can themselves, rather than directing or paying others to do things for them. This works against their need to delegate, even when they're overloaded with simple,

unskilled tasks, adding to their stress and overprogrammed condition.

■ Women owners are persistent to a fault, typically unwilling to give up no matter what the personal cost. This may be the result of not understanding the 80-20 rule and insisting on spending 80 percent more time to polish the last 20 percent of the job. It also makes them great vendors and contractors because they always get the job done.

■ Most women are good at organizing their time. Their preparation for a scheduled conference or bid is usually better than that of most male-run businesses. Yet there's never enough time to give fully of themselves in their multiple roles in business, family, and personal nurturing. The roles of boss, mommy, daughter, and sweetheart compete endlessly for their time and emotional commitment.

But still they get the job done, to the growing annual tune of $1.4 trillion.

If you're a woman business owner, you should join the National Association of Women Business Owners, headquartered at 1100 Wayne Avenue, #830, Silver Spring, MD 20910, 301-608-2590. An extremely good and highly recommended book is *The Woman's Guide to Starting a Business,* by Claudia Jessup and Genie Chipps (New York: Henry Holt and Company, 1991).

Working Capital Turnovers

Your working capital is the hardest-working money you've got. It turns over in the daily conduct of your business. The main three assets are cash, accounts receivable, and inventory, although all your current liabilities are also active deductions from your working capital.

The only absolutely safe way to double your money is to fold it over once and put it in your pocket.

Working-capital turnover starts when you use cash to buy inventory, or to make payroll if you're in a service business. When a customer buys inventory from you or buys your services, your invoice to her becomes an account receivable. When the invoice is paid, which may be immediately in a retail business, cash is received, and the cycle starts over.

Of course, the sale price is for an amount greater than your cost, with enough to pay your overhead, so you skim off a small amount per transaction that becomes your profit. The faster you can repeat this cycle of buying, selling, and collecting cash again, the less working capital you need.

On your balance sheet, cash, accounts receivable, and inventory are combined as current assets. The outgoing side of your working capital—the combined total of accounts payable, accrued payroll and expenses, all short-term notes (less than one year), and the current payment due within one year on any long-term notes—is your current liabilities.

Total current assets less total current liabilities equals net working capital. This is the amount of your own money working in the business. Current liabilities are really someone else's money held by your business that you're temporarily using but haven't paid yet.

Working-capital turnover is the number that results from dividing sales volume by net working capital. In most businesses, it's anywhere from three to ten, but some businesses are much faster or much slower.

You should make a profit on each turnover, so the faster you can turn over your working capital, the better it is for your business. The faster it turns over, the higher the volume you can handle with the same amount of investment.

447

You Are the Sole Guardian of the Bottom Line

IN THE SURVIVAL STAGE and early growth stage, you're the sole guardian of your profits, shown at the bottom line on your operating statement. This is the real solo act of the beginning entrepreneur.

All your employees and managers want more money in their paychecks, more facilities to work with, more employees in their departments, more conveniences, and more things that cost money. You're the one who must say no, or expenses will exceed income. After you get larger, you can get others to help you guard these earnings by giving them an incentive in the form of participation in those earnings.

Until you get large enough to have a mentor, an advisory board, a bonus plan, a board of directors, or other investors, everyone with whom you deal tries to make your bottom line smaller. Every salesperson's story (including yours) is "Buy my product or service with dollars now because, as a result of my product or service, later you will have returned to or retained by your company more dollars than you're giving me now."

Your knowledge of your market, your people, your own business goals, and your problems is the basis of your judgment and decisions. You won't be right all the time, but you must be right most of the time to survive and grow.

Every expenditure you make is either required by law or spent in the expectation that by spending a dollar now you'll ultimately have more than a dollar left over. This applies to people as well. If you don't pay good wages, you won't get good people working for your company.

Sometimes the connection is remote, but the principle remains. Don't spend that dollar unless you see it coming back with an increase in some way. Beware of ego expenditures. Carefully examine discretionary expenditures for productive results. Charity is the exception.

Ideally, you want to create an environment in which your best and brightest people know they're looking after their own best interests while they're also looking after yours. That's when the magic starts to happen.

Motivate salespeople. Compensate them for bringing in business volume at prices and conditions you establish. Then you and others must produce salable services or products in a manner that satisfies the customer and leaves a profit for the company. Incentive programs get others to focus on the bottom line because a piece of it also belongs to them.

Hasten and welcome the day when people besides yourself express concern for the bottom line, because while they're looking after #1, they're also looking after you.

The best, most efficient, most profitable way to operate a business is to give everybody in the company a voice in how the company is run and a stake in the financial outcome—good or bad.

Y

448

Zero-Base Budgeting

THE BUDGETING PROCESS USUALLY STARTS by looking at last year's expenses and then overlaying next year's objectives or changes in plans. If you grow continuously, this is normal and routine.

Unfortunately, traditional budgeting also tends to cause a slow buildup of charges for once-desirable and affordable items—extras such as additional employees in service departments, automobiles, computers, magazine subscriptions, expense accounts, telephones, coffee machines, equipment rentals, and country club memberships and dues.

As time passes, the accumulation of such expenses goes unnoticed. Benefits become institutionalized and taken for granted. Whole departments, procedures, and some employees become sacred cows. This slow buildup of unquestioned, continuing expenses requires drastic surgery when you review it in detail during a business downturn. Reviews should be done routinely and periodically rather than when falling business turns them into crisis management.

Zero-base budgeting means going back to a zero starting point and questioning every expenditure and every staff position to see whether it should be continued or eliminated for the coming budget period. The decisive question is this: If we were starting our present business today with limited funds, would we consider this expense necessary and productive?

If the answer is no, take it out of next year's budget.

> *Any jackass can draw up a balanced budget on paper.*
>
> —Lane Kirkland

Always establish a specified time as a review point for operating decisions, policies, or contracts. Every procedure, program, and decision is considered by your employees as permanent and set in concrete unless you make it clear that such things will be reviewed and revised at some logical point, such as year-end, after six months, or every calendar year.

If you build periodic reviews for revisions into your bonus programs and other commitments, resulting changes cause less surprise or resentment. If they're not scheduled or periodic, such revisions set off alarm bells and cause anxiety among affected employees. Be sure not to leave the impression that you're changing the rules while the game's in progress.

Schedule timely reviews of everything except your marriage.

Z

449

ACKNOWLEDGMENTS

This should be called "How *we* wrote this book," because I've had a lot of help. My lifetime experience has been as a business and professional man and management consultant. My venture into the serious book-writing business has confirmed that there are no such things as writers, only rewriters.

For the once-in-a-lifetime book writer, an experienced editor is absolutely (she told me to take out "absolutely") essential. Lianne Mercer of Fredericksburg, Texas, has guided me with patience and skill, trying to get a readable product from my background and experience. She taught me a tremendous amount about rewriting, as I tried to teach her about entrepreneurship. We hope our joint efforts have melded into a unique format and approach that serves and helps would-be, present, and future entrepreneurs.

Friends and associates have helped me directly and indirectly. They've read parts of the manuscript to be certain that I wasn't making errors or giving bad advice, and they've made suggestions about titles. They have encouraged me in many ways, not the least of which was being impatient with me to complete this lengthy project.

These people are old friends, business friends, new friends, or Silver Fox Advisors who deserve more than just to have their names mentioned. This acknowledgment of their help is to thank them for their contributions to the book and for their friendship, both of which I value.

Ray Arnett

Roman Arnoldy

Ed Bick

Bill Broyles

Charles Carter

Joe E. Chojnacki

Jack Cunningham

Glen Dorflinger

Marcia Faschingbauer

John Fields

Susan Gramatages

Jim Griffing

Jon Hall

Marilyn Hermance

Jeri Howell

John King

Mel Kleiman

Bill Kretlow

Edward Lowe

Ken McDowell

Scott Millican

Phil Morobito

Dennis Murphree

Walter Murphy

Jan Norris

Ed Norwood

Phil Peden

Monte Pendleton

Paul Pond

Bob Pope

Craig Rowley

Steve Scott

Sue Shaper

Bill Sherrill

Gerry Sill

Bill Spitz

Carl Stevens

Pete Whiteford

452

A special thanks goes to Helen Hodges, who contributed the information I could not write myself that is contained in WOMEN-OWNED BUSINESSES (WOBs).

The following students of the Classes of '96 and '97 of the Center for Entrepreneurship and Innovation at the University of Houston have helped proofread the manuscript, checked for clarity, looked up quotations, and laughed at my jokes and recitations of entrepreneurial experiences. They are

Moe Alva

Judy Amonett

Barbara Baxter

Carlos Buchanan

Karla Cummings

Marco Garcia

Raya Kulkarni

Kelvin McKnight

Jeff Megow

Tam Nguyen

Tina Nguyen

Janice Rawls

Claudia Redden

Kevin Schneberger

Nadir Shah

David Spyres

Viviana Vargas

Rickey Vourganas

John Wynn

To the associates, employees, customers, vendors, clients, CEO roundtable members, and even competitors who played the business game with me for so many years . . .

To the hundreds of others who have exchanged ideas, rubbed elbows, and worked for, against, and with me during many happy years of keeping score, who are the sources of the experiences that have been the basis of the knowledge, judgment, and opinions expressed in this book . . .

And to Ray Bard, my publisher, Suzanne Pustejovsky, the jacket and text designer, and Sherry Sprague, the project manager . . .

A VERY BIG THANK YOU!

Although I express sincere thanks to all the above and others for their help in getting this manuscript to print, I accept full responsibility for errors, shortcomings, and omissions. I practice what I've preached; the buck stops with me.

About the Author

Tom S. Gillis has been active on the Houston business scene for 50 years as business owner, entrepreneur, lawyer, CPA, mentor, and management consultant.

His business experience started with a petroleum equipment manufacturing firm and two employees. While president and principal owner, he acquired and sold several small companies and product lines, finally selling the entire company to a corporation listed on the New York Stock Exchange. When he completed his contract as chairman, the company had 400 employees.

His law practice was principally in the corporate and tax field, but also included probate, finance, and corporate mergers during the 1950s. He became a CPA while employed by Ernst & Ernst and had a private accounting practice with several employees. A large portion of his time was spent on systems and management services.

Tom has been director of a downtown bank and of several other corporations. His consulting with the Silver Fox Advisors since 1986 has been in the area of general business management, long-range planning, acquisition and sale of businesses, and business reorganizations.

His education, in addition to a law degree and CPA certificate, includes a B.A. in economics from Texas A&M, where he was corps commander and valedictorian when World War II started. His military service included platoon, battery, and battalion commander and service on the staff of General George Patton during combat in Europe. He was born and raised in Fort Worth, Texas.

Tom continues as an active business consultant, member of several advisory boards, and tennis player. He is also currently serving as an executive professor at the Center for Entrepreneurship and Innovation at the University of Houston.

He can be reached at: 175 Sage Road, Houston, Texas 77056, phone 713-622-2818 or fax 713-622-0887.

INDEX

456

461

463

472

TO ORDER ADDITIONAL COPIES OF

STRAIGHT TALK FOR STARTING & GROWING
YOUR SMALL BUSINESS

Hardcover	$29.95
Paperback	$19.95

VISIT YOUR FAVORITE BOOKSTORE OR

CALL TOLL FREE
1-800-945-3132
24 HOURS A DAY
7 DAYS A WEEK

OR FAX YOUR ORDER TO 512-282-5055

VISA / MASTERCARD / DISCOVER / AMERICAN EXPRESS ACCEPTED

QUANTITY DISCOUNTS ARE AVAILABLE
CONTACT

BARD PRESS
512-329-8373 Phone
512-329-6051 Fax

HG
4027.6 Gillis, Tom S., 1921-
.G55   Guts & borrowed money

1997

Date Due

BRODART INC.   Cat. No. 23 233   Printed in U.S.A.